Jesus People

Jesus People

THE HISTORICAL JESUS
AND THE BEGINNINGS OF COMMUNITY

David Catchpole

Julia

with very best wishes

David

DARTON · LONGMAN + TODD

Baker Academic
Grand Rapids, Michigan

First published in 2006 by
Darton, Longman and Todd Ltd
1 Spencer Court
140–142 Wandsworth High Street
London SW18 4JJ

and

Baker Academic
a division of Baker Publishing Group
PO Box 6287
Grand Rapids
MI 49516-6287

A catalogue record for this book is available from the British Library.

ISBN 0 232 52667 2

Library of Congress Cataloging-in-Publication Data is on file at the Library of
Congress, Washington, D.C.

ISBN 10: 0–8010–3160–5
ISBN 978–0–8010–3160–1

Designed by Sandie Boccacci
Phototypeset in 11.25/14pt Bembo
by IntypeLibra Ltd
Printed and bound in Great Britain by
Page Bros, Norwich, Norfolk

For Esther and Graham

Contents

Preface

Human existence, sometimes beset by bewilderment and loneliness, quite understandably gives rise to the famous dictum, 'I think, therefore I am.' Salvation from illusion about my existence may arrive via the encouraging thought that I am at least conscious that something is happening within my head – or I think I am! But it is a bare and minimal thought, capable of no more than a restricted reach into the richness of human life as we experience it in moments less blighted by loneliness. Would not that richness be better affirmed by means of a bolder dictum, 'I relate, therefore I am'? Would not the network of relationships, of shared experiences, of membership of communities (whether large or small, confident or struggling, supportive or splintered) have to be taken into account in defining who each one of us may be, and how the unfolding life story of each of us progresses from first word to last full stop?

To say 'yes' to that proposition is, however, to venture the capital of self-understanding in a very risky and slippery concept. To define 'community' – think of the myriad ways in which the term is used nowadays: 'the Cathedral community', 'the gay community', 'the Muslim community', 'the rural community', even 'the hunting community' – is a daunting and intellectually intimidating task. Depending on the context in which the term is used, the emphasis may vary – sometimes shared location, sometimes shared genetic inheritance, at other times shared origins, shared interests, shared consciousness of vulnerability and powerlessness *vis-à-vis* another body which (for whatever reason) calls the shots of human life. A 'community' may never meet in order to express its sense of fellowship, or it may not be able to give full rein to that sense without meeting. The members of a community may be 'in there' because they cannot help it, or they may be there because they made a conscious decision to belong. The variety is kaleidoscopic, the common thread a deep-seated sense of some kind of bond with other human beings – a sense that 'we stand together' over against (if necessary, defensively against or even self-assertively against) those who are 'not with us'.

My concern in these studies is to explore what sense of community there may have been in the experience of those who made a conscious decision to adopt some kind of positive stance towards the historical Jesus. Such explorations were encouraged in principle and put on a firm footing as long ago as 1960 in an article by the distinguished East German New Testament scholar, Heinz Schürmann. His article has, as it were, worn well and still today makes good reading. In affirming the importance of 'community' in the development of the tradition of Jesus' sayings, he at the same time subjected to characteristically precise and relentless criticism the uncritical assumption that the community was an exclusively post-Easter phenomenon. His reminder that there was a multi-faceted continuity between the pre- and post-Easter periods had the very salutary effect of rescuing continuity in respect of confession of the special status of Jesus (however that specialness should be defined) and his word, of tradition, and of community life. Many have subsequently built on the foundations of Schürmann's work, and questions about the community brought into being by Jesus continue to stir us into renewed examination of the evidence. What gave those men and women who took him seriously whatever sense they may have had of involvement or participation? What was their 'community', if they had one? What were they doing when they were, as one might put it, being themselves? What were the boundaries of their community, and how did that community relate to other groups who in religious or political or social terms would all have formulated their own version of 'I relate, therefore I am'?

The six studies which form the content of this book are a considerably expanded version of a series of Lent Addresses given in Wells Cathedral in 2003. For the privilege of being invited to speak on such a theme in such a breathtaking and beautiful setting I am deeply grateful, and especially to the then Chancellor, Canon Melvyn Matthews. As well as being delighted to offer some thoughts on 'the Jesus People', I was at the time also very appreciative of the arguments put forward by those who were (shall we say?) less than wholly convinced by every detail of what I said! Their comments helped me to sharpen up and expand my own thinking.

In presenting the material in both its original oral and now written form, I have followed a deeply held conviction that this sort of study of the gospels is well within the compass of thoughtful and questioning Christian people. They may not all have had the privilege that others of us have had, that is, of spending our professional lives in and making a living from doing what we would have wanted to do anyway. But, provided the perspectives of specialist study of the gospels are put across clearly and imaginatively – a worthwhile aspiration, even if it is never fully achieved – they are well capable of thinking their way into the enterprise. So in the face of the criticisms of one reviewer of the companion volume to this one, *Resurrection People*, who dismissed as 'wishful thinking' my suggestion that that book might be used by some who are beginning the process of scientific study of the gospels, I persist. Indeed I persist with a confident optimism, reinforced by experience year after year in the sphere of lifelong learning, that the appetite, the ability, and the aptitude for such technical work is widely present – and, truth to tell, often disappointed by the unwillingness of those in responsible positions of leadership in Christian churches to invest in all three. The questing and the questioning will not be suppressed, and the issues that provoke both will not go away. If this book encourages others to take a deep breath and enter into this most fulfilling of enquiries, it will have served its purpose. Even if the proposed tentative answers to difficult historical questions should not carry conviction, it will be quite sufficient if the search for alternative answers is energetically pursued.

For those who are stirred into beginning the process of scientific study of the gospels, then, it may be a help if I mention that most invaluable of tools, *Gospel Parallels*, London: Nelson, 5th edn, 1992), edited by B. H. Throckmorton, Jr. The process can be set in motion by working with the 'triple tradition' (where Matthew, Mark and Luke all provide parallel versions), underlining precisely and pedantically the words in Matthew and Luke which derive from Mark, and then moving on to the 'double tradition' (where Matthew and Luke correspond), and underlining in Matthew and Luke all words that they have in common. It will then be possible to see at a glance where editorial (redactional) changes have been made. That is the first step in the study of the history of any tradition, and an indispensable first move in the process of checking when and if we are picking up echoes of the voice of the historical Jesus.

Certain standard conventions are followed in the text of this book.

The term 'MarkR' stands for Marcan redaction, and similarly MattR, LukeR and JohnR. The term 'diff', as in 'Matthew 16:16 diff Mark 8:29', refers to the difference between one version and another. The arguments in favour of the view that a second source, Q, was available to Matthew and Luke alongside Mark, and that Luke normally (though not invariably) follows the Q order, are presumed in conventional references like Luke/Q 3:7–9.

A further convention adopted in this book involves setting in bold italics certain parts of some traditions. This is designed to make readily visible how a given tradition has arguably grown in the telling, acquiring additional material as it has moved from one stage to another in its history.

I am grateful to HarperCollins Publishers for permission to quote from Isabel Allende's novel, *My Invented Country: A Nostalgic Journey through Chile*; to J. M. Dent, an imprint of the Orion Publishing Group, for permission to quote from 'Kneeling' and 'Emerging' by R. S. Thomas; to the SCM Canterbury Press for permission to quote from *The Strong and the Weak* by Paul Tournier; and to Stainer and Bell Ltd for permission to reproduce parts of Sydney Carter's 'Lord of the Dance'. The scriptural quotations used in this book are taken from the *New Revised Standard Version, Anglicized edition* (copyright 1989, 1995, Division of Christian Education of the National Council of the Churches of Christ in the USA). On occasion, however, I have incorporated my own rendering of the Greek text.

It has been a genuine pleasure to work with the editorial staff of Darton, Longman and Todd during the period of this book's gestation. Virginia Hearn, Elizabeth Piercy and Helen Porter could not have been more accessible, thoughtful and helpful, and to them I offer my sincere thanks.

I am very grateful to other colleagues, notably Dr David Horrell, Dr James Crossley and Professor Robert Simmons, who made careful and constructively critical comments on some of the material in draft. In what follows, the errors that other sharp-eyed friends and colleagues will detect are not theirs but mine. Less easily defined, but nevertheless very real, is the debt I owe to successive groups of those who, whether in earlier days in Exeter or more recently in Salisbury, have come week by week to share in 'Theology Quest and Questions' and to make the questing and the questioning their own.

Jesus People

Exactly forty years ago Esther and Graham Stanton came to the UK from New Zealand and shared in the work and friendships of the group of New Testament postgraduates in Cambridge at that time. Speaking personally, the trusting and supportive friendship which dates back to those days and bridges the intervening decades has been an enrichment beyond words. It is to them that I offer this small book with affection and gratitude.

Sarum College, Salisbury
October 2005

CHAPTER 1

Of water and a wilderness: from Jesus to John and back

Introduction

In what is probably Thomas Hardy's finest novel, *Tess of the D'Urbervilles*, a baby boy makes a brief and poignant appearance in the story of his young and beautiful unmarried mother. The name of the baby, whose life would fade away in just a few days, was 'Sorrow'. His mother, Tess, had been seduced, and as she trudged home from the scene of her seduction she met a cheerful travelling stranger who spent his life painting judgemental texts on stiles and stones. The meeting with him was for Tess nothing less than one more nail in the coffin of faith, yet another sign that Christianity, at the end of the day, is about rejection and judgement and exclusion by an angry God. As for little 'Sorrow', after his birth he was plainly not long for this world. That being so, Tess for her part was tortured by the thought, the surely unnecessary thought, that her beloved dying baby would be lost if he were not baptized – yet her father was determined that 'no parson should come inside his door'. And so it came about that Tess herself poured some water in a jug, gathered her younger brothers and sisters together in a circle, told them to kneel and put their hands together, with fingers exactly vertical. At that moment a name came into her mind from the book of Genesis, the name she pronounced as she sprinkled water on the head of the dying child: 'Sorrow, I baptize thee in the name of the Father and of the Son and of the Holy Ghost.' 'Say "Amen", children.' The tiny voices piped in obedient response: 'A-men!' Tess went on: 'We receive this child' – and so forth – 'and do sign him with the sign of the cross.' And, so runs the narrative, 'in the

blue of the morning that fragile soldier and servant breathed his last'
(Hardy 1988: 97–101).

Was it a valid baptism? Only with difficulty did the local vicar, conscious of his professional position, bring himself to concede it. Could the
baby be buried in consecrated ground? No, he thought not. Yet we, the
readers, rebel at the thought of a god like his. We feel that such self-
protecting small-mindedness cannot really be at ease with the true intent
of those tear-stained words, gospel words of the Easter Jesus, words
which express the essence of Christian faith and Christian community,
words both individual and inclusive: 'Sorrow, I baptize thee in the name
of the Father and of the Son and of the Holy Ghost.'

But, we may ask, how did those words, and the rite to which they are
classically attached, come to occupy the central position that they do in
Christian experience and community awareness? Our answer will almost
certainly need to highlight two things – the resurrection of Jesus and the
mission of John the Baptist. Behind and before Christian baptism in the
threefold name there was baptism 'in the name of Jesus', and it was the
resurrection that caused the name of Jesus to be invoked. And if the
resurrection created a community demarcated by such a baptism, a
community of 'resurrection people' – and it did – then the roots of
that community were to be found in an earlier community, a gathering
of Jewish people by water and in a wilderness on the initiative of a
charismatic preacher, John the Baptist. Those roots invite us, as it were,
to attend to them.

In attending to those roots we must steel ourselves for a quite fundamental recognition. The dynamic effect of the resurrection of Jesus,
which can be felt by the reader of all four gospels, was not only to
Christianise Jesus – the pre-resurrection person has often been painted
in post-resurrection colours – but also to Christianise John (the sort of
tendency which in Somerset, centuries later, would impact on the communities of Axbridge, Batheaston, Chilcompton, Farrington Gurney,
Glastonbury, Pilton and Pitney, in the form of a dedication of their
Christian parish churches to the memory of *Saint* John the Baptist). It is
safe to say that no one would have been more astonished by that tendency than the historical John! We therefore need to set up stable
methodological scaffolding within which to reconstruct the original
historical buildings of the two missions, first that of John and then

that of Jesus. While emphasising the resurrection as an overwhelming community-forming influence, we must be prepared to get behind it.

The scaffolding of the historian's work is initially provided by *source criticism*, that is to say, the investigation of how the gospels relate to one another and of how they draw on earlier versions of the material their writers use. In the case of the gospels this means:

(i) Mark came first (probably around 69 CE, cf. Hengel 1985: 14–28), and was used independently of one another by Matthew and Luke. Mark's own sources are no longer directly accessible to us, but their existence is beyond doubt and demonstrated not least by the presence in his text of aporias, that is to say, awkward breaks, dislocations, apparent interruptions, and the like. These may well stem from the introduction of favourite Marcan ideas within some of the individual stories which he brings together so creatively and imaginatively to form his overall 'story of Jesus'.

(ii) Matthew and Luke (both probably 80s CE) had a second source, which they used independently, and which we designate Q (probably 50s CE). This hypothesis is a very good one (Kloppenborg Verbin 2000: 11–111), notwithstanding the resistance it sometimes provokes, for it enables us to show proper respect for the editorial integrity and consistency of both the later gospel writers. The alternatives, that Matthew used Luke – but where did all Luke's non-Marcan material come from, and why did Matthew edit Luke in a way that clashed with his characteristic concerns? – or that Luke used Matthew – but where did all Matthew's non-Marcan material come from, and why did Luke edit Matthew in a way that clashed with his characteristic concerns? – carry burdens of implausibility too heavy to be borne.

(iii) John came last (probably 90s CE), very likely appearing in two successive editions ($4G^1$ and $4G^2$). The writer(s) of this gospel may well have known and used one or more of the other three synoptic gospels. Compelling evidence of expansion of an earlier edition is provided by countless dislocations in the text, and fascinating evidence of the gospel writer's awareness of the final editorial changes made by Matthew, Mark and Luke strongly suggests that he knew them all.

There is a good deal more to the scaffolding than these source-critical results, but they will be enough for the present. As we begin to construct the building or, if you like, to pursue the quest of the historical John, in full awareness of the Christianising process that almost certainly changed his image, certain conclusions which bear on the issue of community consciousness will start to emerge.

First, the mission of John was distinct and independent in its own right. A community that consisted of John's people was therefore a genuine possibility.

Second, John's mission was, in a very real sense, a prophetic mission to anyone and everyone in Israel.

Third, the controlling message was not so much new as a prophetic call back to the old and familiar responsibilities of Torah obedience incumbent upon Israel, that is to say, a call to the covenant people of God to be what they were intended to be, indeed what they were committed to being. That call was to a renewal of 'righteousness', both in the sense of the defining relationship between God and his people and also in the sense of harmony and justice in inter-personal dealings. Crucially, that call was backed by the disturbing warning of impending judgement.

Fourth, those who listened and responded positively, and who therefore embraced the offer of escape from the approaching judgement, were not 'new Israel' but rather 'true Israel' or 'restored Israel'. They were a 'community of salvation'. They were distinct from those who, in spite of being part of 'ethnic Israel', were now destined for judgement. In spite of, or indeed because of, this distinction, they embodied 'all Israel', and therefore technically they could be seen as a 'remnant'. As a repentant community within a community, they identified with the alienation of the nation.

Fifth, Jesus, and quite possibly those who came to be close to him, were actively part and parcel of John's prophetic mission. When he set out on a mission that derived from that of John but became independent, he continued to draw upon the central convictions and community consciousness of John.

Sixth, the rite of baptism, which was probably part of Jesus' programme at the outset, did not continue to be so as his more widely itinerant mission developed. Thus John alone was regarded as 'the Baptist'. The change of strategy on the part of Jesus is unlikely to have implied reservation about, still less rejection of, the rite of baptism. It was more likely a matter of resolute missionary pragmatism, and quite possibly a recognition that John himself had made renewal and righteousness primary, and baptism (although important) secondary.

Finally, Easter saw the re-affirmation of that defining rite of baptism as an expression of the same community identity that John the Baptist had fostered. No direct precedent existed for post-Easter Christian baptism other than the baptism of John. So the resurrection of Jesus was seen as an endorsement of the validity and permanent impact of that baptism.

Should that cluster of community-oriented conclusions carry conviction, Christians need to take very seriously indeed their debt to John as well as to Jesus: he contributes to the *continuity* which stretches through from the pre-Easter to the post-Easter phases, and which combines with the newness and *discontinuity* with the past which Easter also brought into being.

There are two more things to add by way of amplification at this early stage: first, it has already been suggested that the John to whom Christians are indebted is very specifically a prophetic figure – and we may say even at this early stage that the excision of the prophetic heart and centre of John's mission cannot be justified on the basis of Josephus' account, to which we shall turn shortly, or by discounting how Christians described him (*pace* Chilton 2002: 26–39). So we must pause to ask what we mean when we attach this term 'prophet' to him, a term so liable to trip off the tongue without sufficient care and precision as to its essential nuances. Before we engage in the quest of the historical John and the exposure of the community dimension of his mission, it had better be clarified.

Clarification can come by way of two complementary perspectives. On the one hand there are the recurrent characteristics of actual persons, most notably from Amos or Isaiah onwards, who represent the classic 'prophetic' tradition. On the other hand there are the sociological types, which are to an extent theoretical models rather than actual persons, and which distinguish 'prophet' from 'priest' (Weber).

In the first scheme the prophet emerges as someone who speaks under divine and sometimes even ecstatic inspiration, receiving the word of God in the setting of a close and intense personal relationship with God. S/he conveys that word to a third party (person or group), addressing the failure of the recipient (person or group) to observe in practice the principles to which they were committed as those who are related to a God of mercy and grace but also a God of not unlimited patience – in short, acting as 'the conscience of Israel' (Schmitt 1992: 485). S/he subjects those responsible for national institutions to critical scrutiny if necessary, though without thereby urging the abandonment of those institutions in principle. S/he acts as the public guardian of basic moral laws which should define the life of the recipients, but which in practice are being flouted. S/he announces imminent and catastrophic judgement in the face of persistent obduracy and unwillingness to reform. Nevertheless s/he looks for the renewal of the relationship between God and his people, offering hope and restoration in the event of a sincere and effective human response or a divine proclamation that 'enough is enough' in respect of judgement, and therefore that God is returning to his people in salvation and righteousness (Isaiah 40—55; Malachi).

In the second scheme, the model/type 'prophet' is distinguished from the model/type 'priest'. The latter is part of an establishment with its own traditions, is legitimated by that establishment, has responsibility to preserve the tradition and maintain the establishment, and is in essence a conservative figure. S/he may have ritual responsibilities, but paradoxically those are not necessarily part of the package, as it were, of 'priesthood' *as a model*. Over against this model/type of the 'priest' should be set the alternative, the 'prophet'. Within this antithesis it becomes possible to see the prophet as someone who in no way derives authorisation from the system or establishment, an individual who possesses a charisma which constitutes his/her endowment for the designated role. Those who are invited to respond to the 'prophet', if they do so, simply recognise that the 'prophet' rings true – true *for them* as the mediator and mouthpiece of God, prepared to mount a sharp and devastating critique of the establishment and/or those who function within it, insistent on fundamental moral values and obligations. On this showing, the prophet is not so much a conservative figure as a figure of protest and change, an outsider to the establishment, for all that s/he appealed to and worked within the defining parameters of the nation's life. Even if, as was from time to time evidently the case, actual prophets were actual priests (e.g. Ezekiel), model/type prophets are to be distinguished from model/type priests, for reasons that will have become clear. Priestly functions, when they do figure, are on this showing accidental rather than essential to prophethood.

At point after point there is an observable match between the actual prophet and the model/type prophet. And at the point of convergence between the two complementary perspectives on what it means to be a prophet stands, if we may risk anticipating later studies, the austere and critical figure of John the Baptist.

The second term needing amplification is the word 'remnant'. In a context determined by human faithlessness and, in the case of Israel, breaches of the covenant and abandonment of 'righteousness', the judgement of God raises a question mark over the very survival of the nation. Repeatedly in narrative and prophetic texts (cf. 1 Kings 19:18; 2 Kings 19:4; Isa. 4:2–4; Jer. 31:7–9) the righteousness of God – that is to say, his faithfulness to his commitments combined with his freedom to judge them for abandonment of theirs – brings about the survival of a portion of the nation as an expression of mercy. Such persons are either faithful and therefore exempt from judgement, or, following repentance, have renewed their commitment to faithfulness (Meyer 1992: 669–71). They are a fraction of Israel numerically but they *are* Israel as representative of the people with whom God entered into, and sustains, a relationship of faithfulness. To anticipate further the outcome of the studies that follow, the idea of a remnant turns out to be deeply embedded in the community consciousness of John.

From Josephus to the historical John

Our first major source of information about John is the Jewish historian Josephus. He includes a substantial report on John in a lengthy review of the events of the first century CE, written in the years 93/94 CE. His view of John is unaffected by Christian theological schemes, and is therefore an independent witness of some importance. What he says is certainly not to be read uncritically, for he has his own axes to grind. Nevertheless many recent participants in the quest of the historical John have quite rightly resisted the temptation to write Josephus off. With a particular interest in observations that have community implications, we shall set out to isolate features of his report which overlap with features included in the gospels; other features which the gospels include but he does not; and finally elements which he includes and the gospels do not.

Josephus and the by no means unanimous gospels agree, as we shall see, (i) on John's being known as 'the Baptist' and so being the personal agent of the baptism of others; (ii) on that baptism's being (implicitly) once for all and initiatory; (iii) on the independence of his mission rather than its being simply the prelude to that of someone else, so that when John is discussed Jesus is ignored, and vice versa (*Antiquities* 18:63–4; 20:200); (iv) on his central preoccupation with 'righteousness', and therefore with a return to moral renewal and covenant faithfulness; (v) on the presence of the offer of forgiveness; (vi) on the absence of any critique of the Temple order as such; (vii) on his message's having a socio-political dimension; (viii) on a John-versus-Antipas confrontation; and (ix) on the substantial public recognition of, and sympathy for, John.

Josephus lacks what the gospel traditions convey concerning (i) his preaching of future judgement and salvation, and therefore his opening up of the possibility that some of the Jewish people might be at risk; (ii) his being a prophet or even in some way an Elijah figure, committed to Israel's restoration; (iii) his asceticism; (iv) his reception by dubious sections of the community, that is to say, tax-collectors and prostitutes; (v) his preparation for a 'coming one', whoever that person might be; (vi) his significance for the mission of Jesus of Nazareth; and (vii) his critical contact with the Judean religious leadership.

The gospels lack what Josephus conveys concerning (i) a formal communal assembly of those submitting to baptism; and (ii) the distinctness of repentance-cum-forgiveness on the one hand and baptism on the other.

Josephus' report concerning John (*Antiquities* 18:116–19; cf. Meier 1992: 233) runs as follows:

> [116]But to some of the Jews the destruction of Herod's army seemed to be divine vengeance, and certainly a just vengeance, for his treatment of John, surnamed the Baptist.
>
> [117]For Herod had put him to death, although he was a good man and had exhorted the Jews, provided that they were cultivating virtue, and practising righteousness towards one another and piety towards God, to come together in baptism. In his view the baptism would only be acceptable to God if they employed it, not to gain pardon for whatever sins they committed, but as a consecration of the body, implying that the soul had already been cleansed by righteousness.
>
> [118]When others too joined the crowds about him, because they were aroused to the highest degree by his words, Herod became alarmed. Eloquence that had so great an effect on mankind might lead to some form of sedition, for it looked as if they would be guided by John in everything they did. Herod decided therefore that it would be much better to strike first and be rid of him before his work led to an uprising, than to wait for an upheaval, get involved in a difficult situation and see his mistake.

[119]And so John, because of Herod's suspicions, was brought in chains to Machaerus, the stronghold that we have previously mentioned, and there put to death. But the verdict of the Jews was that the destruction visited upon Herod's army was a vindication of John, since God saw fit to inflict such a blow on Herod.

This report is framed by the double reference to the widespread popular conviction that the military defeat experienced by Herod Antipas was a divine judgement for his execution of John. This is worth setting alongside the data provided by the gospel writers. It speaks volumes about how highly regarded John was throughout the community, and presumably implies the substantial success of his mission, while at the same time pointing rather obviously to tension between him and Antipas.

The picture of John painted by Josephus portrays him as a sturdy advocate of what Jewish readers would recognise as standard features of the life of the covenant community – 'piety toward God' standing broadly for obedience to the first five of the Ten Commandments, and 'righteousness towards one another' standing broadly for obedience to the second five (cf. Philo, *Who is the Heir* 168–72; Sanders 1992: 193), the two together summarising the essence of Judaism (cf. Josephus, *Antiquities* 15:375; Philo, *Special Laws* 2:63; *Virtues* 175).

Helpful clarification of what Josephus has in mind can be found in, for example, his observation that following military victories and the obvious demonstration that God was on his side, Jehoshaphat 'enjoyed splendid fame because of his righteousness and his piety toward the Deity' (*Antiquities* 9:16; cf. 2 Chr. 20:29–30). It is no different in his portrayal of Jotham, the son of Uzziah (cf. 2 Kings 15:32–8; 2 Chr. 27:1–9). Turning a blind eye to the biblical writers' criticisms of Jotham's reign, Josephus declares that 'he lacked no single virtue, but was pious toward God and righteous toward men' (*Antiquities* 9:236). In the same vein, the rather more admirable figure of Hezekiah is described as 'kindly, righteous and pious'. That added up to his 'considering nothing more necessary or profitable to himself and his subjects than the worship of God', which translated itself into a public demand for 'purification from former pollutions', the restoration of traditional worship and sacrifice in the Temple, and a demand, issued by himself and by prophets, and re-inforced by warnings of divine judgement, for repentance and a return to traditional piety (*Antiquities* 9:260–67). Unsurprisingly, Josiah is in turn praised highly on exactly the same grounds: 'he gave proof of his piety and righteousness' by rooting out the worship of idols, 'which he said were not really gods', by renewing traditional Temple worship, and by meticulous administration of justice, that is to say, 'by following the laws' (*Antiquities* 10:49–56; cf. 2 Kings 22:1–2; 2 Chr. 34:1–2). Much later in history, the Essenes, whose position we can check via the Qumran texts, are said by Josephus to require of each initiate a series of undertakings, reinforced by 'tremendous oaths', and pre-eminent among those undertakings are, first, 'that he will practise piety towards the Deity', and second, 'that he will practise righteousness towards men' (*Jewish War* 2:139).

These are all very positive statements, but their bearing can also be assessed when we note how their *absence* is interpreted. Thus, to give just one example, Josephus heaps reproaches on his erstwhile rival, John of Gischala, rating him lower even than the detested *sicarii*. John had, so declared Josephus, 'dared to practise impiety even towards God (*ton theon asebein*), for he had unlawful food served at his table and abandoned the established rules of purity of our forefathers [thus being] guilty of such mad impiety towards God' (*Jewish War* 7:264). Plainly, 'piety towards God' is just as much about respecting distinctive Jewish identity.

So, when Josephus uses the language of piety and righteousness about John, it becomes clear that the wholeness of covenant-conditioned obedience defines his agenda, and with it the self-consciousness and identity of the Jewish people. John is beyond all doubt in the mainstream of Jewish religious life.

That being so, we probably need to question the distinction Josephus draws between two groups of John's hearers. The first group, he says, listens to a message of 'virtue . . . righteousness . . . piety', and for the authorities there is apparently no problem. The second group listens to John's words and is thought likely to do whatever John advocates, and for the authorities there is apparently a big problem. How may this be explained? After all, righteousness true to its name has, almost by definition, a potential for social and political critique with consequent unease in establishment circles. We should probably infer an artificial distinction promoted by Josephus himself, writing as a socially conservative apologist. He feels trapped between respecting John on the one hand and rejecting socio-political subversion on the other. For the historical John, by contrast, two separate audiences are less likely than two aspects of an integrated message, and it is almost inevitable that such preaching in the region of Galilee/Peraea would be heard as offensively bad news by the tetrarch of the region, for at least two reasons.

First, Antipas stood convicted of infringements of the first part of the Decalogue, having used 'representations of animals' in breach of the second commandment (Josephus, *Life* 65; cf. Exod. 20:4) in his palace. He came close to an infringement of the second (Exod. 20:14) by having married Herodias, the wife of his half-brother, Herod (Josephus, *Antiquities* 18:109–10; cf. Lev. 18:16; 20:21). Moreover, he flouted the purity laws by abandoning his old capital, Sepphoris, on which he had spent a great deal of money, and building a new one, Tiberias, on ground which had formerly been a cemetery (Josephus, *Antiquities* 18:36–8; cf. Num. 19:11–14). To such a person, the reverberations of John's preaching would be unsettling indeed.

Second, Antipas also stood convicted of ostentatious wealth, so much so that Jesus of Nazareth voiced a barbed question about his style (Luke/Q 7:25). Again, to such a person the reverberations of John's preaching, as we shall be able to uncover it, would be a cause of serious concern, especially since Galilee was during that period marked by acute social tension.

For Josephus, then, a religion centred on 'virtue . . . righteousness . . . piety' was wholly admirable, but a religion which risked destabilising an already brittle and insecure regime (Theissen/Merz 1998: 173–5) was too prophetic to be comfortable. Antipas and his loyal entourage, like those whom he settled in his new capital, probably picked up echoes of a message advocating socio-political reversal, and they were quite right to be worried. So by creating two distinct audiences Josephus invites his readers to share both his approval of classic Mosaic religion and his disapproval of any tampering with the *status quo*. For the less prejudiced historian, the prophetic strain in John's message, which Josephus brushed out, needs to be brushed back in again.

That said, we must give Josephus substantial credit for an otherwise plausible account. His John stands in the classic tradition of Old Testament prophecy (though that dangerous word does not appear), with his fierce insistence that forgiveness of sins would not be supplied by an 'external' rite. Instead, his hearers must listen first to the call for a return to 'righteousness', something dictated by the covenant and demonstrated in appropriate inter-personal human behaviour. On that basis alone they can receive forgiveness and the inner cleansing that goes with it. *After that*, they can share a washing rite that, like all Jewish washings, has to do with cleansing of the body (Taylor 1997: 58–64). The baptism itself, be it noted, does not deal with the moral problem. It comes into its own after the moral problem has been addressed.

At this point we may pause to consider whether it would be a correct inference from Josephus' account that John's baptism was deliberately intended as some kind of alternative to the sacrificial system. Was he undercutting in any way the Temple, where that system held sway and performed a central and essential function in the life of Israel? Such a view has gained ground in recent writing about John. We read repeatedly of a 'significant parallel to the atoning sacrifices . . . an alternative to the temple's sacrificial system as a means of forgiveness' (Webb 1991: 203); of 'a clear alternative to the Temple' (Wright 1996: 160); of how 'baptism for the forgiveness of sins is *de facto* a ritual to rival the temple cult; for here the forgiveness of sins was really offered' (Theissen/Merz 1998: 436); and most recently that 'in a sense, baptism took the place of the sin offering [so that] John offered his own ritual as an alternative to the Temple ritual' (Dunn 2002: 459–60). With all due respect to these proposals, it may be doubted whether Josephus intends to say anything of the kind.

First, it is assuredly significant that his terminology in the statement that baptism 'would only be acceptable to God if they employed it, not to gain pardon for whatever sins they committed but . . .' draws on the vocabulary of sacrifice, specifically his own descriptive language for the sin offering (cf. *Antiquities* 3:204, 230, 238–40; Dunn 2002: 459). But the significance is that John reportedly *denies* that such sin-offering-type thinking is appropriate to his baptism.

Second, if, as we shall see, John's baptism was for each person a one-off act of commitment, we must ask what happened after that? Was the problem of subsequent sinful actions simply not to be part of the religious equation? If they remained an issue, how would they be dealt with? Was attendance at the daily sacrifices, the festivals, the Day of Atonement, something inappropriate and to be undertaken as a matter of pragmatism rather than principle? Neither the gospel traditions, sparse though they are, nor Josephus encourage such radical thinking, let alone action. On the contrary, the implications of Josephus' report of John's exhortation would seem to be that while the Temple and all that *neces-*

sarily happened there by way of worship and sacrifice was taken for granted, the prime necessity was not deflection from a worship system authorised by God but the reform and renewed commitment of the worshippers.

Third, deflection from that worship system would, in Josephus' terms, be an abandonment of 'piety' (*eusebeia*), for he repeatedly uses that term to express unqualified devotion to Temple worship (e.g. *Antiquities* 8:51–6; 12:140). Indeed, in a striking phrase assigned to Herod the Great in his announcement of the planned reconstruction of the Temple, the building itself is described as 'this first archetype of piety' (*to prōton tēs eusebeias archetupon*) and the work itself as an act of gratitude and piety (*Antiquities* 15:386–7). That same reverence for the Temple and all that it represents is by implication John's position. His baptism is therefore to be seen as a supplement rather than a substitute for the Temple ritual, a complementary corrective rather than a critique.

This John is a true successor of Isaiah (Taylor 1997: 90), who had spoken dismissively of the standard practices of religion by people who needed a rough reminder of the non-negotiable prior conditions of acceptable worship:

> [16]Wash yourselves; make yourselves clean; remove the evil of your doings from before my eyes; cease to do evil, [17]learn to do good; seek justice ... [18]Come now, let us argue it out, says the Lord: though your sins are as scarlet, they shall be like snow ... [19]If you are willing and obedient, you shall eat the good of the land; [20]but if you refuse and rebel, you shall be devoured by the sword ... (Isa.1:16–20)

According to John, only after just such an 'internal' cleansing, which showed itself in action, could another 'external' cleansing be undergone, one that could be understood in terms of Israel's commitment to holiness and separation. As has been convincingly argued, 'Josephus ... tells us that it was a turning to righteousness that effected remission of sins or soul-cleansing. Baptism was for the body's purification and followed from this' (Taylor 1997: 96).

Josephus also says of John that he was 'surnamed the Baptist'. This is important. It serves to open up a gap between him and, say, the famous Bannus (cf. Taylor 1997: 32–42), who had been Josephus' mentor for three years:

He lived in the wilderness, wearing only such clothing as trees provided, feeding on such things as grew of themselves, and using frequent ablutions of cold water, by day and night, for purity's sake. (*Life* 11)

Bannus apparently baptized nobody. So similarities there may be, but in addition to public impact two dissimilarities are crucial: first, that personal involvement in the baptizing of others, and second, provision of what turns out to be effectively an initiatory rite. On the first point, we are reminded of the saying 'I baptize (*or* have baptized) . . .' (Mark 1:8; Luke/Q 3:16), sufficient in itself to distinguish John from the host of other seriously religious people who made much of ongoing purificatory washings (Webb 1991: 180–81). On the second point, even if those who freshly committed themselves to 'righteousness' proceeded also to renew their commitment to the standard routine of washings in second-Temple Judaism – and they could hardly do otherwise if they were religiously serious – this baptism by John represented a new and therefore unique beginning. In this respect it had some resonance with the regime at Qumran – an initiatory washing for those who might have thought they were clean because they were part of Israel, but who from the point of view of the sect were not, and the beginning of a routine of washings that constituted a regime of holiness (Taylor 1997: 76–88). Such a routine, it must be remembered, does not exclude a rite of initiation (rightly, Evans 2002: 44–71).

But, we may ask, into what were they being initiated? There is no evidence of any kind of sectarian Baptist-centred community with well-defined boundaries like that at Qumran. Further, the 'disciples of John' may have formed some sort of gathered group, committed to John as learners to teacher, but not everyone who underwent his baptism would be initiated into discipleship in that sense. The answer to our question perhaps emerges when we consider that there were doubtless many in Israel who personally needed no exhortation from John to respect 'virtue . . . righteousness . . . piety' and to repent, but they would not thereby be beyond the horizon of his message and his hope. They could identify with all he stood for; they could share in the penitential commitment for which he called, for that call was very probably to be understood in more than personal terms. In a movement which is born within an alienated people standing under judgement, and which looks forward to a decisive intervention by that people's God, the sense of community takes precedence over the sense of personal individuality. As has rightly been observed:

> John's summons to baptism in the wilderness was directed not simply to all Israelites but to all Israel, i.e., to the nation as an ecclesial entity or to Israel as the people of God. The response to his summons therefore could not be merely so many responses of individuals within Israel; it had to be the response of Israel as such. (Meyer 1979: 118)

Two hundred years before John, Daniel had been written up as a paradigm of personal obedience and a model of those who needed no repentance. But because he also embodied the longing of his community for liberation, he was made to express solidarity rather than separation, and to voice a lengthy prayer of penitence:

> ^{3}I turned to the Lord God, to seek an answer by prayer and supplication with fasting and sackcloth and ashes. ^{4}I prayed to the Lord God and made confession . . . ^{20}I was praying and confessing my sin and the sin of my people Israel. (Dan. 9:3–4, 20)

Add these considerations together, and the likely conclusion is that John's community is *an open and penitential group within Israel, freshly committed to the fundamentals of Israel's existence and contributing to the renewal of the 'righteousness' of the nation.* Numerically, those who respond may be part of the people. Ideologically and in representative terms, they are the whole of the people. They are what John's prophetic predecessors described as 'the remnant' (Meyer 1979: 118–22).

This brings us to one priceless piece of historical information conveyed by Josephus that, if we only had the gospels, we might have missed. He speaks of how people were being asked by John to 'come together' in baptism (*baptismōi sunienai*). Such assembling together in an ordinary and matter-of-fact sense had already taken place when people came to hear John, or were called and led by him to the Jordan river. This assembling, however, seems to be something more intense, more formal, and we note (cf. Webb 1991: 199–201) the loaded significance of the verb *sunienai*.

A 'coming together' is (i) what happened when all the people *came together* to Gilgal for the anointing and proclamation of a new king

---

(*Antiquities* 6:83) or the dedication of a temple (*Antiquities* 8:100; 13:67); (ii) it is what formally happens when factions are formed, whether for peace or war (*Jewish War* 4:132); (iii) it is what Essenes do when they *assemble* in one place for ritual washing (*Jewish War* 2:129); and (iv) it is what pilgrims do when they are '*meeting* and feasting together' at the pilgrim festivals (*Antiquities* 4:203). In short, it stands for the active realisation of a sense of community.

Consequently, when this happens in the context of John's mission, it is no shapeless or randomly spontaneous gathering of Jewish people, but a somewhat formal gathering on a set basis and for a set purpose. The basis is the prophetic message, and the purpose the corporate baptism. One should not, therefore, think of John as some kind of lone ranger, baptizing in a 'here a person, there a person' style. A corporate body is in view. It first commits itself to repentance and renewal of the principles and responsibilities enshrined in the covenant ('righteousness'). That means that it is united in receipt of divine forgiveness of openly acknowledged human failure. And then it seals its fresh start – doubtless both individual and communal – in a public and corporate baptism. That being so, John emerges quite unambiguously as a man with a mission that has to do with the assembling of a 'community of salvation'. That community of salvation, defined in terms of the normal parameters of Israel's existence, is representative of the wider community and expressive of the hope that remains available to the wider community. For that to be true it must be clear that John is not, repeat not, a man with a monotonous and monochrome preoccupation with judgement. Like many a prophet before him – one thinks of Jeremiah, with his uncompromising warnings about judgement, warnings into which there is built conditionality and therefore the possibility of mercy for those who will truly attend to his message – John is about judgement on the unrepentant, and judgement as a spur to repentance. That has to be his starting point, yes, but from there his message is all about salvation for the renewed people of God.

From the gospels to the historical John

From Josephus as an important source of information about the Baptist, we now turn to the gospels and first of all to the gospel of John. This gospel engages in a 'Christian take-over of John the Baptist' (Theissen/Merz 1998: 205) and insists that John is *not* the light, *not* the royal messiah, *not* Elijah, and *not* the Moses-like prophet – just a voice located in the wilderness and speaking persistently about, pointing incessantly to, Jesus (John 1:20–23). He has disciples, but his supreme concern is to detach them from himself and attach them to Jesus. All this is patently Christian. Nevertheless, some further precious nuggets of historical fact are conveyed to us.

First, John's baptism provoked controversy: 'A discussion about purification (*zētēsis . . . peri katharismou*) arose between John's disciples and a Jew (*or the Jews*)' (3:25). The dislocation between verse 25 and the following verses has often been noted: rather oddly, given the frequency of irremediable dislocation in the fourth gospel as a whole, considerable effort has been made by commentators to remedy this one. They should not bother! As it stands and without accommodation or hypothetical emendation, verse 25 survives in spite of the tendency of the following narrative to become an apologia for the superiority of Jesus to John (3:26–30). The dispute is about purification, the nuances of which are made clear in advance by the reference to 'the Jewish rites of purification' (2:6). The actual term used (*zētēsis*) is a strong one. It indicates very firmly held opinions on both sides about what is perceived to be a matter of fundamental theological importance. The same word does duty in Acts 15:7, referring to 'no small controversy and dispute (*zētēsis*)' between Paul and Barnabas and the theological traditionalists in Jerusalem, which, being interpreted, means a ferocious set-to. We may be sure in John 3:25 that heated disagreement about the interpretation of John's baptism, and its apparent dissonance with the standard regime of washings in Judaism, was involved. This is of a piece with our findings so far, and also with the polemic documented in Luke/Q 3:7–9.

At the same time we must notice that John was, at least for a time (John 5:35: *pros hōran*), respected by at least some of the leaders of the Jewish community, themselves carefully engaged in assessing the validity of religious teachers. This is of a piece with the approval of John by the former Pharisee, Josephus, and the later alliance between Pharisees and followers of John (cf. Mark 2:18).

Such warm approbation of John, documented in John 5:31–6, is so formulated by Jesus as to suggest his having the Elijah profile in mind: 'He was a burning and shining lamp [cf. Sirach 48:1], and you were willing to rejoice for a while in his light.' Given the contrast between what the Baptist is made to say about himself (1:21) and what the Johannine

Jesus is made to say about him, not to mention the contrast between what the Baptist in the fourth gospel does and what Elijah in the tradition is expected to do, the John/Elijah correspondence certainly looks pre-Johannine, but that simply takes us back to what the synoptics say – some, even if not all, of the time. At this stage we have to defer a decision about whether that correspondence goes back even further to the historical Jesus and even the historical John.

Second, the fourth gospel indicates that the Jesus movement did in all probability derive from the mission of John, for otherwise it is hard to explain the strength of the effort made to subordinate John to Jesus.

Third, the Jesus movement – Jesus' disciples, at the very least – were involved in baptizing activity. The evangelist protests too much by allowing that Jesus was thought to have been baptizing, but then semi-retracting it by insisting that it was Jesus' disciples who were carrying out baptisms (4:2). As if that could in principle drive a wedge between Jesus and what was taking place, or erase the memory of the explicit statement that 'Jesus and his disciples went into the Judean countryside, and he spent some time there with them and baptized' (3:22, 26)! And if Jesus baptized within the general ambit of John's mission, the implication is that he did so on behalf of John – he alone was 'the Baptist' – and in recognition of the authority of John. That fact, so awkward from the evangelist's point of view, must be why he works hard to obscure reality.

Overall, however important these nuggets of historical memory are, it remains true that they are set within a story that is absolutely overwhelmed by Easter-influenced interpretation of Jesus. The fourth gospel takes striking liberties with history in order to make John, like Jesus, concerned only to focus on the earthly presence of the heavenly Son of God. Most of what John says about Jesus can scarcely be harmonised even with the synoptic gospels, let alone with historical reality. But we are grateful for the precious historical nuggets which still survive and to which we shall return.

From the fourth gospel to the gospel of Matthew. This gospel writer correctly sees the status of baptism as expressive of the status of the baptizer. To baptize is to presume a position of authority. Hence there is a problem when Jesus comes to be baptized by John. It seems to place on an inferior level the person whom Matthew regards as superior. That cannot be! So three things happen to the Baptist (see Matthew's insertion in 3:14–15). First, he is made to recognise the existence of a real (Christian!) problem. Second, he is made to hesitate over whether it is right for Jesus to be baptized at all. Third, he is given reassurance that for the sake of conformity to God's great programme – summed up in the favourite Matthean notion of 'righteousness' – the baptism should take place. Again there are clear signs of later concern in the mind of Matthew, but we nevertheless note some more priceless historical nuggets in a gospel whose writer is clearly aware of ideas that are floating around in Palestine.

The first is that indeed there was in the baptism of John a clear sense of special authority attaching to the person of John himself, that is to say, to be baptized by him was to acknowledge the authenticity of his calling.

The second is that Jesus was indeed baptized by John, and that this was a serious problem for thoughtful Christians – not because of any conviction they may have cherished that Jesus had no need to repent (where is the evidence of such a view of him?), but because of their christological convictions that 'Jesus is the greatest, not the greatest but one.' Of course, it should not have been a problem at all, for to undergo baptism was to identify with the representative penitence of a community.

The third is that there was a great deal of continuity between John and Jesus as preachers, so much so that often when Jesus spoke, the voice was the voice of Jesus but the words were uncannily like the words of John.

From John and Matthew we move on. The gospel of Luke gives us more raw material on the Baptist than any of the other gospels. But while stressing simultaneously the greatness of John and his inferiority to Jesus – remember how even before birth he kicks within the womb of his mother in order (allegedly!) to signal his recognition of Jesus – Luke gives us even more precious nuggets of historical information than the others do. This emerges from a study of Luke 1 (cf. Catchpole 2000: 111–16, drawing on Vielhauer 1965: 28–46), in which the following key factors come to light: (i) the extremely close and extensive parallelism between the John-story and the Jesus-story, a closeness which can hardly fail to suggest that one of the stories has been written up in imitation of the other; (ii) the clarity with which the Jesus-story reflects Luke's favourite ideas about Jesus, whereas the John-story is at significant points out of line with Luke's views and indeed appears completely untouched by distinctively Christian views; (iii) the consequent likelihood that pre-Lucan source material is available to us in the annunciation in verses

5–25, the song of Elizabeth (*sic*) in verses 46–55, the birth and naming of the new baby in verses 57–66, and the second half (at least) of the song of Zechariah in verses 76–9; (iv) the likelihood that the preservation of this narrative/song sequence material would have been within the community of ongoing disciples of John, whose separate existence is admitted in Mark 2:18 and Luke/Q 7:18; and (v) the unlikelihood that a narrative which uses such standard and classical forms as angelic appearance stories is straightforwardly historical, and yet the strong possibility that in this tradition, preserved by the community of John's disciples, there would survive genuine historical memories of the central convictions and concerns of the prophet John.

In passing, a note about the Magnificat as the song of Elizabeth, a proposal which stems from several considerations:

(i) There is variety in the manuscript tradition of verse 46, with a significant minority of manuscripts reading 'And Elizabeth said . . .' over against the majority reading 'And Mary said . . .' It is easier to think of manuscript copyists changing from Elizabeth to Mary than the other way round. What would be the motive for that?

(ii) After the Magnificat we read (v. 56) that 'Mary stayed with her . . .', which presumes that Elizabeth was the previous speaker. Otherwise, verse 56 should read, 'She stayed with Elizabeth . . .'. It doesn't.

(iii) The strategy of the Magnificat is to move from the situation of a woman to that of the nation, and the woman's position is defined in verse 48 as 'humiliation' (*tapeinōsis*), a term which, within a culture which saw infertility as the 'fault' of the woman and a cause of shame, fits the predicament of Elizabeth and not in any way at all the situation of Mary.

(iv) The strongest biblical echoes that can be detected in the Magnificat come from the song of Hannah (1 Sam. 2:1–10). Elizabeth's problem matches that of Hannah: Mary's situation is not parallel at all. In this vein it is striking that after the birth of John, Elizabeth's friends and relatives 'heard that the Lord had shown his great mercy to her' – and mercy is the great and overarching theme of the preceding song, the Magnificat: 'His mercy is for those who fear him from generation to generation . . . He has helped his servant Israel, in remembrance of his mercy' (vv. 50, 54).

The pre-Lucan material in Luke 1 does not mention the rite of baptism or John's status as baptizer. It lays all the stress on his preparation of

Israel for the Lord. He acts in the mode of Elijah. The formulation 'with the spirit and power of Elijah he shall go before him' recalls the historical Elijah as a figure of the past whose spirit could be bequeathed and whose actions could be replicated: thus, the Jericho prophets had commented that 'the spirit of Elijah rests on Elisha' (2 Kings 2:15) and the following narrative had represented some of Elisha's subsequent actions as more or less carbon copies of what Elijah had done. But Luke 1:16–17 goes further than this, as can be seen when the amplification of John's programme is set alongside the text of Malachi 3:23–4/4:5–6:

> [16]He will turn many of the people of Israel to the Lord their God. [17]With the spirit and power of Elijah he will go before him, to turn the hearts of parents to their children, and the disobedient to the wisdom of the righteous, to make ready a people for the Lord. (Luke 1:16–17)

> [23/5]Lo, I will send you the prophet Elijah before the great and terrible day of the Lord comes. [24/6]He will turn the hearts of parents to their children and the hearts of children to their parents, so that I will not come and strike the land with a curse. (Mal. 3:23–4/4:5–6)

The correspondence between these two texts serves to set John not simply in the tradition of a figure of the past but also to link him directly with the ultimate figure of the future – none other than God himself. That 'the Lord' is God becomes clear when Luke 1:17 is read in the light of 1:16, and 1:76b in the light of 1:76a. Of course, God (1:76: 'the Most High') may be thought to act through divinely appointed agents, but it is essentially the coming of God that John's mission is all about.

The full impact of the correspondence of these two texts can be detected by giving due weight to the fact that Malachi 3:23–4/4:5–6 is probably part of a later appendix to the book of Malachi, which originally ended with 3:19–21/4:1–3, and that in commenting on 3:1a in particular, it is picking up not just a single verse but a whole oracle consisting of 2:17—3:5 (cf. Hill 1998: 267–8):

> [17]You have wearied the Lord with your words. Yet you say, 'How have we wearied him?' By saying, 'All who do evil are good in the sight of the Lord, and he delights in them.' Or by asking, 'Where is the God of righteousness?'

^{1a}See, I am sending my angel/messenger to prepare the way before me, ^{1b}and the Lord whom you seek will suddenly come to his temple. ^{1c}The angel/messenger of the covenant in whom you delight – ^{1d}indeed, he is coming, says the Lord of hosts.

^{2}But who can endure the day of his coming, and who can stand when he appears? For he is like a refiner's fire and like fuller's soap; ^{3}he will sit as a refiner and purifier of silver, until they present offerings to the Lord in righteousness. ^{4}Then the offering of Judah and Jerusalem will be pleasing to the Lord as in the days of old and as in the former years. ^{5}Then I will draw near to you for judgement; I will be swift to bear witness against the sorcerers, against the adulterers, against those who oppress the hired workers in their wages, the widow, and the orphan, against those who thrust aside the alien, and do not fear me, says the Lord of hosts.

Malachi 3:1 is not the easiest text in the world to analyse, and its ambiguities make for some considerable difficulty for any interpreter (Hill 1998: 265–71, 286–9), with its reference to three figures whom some think coalesce with one another in one way or another. For our purpose we need only note that 'the angel/messenger who prepares the way' (v. 1a) is distinct from, and works in advance of, 'the Lord who will suddenly come to his temple' (v. 1b), who in turn may or may not be the same as 'the angel/messenger of the covenant in whom you delight' (v. 1c). The messenger who 'prepares the way', and who comes to be equated with Elijah, has the task of achieving inter-generational harmony. This is the prelude to 'the great and terrible day of the Lord', which is amplified in the oracle of 2:17—3:5.

That oracle outlines what happens when the absent God, no longer present in his Temple, comes back (Hill 1998: 267). There is nothing wrong with the Temple itself – it remains '*his* temple' (Malachi 3:1b) – but there is a great deal wrong with those who use it and/or lead its worship. Acceptable worship presupposes acceptable worshippers, and because righteousness is a casualty, the worship is unacceptable and the purifying fire of judgement a certainty (v. 3). So it is imperative that the covenant relationship between God and Israel, including that between God and Levi in particular, should be revived; the worship purified (v. 3); the agenda of social justice addressed (v. 5); abuses corrected; and righteousness restored (v. 3). Two great themes – righteousness (v. 3), reinforced by repentance (v. 7) – dominate the message of Malachi, the non-negotiable demand of God, and the refining judgement in prospect. When repentance is forthcoming, and righteousness re-established, then and only then will safety and protection from the divine fire be achieved. Not that everyone can realistically be expected to respond: the following oracles acknowledge that there will still be a visible difference 'between the righteous and the wicked, between one who serves God and one who does not serve him' (3:18). But those who *are* righteous and who *do* serve God, those people *within* a people, who essentially *are* the people, will give effect to the defining reality of their lives, that is, that they are *covenant* people.

So the preparatory figure of Elijah must be set in the context of a community under threat. The coming day of the Lord, for which he prepares, is both great and terrible. His mission is to bring about the changes of heart and life, specifically the healing of inter-generational discord and conflict, which are the first priority in the face of the terror. That is what Malachi 3:23–4/4:5–6 could not but feed into the definition of John's task in Luke 1:16–17.

Long before Luke 1:16–17 had been written, the Malachi text had been picked up by Sirach 48:10–11, and the impact of the coming Elijah had been extended to include the resurrection of the dead and the final gathering of scattered Israelites. He had become part of, rather than preliminary to, the final events. Luke 1:17 retreats from that development, and retains the more limited definition provided by the original Malachi text (Bryan 2002: 92–4). But in just one respect the text of Luke 1:17 is formally comparable with Sirach 48:10. It replaces the second part of the parallelism in Malachi 3:24/4:6 which read 'and the hearts of children to their parents'. The replacement turns out to be remarkably close in content to the different replacement found in the LXX version of Malachi's text: 'who will restore the heart of father to son *and the heart of a man towards his neighbour*'. The strikingly comparable replacement in Luke 1:17 reads 'and the disobedient to the wisdom of the righteous'. This plainly shows sensitivity to Malachi's vision of a harmony extending beyond inter-generational family relationships to those of the wider community. And, we observe with interest, the emphasis in this statement of intent matches precisely Josephus' report that practising 'righteousness towards one another and piety towards God' was central to John's preaching.

Someone who shared the assessment of the spiritual health (or otherwise) of Israel, who was convinced of the imminent intervention of God in judgement, who felt impelled to carry out a preparatory mission in advance of the fearfully imminent and purifying God, and who was inspired by 'zeal for the law' as Elijah had been (1 Macc. 2:58; cf. Mal. 3:22/4:4, 'Remember the teaching of Moses . . .'), could in a real sense be 'Elijah for a later and final era'. The profile was plain and the mandate precise. All that was needed was for someone to enter the space within the divine programme, and it hardly needs saying that someone with an intensely prophetic self-awareness and a negative diagnosis of the nation's health (for whatever reason) would be more than appropriate. This is where John the Baptist comes on stage.

Luke 1 is, when treated in this way, full of yet more of the most price-less historical nuggets (*pace* Theissen/Merz 1998: 198), which happen not only to expose the convictions of John but also to respect the independence and the integrity of his work. If his work is a warm-up operation for someone, then that someone is God. And the great central themes of John's mission, recollected by those who preserved the material, emerge in the message of the angel and the inspired songs of his parents. We should pause to recall that just as angelic pronouncements cannot but be taken with the utmost seriousness as divinely initiated revelation, so too songs – formally poetic and implicitly inspired – must be taken as incalculably more than incidental human exclamations. Here are thoughts that originate in the mind of God. And all those thoughts must be heard in the summarising conclusion of the second song:

> [78]By the tender mercy of our God,
>> the dawn from on high will break upon us,
> [79]to give light to those who sit in darkness and in the shadow of death,
>> to guide our feet into the way of peace.

This climax to a Malachi-inspired, Elijah-conditioned tradition recalls the words of Malachi 3:20/4:2, with which that book originally reached its climax: 'for you who revere my name the sun of righteousness shall rise with healing in its wings'. That is what gave a sense of direction to the mission of John. With the healing would come the righteousness.

So, in conclusion, this very important Lucan source material dovetails impressively with the evidence provided by Josephus. John's community is Israel, but an Israel that has received forgiveness specifically by means of the mission of John himself. We already know from Josephus about John's commitment to the priority of 'righteousness'. We also know already about the community dimension of his work, and his purpose to cause Israel to be what it was intended to be. Finally, given the habitual tendency of God across the generations to overturn the established hierarchies, that too is part of the view opened up by John's mission. No wonder Antipas fretted if this sort of thing got through to him, and no wonder the religious establishment in Judea was, as we shall see, unsympathetic!

Finally, we turn to the gospel of Mark. If we only had Mark, we would know singularly little about John's preaching. But we would know a little more about what people thought of him. Whereas Matthew and Luke both use their non-Marcan source, Q, to extend the coverage of John's preaching, so that we know rather more about his presentation of judgement and salvation – chaff and wheat, fruit-bearing and fruitless trees, water versus Spirit and fire – Mark sets up a contrast between the comparatively inferior John and the superior figure of Jesus, and between two baptisms, and that is that – until, that is, Jesus himself provides an extremely significant appraisal of John's mission! On the preaching front, as far as John himself is concerned, the rest is silence. What little there is about him is brought under the control of Christology: the only things worth hearing from John are things about Jesus! That represents in microcosm the tendency that would prevail in the fourth gospel. And yet we know from John's address to the people attending his baptism that there was more to him and his public utterances than that. So again, the tendency to make the much-reduced story of John only the first chapter of, or the prologue to, the story of Jesus is on display. That is the way the Christians stripped John of his essential independence.

In spite of that tendency there are, however, three extra traditions in Mark which supplement what is said about John's mission and preaching: the account of the circumstances of his execution by Antipas (6:17–29), the evaluation of his work by Jesus (9:9–13), and the controversy about Jesus' own authority (11:27–33). The first can be set alongside the report of Josephus, with which it is in some tension – did Antipas intervene because John criticised his behaviour or because he was perceived as a threat to the regime? – and the third implicitly attests both the priority and independence of his mission in relation to that of

Jesus, and also the volume of popular support for John. But the second is particularly interesting, not least because Jesus' view of John and his role within the community of Israel matches the view maintained in Baptistic circles (cf. Luke 1:17). This is a convenient moment to antici-pate later studies by examining the history of the tradition that we owe to Mark.

> [9]*As they were coming down the mountain, he ordered them to tell no one about what they had seen, until after the Son of Man had risen from the dead.* [10]*So they kept the matter to themselves, questioning what this rising from the dead could mean.* [11]Then they asked him, 'Do not the scribes say that Elijah must come first?' [12a]He said to them, 'Elijah does indeed come first to restore all things. [12b]*How then is it written about the Son of Man, that he is to go through many sufferings and be treated with contempt?* [13]But I tell you that Elijah has come, and they did to him whatever they pleased *as it is written about him.*' (Mark 9:9–13)

As it stands, this unit of material features both literary lurches and Marcan motifs. First, ever since the recognition that the Marcan secrecy scheme is most of the time the evangelist's creation, and is explained above all by 9:9 (Wrede 1971: 67), it has been more than a little difficult to assign verses 9–10 to pre-Marcan tradition. All the more is this the case when the disciples' incomprehensible incomprehension about resurrection, that is to say, the resurrection of Jesus, resurfaces in Marcan redaction shortly afterwards in 9:32: 'They did not understand what he was saying and were afraid to ask him.'

Second, the question about the sufferings of the Son of Man in verse 12b is characteristically Marcan and also plainly interrupts the smooth passage from verse 12a to verse 13. Matthew, who is admittedly not always a sure guide in these matters, recognised and responded to the awkwardness by simply omitting verse 12b from Matthew 17:11.

Third, the concluding 'as it is written about him' is artificial, since there is no pre-Christian warrant for the idea of a suffering Elijah. That is not, however, the main ground for regarding it as a later addition. In fact, it matches the 'as it is written about the Son of Man' and promotes the parallelism between the fates of John and Jesus, which was already signalled early in Mark's narrative in the statement about John's having been 'handed over' (1:14) just as Jesus himself would in due course be 'handed over' (3:19; 9:31; 14:21). It also reminds the reader of the artificial attachment of the classic Elijah text of Malachi 3:1 to what would otherwise read smoothly at the very beginning of Mark's narrative: '. . . as it is written in Isaiah the prophet . . . The voice of one crying in the wilderness . . .' (1:2–3).

Three details require clarification in the disciples' question and Jesus' answer. First, the form of the question, 'Do not the scribes say that . . .?' brings 9:11 alongside 12:35, where Jesus himself asks, 'How can the scribes say that the Messiah is the son of David?' In the latter case there is no intention to dispute the correctness of the scribes' observation, only an intention to clarify *the sense in which* it is true. Hence, we expect in 9:12a, 13 a similar clarification of the sense in which it is now appropriate to say that 'Elijah must come first'. That is indeed what the affirmation that John has performed Elijah's designated task does.

Second, the key word 'first' in 'Do not the scribes say that Elijah must come first?' makes clear that the disciples' question has to do with timing and picks up certain assumptions (Bryan 2002: 90). The scribes can very easily say what they do because according to Malachi the coming of Elijah precedes the coming of the Lord in judgement. But we ourselves may ask why this should be an issue for the disciples of Jesus. The answer may well be that Jesus, like John before him, is announcing the coming of God in judgement and kingship – there is abundant warrant for saying that – but the difference is that Jesus, unlike John before him, has affirmed that God's kingly rule is already making itself felt in his own mission. Is there room for another key figure like Elijah, given the special significance of Jesus himself as the inaugurator of the final act of God? Should even the possibility that Jesus himself is Elijah (cf. Mark 6:15; 8:28) be entertained? These are entirely reasonable questions, and it enables the answer of Jesus to seem reasonable too. One may add to that observation that taking 'first' as meaning 'prior to the resurrection of the dead' (thus, 9:10) means working not with a primary and distinct *pre-Marcan* unit but with the secondary *Marcan* setting.

Third, the answer of Jesus might be understood as new in content, or an indication that the disciples do not equate John with Elijah except with Jesus' prompting (Bryan 2002: 100). And if disciples of Jesus had a background in the mission of John, that might indicate that John himself never adopted the Elijah role. However, it is perhaps more likely that Jesus, who not only begins to inaugurate the kingdom of God in the *present* but also still announces the kingdom as *future* (cf. Mark 1:15), has neither excluded the Elijah expectation because of the present kingdom nor set himself to fulfil that role in relation to the future kingdom. On that basis he confirms a claim that is already known, namely, that the Elijah figure who prepares for God's coming is indeed John the Baptist.

The tradition that comes into view when Marcan additions are subtracted is as remarkable as that recording Jesus' assessment of John in Luke/Q 7:24–8, to which we shall soon turn. In this case, as in the other, there can be very little doubt that we hear the words of Jesus (Bryan 2002: 89). Would a Christian person or community declare that the 'restoration of all things' is a firm achievement of the now completed mission of John the Baptist? Would anyone focused exclusively on the allegedly unique achievement of Jesus give John such unqualified endorsement, even if it were formulated implicitly rather than explicitly? Surely not. But then the question again arises as to the content of that restoration which is said to have been achieved. It looks as if it consists of a successful drive to bring about what Malachi defined as a return to covenant faithfulness, of which reconciliation in families is a token and sign (Bryan 2002: 92). That reconciliation can easily be seen as obedience to the fifth commandment (Exod. 20:12; Deut. 5:16) covered by John's emphasis on the Ten Commandments. If so, John is here acclaimed by Jesus for the gathering of a community of those who are committed to one another in 'righteousness' and committed afresh to the coming God of Israel (Bryan 2002: 128). It is a community from within Israel, committed to being Israel.

In sum, therefore, the evangelists all have their own axes to grind, but they do still provide us with pricelessly important evidence about John. They manifestly wish to convey to their readers that the superiority of Jesus to John had all along been part of the historical and theological package. John himself, they claim, had recognised it. For them, John was part of the story of Jesus, and no one should think otherwise. But the truth of the matter, as we have been able to recover it, is different. Jesus belongs primarily to the story of John rather than vice versa. If we give John back his independence and distinct integrity, then we are in a position not only to work from the nuggets of historical reality that can be located here and there in the four gospels but also (as we have seen) to bring into the reckoning the testimony, duly scrutinised and sifted, of Josephus. And as part of the process of making contact with John, as it were, we have been able to determine his Israel-centred community-consciousness.

John as prophetic insider and outsider

The evidence we have surveyed so far confirms that a considerable proportion of the population at large recognised John's authenticity. He was not, like so many prophets, at odds with his community as a whole.

This conclusion is reinforced by one of the most striking traditions in the gospels, one which has very probably been expanded editorially by the compiler of the Q source, but one whose earlier contours can fairly easily be discerned (Luke/Q 7:24–8). Not only do we encounter here further impressive evidence to add to that of Mark 9:11, 12a, 13a of Jesus' retrospective endorsement of John – and therefore of the status of his mission and baptism – but we also see that Jesus is able to count on the sympathetic agreement of his audience on the basis of their first-hand experience. Everyone apparently agrees that John was a prophet, and also that there was an implicitly anti-Antipas flavour to his mission:

> [24]Jesus began to speak to the crowds about John: 'What did you go out into the wilderness to look at? A reed shaken by the wind? [25]What then did you go out to see? Someone dressed in soft robes? Look, those who wear soft robes are in royal palaces. [26]But what did you go out to see? A prophet? Yes, indeed, I tell you (*nai legō humin*), and more than a prophet. [27]***This is the one about whom it is written, "See, I am sending my messenger ahead of you, who will prepare your way before you."*** [28a]Truly I tell you, among those born of women there has not been raised up anyone greater than John. [28b]Yet the least in the kingdom of God is greater than he.' (Luke 7:24–8)

This tradition is, first, shaped by a trio of questions, the answer to each of which is agreed between the hearers and Jesus. The answers are 'no', 'no' and 'yes', with the third being especially emphatic (cf. the force of the word *nai*, translated 'yes, indeed' in Gen. 42:21; Job 19:4; Judith 9:12; Luke 11:51; 12:5). En route to the 'yes, indeed' affirmation, the two preliminary questions carry loaded references to that same Antipas who would finally bring, or had already brought, the life of John to a bloody end. Reeds are found in the wilderness, but anyone clothed in rich splendour is certainly not. So why mention such a person? To do so is gratuitous unless, that is, a sideswipe is being taken at a known figure. The identity of that figure emerges pretty clearly when we recall the use of the reed on the coinage Antipas issued when he founded his capital city Tiberias in the year 19 CE, not to mention his adaptable and self-serving political strategy ('a reed shaken by the wind') (Theissen 1992: 26–42). The essential character of John's mission becomes clear by implication: (i) prophetic, as shown by appropriate, emphatically non-royal, clothing (cf. 1 Sam. 28:14; Zech. 13:4), and by the highly charged setting in the wilderness; (ii) opposed to Antipas, and offering a better hope for the future than any Antipas-like figure could ever do; and (iii) affirming the judgement which traditionally overtakes those in power who are compared to 'shaken reeds' (Theissen 1992: 27: Jereboam and Israel in 1 Kings 14:15; Philopator in 3 Maccabees 2:22).

That brings us, second, to the matter of geography. While neither Josephus' report nor John's own speech define the location of his activity, only the fact that sufficient water would need to be available to effect the statement that 'I baptize you with water', Jesus' testimony to John specifies the desert/wilderness. Is this significant, and if so how?

(i) All four gospels, and indeed Q before them, make much of Isaiah 40:3 when interpreting the Baptist's activity, and the fourth gospel even places a quotation of this famous text on the lips of John himself (Mark 1:2; Matt. 3:3/Luke 3:4; John 1:23):

> In the wilderness prepare the way of the Lord,
> make straight in the desert a highway for our God.

The text is always adjusted to make it fit the Baptist by omitting the phrase 'in the desert', thus destroying the parallelism with 'in the wilderness'. In the original text of Isaiah the Lord will come to Zion, and the herald of his coming may well be positioned in Zion, too. It is the process of preparation that is set in the wilderness/desert. This opens up two possibilities as far as John is concerned: *either* he went to work in the desert under the conscious influence of an adjusted version of Isaiah 40:3, *or* he worked in the desert for different reasons, and the application of the adjusted text of Isaiah 40:3 derives from later interpretation. In the first case, the text generated the historical fact; in the second the historical fact gave rise to the use of the text. The second option reminds us of how in just the same way the Qumran community, having moved

Study Philosophy Online!

www.conted.ox.ac.uk/ad/on1   Join our free e-mailing list

Teaching AS/A2 Philosophy?

Then you might be interested in (and enjoy) our online courses

These ten week courses cover key topics such as religion, free will and determinism, our knowledge of the external world and utilitarian ethics and they do so by encouraging participants to think for themselves and discuss the issues by way of class and group discussion boards.

The beauty of doing an online course is that you choose when to do the work (although you will have to work within the constraints of the ten week timetable), and you choose whether or not to do the optional assignments (some assignments are required because we find that participants get much more out of the course if they have to engage with others). Furthermore you don't have to *go* anywhere to do the course. Do it from the comfort of your own home, with your own mug of coffee beside you!

NEW - While you take the courses you have **free access** to Oxford University Press's online reference resources (see the website for details).

We're pleased to announce two new philosophy courses:

Philosophy of Religion by Dr Tim Mawson (Oxford). If you're interested in delving into the philosophical issues and arguments surrounding the claim that there's a God, then this is the course for you. Together, we shall look at what, if anything, it is that Jews, Christians, and Muslims are agreeing about when they claim that there is a God; and we shall look at what, if any, prospects there are for rationally defending or attacking this claim.

Introduction to Political Philosophy by Professor Jonathan Wolff (UCL). Political philosophy contains some of the greatest writings in the western intellectual tradition, as well as highly stimulating contemporary contributions

Also: The **Philosophy Gym** written by Stephen Law around his book of the same name, **Introduction to Philosophy** by Annamaria Carusi, and **Introduction to Philosophy of Mind** by Marianne Talbot. **Coming later: Philosophy of Knowledge**

We also offer short courses on visual arts, archaeology, English literature, and nanotechnology plus a range of longer courses in computing, local history – visit our website for details and leave your email to get updates

---

Enrol today at: **www.conted.ox.ac.uk/ad/on1**

Department for Continuing Education, University of Oxford, 1 Wellington Square, Oxford OX1 2JA

location, proceeded to attach the text of Isaiah 40:3 to where they settled:

> [12]And when these become a community in Israel [13]in compliance with these arrangements, they are to be segregated from within the dwelling of the men of sin to walk in the desert in order to open there His path. [14]As it is written, 'In the desert, prepare the way of ★★★★, straighten in the steppe a roadway for our God.' [15]This is the study of the law which he commanded through the hand of Moses . . . (1QS 8:12–15: text in Martínez/Tigchelaar 1997: 89)

Whereas the influence of Malachi 3:1a in the traditions concerning the Baptist is strong, the influence of Isaiah 40:3 is by comparison quite weak, and the substantial overlap between the two – 'See, I am sending my messenger to *prepare the way* before me' – could have encouraged the later introduction of the weaker text as a means of interpreting the location of John's activity. This means that we must be prepared to look elsewhere for the significance of John's choice of location.

(ii) Not long after John, other prophetic figures – often referred to as 'sign prophets' – would call as many as would listen to assemble in the desert/wilderness. These people chose their location deliberately: this was the place to see vindicated 'the belief that God would there give them tokens of deliverance' (*Jewish War* 2:258) or 'unmistakable marvels and signs that would be wrought in harmony with God's design' (*Antiquities* 20:168). For them the desert/wilderness was a strategic focus, and the Jordan the setting for exodus-type 'signs which would effect deliverance in the manner of the theophanic miracles of the Exodus/Conquest' (Bryan 2002: 34–9). Sadly for them, no signs occurred, nor any divinely stimulated reed sea-type event at the Jordan, only a devastating silence and a depressing (for them) lack of divine activity. No interventions came, except from the prefects, who brought matters to a uniform and abrupt conclusion.

To set these later prophetic figures alongside the Baptist is to be impressed by some points of agreement. He and they set about assembling people in the wilderness, and were energised by an eager longing for divine intervention. But crucial points of disagreement prevent John from being seen as their prototype. He was a preacher of judgement and repentance in the way that they do not seem to have been. For him there was no thought of signs initiating the expected act of God, and almost inevitably serving secondarily to confirm his own charisma-determined authenticity, whereas for them the signs were essential. Above all, John was a baptizer, and they were not. For him the wilderness, while not without its own intrinsic significance, seems to have been more notable strategically for the water of the Jordan river than for anything else. So, for all the points of agreement between John and the 'sign prophets', the distinctiveness of John over against them leaves the stronger impression.

(iii) We should probably do no more – but certainly no less! – than note that by opting to work in the wilderness, and by calling others to the wilderness, John was identifying with a long tradition of piety, protection of purity, and protest against the wielders of power. This was, after all, the place to which Elijah had fled under threat from Ahab (1 Kings 19:4). It was the place to which the Maccabean loyalists, the 'many who were seeking righteousness and justice [who] went down to the wilderness to live there . . . because troubles pressed heavily upon them', had resorted under threat from Antiochus Epiphanes (1 Macc. 2:29; 2 Macc. 5:27). It was the preferred place of the Qumran community, led by the 'Teacher of Righteousness', and resisting the threat of Jonathan Maccabeus, just as Jonathan himself had previously fled there from the threat of Bacchides (1 Macc. 9:33). It was the setting for the quasi-hermitic Bannus (Josephus, *Life* 11). We infer that resort to the desert/wilderness was yet another sign of the intensity of John's devotion and loyalty to the fundamental principles of Judaism.

The tradition in Luke/Q 7:24–8 has, third, been expanded, with verse 27 (in bold italics) interrupting the original sequence from verse 26 to verse 28. It fuses Malachi 3:1a and Exodus 23:20, the text that in any case influenced Malachi 3:1a, in order to relate John to Jesus. Thus, 'before me' (i.e. God) is replaced by 'before you' (i.e. Jesus). That has not been the concern of the material up to this point. While verse 27 cannot be the original sequel to verses 24b–26, it is plain that without *some* sequel the sayings would hang in the air. A few ancient manuscripts recognised the problem by putting verse 28a next to verse 26. It may have been a true instinct that led the copyists of those manuscripts to separate verse 28b from verse 28a, for the tendency in verse 28b to reduce John by means of an adverse comparison matches verse 27 and is not prepared for in verses 24b–26, 28a. It must be admitted, however, that such a 'solution' remains controversial among New Testament specialists, and verse

28b is more likely to be the original sting in the tail of what Jesus says. It expresses the self-awareness and mission-consciousness of a person who presumes to make such an authoritative evaluation of John, and then goes on to register the conviction that through his own mission God's rule is not just announced but also made available. With the former we can compare the thinking which seemed to underlie Mark 9:13a; with the latter we may correlate whatever it was that caused the disciples and then Jesus to use the word 'first' in Mark 9:11–12a.

In detail, the terms 'born of women' and 'raise up' are idioms referring respectively to humankind as such (cf. Job 14:1: 'A mortal, *born of woman*, few of days and full of trouble') and to divine appointment to a particular role (cf. Sir. 10:4: 'The government of the earth is in the hand of the Lord, and over it he will *raise up* the right leader for the time'). Jesus' very emphatic endorsement of the widespread view of John as within the prophetic succession, and his additional declaration that he was in fact greater than all his predecessors within that (or any other) succession, is startling indeed. Even if there follows the suggestion that the post-John era is an even better time, a time when God's kingship can be experienced and entered, the affirmation about John himself could scarcely be outdone. Doubtless it should be linked with Jesus' having personally undergone John's baptism, and very probably having been among the disciples of John, absorbing so much of his teaching that he could make it his own. Perhaps the thought of the John/Elijah equivalence is not too far away.

So in speech, in appearance, in anti-establishment orientation, John was a prophet. Despite the negativity of the political elite, he made a significant impact on the community.

Tension with those in a different position of authority, this time religious authority, within the community is implied by another tradition, this time the record of John's preaching preserved in Q (Luke/Q 3:7–9):

> 7bYou brood of vipers! Who warned you to flee from the coming wrath? 8Bear fruits worthy of repentance. Do not presume to say among yourselves, 'We have Abraham as our ancestor'; for I tell you, God is able from these stones to raise up children for Abraham. 9Even now the axe is placed at the root of the trees; every tree therefore that does not bear good fruit is cut down and thrown into the fire.

In respect of this tradition, first, Matthew and Luke disagree in the introduction they provide: 'When he saw many Pharisees and Sadducees
coming to his baptism . . .' (Matthew) versus 'He said to the crowds that
were coming out to be baptized by him . . .' (Luke). Each evangelist has
reworked the introduction according to his own interests. The introduction in the Q source may have been how Luke presents it – 'the
crowds' – in similar vein to Luke/Q 7:24, where Jesus speaks to 'the
crowds' who evidently have first-hand experience of John, though those
'crowds' seem markedly more favourable to John than the audience of
Luke/Q 3:7–9 here. Alternatively, it may have been, though this is not
very likely, how Matthew presents it – 'Pharisees and Sadducees'. It
might even, bearing in mind how Matthew likes to set up such a
pairing with Pharisees, be simply 'Sadducees' (so, Webb 1991: 175–8).
We can only guess, and guess rather ineffectually, but in any case it is the
substance rather than the setting of the sayings that takes us forward.

Second, those addressed as 'brood of vipers' are unlikely to be the general audience to whom an appeal is being made, nor persons who have
come in order to be baptized, but rather persons in authority who are
checking out the whole situation (cf. John 1:19) and who are being
addressed ironically. Matthew reflects this in using the verb 'come to'
(*erchomai epi*), which usually refers to making contact and not necessarily
any more than that (cf. Matt. 21:19; Mark 16:2). The saying beginning
'We have Abraham as our ancestor' is best understood as a putative argument *against* involvement in John's baptism, rather than a thought in the
mind of anyone of serious and sympathetic disposition who is coming
for baptism. It may express a sense that the faithfulness of Abraham in
offering his son Isaac as a sacrifice represented a quite sufficient 'benefit'
that accrued to the advantage of later generations of his people (Taylor
1997: 124–30). Or, perhaps more likely, it is the sort of thing that comes
across in Josephus' amplification of the speech made by Nehemiah on
arrival in Jerusalem:

> Fellow Jews, you know that God cherishes the memory of our fathers
> Abraham, Isaac and Jacob, and because of their righteousness does not
> give up his providential care for us. (*Antiquities* 11:169; cf. Neh.
> 2:17–18)

Over against such an appeal to Abraham, which bases the confidence of the present generation on security achieved by the righteousness of the patriarchs in the past, and which would supposedly make repentance and baptism unnecessary, John insists that the present generation must accept responsibility on its own account for the achievement of 'righteousness'. 'We have Abraham as our ancestor' is, after all, a plural statement. In it a community speaks, defending itself against the need to repent and undergo baptism. That means a tacit recognition that John's mission is emphatically *community*-oriented, *Israel*-oriented. So in Luke/Q 3:7–9 we have a critique of those who claim to represent a community and who have no intention whatever of being baptized, because their security is, they believe, well grounded and in no kind of jeopardy. John's address to them is very much *ad hominem* and is not part of his general and public preaching of baptism. For that we are left with Luke/Q 3:16b–17 alone. The contrast between the identities of the two audiences designated 'you' (Luke/Q 3:7b, 16b) could not be more pointed.

Third, John's profile is here again that of a prophet – and his purpose typically prophetic: short-term expectation of an intervention of God; an attack on religious complacency grounded in a sense of the special relationship between God and his people; the presence of both salvation and judgement in the message, but with the accent placed unmistakably on judgement, that is to say, more concern to disturb the comfortable than to comfort the disturbed; and an overarching purpose of getting the people of God to be what they are intended by God to be.

In sum, then, John's profile can be defined thus: he was a prophet, who carried conviction with the community to which he spoke, but stood in some tension with those who exercised power and authority. His mission to prepare for the coming of God was not to be pursued inside the regular religious and priestly structures within which, according to Luke 1:5–23, his family life was so firmly embedded. From priestly stock he came; to a prophetic vocation he gave himself.

John the Baptist in community context

The case for Isaiah 40:3 as a formative influence on the historical John turned out to be not impossible but nevertheless frail. The case for Malachi 3—4, the classic passage referring to an Elijah figure, as such an influence appeared to be much stronger (cf. Trumbower 1994).

It may well not be coincidental that the Jordan should figure so prominently in the missions of both Elijah and John (Trumbower 1994:

36–7; Evans 2002: 49): a setting on the *eastern* side of the river (because John has to be set in Perea, the domain of Herod Antipas) recalls the hiding-place of Elijah (1 Kings 17:5) and the place to which Elijah crossed the river prior to his ascent (2 Kings 2:6–8). Not perhaps entirely irrelevant is another consideration: it was the mission of Elisha as successor to Elijah, and son-like inheritor of his legacy of prophetic spirit (2 Kings 2:9–15), that included a call for Naaman's washing and cleansing in the Jordan (2 Kings 5:10–14; Evans 2002: 49).

This is the point at which we can move to an assessment of the 'two baptisms' saying, the study of which is complicated by the difficulty of establishing the original wording of Q, and by Mark-versus-Q discrepancies. If we follow the principle of moving from the clear to the unclear, the place to start is of course Mark 1:7–8:

7aThe one who is more powerful than I is coming after me;
7bI am not worthy to stoop down and untie the thong of his sandals.
8aI have baptized you in/with water;
8bbut he will baptize you in/with holy spirit (*pneumati hagiōi*).

Mark has two separate sayings, the first dealing with the two contrasting figures, John and a 'coming one' (Mark 1:7), and the second with two contrasting baptisms (Mark 1:8). In line with the absence from Mark of any explicit preaching of judgement by the Baptist, the future baptism is 'in holy spirit'. From the immediately following tradition of Jesus' own post-baptismal endowment with the Spirit, we must infer that the coming baptism has to do with salvation, and that the greater strength of the coming one as over against John has to do with the creation of a Spirit-endowed community. John's community of repentant and forgiven persons (cf. Mark 1:4) is subsumed in the future community of Spirit-endowed persons, of whom Jesus is both prototype and creator. That is Mark's view.

From Matthew and Luke, on the other hand, we are able to infer that Q has the same two sayings about the two figures, John and the 'coming one' (Luke/Q 3:16c), and the two baptisms (Luke/Q 3:16bd), but in this presentation the two form a sandwich structure. The most serious difficulty is how the future baptism was defined in Q. It was clearly a baptism 'in fire' – on that much Matthew and Luke agree – and the meaning of that fiery process is conveyed by talk of winnowing and cleansing, and then finally of burning and gathering (Luke/Q 3:17). But did it involve nothing other than fire – for it might in principle be that Matthew and Luke both owe their references to 'holy spirit' to Mark 1:8 – or was it also a baptism 'in spirit', or even 'in holy spirit'? Gospels specialists opt, with carefully reasoned arguments, for each and every one of these theoretically possible conclusions. But while all are genuinely possible, greater probability arguably attaches to 'in holy spirit': first, the two halves of the saying share a common reference to 'you', and it would be odd if judgement alone were the prospect for those who had committed themselves to the salvific experience of John's baptism; second, it would be without precedent for a prophet to summarise his view of the future in terms of judgement alone (cf. Taylor 1997: 7). Even Amos, of whom John reminds us not infrequently, and whose preoccupation with judgement was fierce and firm, still 'presents a ray of hope' in his 5:4–6, signalling that

> the final death sentence has not been signed . . . the divine judgment is not irrevocable . . . for the decision of God is very often subject to change, but the change is contingent upon the people's return . . . [for] repentance has the power to abrogate the death sentence for the individual as well as for the entire nation. (Paul 1991: 161–2)

The oracle in question, 'Seek me *and live* . . . seek the Lord *and live*', followed by more of the same, 'Seek good and not evil, *that you may live*; and so the Lord, the God of hosts, will be with you' (Amos 5:14), is probably not to be set aside as a post-Amos intrusion (Paul 1991: 164). By referring, albeit using different imagery, to fruitful trees and gathered wheat, John signals just such an expectation of restoration and return.

The Q version of the saying can, subject to these uncertainties, be shown to harmonise most naturally and easily with what we have so far recovered concerning the mission of the historical John. So that version can form a working basis for further reflection:

> [16b]I on the one hand baptize you in water; [16c]on the other hand the one who is coming after me is stronger than I, of whom I am not worthy to carry/loosen his sandals; [16d]that person will baptize you in holy spirit and fire; [17]whose winnowing-shovel is in his hand, to cleanse his

threshing-floor and to gather the wheat into his granary, but to burn the chaff with unquenchable fire.

Certain risks are necessarily involved in interpreting this saying, and specialist study has continued to exhibit cracks and conflicts within it. But something must and can be said.

First, the saying about the greater strength of the coming one (Luke/Q 3:16c) is extremely serviceable to Christians, keen as they would be to affirm John's inferiority and Jesus' superiority. It may even be an editorial construction at the Q stage, preparing for the rather artificial question directed by the Baptist to Jesus, 'Are you the coming one, or should we look for someone else?' (Luke/Q 7:19), with which the later long Q section concerned with the relationship between John and Jesus begins (Luke/Q 7:18–35). Whoever 'the coming one' may be, the insistence on John's inferiority seems unnecessary and therefore, to repeat, artificial. But in its present setting the greater strength is understood to consist primarily not in who the person is but in what the person does, that is, 'baptize' with holy spirit and the fire which, in a Malachi-conditioned context, means purification and judgement.

Second, while it is not spelt out explicitly that 'I baptize with water' (Q's verb in the present tense) refers to an immersion (cf. Jesus' coming up [*anabainōn*] out of the water, Mark 1:10) which is once for all, this is much more likely than the alternative of a constantly repeated sequence of purificatory washings. Crucial here are two considerations: (i) that Mark's wording is not 'I baptize [*baptizō*] you . . .' (Mark 1:8) but 'I have baptized [*ebaptisa*] you . . .', that is, a once-for-all past event, and (ii) that John is called both by gospel traditions and by Josephus 'the Baptist'. As we have already seen, this sets him apart from Bannus, the revered teacher of the young Josephus, and his baptism from any other purificatory regime in the Jewish community. The impression conveyed is of a once-for-all initiatory rite, carried out by John – after all, he can hardly have been actively engaged in repeated washings of all those who attached themselves to him and affirmed their conviction that he was the prophet for their time.

By undergoing such a baptism, and thereby affirming John's prophetic status, they were recognising that his action was in a real sense an action of God. They were therefore receiving a divine seal of the forgiveness, following on repentance and renewal, which they had already sought.

John's rite cannot therefore be classified simply with those rites of purification which deal with purity alone and have no moral concern. Those who undergo it are not in a state of impurity in the standard sense of that term. They have a different sort of problem, which has been dealt with *and effectively shown to have been dealt with* by the baptism.

Third, that theme of the forgiveness of sins is all-pervasive in connection with John's baptism: only with dogged obduracy can the phrase 'a baptism of repentance for the forgiveness of sins' be read as no more than a throw-back from a later Christian baptismal theology, 'the anachronistic assignment to John of an element of the language of catechesis within early Christianity' (Chilton 2002: 35). Zechariah's song, the Benedictus, has at its centre the theme of the forgiveness of sins as the content of 'the knowledge of salvation', the turning point in Israel's experience *en route* to the coming enjoyment of light and peace (Luke 1:77); Mark makes it the content of John's preaching (Mark 1:4); Josephus, as we have seen, insists that it was the very core of John's appeal (*Antiquities* 18:117). All the evidence at our disposal therefore encourages us to think of the baptism as a confirmation of the removal of that uncleanness which results from moral alienation, and thus the recovery of a state of holiness that extends far beyond the sphere of purity. Israel is being asked to be once again what Israel must be, a people that is 'holy because I am holy' (Lev. 11:44). This is the burden of the message of Malachi, which the Baptist revived so forcefully.

If all the evidence at our disposal encourages us to think about the historical John in this vein, we must repeat that only by a serious over-interpretation of that evidence can we find in the forgiveness-cum-baptism theme the suggestion of a subversive movement 'aimed not at renewing the existing structures, but at replacing them . . . a clear alternative to the Temple . . . an implicit counter-Temple movement' (Wright 1996: 160, 497). Nor can we legitimately find in the warning to the inspectors, 'Do not presume to say among yourselves, "We have Abraham as our ancestor" . . .' any insistence on a redrawing of the boundaries of Israel (Wright 1996: 323). Nor is repentance as understood by John a matter of abandoning revolutionary zeal (Wright 1996: 250). If John revived the approach of the prophets, who were scarcely engaged in counter-Temple movements; if he, like many before him, attached forgiveness to a genuine change of heart and conduct on the part of the religiously complacent and negligent; if he, like many before him, warned

---

that even the most prized features of Israel's covenant relationship must not be taken for granted; if he achieved something of an alliance with at least some Pharisees (Mark 2:18) and gained the respect of Josephus and indeed some at least of the contemporary religious leaders; if his message of repentance made an impact on those with a moral problem (prostitutes) and implicitly pro-establishment collaborators (tax-collectors), for whom a call to repent of revolutionary zeal would have little purchase; then it is more prudent to stay within the confines of what the evidence, straightforwardly interpreted, demands – John was truly in the prophetic succession, calling Israel to take stock and take seriously the divine demand to be in practice what they were in principle, the people of God.

Fourth, the relationship between John's baptism and that future baptism which God will effect is naturally a function of whatever the 'baptism in holy spirit and fire' was about. It is also a function of how the plural 'you' who receive the future baptism are related to the plural 'you' whom John baptizes. We have already seen that it would be a mistake to see the future baptism as involving judgement alone, since it is clearly in prospect for those forgiven by God and baptized by John, and second, that if 'you' in both cases stands for Israel, room is left for a sense that the people as a whole are both faced with judgement and also offered salvation. In other words, paradoxical though it might seem, those who respond to John can be distinguished from those who do not so respond, but have not thereby lost their identification with the nation to whom they all belong. The upshot is that, although Israel must pass through the divine fire, the firm promise to Israel, anticipated already in the group assembled around John, is of an endowment with God's spirit which signals the new people in the new era (cf. the range of texts cited in Webb 1991: 224–7: Ezek. 36:26–7; *Jubilees* 1:23; Joel 2:28–9; 1QS 4:20–21). From these considerations we can conclude in the latter case that John's baptism is an anticipation of the life of the new era, and a protection from the peril of divine judgement for those who listen and respond to him as prophet and baptizer. In their life and religious experience they anticipate the community life of the new era.

But if the corporate body undergoing baptism does so in anticipation of being allowed to experience the new post-judgement era, and if they are (as it were) a microcosm of the Israel that benefits from divine intervention, what will life in the new era be like? What are the promises? What are the demands? How, too, does the future impact on the present?

First, the beginnings of an answer are contained in the celebration contained in the Magnificat, a message that started with the humiliation of John's previously childless and therefore (according to current cultural norms) shamed mother, and moved from her to the predicament of Israel. The key theme of the Magnificat is 'mercy': 'His mercy is for those who fear him from generation to generation . . . He has helped his servant Israel in remembrance of his mercy' (Luke 1:50, 54), and in case the reader misses that fact, mercy is what Elizabeth/Israel is declared to have received: 'The Lord had shown mercy to her' (v. 58). That is to say, the covenant relationship is being honoured in full.

Second, the message conveyed by the Magnificat is uncompromising in its traditional treatment of human structures and suffering. The rich, proud and powerful will be cut down to size; the lowly and the hungry will be raised and fed. The Benedictus is equally direct: light will shine where darkness and death have hitherto held sway. Liberation and salvation from the control of foreign powers will enable the nation's service of God to take place in peace and complete freedom from fear. Thus flesh is put on the bones of the expectation of social and political reversal and displacement.

Third, there is the recurrent theme of 'righteousness', that key covenant concept. We note the unmistakable 'atmosphere' of righteousness with which the scene for the drama of the Baptist's mission is set: his parents were 'righteous before God', and walked before God blamelessly in all the commandments and 'righteous regulations' (dikaiōmata) of the Lord (Luke 1:6). The terms of reference of John's public work are defined in precisely that way: the preparation of the Lord's people by 'turning the hearts of the disobedient to the wisdom of the righteous' (v. 17). Josephus' account of him is shot through with recurrent references to righteousness. And it can scarcely be ignored that in later gospel traditions 'righteousness' keeps obtruding in connection with John: the Matthean construct of the John/Jesus conversation resorts to it (Matt. 3:15); a Q tradition (Matt. 21:32/Luke 7:29) associates John with 'the way of righteousness' or the reaction of 'righteousing' God for what has happened with John; a further Q saying concludes the survey of the whole John/Jesus question with the comment that 'Wisdom is righteoused by her children [that is to say, those who *listen* to Wisdom, whose mouthpieces are John and Jesus]' (Luke/Q 7:35). John and his mission left an unmistakable, righteousness-shaped footprint in the sand of first-century memory.

Fourth, the recognition of, and return to, righteousness in repentance and practical behaviour has further implications. In the context of a call to the whole community to *be* what that community, at least potentially, *is* in the presence of God, a remarkable inclusiveness becomes the order of the day. That inclusiveness can certainly be seen in the brilliantly improved prospects of the poor, who all too easily become marginalised and scarcely acknowledged. They could not be more firmly acknowledged than they are in the song of Elizabeth: the poor *belong to* Israel, but in a deeper sense the poor *are* Israel. More adventurous and controversial is the inclusion of the tax-collectors, the sinners and the prostitutes (cf. Matt. 21:32/Luke 7:29–30) – drawn in on the basis of repentance, acknowledging that in the work of John the work of God can be seen and known.

Fifth, given this overall tenor of John's mission, the hopes for the future of Israel that he stirred up, and the traditional Torah-based ethics that he championed, the indicative for the future could not but dictate an imperative for the present. Thus, no one could take seriously his equation of the poor with the community without at the same time giving active attention to the plight of the poor within the community. No one could take seriously his resolute reaffirmation of righteousness without attending to the obligations laid down in his so–called sociological preaching (Luke 3:10–14) – obligations imposed on the audience as a whole (distribution of property in food and clothing), and on the agents of authority in particular: (i) tax-collectors, who are called not to abandon tax-collection but to practise justice, and to avoid graft and greed, and (ii) the military, who are called not to abandonment of military service but to contentment and the avoidance of bullying. The soldiers in question were doubtless in the employ of Herod Antipas, their presence confirming the close interest Antipas was taking in the activities of John, and also the direct impact that his mission clearly had on the regime of Antipas. In all these respects, he is a typical 'back to basics' prophet.

Jesus in the context of John

We return to the full-hearted public endorsement of John by Jesus (Luke/Q 7:26, 28), with which we can associate an enigmatic saying which has caused more than a little trouble to interpreters (Matt. 11:12–3; Luke/Q 16:16):

> [26]But what did you go out to see? A prophet? Yes, indeed, I tell you (*nai legō humin*), and more than a prophet. [28a]Truly I tell you, among those born of women there has not been raised up anyone greater than John. [28b]Yet the least in the kingdom of God is greater than he.

> [16a]The law and the prophets until John: [16b]from then on (the gospel of) the kingdom of God has suffered violence, and the violent take it by force.

This reconstruction of the original wording of the latter, enigmatic saying has built into it several detailed decisions: (i) Luke's order, with verse 16b following verse 16a, rather than Matthew's reverse order is more logical and more likely to be original. (ii) Matthew's emphasis in his 11:2–19 on prophecy probably accounts for his non-idiomatic 'all the prophets and the law' and his use of the verb 'prophesy'. The close relationship in sequence between Matthew 5:17, 18, 31 and Luke 16:16, 17, 18 serves to provide confirmation of the original presence of 'the law and the prophets' (Matt. 5:17: cf. Schürmann 1968: 126–32). (iii) Matthew's version of Luke/Q 16:16b is much the more difficult, and Luke's clarifying, though not at all inappropriate, introduction of the term 'gospel' may well be a reminiscence of 'the poor have the gospel brought to them' (Matt. 11:5/Luke 7:22), and at the same time a sign that this saying originally belonged where Matthew has positioned it.

It is unlikely that this very probably authentic 'law and prophets' saying was originally an extension of the acclamation of John by Jesus. Nevertheless, it has some of the same features: a review of previous history, a sense that John stands at the end of that historical sequence, an implicit identification of the speaker with John, and a sense that the era of John – or is it the era after John? – is kingdom-centred. That being so, it may be that we can see how Luke/Q 16:16 would work if Luke/Q 7:26, 28 were allowed to help resolve some of the enigmatic details. In themselves, the two terms 'until' and 'from then on' could equally be inclusive or exclusive; the designation 'the law and the prophets', followed by the suggestion of the dawning of a new era, could in principle be taken to mean abrogation or at the very least subordination.

Several key references to 'the law and the prophets' in biblical literature combine to point up how they together represent the centre of gravity of Jewish religious faith and practice. Jesus ben Sirach follows his devoted study of 'the great teaching given to us through the law and the prophets' by offering further teaching and wisdom as an amplification and application of all the content of that body of material (Sirach: prologue). Judas Maccabeus uses 'the law and the prophets' to encourage his army to believe in their coming victory (2 Macc. 15:9). The father of the seven martyrs is said by their mother to have educated them all most thoroughly in 'the law and the prophets', as a result of which they are able to recall the heroes of faith in a God who brings the righteous through even the most awful experiences of suffering (4 Macc. 18:10–19). Those heroes include kings, prophets and sages – in short, notable personnel in a review that matches the panoramic reference to 'those born of women' in Luke/Q 7:28a. In the light of the evidence of Jesus' attitude to the traditions of Israel, which will be examined shortly, it is likely that Luke/Q 16:16 is not in any way playing down 'the law and the prophets' by signalling the dawn of a new era. Rather, the intention is to see that new era, epitomised in the prophetic message of 'the kingdom of God', announced initially by John and with even greater effect by Jesus, as the new centre of gravity of faith. It does not set aside what had previously been in place but builds on and extends it, even in the teeth of fierce conflict. The saying allows two complementary perspectives: from one angle, John is on a line of continuity from 'the law and the prophets' to Jesus, while from another angle, John belongs with 'the law and the prophets' as preliminary to all that Jesus is, represents, and says. Perhaps the saying is intended to discourage its audience from making a choice, for both perspectives contain truths that Jesus seems to want to communicate. But above all, Jesus associates himself with John in trying to shift the centre of gravity of faith. With no disrespect for the tradition, the faith it shaped and the hope it encouraged, there is now a new focus. Nothing should distract from the gospel of God's kingdom, the future coming of God to his people as announced by John and Jesus.

From this conclusion we can retrace our steps to what is historically as near as may be beyond dispute, namely that Jesus who spoke in this way had previously been baptized by John. No Christian inventiveness could account for this tradition. No holding back on Jesus' part is conceivable in view of the unstinting praise he heaped on John in Luke/Q 7:26, 28.

Jesus' baptism by John cannot but signal agreement with his outlook and acceptance of his message, including the need for repentance and forgiveness (Taylor 1997: 11). He was almost certainly a disciple of John. On such a basis we can understand why in the gospel tradition the voice is often the voice of Jesus and the words uncannily like words of John. One thinks of the prophetic announcement of the near kingdom: 'The kingdom of God has come near' (Mark 1:15); the characteristic summons to repentance (Luke/Q 10:13; 11:32; Luke 13:3, 5; 15:7, 10; 16:30), with just too many traditions insisting on the need for repentance – not necessarily individual, and often collective and communal – for this theme to be detached from Jesus; the loud echo of John's expectation of social and political transformation and reversal in the earliest version of the beatitudes (Luke/Q 6:20b–21), to which we shall return in due course (see pp. 210–14); the parables which warn of future separation (Matt. 13:24–30, 47–8) and unmistakably repeat John's announcement that the coming one 'will gather his wheat into the granary, but the chaff he will burn with unquenchable fire' (Luke/Q 3:17); and the intense longing for the lighting of the divine fire (Luke 12:49):

> I came to bring fire to the earth,
> and how intensely I wish it were already kindled!

So the primary influence on Jesus becomes ever more clearly detectable. It was assuredly his prophetic teacher, the Elijah-like prophet who had baptized him.

The baptismal experience of Jesus, however, is a truly vital piece of evidence. It has rightly been described as 'a bedrock historical datum' (Marcus 1995: 512). By means of it, Jesus identified with an alienated people in need of repentance followed by purification, and committed himself to renewal (Mark 1:9–11).

> [9]In those days Jesus came from Nazareth of Galilee and was baptized by John in the Jordan. [10]And just as he was coming up out of the water, he saw the heavens torn apart and the Spirit descending like a dove on him. [11]And a voice came from heaven, 'You are my Son, the Beloved; with you I am well pleased.'

What is additionally important for the understanding of the mission of

Jesus is the consequent and very private visionary experience that overtook him after the baptism itself. There are two versions of that visionary experience made available by the gospel tradition – Mark 1:10–11 and Luke 10:18 – and it may well be that as historians we have to choose between them.

The experience as detailed by Mark needs first to be considered. The later evangelists go in for an expansion of the circle of awareness of what happened to Jesus. They should not have done. Mark reports a public baptism, yes, but a public post-baptismal experience, no. It is in strictly limited terms an experience of Jesus. How may we classify and interpret that experience?

A close and instructive parallel is found in the visionary experience of Peter, which is described in Acts 10—11, and which in turn is compara-ble to the visionary experience of Paul in the Temple in Acts 22. Peter's experience is variously termed a trance (*ekstasis*: Acts 10:10) or vision (*horama*: Acts 10:17, 19): 'In a trance I saw a vision' (*en ekstasei horama*: Acts 11:5). In the two parallel stories there are three crucial and defining features. The first is an opening of the heavens (Mark 1:10; Acts 10:11). The second is the sight of something recognisable descending: 'some-thing like a large sheet' (Acts 10:11; 11:5) *or* 'like a dove' (Mark 1:10). The third is the sound of a voice from heaven, speaking personally to the recipient: 'Rise, Peter, kill and eat . . . what God has made clean, you must not call profane' *or* 'You are my Son, the beloved; with you I have been well pleased.'

This suggests an ecstatic dimension to the religious experience of Jesus at the moment when his mission is inaugurated. It would centre on a sense of his being endowed with the Spirit for whatever was in store. If the heavenly voice did indeed say what Mark claims, adroitly combining (in the view of most interpreters) Psalm 2:7 and Isaiah 42:1 in 'You are my son, the beloved; with you I have been well pleased,' it would also imply that the mission was from the start informed by a substantial Christology.

The heavenly declaration has recently been examined in a fresh way (Taylor 1997: 264–77), concentrating on the ideas involved, playing down the interpretation that relies on the detection of the two Old Testament texts, and playing up a more prophetic pattern. The argument runs as fol-lows:

(i) To be a 'son of God' is to be an Israelite, and on occasion an Israelite specially singled out as 'righteous' and close to God. The case of Honi the Circle-Drawer, famous man of prayer and martyr in the first century BCE, is instructive: Josephus describes him as 'a righteous man and dear to God' (*Antiquities* 14:22–4), and the Mishnah records in connection with his intimate prayerful relationship with God that, in his words, 'I am like a son of the house before you,' and in the words of Simeon ben Shetah, 'You plead with God and he performs your will, like a son that pleads with his father and he performs his will' (*m. Taanith* 3:8).

(ii) To be 'beloved' can be interpreted along the lines of Daniel 9—10, where the prophet, after confessing the sins of his people and praying for forgiveness, is visited in a vision by the angel Gabriel. The visitation leaves Daniel endowed with wisdom and understanding, and given 'the word and the vision' because 'you are greatly beloved' (Dan. 9:20–23).

(iii) The divine Spirit, often associated with Wisdom who 'passes into holy souls [and only such souls] and makes them friends of God and prophets' (Wisd. 7:27), is the standard endowment of the prophet. An 'anointing' takes place to equip the prophet for the forthcoming task (cf. 1 Kings 19:6).

Finally, (iv), the affirmation that 'with you I have been well pleased' picks up the preceding hints of the recognition of 'righteousness', and by virtue of the aorist form (*eudokēsa*) points to a distinct one-off occasion, which must be the baptism itself. This is not a statement of *extended* approval but rather of a past *moment* of approval.

Points (iii) and (iv) certainly carry conviction. That Jesus should embark on the mission that he did, with a strong sense of Spirit-endowment is multiply attested and virtually beyond doubt. That he should undergo baptism for genuine personal reasons, and not just for detached pragmatic or programmatic reasons, would make sense in the light of his neither claiming perfection (cf. Mark 10:18; see Taylor 1997: 11) nor acting perfectly (cf. Mark 7:27; see below, p. 176). That said, it seems a touch risky to rely too heavily on the heavenly voice's choice of a Greek aorist – just as risky as reliance on Gabriel's choice of a perfect participle (cf. Luke 1:28; see below, p. 116)! But arguments (i) and (ii) cause more hesitation: the echoes of Psalm 2:7 and Isaiah 42:1 are exceedingly strong – do all the multitudes of commentators who have picked them up have a hearing problem? – and the christological terminology not only seems higher-powered than is suggested but also rather consonant with Mark's own royal and more-than-Israel Sonship Christology.

At this point the experience detailed by Luke (10:18) needs to be considered:

I watched Satan fall from heaven like a flash of lightning.

In its present context, the disciples have returned from mission in joyful spirit, and their joy becomes the basis for a salutary comment by Jesus (vv. 17, 20). They are also, somewhat oddly, authorised *post eventum* to gain mastery over hostile and threatening forces (v. 19). But verse 18 stands out as a disclosure of a very personal visionary experience of Jesus himself, one which it is wholly appropriate to link to his baptism and the inauguration of a mission during which the forces of evil would be confronted and confounded (cf. Marcus 1995: 516–20). Such a suggestion makes comprehensible the fact that the hostile comment by those close to him, 'He has gone out of his mind [*exestē*]' (Mark 3:21), is, at least in Mark, attached to the debate about the agency of Jesus' exorcisms. It also coheres without any awkwardness with Jesus' conviction that if he by the Spirit of God cast out demons, then the kingdom of God had come upon people (Luke/Q 11:20, following the Matthean wording).

Here then, in a combination of the motifs of Mark 1:10 and Luke 10:18, we detect the historical evidence about the beginning of a prophetic mission. And this is where we may usefully return to the primary and fundamental reality about a prophet. S/he lives on the boundary between the human and divine worlds, and 'enjoys' (though not always pleasurably) *an intimate relationship with God*, whose intention and providence are wrapped in secrecy (cf. Amos 3:7: 'Truly the Lord God does nothing without revealing his secret to his servants the prophets'). S/he both receives and transmits revelatory messages from God (cf. 1 Sam. 9:15; Isa. 50:4–5). This intimate relationship between a prophet and God gives rise to the notion of the true prophet as 'sent', and in consequence the characteristic introductory formula, 'Thus says the Lord'. Moreover, the notion of a call is expressive of *independence of all human authorities*, and *a charismatic appointment* which is not part of any succession: see Amos 7:14–15:

14I am/was no prophet nor a prophet's son; but I was a herdsman . . .
15and the Lord took me from following the flock, and the Lord said to me, 'Go, prophesy to my people Israel.'

The essence of such a call can be discerned from Micah's oracle against false prophets, drawing together such themes as vision, revelation, endowment with power and the divine Spirit, and the commission to call a nation to account (cf. Mic. 3:5–8):

> 5Thus says the Lord concerning the prophets who lead my people astray, who cry 'Peace' when they have something to eat, but declare war against those who put nothing in their mouths. 6Therefore it shall be night to you, without vision, and darkness to you, without revelation . . . 8But as for me, I am filled with power, with the spirit of the Lord, and with justice and might, to declare to Jacob his transgression and to Israel his sin.

This is the world of experience and thought within which Jesus' post-baptismal crisis belongs. He was deeply rooted in the mission of John, and he took from that mission many of its defining features. Then he was launched on his own prophetic mission by an ecstatic-mystical call-type vision that contained within itself an endorsement of John as well as a call to himself. For all that the 'disciples of John' did not all identify with the mission of Jesus and the disciples he gathered around himself, the work of John was powerfully formative for the work of Jesus. And when, after the mission of Jesus was complete and had been overtaken by his death and resurrection, the new community of 'resurrection people' was given its identity, at least in part, by a baptism which was in continuity with the baptism of John.

John the Baptist in resurrection perspective

Christian belief is bound to view all that had happened prior to the resurrection of Jesus with a keen awareness of continuity-cum-discontinuity. Not everything that happened prior to Easter either can or should be re-licensed, as it were, for the post-Easter world. It is perfectly possible in principle that, just as with some things said and done by Jesus, so also anything or everything said or done by John *might* have to be assigned to the discontinuity column and abandoned. Possible, but perhaps not probable, because of the way in which the foundational experiences of the risen Jesus are described.

Resurrection belief itself is most firmly and broadly rooted in an appearance to a group of disciples. That appearance is hinted at in Mark

16:7, affirmed in 1 Corinthians 15:5, 7, and told in narrative form in three versions elsewhere: Matthew 28:16–20; Luke 24:36–49; and John 20:19–23. Notwithstanding very considerable variation between the stories, some themes recur: (i) *repentance* (Luke 24:47); (ii) *forgiveness of sins* (Luke 24:47; John 20:23); (iii) *baptism* (Matt. 28:19, but see Luke's alternative formulation in Acts 2:38: 'Repent, and be baptized every one of you in the name of Jesus Christ for the forgiveness of your sins; and you will receive the gift of the Holy Spirit'); and (iv) the *Spirit* (Matt. 28:19; Luke 24:49; John 20:22). These themes remind us of key elements in the mission of John, key features in the process of community definition.

In one way or another, then, the voice of John was once again heard in the land as the earliest post-resurrection Christians adopted a rite, which had not only been definitive for John's mission but also very probably continued, at least for a time, as part of the mission of Jesus. When therefore we set in a Christian context the formal liturgical phrase, 'baptizing them in the name of the Father and of the Son and of the Holy Spirit', we are placing ourselves in a line of religious experience that is ultimately indebted to the ministry of John.

We also place ourselves in a line of religious obligation focused on John's keynote theme of 'righteousness'. This term indeed stands for more than a commitment to moral integrity and behavioural obedience to the will of God, defined by the last five of the Ten Commandments, but it certainly does not stand for less. The voice of the prophet, resounding across time to those who submit to the baptism which John inaugurated, is a voice which cuts through casuistry, calls for respect for the 'big principles', and lays down commitment to 'the good life' of righteousness as the *sine qua non* for the candidate for that baptism. It is a voice that calls for unending exposure to the discomfort of a prophetic call for renewal.

This, however, might suggest an undue preoccupation with where and how the individual stands before God. That is certainly involved, but even more prominent is the appropriate community awareness. John's mission, encapsulated in his baptism, was all about bringing to effect what it means to be the people of God. How does the community awareness, and a comparable realisation of what it means to be the people of God, work out when baptism is set in a post-resurrection religious context? To answer this question we would be well advised to turn to Paul, keenly aware that for him the resurrection established Christ as the defining figure for *the whole world* and the *corporate* embodiment of a new world and a new community.

For Paul the resurrection of Christ was *a past event* in the experience of an individual which could be viewed (as it were) from afar. But at least equally importantly it was also *a present and inclusive experience in which others could participate.* None of Paul's contemporaries, as far as we can piece together their positions, achieved such profound insight as he did into the implications of a faith-baptism initiation into the risen Christ. Faith in the risen one *alone*, realised in the death-and-resurrection-effected experience of baptism, achieves (in Paul's view) entry into that regularity of relationship which is the meaning of 'righteousness', the relegation to a past era of that life whose last term is death, and the participatory and transformative involvement in the risen Christ who embodies 'new creation'. To take a classic statement of the position:

> [17]If anyone is 'in Christ', new creation! The old things have passed away: look, new things have come into being . . . [21]Him who did not know Sin, he made to be Sin for us, that we might become 'the righteousness of God' in him. (2 Cor. 5:17, 21)

First, this 'new creation' in which people share is God's new beginning, effected for those who represent the new version of humankind: they personally are no longer primarily defined by the old concept of the people of God, and therefore by the Jew/gentile distinction, nor do they define others in that 'according to the flesh' way (2 Cor. 5:16). The corporate Christ, who now dominates the theological and religious horizon, is inclusive and therefore no longer to be defined as 'Jesus the Jew', for all that we cannot stress too heavily that the pre-Easter prophetic Jesus was indeed 'Jesus the Jew'. Second, as the spotlessly law-keeping one he was nevertheless (says Paul) 'made to be Sin', that is to say, to come under the authority of the personalised being, Sin. That can only mean that he submitted to Sin, not by sinning but by dying (v. 21a). But in that case the meaning of the matching counterpart statement that we 'become the righteousness of God in him' must be essentially a matter of sharing in the great event which followed on from his death, namely his resurrection.

By means of this argumentation, and in the light of the post-resurrection experience of the Spirit, it becomes evident that the baptism and prophetic message of John for Israel can be, and is, overtaken by Christian baptism within the parameters of the post-Easter gospel for the world.

Perhaps there are other respects in which the dependence of Christian baptism upon John's rite, as well as its development beyond that rite should send a salutary message to the contemporary Church:

Once a community becomes institutionalised – 'routinised', in the rather apt language of sociology – the voice of prophecy all too easily fades into a mere echo, and maybe even less than that. But attending to the critique of the prophet, to the disturbing non-establishment message recalling the community to principles both big and basic, to belief and hope in a future dominated by a discontented God who is the author of change, to the insistence that regularity and routine piety are not enough, to the summons truly to 'be the people of God' and to exhibit the beauty of holiness – perhaps in those areas the mission of John can and should be a mission to us. Surely nothing less is demanded by the resurrection of the one who declared, 'Of those born of women there has never been raised up a greater than John.'

CHAPTER 2

New life, new labour:
terms of reference for 'following Jesus'

Introduction

One of the most striking features of the beautiful Cathedral in Wells is the pulpit. Entered through the chapel dedicated to St Edmund of Abingdon, who was Archbishop of Canterbury during the years 1233–40, the pulpit is connected to the tomb of William Knight, Bishop of Bath and Wells during those years so crucial in the story of the English Church (1541–7). Under the cornice of the pulpit is engraved the text of 2 Timothy 4:2:

> PREACHE · THOV · THE · WORDE · BE · FERVENT · IN · SEASON · AND · OVT
> · OF · SEASON · REPROVE · REBVKE · EXHORTE · WYTH · ALL · LONG ·
> SVFFERYNG · & · DOCTRYNE · 2 · TIMO.

Facing outwards, the text is nevertheless directed inwards towards the preacher. He or she is brought back in salutary fashion to the New Testament's manual of Christian ministry.

An oily and self-righteous young clergyman, prematurely promoted to be the Bishop's Chaplain, engineered for himself an invitation to climb into the pulpit of another of the most awe-inspiring cathedrals in the land in the presence of the Bishop and the Dean and Chapter. This ambitious young clergyman preached a provocative sermon on another text from the New Testament's manual of ministry, a sermon which the Bishop's wife loved – 'Bishop,' she enquired, 'did you ever hear a more sublime, more spirit-moving, more appropriate discourse than that?' – but it hurt the Precentor deeply, enraged that high and mighty, if somewhat peppery, potentate, the Archdeacon, and landed the Bishop in one almighty load of trouble. It was a pretext for Anthony Trollope to dip his pen in vinegar and write:

> There is, perhaps, no greater hardship at present inflicted on mankind in civilised and free countries, than the necessity of listening to sermons. No one but a preaching clergyman has, in these realms, the power of compelling an audience to sit still, and be tormented. No one but a preaching clergyman can revel in platitudes, truisms, and untruisms, and yet receive, as his undoubted privilege, the same respectful demeanour as though words of impassioned eloquence, or persuasive logic, fell from his lips! . . . He is the bore of the age . . . the nightmare that disturbs our Sunday's rest . . . (1978: 46–7, 72)

Inveterate listeners to sermons may be forgiven a wry smile when reading those words. Doubtless no such thought would ever flash into the minds of those who Sunday by Sunday attend the Cathedral in Wells, for no preaching clergyman or woman would match the performance in the pulpit of the oily young Chaplain to the Bishop of Barchester, the Revd Obadiah Slope, bless his heart, as he preached his angry-making sermon. And in fact we must not stay long with the Revd Obadiah Slope – no longer than to notice that his text ('Study to show thyself approved unto God, a workman that needeth not to be ashamed', 2 Tim. 2:15), like that engraved on the pulpit in Wells, belongs to a setting in which there is a well-defined institution, a well-ordered succession and indeed hierarchy of leaders, a well-respected tradition, and – if the author of 2 Timothy has his way – a well-maintained process of highly committed guardianship and explanation of the tradition. That is the world of the semi-Pauline writer of the pastoral letters: that is the world of the hen-pecked Bishop and his haughty Chaplain, for all that they became locked in bitter conflict with the erstwhile establishment of the Diocese of Barchester. A very admirable world, no doubt, and a very safe world too for all the forces of ecclesiastical conservatism, even (one might say) in the long term very necessary – but more 'routinised' than 'charismatic', and worlds away from the manner and the matter of the missions of the historical John and the historical Jesus, and therefore of the group of those who followed, the nucleus of the 'community of Jesus people'.

We have seen that if we want a category in which to place Jesus and those who were at the centre of his movement it would be the same word as came to mind with John the Baptist: 'prophet'. And we recall that Jesus' movement was an offshoot, indeed in many ways a continuation of, the movement of his predecessor, whom he and the population at large regarded as a prophet. So the ground is prepared for a study of what it meant to be closely associated with the second of these charismatic figures.

On making contact with the historical Jesus

We need at this point to pause over the whole question of how we will gain access to the historical Jesus. The gospels are our main resource, but they are dedicated to promoting resurrection-focused understandings of Jesus, contributing to post-resurrection controversies, responding to post-resurrection impulses and obligations.

Is this, some might ask, a problem? Not for everyone, though it is for anyone who is convinced that the centuries-long journey of critical scholarship towards the goal of recovering the historical Jesus has not been a perverse waste of time. Those for whom there is no problem can – unwisely! – take heart from the eloquent, enthusiastic but (dare one say it with respect?) exaggerated case that has recently been mounted along the following lines:

> First, the culture of Jesus' time was primarily oral and securely reten-
> tive, and therefore such as to safeguard the memory of what Jesus said
> and did. (Wright 1996: 133–7)

Second, the exponents of 'tradition history' have condemned themselves out of their own mouths by dismally failing to show that their method produces assured results. The whole gamut of source criticism, form criticism, redaction criticism and the like is the diet of those of us who have 'wasted our substance on riotous but ruinous historicism' (Wright 1996: 662): we need to take a leaf out of the book of the prodigal son who repented and came home – home for a mainstream critical scholar being an encounter with Jesus as he really was, accessible without more ado through the gospels as they stand. In this serene setting, as has accurately been noticed, s/he would be spared the necessity of ever saying 'Jesus did not say this' or 'Jesus did not do this' or 'This did not happen' (cf. Borg 1999: 231).

Third, the variations within the gospel tradition are to be explained by Jesus having said more or less the same thing once, twice, three times . . .

Fourth, there is nothing in the gospels which needs to be set aside on the basis of a post-Easter *versus* pre-Easter discrepancy. All we need to do is recognise that the historical Jesus, who specialised in 'cryptic and coded riddles and stories . . . cryptic and subversive wisdom' (Wright 1996: 591, 606), and who should not be set over against the evangelists, can now at last be understood – the implicit and hidden has simply been overtaken by the explicit and open. From the three gospel mines – who knows, it may be four? (Wright 1999: 251–2) – we can without differentiation bring up to the surface the historical gold. So away with sources! Away with strata! Away with sifting! Above all, away with scepticism!

One has to say, with genuine admiration, even if that admiration is tinged with exasperation, that the boldness of it all is breathtaking. But it simply will not work. First, the culture of Jesus' time doubtless ensures that *some* – even a great deal – of the Jesus tradition stems from him, but it cannot – should not – be overworked to guarantee *all* of that tradition. Some of the traditions in our possession serve as compelling and even devastating counter-examples which undermine that whole approach. One has only to turn to the infancy narratives. Unrelated to one another in literary terms (though as a matter of fact not necessarily lacking signs of literary expansion), agreeing over a limited range of data, disagreeing over a much wider range, incapable of being harmonised with one another and therefore incapable of *both* being historical, supported (one might argue, appealing to Acts 1:14; 1 Cor. 15:7; Gal. 1:19; 2:9, 12) by the long-term presence of members of Jesus' family in the earliest Christian community, they demonstrate perfectly why an investment in orality is likely to yield exceedingly poor dividends for the historian's capital. If that is so in one possible case of oral transmission, why not in any number of others?

Second, even when we have shown due deference toward the contribution – no more – of orality, the most significant fact is that we have to work with *documents* which can be shown by the study of often massive agreement in the wording and the ordering of their component traditions to be *interrelated* and composed of material which has often manifestly grown in the telling.

Third, the 'Jesus might have said it twice' working hypothesis is seductively sensible *prima facie*, but again it has a habit of collapsing under the weight of those who lean on it. Take the variant versions of Jesus' visit to Nazareth (Mark 6:1–6a; Luke 4:16–30) – sufficiently over-lapping to be quite clearly alternative accounts of one visit, and scarcely open to being ordered historically so that the 'event' described by Luke preceded the 'event' described by Mark, yet sufficiently discrepant to justify a literary-critical evaluation rather than an oral one.

Fourth, disagreement among critical scholars proves nothing more than the insufficiency of the resources available to them, coupled with their human frailty, a quality not lacking in conservative scholars, who also – believe it or not! – often disagree about the interpretation of that which they confidently accept as historical. The work of neither group is invalidated by involvement in ongoing dialogue, proneness to error, and a capacity for disagreement.

Fifth, the neo-conservative, anti-critical procedure simply proves too much. Thus, to take one example, within the envelope of acceptance of Jesus as a performer of acts of power – it matters not whether magic or miracle be the label attached by reporters – not an eyelid is batted over the historicity of 'Jesus' touching of the dead and raising them to life . . . signs of covenant renewal [which] include the multiplication of bread in the wilderness, and the stillings of the storms, both carrying overtones of the exodus' (Wright 1996: 192–3). No versatility can cloak the under-lying reality that, for most thoughtful modern people, that way lies credulity. We had better settle for a world that thrives on such risky things as possibilities and probabilities, and – let us not be too coy about it – improbabilities. So, tradition history, we cannot do without you! Come back, sources! Come back, strata! Come back, sifting! Come back, that sensible and constructive scepticism which recognises that the first-century world of the documents is not identical with the twenty-first-century world of those who study the documents.

So we return to the need to face squarely the reality – the *brutum fac-tum*, as one might say – that our main resource consists of documents that in whole and in part promote resurrection-focused understandings of Jesus. This means that the stories and sayings in them have often been coloured and conditioned – maybe sometimes created – by a set of con-victions about Jesus *as he had come to be acknowledged and experienced after Easter*. Those convictions about Jesus have also brought fundamental change in the presentation of the followers of Jesus, who have been made to react to him as someone who belongs to the transcendent world of divine beings, which in Jesus' case means his post–resurrection existence. So the material the gospel writers provide has often grown in the telling, both quantitatively and qualitatively. It must therefore be sifted carefully by the historian, using defensible criteria.

The criteria of authenticity have of course to be used on the *earliest* version of any material, not material at a later stage of growth and development. And those criteria themselves can be set out as follows:

First, the *criterion of Palestinian context*: a tradition must presuppose a setting in the world where Jesus always worked. That is obvious and non-contentious. It is not the same as the suggestion that when, for example, a saying works well in Jesus' own mother tongue, Aramaic, it must have been said by him. That is a glaring *non sequitur*, for most of the earliest associates of Jesus, and plenty who were not associated with him at all, were just as much Aramaic speakers as he was.

Second, the *criterion of multiple attestation*: a saying, an action, a theme present in a plural number of independent (*sic*) units of tradition, may well be historical. It does not automatically follow from multiple attestation that material is authentic, nor contrariwise is multiple attestation a *sine qua non* for authenticity, but it helps, strengthens the possibility, bolsters the historian's security in supporting historicity, if it is there. Thus, there are countless sayings attributed to Jesus which indicate, explicitly or implicitly, that he saw God's kingly rule as a future hope, and one that was already penetrating the present (cf. Mark 1:15; Luke/Q 11:20). In the face of such multiple attestation, the historian can scarcely hold back from voting for general authenticity, even if s/he is not thereby compelled to back the historicity of each and every specific case. After all, the earliest Christians seem to have thought that way, too. At the same time, multiple attestation covers sayings which deal with the delay in the realisation of that great future hope (for example, the parables in Matt. 25:1–13; Luke/Q 12:42–6; 19:12–27), and thereby shows itself to be insufficient as a demonstration of historicity. Multiple attestation also supports the idea that Jesus brought really and demonstrably dead people back to life (cf. Mark 5:21–4, 35–43; Luke 7:11–17; Luke/Q 7:22), which is frankly incredible.

Third, the *criterion of dissimilarity*, that is to say, distinctiveness over against contemporary (second-Temple) Judaism and emergent Christianity. This runs the risk of assuming in advance that what is most characteristic of Jesus is distinctive in relation to either the Judaism of his time or the beliefs of his followers in the post-resurrection era. So inherently implausible an assumption, which tends in any case to maximise unrealistically our knowledge of the diverse phenomena which were Judaism and Christianity, suggests that this criterion would be better replaced by the *criterion of embarrassment*, which takes seriously any evidence of an outlook or practice which went 'against the grain', as it were, and tended to cause the early Christians difficulty, and which they may have tried to play down (Sanders/Davies 1989: 304–15). Thus, we can see from the various versions of the so-called equipment rule in Jesus' mission charge to the disciples (Mark 6:8–9; Luke 9:3; Luke/Q 10:4), that a strict and uncompromising set of requirements, while not unparalleled in contemporary Palestine (cf. Josephus, *Jewish War* 2:124–6), gave the gospel writers cause for pause, and that 'embarrassment' with the ultra-rigorous version brought about a certain softening. In similar vein, the remarkably varied reports of Jesus' treatment of divorce (cf. Mark 10:2–9, 11–12; Matt. 5:32; 19:3–9; Luke 16:18) show the difficulty that was caused by the tough and unyielding versions on the one hand, and the realistic instinct to replace toughness with a slightly softer and more accommodating position. *Mutatis mutandis*, that means that the stiffest and toughest demands in both these representative cases, the most 'embarrassing' ones, have a good claim to be regarded as historical.

Fourth, the *criterion of plausible historical continuity*: a tradition must lead straightforwardly towards later securely established historical events. Thus, as has often been remarked, the agonies of early Christianity over the question of Christian commitment or non-commitment to unrestricted Jew/gentile table fellowship, and over the understanding of the identity of the people of God which the food laws articulate (cf. Gal. 2:1–10, 11–14), virtually demand that Jesus should not (*pace* Mark 7:19, interpreting or conceivably misinterpreting 7:15) have abrogated them.

Finally, the *criterion of coherence*: does a tradition agree with material already accepted? Coherence can extend to *overall profile* (an 'explanatory paradigm': Allison 1998: 36) as well as to *particular detail*. Thus, the recognition of the centrality of the proclamation of the imminent arrival of the kingdom of God enables us to see Jesus as a prophet – and that itself becomes in turn a criterion (does a tradition match the profile of an eschatological prophet?). This has a certain circularity about it – but it is not a vicious circle, it's a virtuous circle!

Before taking the investigation forward, we should recognise afresh that the question of historical authenticity is bound to be acute in connection with the presentation of discipleship. Gospel writers, readers and hearers would inevitably identify with those who were in a committed relationship to Jesus. That would almost certainly mean that, just as the Jesus they portrayed would be painted in Easter colours, so too the disciples would be presented under the influence of the problems and possibilities of their own situations.

An example of the delicacy of the process of historical sifting can be seen in the gospel of Mark. The negativity which occasionally surrounds the characterisation of the disciples − bewilderment, misunderstanding, fear, and finally cowardly abandonment of Jesus to his fate − leads some to see those companions of Jesus as 'straw men', that is, the embodiment of a theology of which *Mark* strongly disapproved. Not the followers of the historical Jesus but the opponents of the controversial Mark!

In fact, this interpretation is more than a little one-sided, even skewed. This is because the disciples are for the evangelist the crucial witnessing link with Jesus, the guardians of the tradition upon which the Marcan Christians depend. If they are fearful it is because they are *intended* to be fearful and *must* be fearful, for they are the human witnesses to events in which the divine comes awe-fully near. In the person of Jesus, as interpreted by Mark, they are faced with the *mysterium tremendum et fascinans* (Otto 1958: 12−24, 31−40) of God's presence. But such awe takes us back to where we started, for the awe-inspiring Jesus is likely to be the post-Easter Jesus. We do well therefore to see in the disciples something of a combination of how the original followers of Jesus were and how the believing members of later post-Easter Christian communities had come to be, just as the Jesus of the gospels is a combination of how he originally was and how he had come to be viewed when lit up with resurrection splendour. To distinguish between the two − that is the problem!

Disciples and followers

Those who committed themselves to Jesus and his mission, and whatever community consciousness was involved, had already before them the model of community that defined the mission of John. The evidence concerning John the Baptist suggests to us a pattern of concentric circles for the sense of 'community' that he engendered. At the centre there was John himself. An outer circle consisted of the widely drawn community of those who, after hearing the call to come to the wilderness, committed themselves in a repentant spirit to 'righteousness', to share in the baptism, and then to disperse to their homes and regular occupations (cf. Luke 3:10–14). They dispersed to live as 'Israel within Israel'. But rather closer to John was an inner circle, the more precisely defined group called 'disciples of John' (cf. Mark 2:18; Luke/Q 7:18), who were learners in relationship to him as teacher and prophet (cf. Luke 11:2).

In a rather similar way, there stands the figure of Jesus at the centre of his mission. An outer circle consisted of those who doubtless responded with repentance and a commitment to righteousness to his message of God's kingdom and peace, but whose living as 'Israel within Israel' did not involve moving outside the parameters of normal human life. As we shall see, far from leaving their homes, these sympathisers with Jesus' mission remained in place to welcome and offer their hospitality to others, at times more peripatetic and embracing insecurity, who formed an inner circle around Jesus (Theissen 1993: 46–50). Evidently, not everyone who was called to respond to the message of the kingdom was called to follow Jesus. Nevertheless, the defining principles that stand at the heart of Jesus' mission, and the community implications of that mission, emerge with particular clarity from a study of his inner circle, the precisely defined group of 'disciples of Jesus', those who were learners in relation to him as teacher and prophet.

The essence of the experience of discipleship emerges from a series of one-to-one encounters with Jesus. In them all, his call is addressed not to anyone and everyone who may choose to share in a large group response: it is always individualised. The gospel traditions that exemplify this are probably the best place to begin. They pass all the authenticity tests with flying colours: they are Palestinian, multiply attested, coherent, at home in the setting of a prophetic mission, and at times embarrassing to the early Christians. We turn first to Luke/Q 9:57–8:

> [57]And as they were going in the way, a certain person said to him, 'I will follow you wherever you go.' [58]And Jesus said to him, 'Foxes have holes and the birds of heaven have nests, but the Son of Man has nowhere to lay his head.'

Here is, first, evidence of Jesus' strategy of itinerancy: 'wherever you go . . . nowhere to lay his head'. The implications should not, however, be exaggerated. We have the impression that Jesus left Nazareth, his hometown (Mark 6:4), and settled in Capernaum. This is where a series of recorded incidents are placed. This is also the place which receives the fiercest denunciation for non-receptivity (Luke/Q 10:15), which would presumably only be justified if Capernaum had been linked to Jesus with special intensity. Capernaum was therefore very likely the place where Jesus did normally have somewhere to lay his head. Consequently the saying which says otherwise must presuppose the very special setting of mission. Jesus, we may be sure, takes active steps to reach the whole of Israel, and such is the essential setting for this saying. That 'migratory' setting is almost certainly envisaged by what is said about animals and birds (Casey 1985: 8–9).

Second, the allusion to 'foxes . . . birds of heaven' rather surprisingly selects from biblical tradition some creatures that are regarded with undisguised distaste. For the foxes, a term which probably includes jackals (Casey 1985: 8), it is not too strong to speak of their being 'notorious, unclean and noisy animals' (Casey 1985: 9). Typical texts would be Psalm 63:9–10, 'Those who seek to destroy my life . . . shall be a prey for foxes', and 1 Enoch 89:42, 'The dogs and the foxes and the wild boars began to devour those sheep.' For the 'birds of heaven', when paired with animals and regarded as predators, we can take our cue from typical texts like Deuteronomy 28:26, 'Your corpses shall be food for every bird of the air and animal of the earth, and there shall be no one to frighten them away'; or Jeremiah 15:3, 'I will appoint over them four kinds of destroyers, says the Lord: the sword to kill, the dogs to drag away, and the birds of the air and the wild animals of the earth to devour and destroy.' It would have been possible for Jesus to choose what might be termed more neutral examples from the created order to make the point about homelessness: the fact that he chooses the particular examples of 'foxes . . . birds of the heaven' adds a new dimension and constitutes a warning that involvement with him and all he stands for carries no human plaudits and opens no access to honour and prestige.

Third, here is the term 'Son of Man', a translation of the Aramaic phrase *bar (e)nash(a)*. This is an idiom, whose usage can be seen in some parallel texts, in which the speaker formulates a generalisation whose scope is indicated by the context, a saying which *may* apply to himself, perhaps even to himself in circumstances of humiliation, threat or danger (Casey 1987: 23–7). Whether there *must* be a tacit self-reference is arguably less certain. Two examples are worth quoting:

> Rabbi Ze'ira ... wished to buy a pound of meat from a butcher. 'How much is this?' he asked. '50 *minas* and a lash,' was the answer. The rabbi offered 60, 70, 80 and finally 100 *minas* to escape the lash, but to no avail. In the end he said, 'Do as is your custom!' In the evening he went to the house of instruction and said, 'Rabbis, how wicked is this land that *bar nash* cannot eat a pound of meat until he has been given a lash!' (*j. Berakoth* 2.8.5c)

What is clear here is that Rabbi Ze'ira draws on his experience of making a purchase from the maverick local butcher. He reports on what he believes he has discovered to be a non-negotiable 'custom', and sums up the situation in an inferential generalisation for the benefit of his colleagues. But the generalisation in the *bar nash* saying is true for anyone who wants to purchase meat in that specific situation. It *happens* to reflect his experience, but it would still have been true if he, the speaker, had not wanted to purchase any meat. The *bar nash* saying applies definitively to people in general in 'this place' – but only coincidentally, only secondarily, and not intrinsically, not of necessity, to the speaker.

> Rabbi Kahana said to Rabbi Johanan, 'If *bar nash* is despised by his mother but honoured by another of his father's wives, where should he go?' 'He should go where he is honoured,' replied Johanan. Thereupon Kahana departed. Rabbi Johanan was then told, 'Kahana has gone to Babylon.' 'What?' exclaimed Johanan. 'Has he gone without asking my permission?' 'The story he told you,' they replied, 'was his way of asking permission.' (*j. Berakoth* 2.8.5c)

This time the answer to the initial question from Rabbi Kahana is couched as a statement of general principle (Lindars 1983: 20). The presumed setting is one in which authoritative teacher and subordinate disciples together discuss general principles of behaviour. The principle laid down by Rabbi Johanan happens to be applied by Rabbi Kahana to himself, but it did not have to be, and Rabbi Johanan was clearly surprised when it was. In order that it should be, the saying had to be understood parabolically, and that was neither natural nor necessary. But when it was, then Rabbi Kahana took the role of a son, gave the primary role of mother to his present teacher, Rabbi Johanan, and the role of alternative wife and step-mother to another more appreciative teacher in Babylon. Just as with Rabbi Zeira's generalisation, it becomes clear that a *bar nash* statement is a generalisation which primarily has no concern with the speaker, but secondarily it *may* do. The context will indicate whether it does or not.

So in similar vein the *bar (e)nash(a)* saying in Luke/Q 9:58 is setting out a fundamental principle which applies primarily to anyone who 'follows' and shares in Jesus' mission. 'The generic usage is *essential* to the purpose of the saying' (Lindars 1983: 30). That, after all, was the matter under consideration in Luke/Q 9:57. We feel under pressure to include the speaker, but not because of the saying in and of itself – only because an imaginative hearing of the saying suggests that what is true for any follower cannot but be true for the one being followed. From here we can move on to Luke/Q 9:59–60:

> [59]He said to another person, 'Follow me.' And he said, 'Allow me first to go away and bury my father.' [60]He said to him, 'Leave the dead to bury their own dead, and you go away and announce the kingdom of God.'

This tradition is one of two that have in recent years tended (probably mistakenly) to be seen as evidence for a break between Jesus and Torah piety, because of the call to substitute 'following Jesus' for family commitments (Hengel 1981: 8–15). But this discipleship saying must be balanced by other traditions affirming family obligations: Mark 7:9–13; 10:17–22. In these traditions the *law* relating to honour and care for parents is cited and respected. This enables us to see that in the tradition we are considering Jesus is not voicing a law but *a prophetic demand*. We may add that the pro-parents traditions are all the more impressive in view of the breach between Jesus and his own family (cf. Mark 3:20–21, 31–5; 6:4), and the current allegation against him that he was equivalent to the 'stubborn and rebellious son' (Luke/Q 7:34; cf. Deut. 21:18–20).

Three clusters of texts combine to sketch in the background of this prophetic demand of Jesus. (i) There are many texts confirming burial as the final act of respect (e.g. Tobit 1:17–18; 2:4–9; 12:12–13; Sir. 38:16), and others which see lack of burial as intensely shaming and repugnant (e.g. 2 Kings 9:10; Psalm 79:3), an offence against nature, a defilement of God himself, and an exhibition of barbarity (Josephus, *Jewish War* 4:380–83). Then (ii) there are texts affirming the special responsibility of a son to bury his parents: instructions are given by fathers to sons (Gen. 47:29–30; Tobit 4:3), and the pain of a son's unavailability can be illustrated by the anguish of Josephus' mother, who appears oddly forgetful of her other son, Matthias (Josephus, *Life* 8), when she thought he had been fatally wounded during the Roman siege of Jerusalem:

> 'This then is the fruit that I reap of my blessed childbearing that I am denied the burial of my son by whom I hoped to have been buried.' (Josephus, *Jewish War* 5:545)

Finally, (iii) there is legislation giving the burial of relatives priority over major religious obligations:

> He whose dead lies unburied before him is exempt from reciting the *Shema*, from saying the *Tefillah*, and from wearing phylacteries. (*m. Berakoth* 3:1; cf. Lev. 21:1–2)

So much for the background. But the essential thrust of the exchange between Jesus and a possible follower is not just in the contrast between burying parents and following Jesus. There is one implicit detail, not spelt out, to which it may be important to give due weight. The potential disciple is apparently not engaged *at the moment* in the process of mourning; therefore, the father has not died; therefore the request is tantamount to saying, 'I will come and be a disciple at some unspecified future time – maybe soon, maybe not so soon' (Bailey 1980: 26). Urgency is simply not in his mind. But it looms large in the mind of Jesus. The kingdom is coming soon. That means that Q, the source of Matthew and Luke, is almost certainly right in making separation from home/family relationships (Q 9:57–60) lead into the mission charge, centred on the message, 'The kingdom of God has come near to you' (Luke/Q 10:9, 11; cf. Mark 1:15). This is a blueprint for a strictly select group and not a general rule or law. It is an imperative generated by *urgent prophetic commitment to the near kingdom.*

A final example of a tradition about a one-to-one encounter between Jesus and a potential follower is found in Luke 9:61–2:

⁶¹Yet another person said, 'I will follow you, Lord, but allow me first to go and say goodbye to those in my home.' ⁶²And Jesus said to him, 'No one who puts his hand to the plough, and who looks back behind him, is fit for the kingdom of God.'

The themes of commitment to the kingdom of God and radical separation from family, home and work are once again present. The separation is this time conveyed rather powerfully by the refusal of the request to say goodbye. What does this refusal imply?

First, it has been pointed out that the process of leave-taking involves more than words of farewell by the one party: those who are left are in a position of some power and control, and their permission and prayerful goodwill is rather important (Bailey 1980: 27–9). This can be illustrated from the book of Tobit: (i) In commissioning his son Tobias to travel to obtain money left in trust in Rages in Media, Tobit makes a farewell speech, replete with instructions about upright living, and giving priority to the obligation to give both him and his wife an honourable burial. He also makes detailed plans for the safety of his son while travelling, and sends him and his companion away with prayer to God for safety on the way out and on the way back (cf. Tobit 4—5). (ii) After marrying Sarah, the daughter of Raguel, Tobias wants to go home, but *he has the utmost difficulty in getting away*! After fourteen days of wedding celebrations it is a matter of 'Send me back . . . I beg of you, father, to let me go . . . No, I beg you to send me back . . .' (Tobit 10:7–9). From this story it is clear that the farewell procedure includes an active role, something between permission and commission, for the *paterfamilias*.

Second, what is new is the clarification of the *model* that is being used for the relationship between Jesus and a typical follower. See 1 Kings 19:19–21:

> ¹⁹So Elijah set out from there and found Elisha the son of Shaphat, who was ploughing. There were twelve yoke of oxen ahead of him and he was with the twelfth. Elijah passed by him and threw his mantle over him [a sign of taking possession and also of the communication of prophetic power, cf. 2 Kings 2:8, 13–14; Josephus inserts at this point the comment that 'thereupon Elisha immediately began to prophesy', *Antiquities* 8:354]. ²⁰He left the oxen, ran after Elijah, and said, 'Let me kiss my father and mother, and then I will follow you.' Then Elijah said

to him, 'Go back again; for what have I done to you?' [21]He returned from following him, took the yoke of oxen, and slaughtered them; using the equipment from the oxen, he boiled their flesh, and gave it to the people, and they ate. Then he set out and followed Elijah, and became his servant.

Just as John the Baptist had probably understood his mission as a reactivation of the Elijah/Elisha model (cf. Luke 1:17), so too does Jesus, whose self-understanding includes the idea of prophetic charisma and possession of God's Spirit. But we need once more to take particular note of the family dimension. The point about the break with the family is made even more firmly: what Elijah allows, Jesus disallows and thereby aligns himself with a widely attested tendency to give religious commitments priority over natural family ties (Barton 1994: 23–56). Furthermore, while Elisha understands the relationship between himself and Elijah as one of kinship – thus, 'a double share of your spirit' (2 Kings 2:9–12; cf. Exod. 21:17) – for Jesus and his followers a new kinship relationship is indeed established, though not one in which Jesus occupies any kind of parental position.

New life, new labour

The call to belong to the very close circle of Jesus' associates was a call to be and also to do. It would be very one-sided to define their role as that of watching and witnessing: rather, they were by definition also required to work – not just seeing but also sharing in Jesus' prophetic work. A series of traditions provide multiple attestation in support of this conclusion, and a sample may helpfully be examined. The first is Mark 1:16–20:

> [16]As Jesus passed along the Sea of Galilee, he saw Simon and his brother Andrew casting a net into the sea – for they were fishermen. [17]And Jesus said to them, 'Follow me, and I will make you fish for people.' [18]And immediately they left their nets and followed him.
> [19]As he went a little further, he saw James son of Zebedee and John his brother, who were in their boat mending their nets. [20]Immediately he called them; and they left their father Zebedee in the boat with the hired men, and they followed him.

Features that have by now become familiar reappear in this two-in-one tradition – the authoritative call, and the break with family and work – but at the same time two new features come to light.

First, those called were certainly not all among the 'have nots' of society. When a few years later other would-be prophetic leaders called people to 'follow' them, those called are said to have taken with them all their possessions (Josephus, *Antiquities* 20:97), which must mean that they had possessed no more than they could carry, or they are described as 'simple people' (*Antiquities* 20:197) or as 'not a few of the indigent class' (*Jewish War* 7:438). This is not the profile of those called by Jesus, some at least of whom make a living from the vital fishing industry and belong to households with hired servants. If at any time we find these 'haves' appearing as 'have nots', it is because they have chosen to be such (Theissen 1993: 85). Incidentally, we should not take too seriously Luke's breathtaking inventiveness (5:1–11) in transforming Mark's story so that the fishermen's failure at work was the occasion of their accepting Jesus' summons!

Second, special prominence is given to the call to engage in mission: 'I will make you fish for people.' This call to mission can be clarified in a number of ways, especially by studying the mission charge that is doubly attested in the gospels (Mark 6:6b–13; Luke/Q 10:2–16). The different versions have to be played off against one another, and the intervention of each of the gospel writers allowed for, in order to reconstruct what Jesus' original instructions comprised. The overall conclusion should probably be that Mark's version is on the whole a modified, even softened, version, and that the Q version has itself probably grown. This version (Luke/Q 10:2–16) probably ran as follows:

> **[2]He said to them, 'The harvest is plentiful, but the labourers are few; therefore ask the Lord of the harvest to send out labourers into his harvest.** [3]Go on your way. See, I am sending you out like lambs into the midst of wolves. [4]Carry no staff, no purse, no bag, no sandals; and greet no one on the road. [5]Whatever house you enter, first say, "Peace to this house!" [6]And if anyone is there who is a "son of peace", your peace will rest on that person; but if not, it will return to you. [7]Remain in the same house, eating and drinking what they provide, for the labourer is worthy of his hire. [8]Whenever you enter a town and its people welcome you, [9]cure the sick who are there, and say to them,

"The kingdom of God has come near." [10]But whenever you enter a town and they do not welcome you, go out and say, [11]"Even the dust that clings to our feet, we wipe off in protest against you." [12]I tell you, on that day it will be more tolerable for Sodom than for that town.

[13]*'Woe to you, Chorazin! Woe to you, Bethsaida! For if the deeds of power done in you had been done in Tyre and Sidon, they would have repented long ago in sackcloth and ashes.* [14]*But at the judgement it will be more tolerable for Tyre and Sidon than for you.* [15]*And you, Capernaum, will you be exalted to heaven? No, you will be brought down to Hades.*

[16]'Whoever listens to you listens to me, and whoever rejects you rejects me, and whoever rejects me rejects the one who sent me.'

There are several important elements of this tradition to take into account: First, the two bold italicized sections are later additions, because (i) an instruction to pray that the Lord of the harvest will send out reapers (v. 2) is directed at a community supporting a mission rather than at the missionaries themselves, and (ii) the woes directed to the towns of Galilee (vv. 13–15) look back rather than forward, and presume rejection as having already taken place. At the very least, these two sections did not originally belong in their present context.

Second, 'I send you out as sheep among wolves' (v. 3) picks up the standard association of wolves with rapacity, destruction and devastation (cf. Gen. 49:27; Isa. 11:6, where it is only in the context of a new order of creation that wolves will be no threat to lambs; Jer. 5:6; Acts 20:29). Here is a warning of the traditional negativity that prophetic emissaries tend to encounter. This is paralleled in other sayings of Jesus – see especially Luke/Q 16:16, where 'the kingdom of God suffers violence, and violent men take it by force' in the missions of John and Jesus – and matches the outlook of the 'foxes . . . birds of the heaven' saying, which we have already studied. The criterion of multiple attestation encourages us to conclude that we are hearing the voice of Jesus.

Third, the equipment rule forbids staff, purse, bag and sandals (v. 4). So tough a requirement was problematic to at least some early Christians, as Mark's revision (6:8–9) confirms, so the criterion of embarrassment is very much apropos. The earlier Q version of the rule takes us directly into the neighbouring world to that of the Essene travellers, of whom it was said:

[124]On the arrival of any of the sect from elsewhere, all the resources of the community are put at their disposal, just as if they were their own; and they enter the homes of those they have never seen before as though they were their most intimate friends. [125]Consequently, they carry nothing whatever with them on their journeys, except arms as a protection against brigands. In every city there is one of the order expressly appointed to attend to strangers, who provides them with raiment and other necessities. [126]In their dress and deportment they resemble children under rigorous discipline. They do not change their clothing or shoes until they are torn to shreds or worn threadbare with age. (Josephus, *Jewish War* 2:124–6)

But the quite distinctive atmosphere of Jesus' and his disciples' mission quickly becomes clear.

The absence of a staff highlights the central principle of the 'peace people' (cf. vulnerability to insult and mistreatment, and non-retaliation: Luke/Q 6:27–30) and the character of the era of God's kingly rule as an era of peace (cf. Isa. 52:7). But special interest attaches to the insistence that the messengers must not take purse, bag or sandals. The implication is that those who bring the message of the kingdom identify with those to whom the message is directed, i.e. the poor, the hungry and the mourners (cf. Luke/Q 6:20b–21). The reasons for saying that are as follows.

The absence of a purse, and therefore of money, means that the disciples appear as voluntarily poor, persons who have abandoned concern with material wellbeing in the present era.

The absence of a bag, which is the container for food (see Judith 10:5; 13:10), means that the missionaries identify with the hungry. They have to be prepared for hardship, and are totally dependent on hospitality offered by others (Luke 10:5–7). Later rabbis dismissed dependence on someone else's table as 'life that is no life'.

R Nathan b. Abba said in the name of Rab: He who is dependent on another's table, the world is dark to him, for it is said [Job 15:23], 'He wanders abroad for bread: "Where is it?"' He knows that the day of darkness is ready at his hand. R Hisda says: Also his life is no life. (*b. Bezah* 32b).

Our rabbis taught [1st–2nd centuries CE]: There are three whose life is no life, and they are: He who is dependent on the table of his neighbour; he whom his wife rules; and he whose body is subject to suffering. And some say: Also he who possesses only one shirt. (*b. Bezah* 32b)

The lack of sandals means that they go barefoot and therefore look like mourners (cf. 2 Sam. 15:30; Isa. 20:2–3). In biblical tradition this means the absence of a quite basic necessity (Amos 2:6; Sir. 46:19), and also, according to some later rabbis, openness to insult and shame, and a life that is worse than being dead and buried.

Rab Judah said in Rab's name: One should always sell [even] the beams of his house and buy shoes for his feet. If one has let blood and has nothing to eat, let him sell the shoes from off his feet and provide the requirements of a meal therewith. (*b. Shabbat* 129a)

[R Joshua b. Karhah, mid-2nd century CE:] He who rides on a horse is a king; upon an ass, is a free man; and he who has shoes on his feet is a human being. But he who has none of these, one who is dead and buried is better off. (*b. Shabbat* 152a)

Three are banned by Heaven: A Jew who has no wife; he who has a wife and no children; and he who has children but does not bring them up to the study of the Torah; and he who has no phylacteries on his head and no *mezuzah* on his door, and he who denies his feet shoes. And some say: Also he who never sits in a company assembled for a religious purpose. (*b. Pesahim* 113b)

These rabbinic texts should not be pressed too hard, for their dating may be problematic, and the discussions they record may be theoretical and sometimes even playful. To use a contemporary analogy, they may belong more to the to-and-fro exchange of ideas in a seminar than to the self-conscious decisions of a synod. Their usefulness is not so much in the 'rulings' they lay down as in the evidence they provide of long-lasting cultural assumptions.

Fourth, the heavily loaded peace greeting, which may or may not be reciprocated in the form of hospitality (Luke 10:5–7), points to the dependence of the itinerant emissaries, and is a reminder of the existence of a network of supporters, like the network upon which Essene travellers could depend. It also points to an understanding of 'the kingdom of God' as defined by 'peace' (cf. Isa. 52:7), which again points to the historical Jesus on the basis of the criteria of multiple attestation and coherence.

Fifth, the word-and-action presentation of the message of the kingdom (Luke 10:9) points to the disciples' responsibility to disseminate the message of Jesus, and therefore to their role in the preservation and transmission of material, such as parables, with which Jesus filled out his own message that 'the kingdom of God has come near to you'. It is also an indication of an amply attested healing ministry of Jesus, in which those who are endowed by extension with his Spirit-charisma are empowered to share.

Sixth, the warning of judgement on the unresponsive (Luke 10:12), again satisfying the criterion of multiple attestation, runs, 'I tell you that it will be better for Sodom in that day than for that city.' Here Jesus picks up the notoriety of Sodom as 'the incarnation of wickedness' (see Gen. 13:13; 18:20; 19:13; Jer. 23:14). The wickedness consists not only of sexual licence, illustrated in a disgusting incident of rape, and therefore receipt of judgement by fire (Isa. 1:9; Lam. 4:6; Amos 4:11), but also of the refusal of hospitality. Thus:

> Do not become like Sodom, which did not recognise the Lord's angels and perished for ever. (*Testament of Asher* 7:1; cf. Ezek. 16:49)

Finally, the climactic punchline (Luke 10:16) draws on the Jewish *shaliah* idea of an equivalence between the sent person and the sender, and also expresses Jesus' fundamental awareness, attested times without number, of divine authorisation for his mission. Vital for the disciples is the astonishing affirmation that human reaction to them and their message is nothing other than reaction to Jesus and indeed his God.

The precarious and dependent situation of the followers of Jesus as they engage in mission is therefore conveyed powerfully by the earliest version of the mission charge. Further confirmation is provided when we consider another of the most famous of gospel traditions (Luke/Q 12:22–31), reconstruct its history, and ask about its original setting. What emerges is teaching that has a prophetic context and the strongest possible credentials for authenticity. Prophetic in its presuppositions, it asks, in the way of the wisdom tradition, for reflection about the created order. One thinks of Thomas Hardy's fine poem, entitled 'Afterwards':

When the Present has latched its postern behind my tremulous stay,
　　And the May month flaps its glad green leaves like wings,
Delicate-filmed as new-spun silk, will the neighbours say,
　　'He was a man who used to notice such things'?

If it be in the dusk when, like an eyelid's soundless blink,
　　The dewfall-hawk comes crossing the shades to alight
Upon the wind-warped upland thorn, a gazer may think,
　　'To him this must have been a familiar sight.'

If I pass during some nocturnal blackness, mothy and warm,
　　When the hedgehog travels furtively over the lawn,
One may say, 'He strove that such innocent creatures should come to no harm,
　　But he could do little for them; and now he is gone.'

If, when hearing that I have been stilled at last, they stand at the door,
　　Watching the full-starred heavens that winter sees,
Will this thought rise on those who will meet my face no more,
　　'He was one who had an eye for such mysteries'?

And will any say when my bell of quittance is heard in the gloom,
　　And a crossing breeze cuts a pause in its outrollings,
Till they rise again, as they were a new bell's boom,
　　'He hears it not now, but used to notice such things'?

The sayings about the ravens and the lilies are an invitation to 'have an eye for such mysteries . . . to notice such things', to reflect upon the creation as anyone possessed of true wisdom will always do (cf. 1 Kings 4:33), and to find in the natural world the disclosure of eternal truths. For those who reflect in such a way, for the naturally and humanly anxious missionaries, the sayings about the ravens and the lilies are designed to bring reassurance:

---

^{22}Do not be anxious about your life, what you will eat, or about your body, what you will wear.

^{23}*For life is more than food, and the body more than clothing.*

^{24}Consider the ravens: they neither sow nor reap nor gather into barns, and yet God feeds them. Of how much more value are you than the birds!

^{25}*And can any of you by being anxious add a single hour to your span of life?* ^{26}*If then you are not able to do so small a thing as that, why do you worry about the rest?*

^{27}Consider the lilies, how they grow: they neither toil nor spin; yet I tell you, even Solomon in all his glory was not clothed like one of these. ^{28}But if God so clothes the grass of the field, which is alive today and tomorrow is thrown into the oven, how much more will he clothe you – you of little faith! ^{29}Therefore do not be anxious, saying, 'What shall we eat? Or what shall we drink? Or how shall we be clothed?'

^{30a}For *after all these things the gentiles seek;*

^{30b}your Father knows you have need of these things.

^{31}But seek his kingdom, and all these things will be yours as well.

The underlying shape of the main teaching unit can be discerned by removing the bold italicized sections. Now, one always has to allow for the possibility of an ongoing process of transmission whereby a tradition's original 'roughness' is 'smoothed', as with pebbles. But in this case the content of the tradition almost certainly suggests an original 'smoothness' which later editorial activity 'roughened' and marred somewhat: (i) verse 23 is more naturally addressed to the well-off who do not have reasons for anxiety than to the poor who do; (ii) verses 25–6 argue in a quite different way from the surrounding material, and insist on the *ineffectiveness* of anxiety rather than its *inappropriateness*; and (iii) verse 30a is in the wrong place, that is to say, within the concluding appeal rather than in the main argument, and it also introduces a quite alien attempt to impose a higher standard than that observed by the gentiles. There is a slight shadow of doubt about the call to 'seek his kingdom . . .' in verse 31, which might be deemed extra to the core unit, but on the other hand there is precedent for a concluding punch-line about the kingdom (cf. Luke/Q 7:28b). All in all, with the removal of the extraneous additions there remains a call to avoid anxiety, then two examples from the created order which give reasoned reinforcement to the call, and then finally a rounding-off repetition of the call. The tradition is neat, symmetrical, and coherent.

What is left is notably paralleled in sayings attributed to the second-century CE Rabbi Simeon ben Eleazar, who was based in Tiberias, just a little further south along the shore of the Sea of Galilee from Jesus' own main base, Capernaum. These sayings moved the contributor to the *Encyclopaedia Judaica* to pay a warm tribute: 'His statements are permeated with deep wisdom and sublime faith.' What Simon said was:

> Have you ever seen a wild animal or a bird practising a craft? – yet they have their sustenance without care, and were they not created for no other purpose than to serve me? But I was created to serve my Maker. How much more then ought not I to have my sustenance [without care]? But I have wrought evil, and [so] forfeited my [right to] sustenance [without care]. (*m. Kiddushin* 4:14)

The modes of argument used by Jesus and Simon ben Eleazar are very similar. In dealing with concern about the provision of basic human necessities of life, both argue from the natural world, where work does not happen, and both use 'from the lesser to the greater' logic in order to establish the special position of a human person. But the provision of care for the non-working human person is forfeited, according to Simon, by human wrongdoing, whereas, according to Jesus (who has no illusions about human evil as such, cf. Luke/Q 11:13), it is not forfeited at all – at least, not for those to whom he speaks. For all that they may receive support from sympathisers dispersed here and there (Luke/Q 10:5–7), and even from a small number of well-off women (Luke 8:1–3), the basic fact is that they correspond to the ravens and lilies by virtue of not engaging in farm or home work.

Such disengagement from life-supporting work recalls a lofty and somewhat patronising picture painted by Jesus the son of Sirach (38:24–39:5; cf. Freyne 2004: 48). For that writer, content with his own lot within the ruling class, great credit could be given to ploughmen, artisans who labour night and day, smiths and potters, who rely on their skill with their hands and show admirable wholeheartedness in their search for excellence. Such persons 'are skilful in their own work' and – here's the rub – 'wherever they live, they will not go hungry' (38:31–2). Over against them, and evidently superior to them, stands the scribe, 'depending on the opportunity of leisure and [having] little business' (38:24), dedicated to the achievement of wisdom, preoccupied with prophecies, devoted to the study of the law of the Most High, disciplined in prayer (39:1–5). Such a person can confidently count on the supply of all his needs. But the people addressed by Jesus are more exposed, more vulnerable, more insecure, more prey to anxiety. They have not, as crafts-men might have done, taken the tools of a trade with them in order to support themselves as itinerant workers (cf. Theissen 1993: 52), for the fact is that they are, as far as we know and with the exception of Jesus himself (Mark 6:3), not craftsmen. They have stopped working, whatever their work may have been. They have voluntarily abandoned the normal support systems of life – whether those be, typically, farming (therefore men) or spinning (therefore women, too: cf. Prov. 31:13, 19, 22, 24). They have joined the ranks of the poor and embraced the insecurity of asso-ciating with Jesus, a person committed in his own way to wisdom and prophecy, but still an outsider, not an insider. They have committed themselves to a plan so perilous that it could not last for more than a rela-tively short time, that is to say, the higher and short-term cause of God's imminent kingdom. These men and women (*sic*) are most probably the followers of Jesus who have left home and family to share in his intensely kingdom-focused mission.

In conclusion, that implicit involvement of women as well as men in the community of followers should not be passed over too quickly. It scores well in terms of criteria like embarrassment and multiple attesta-tion, for early Christianity was on the whole not a hotbed of anti-discriminatory gender-blind liberalism. Moreover, what is implicit in the tradition about the lilies is explicit elsewhere. Thus, a trio of named women stands out from a wider group of Galilean female followers, attached (Mark 15:40–41) to the story which ends with the centurion's acknowledgement of Jesus' divine sonship (15:22–39). Similarly, a pair of named women is mentioned in an appendix (15:47) to the story of Jesus' burial (15:42–6). In neither case is the appendix integral to the preced-ing story. The situation is different in the case of the tradition of the Easter morning visit of the women to the tomb: there, in a tradition which on literary grounds can be recognised as an edited version of a pre-Marcan story, the women are mentioned and indeed belong to the fabric of the story (Catchpole 2000: 4–7). That suggests that the list of named women was probably an original part of the archetype of Mark

16:1–8, and that the two other lists are derived selectively from it. If that is correct, it probably consisted of 'Mary Magdalene, and Mary the mother of James [the younger and of Joses], and Salome.' With this list stands Luke's probably independent list of women (Luke 8:2–3): 'Mary Magdalene, from whom seven demons had gone out, and Joanna, the wife of Herod's steward Chuza, and Susanna . . .'

The impression conveyed by these two lists is that some specific women, singled out by name from a rather larger number of women associated with Jesus, are well known in the circles of those reading the gospel texts. They, or the men who are mentioned to give the identity of some of them greater precision, may have held positions of leadership in early Christianity. Their original significance lies, however, in their having benefited from Jesus' gift of healing, and thus having experienced in advance the power of God's kingly rule. Particular prominence is achieved by the Mary who comes from Magdala at the western extremity of the lake of Galilee. She has no male attachment – so is probably either single or divorced. She is always the first named of a duo or trio – so is probably viewed as a leading witness (cf. Deut. 19:15; see Bauckham 2002: 295–304). She had suffered exceptionally serious ill health ('seven demons'; cf. all that is said about legion, Mark 5:1–9). She figures in a tradition which has a very good claim to historicity, and thus attests a movement of the Galileans around and with Jesus to the capital city of Jerusalem for the crucial Passover festival.

The experience of involvement in the community of Jesus people, both female and male, must have been determined by the atmosphere created by his contacts with women other than those who became followers, and also by the general tenor of those of his sayings which allude to women. To this theme we shall return in a later chapter.

Following and eating together

In Mark 2:13–17 there is a tradition which matches those dealing with the two pairs of brothers (Mark 1:16–20). Jesus again goes to the edge of the sea, and

> as he was walking along, he saw Levi son of Alphaeus sitting at the tax booth, and he said to him, 'Follow me.' And he got up and followed him.

In itself this tradition is no more remarkable than the one dealing with the call of Simon and Andrew, James and John. Levi is called to follow, just as the two pairs of brothers had been. We note *en passant* that he is not listed as they were in the twelve (Mark 3:13–19; cf. 'James the son of Alphaeus', v. 18), so while the twelve have a very special future destiny, they are not the only 'followers'.

The sequel to Jesus' calling of Levi, however, takes us to one of the more contentious aspects of Jesus' mission, one whose historicity is supported by all the standard criteria of authenticity. This is the shared table fellowship – whether as host or guest – with tax-collectors, and also the sinners with whom tax-collectors are frequently linked. Over against them there stand in polarised confrontation the Pharisees. The scribes are also mentioned – a partially but not completely overlapping group, since 'not all Pharisees are scribes, and not all scribes are Pharisees' (Theissen/Merz 1998: 226) – but the Pharisees are the ones who, on any showing, make the running here. They clearly expect Jesus to respect the principles that to them seem obvious as a means of effecting the holiness of Israel (Lev. 11:44). Instead, he appears to build into the community of his associates and followers someone who represents *from the Pharisaic point of view* the damning features of a 'sinner', far removed from any commitment to holiness.

Plainly something more is being conveyed by that word 'sinner' than the fact that all humankind falls short of the glory of the God in whose image they are created. The sinners seem to be a special group. Their image, and doubtless the reality that lay behind the image, involved (i) wilful and deliberate Zacchaeus-type lapses in ethical behaviour (cf. Luke 19:1–10); and (ii) existence in practice on the boundaries of Israel, that is, even if s/he is by birth Jewish his/her effective status is gentile. Doubtless, it did not help that in Galilee the tax-collectors were the financial hatchet men of the client tetrarch authorised by Rome, Herod Antipas, and in Judea uncongenial agents of direct Roman authority and rule.

That is the broad context in which to set the Marcan tradition of the call of Levi and its sequel:

> [15]And as he sat at table in Levi's home, many tax collectors and sinners were also sitting at table with Jesus and his disciples – *for there were many and they followed him.* [16]When the scribes and the Pharisees saw

that he was eating with sinners and tax collectors, they said to his disciples, 'Why does he eat with tax collectors and sinners?' [17]When Jesus heard this, he said to them, 'Those who are well have no need of a doctor, but those who are ill; *I have come to call not the righteous but sinners.*' (Mark 2:15–17)

The bold italicized statement is typical of Mark's style and interest, and is unlikely to be original. Its removal enables us to attend to the essential tradition without distraction.

The polarisation between Pharisees and sinners documented here has to be seen against the background of how 'sinners' are treated in the so-called Psalms of David in the Old Testament (cf. Sanders 1993: 227), and even more in the so-called Psalms of Solomon, which probably preserve the Pharisaic/Essene point of view in the middle of the first century BCE (Wright 1985: 641).

From the so-called Psalms of David, a stereotypical profile of 'sinners' can be assembled. (i) Non-Israelites are often intended (Ps. 3:7; 7:9; 9:16–17; 125:3), but often Israelites too (50:16; 101:8), so some uncertainty – significant uncertainty – persists as to whether gentiles or wicked Israelites are in mind (10:3–4; 11:5–7; 28:3).

(ii) The opposite category is typically 'the righteous' or the persons who can count on 'steadfast love', or those who inherit the land (Ps. 37:11–12, 21) that is, those who belong to the people of God and attend to the law of God (1:1, 5; 11:3; 112:6–10).

(iii) When (as is often the case: cf. Ps. 73:3, 12) possessed of power and prosperity, these people tend to oppress the weak and poor and vulnerable, to behave with injustice and cruelty, and to set up legal proceedings against them (37:14, 16, 32–3; 71:4; 82:4).

(iv) 'Sinners' include those who have made a full frontal attack on the religion of Israel (Ps. 74:4–11), or who abandon the law (119:53, 155), persons who because they are the enemies of Israel are also the enemies of God, and vice versa (92:5–11).

(v) These people will ultimately come under the judgement of God (Ps. 146:9; 147:6), and experience torments imposed by him (32:10; 37:34; 58:10; 68:2) in answer to the prayers of their pious opponents (139:19; 141:5).

When we move from this forest of anti-sinner sayings in the supposed Psalms of David to the supposed Psalms of Solomon, we move forward to 63 BCE and the time of the high priest Aristobulus II, when Pompey captured and entered the city of Jerusalem. With a terrifying resonance of the conduct of Antiochus Epiphanes almost exactly 100 years earlier, he was welcomed by some of the residents (Psalms of Solomon 8:16–17), and then with the aid of reinforcements overcame resistance in the Temple, which he proceeded to enter and desecrate (8:22). Some fifteen years later he met his death in Egypt. These Psalms of Solomon preserve the Pharisaic/Essene reaction to yet another national trauma. Unsurprisingly, the familiar polarisation between the sinners and the righteous reappears:

> The Lord's mercy is upon those who fear him with judgement, to separate between the righteous and the sinner to repay sinners for ever according to their actions. (Psalms of Solomon 2:23; cf. 3:11; 13:6–12)

The certainty of divine judgement on those (whether Jewish collaborators or gentiles) who have in effect set themselves up against a holy people, also reappears. The sinners, that is to say, gentiles, have 'exalted themselves to the stars' (Psalms of Solomon 1:5; cf. Isa. 14:13; Luke/Q 10:15), trampled under foot the worship of God (Psalms of Solomon 8:22), and engaged in unprecedented moral turpitude (1:7). The sinners, this time priestly Jews, have desecrated the Temple and the sacrificial order (2:3–5; 8:11–12), engaged in law–breaking (4:1), embraced moral recklessness and fecklessness (2:11–13; 4:3–8; 8:9–10), immersing themselves in a host of deviant activities.

What is clear from these psalms is that a group who are *part of* Israel is speaking and acting on the premise that they *are* Israel, and they reserve special venom for those who allegedly compromise the definitive specialness of Israel. In their view these people can be categorised along with the gentile oppressors. 'Sinners' are people who have sold their birthright.

So the typical approach of the biblical psalms, renewed and revived in the Pharisaic Psalms of Solomon, serves to convey a clear and consistent message. Because set in liturgical texts there would be a regular re-inforcement of the polarised and at times paranoid self-consciousness of the 'righteous' in Israel. Naturally, the 'sinners' are people that we only hear about from their 'righteous' and 'holy' opponents, just as we find the classic statements about sinners in the gospels being placed on the lips of critical Pharisees.

That point needs to be clearly understood. The worship texts – psalms, whether attributed to David or to Solomon – provide the vocabulary that can be used in subsequent polemic. Most particularly, the Pharisaic psalms are available to serve later Pharisaic purposes. But are the so-called sinners actual sinners or simply alleged sinners? There must be a strong suspicion that the most important feature of a sinner is that, viewed from the standpoint of a sectarian or special interest group, s/he is not 'one of us'. It may not be the only feature, but it may be more significant than many other features. One has always to ask: how would the people themselves, whose position is being lambasted by others, have defined their own position if given the chance to do so? It might not be the same. So in all talk of the so-called sinners we have to bear in mind that the issue is probably the drawing of a line around the authentic people of God, or the defining of the boundary of that people *on the basis of Pharisaic convictions.* The case of Levi suggests a radically different mind-set for Jesus on this matter, even if on other matters there was much in common.

What then can we infer from Jesus' controversial weaving of a tax-collector into the fabric of his community of followers, and his preparedness to establish on the basis of shared meals a bond with the 'sinners'? Well, for a start, there is absolutely no hint of Jesus' table fellowship's having 'virtually replaced the food laws' (Wright 1996: 432). Nor is there a root-and-branch dismissal of Pharisees as such, however critical they may be. He tacitly concedes that they represent the 'healthy' and the 'righteous', in just the same way as a famous parable acknowledged as secure the relationship of the elder brother of the prodigal son with his father (Luke 15:31), notwithstanding his view that parties for prodigals were distasteful and better shunned. But for all the closeness of Jesus to the Pharisees, his position was distinct in quite fundamental ways, especially in respect of the strategy of *inclusiveness.* Those who respond to the call for repentance are made, like the prodigal son himself, full partners in the table fellowship. They find themselves bound together in an unexpected way. Their sense of community, visible for all to see, is controversial but demonstrative of a fundamental principle. And one at least of those who followed personified that principle.

Jesus' controversial but principled offer and acceptance of hospitality to and from sinners is therefore a gesture of acceptance of those whose status as true Israelites is, *from their critics' point of view,* in question for one reason or another. That gesture is set, as it were, on the boundary of national self-consciousness and gives effect to a strategy of inclusiveness. Those whom the separated ones set apart, he brings in. Those whom the holy ones write out of the script, he writes in.

Further attestation of this position emerges powerfully in some of the parables, typical of which would be the parables of the lost sheep and the lost coin (Luke/Q 15:4–10).

These two parables form a typical male/female pairing, a pattern well known to readers of both Luke and Q (compare Luke/Q 11:31–2; 13:18–19, 20). Matthew's version of the parable of the sheep is in several, though not all, respects a later assimilation to the concerns of pastoral oversight of a Christian community, some of whose members are being enticed away to an alternative allegiance.

(i) He relocates the parable in his most church-preoccupied chapter, and places it under the heading, 'See that you do not despise *one of these little ones*', the latter term being a favourite descriptive term for Christians (Matt. 18:10, 14). So, according to him, we are *intra muros*, within the Christian community, and no longer engaging with a problem intrinsic to the Jewish community.

(ii) The problem for Matthew's sheep is not just their being lost but, more specifically and more sinisterly, their being 'led astray'. That is heavily loaded language, the sort of language applicable when alien influences have enticed people from the true faith (cf. Deut. 13:1–11). That very issue is of deep concern to Matthew: his blood pressure rises to a dangerous level, as it were, when he warns against charismatic Christian liberals who are (allegedly) theologically unsound on the revelation given once for all (allegedly) in the law: cf. Matthew 7:15–23/Luke 6:43–6. By contrast with all of that, Luke's version can claim to respond directly to a situation earthed in the mission of the historical Jesus.

No process of reconstruction is risk-free, but a good case can be made for the following original underlying the two later versions of Matthew and Luke:

> [4]Which man of you, having a hundred sheep and having lost one of them, does not leave the ninety-nine in the desert and go for the one that has been lost until he find it? [5]And having found it [he lays it on his shoulders] rejoicing, [6]and on arriving home he calls together his friends and neighbours, saying to them, 'Share my joy, because I have

found my sheep which had become lost.' [7]Just so, I tell you, there is joy in heaven over one sinner that repents rather than over ninety-nine righteous people who do not need to repent.

[8]Or what woman having ten silver coins, if she should lose one such coin, does not light a lamp, sweep the house, and search carefully until she finds it? [9]And having found it she calls together her women friends and neighbours, saying, 'Rejoice with me, because I have found the coin that I had lost.' [10]Just so, I tell you, there is joy in the presence of the angels of God over one sinner that repents.

A number of considerations influence the interpretation of these two parables. First, the 'which of you . . .?' introduction not only asks for a decision by all the listeners but presumes that the story in every respect rings true to their experience. The speaker asks the hearers to confirm that in the circumstances he is about to describe they would think or act in the same way (cf. Luke/Q 11:11; 12:25; 14:5; Luke 11:5; 14:28). Faced with the loss of a valuable item, each of them would search resolutely until that search achieved success. That is the main point. The follow-up point is the hosting of a celebratory meal, probably implicit in the calling together of friends and neighbours. This is sometimes judged 'over the top' and a secondary accommodation to the criticism recorded in Luke's editorial introduction: 'This fellow welcomes sinners and eats with them' (cf. Jesus as host in Mark 2:15–17 versus Jesus as guest in Luke 19:5). But such a judgement is probably mistaken:

> Village men gather almost nightly to discuss the events of the village, recite poetry, and tell stories from the oral tradition. It is fully as natural for the shepherd to call in his friends for a little celebration as it is for the woman in the parable of the lost coin. (Bailey 1976: 153)

Second, the size of the flock makes it unlikely that only one shepherd would be involved (cf. Luke 2:8), therefore the fate of the ninety-nine is not made problematic by the search for the one. On the contrary, those who share the care of the ninety-nine would bring them back home at the end of the day (Bailey 1976: 149). Therefore the successful search – and in this respect it is the same with the one coin as with the one sheep – brings with it a restoration of the wholeness of the original set. Without the one item – whether sheep or coin – there is an incompleteness which is now remedied.

Third, the detail of each story should not in each and every respect be pressed. Thus, the responsibility of the owner for the loss is implicit in both scenarios (Bailey 1976: 149), but this does not transfer into the 'just so . . .' part of the tradition. Similarly, there is nothing within the stories which precisely matches the repentance theme in the 'just so . . .' stage.

Finally, the most important thrust of the two parables is that Jesus in his mission engages in a search for those who originally belonged, and without whom the original whole is incomplete. In acting thus, he is bringing about divine joy. This will occasion no surprise in anyone who recalls the biblical insistence on God's own searching for the lost sheep (Ezek. 34:11–16). So the sinners are not extraneous to Israel but an essential part of it, notwithstanding their temporary state of being lost. Such persons could look at the community of Jesus' followers, and see there a confirmation in person of the fact that they were 'in'.

Old family, new family

From the theme of feasting we turn to that of the break with the birth family, which has been recurring regularly in traditions concerned with 'following'. The place to begin is, perhaps surprisingly, the birth family of Jesus himself, for all that the retrieval of firm information about it is exceedingly difficult. What begins to emerge from the complexities of the traditions, however, is that Jesus' family seems to have been deeply affected, and not for the better, by his commitment to a prophetic and kingdom-centred mission, in the context of which he issued to others a call to follow.

The traditions which provide revealing evidence deal with Jesus' visit to his hometown Nazareth (Mark 6:1–6a) and, earlier in Mark's sequence, his true family (3:31–5). In both, there appear on stage his mother, his brothers and his sisters, though not his father. Especially in the latter story, it is evident that a true family unit is in view, and that it functions as the frame of reference for the 'new family'. We can say at once then that the brothers and sisters cannot be cousins of Jesus (cf. Bauckham 1994: 694). They need to share at least one parent with Jesus for the tradition to work. But talk of parents pushes us towards an almighty dilemma. Who are we talking about?

We are certainly talking about Mary. The unnamed mother of Mark

3:31–5 is named in 6:3. With the term 'son of Mary' the tradition takes us into the world of matronymics, with significant implications concerning Jesus' father. Some conjecture that the term 'son of Mary' implies that by the time of Jesus' public mission, his father is no longer alive. However, 'son of the father' labels persist even after the father's death, so this conjecture is not well grounded (Ilan 1992: 23). Failing that, the term 'son of Mary' might point to Jesus' mother as being of higher status than his father. When Antipater is called 'the son of Salome', this is the case. She was an infamous woman, yes, but the sister of Herod the Great and therefore a person of notable rank (Josephus, *Jewish War* 2:26; Ilan 1992: 29–30). But the case of Jesus is unlikely to be comparable, since a whole series of independent (though by no means all historical) traditions connect Joseph, and not Mary, to the family of David (cf. Matt. 1:2–16, 1:18–25; Luke 1:26–38; 3:23–38; Rom. 1:3). Status-wise, that connection could scarcely be bettered. 'In the pedigree hunt, royal lineage is the greatest merit one can boast of' (Ilan 1992: 43). And Mark, whose horizon does not include the notion of a virginal conception, would see the unnamed father as the link between Jesus and David, thus justifying the acclamations in Mark 10:47–8; 11:10 (Bauckham 1994: 698–9). 'Son of Mary', therefore, does not mark her out as a person of superior social status. So if the unnamed father is neither dead nor a person of inferior standing, could it be that Mary was not the only wife of that father? Maybe Jesus is called 'son of Mary' because other siblings are children of another wife. The possibility cannot be discounted. There are many biblical and rabbinic instances of matronymics to distinguish the sons of different mothers, for example, Hur, 'the firstborn of Ephrathah' (1 Chr. 2:50), Adonijah as 'the son of Haggith' (1 Chr. 3:2), Abishai as 'son of Zeruiah' (1 Sam. 26:6), to name but three (cf. Bauckham 1994: 699–700). In the case of Jesus' family, this would mean a common father for all those listed in Mark 6:3, but more than one mother. Mary may not have been the only wife of Joseph. While this is certainly conceivable – pardon the pun! – it is hardly a compelling hypothesis. Perhaps we should settle for a more commonsense-type explanation. The naming of Jesus' mother, like the naming of Jesus' brothers, serves simply and solely to make personal and precise the Nazareth people's close and personal knowledge of the family – here the contrast between Mark 3:31 and 6:3 is striking – and maybe no more should be read out of the text than that.

There remains the most delicate of all the possibilities concerning

Mary's motherhood. A veritable cluster of traditions take it for granted that Joseph is the birth father of Jesus, and therefore that Jesus was Mary's legitimate son. It is arguable that this is so even in the case of that tradition in Luke 1:26–38 which has in the history of Christian thought formed the bedrock of mariological piety. When the tradition refers to divine Sonship, the parallelism between 'he will be called the Son of the Most High, and the Lord will give him the throne of his ancestor David' (v. 32) and 'he will be called Son of God' (v. 35) is the crucial consideration. We are drawn into the sphere of Israelite kingship, where the expected Davidic promise is about to be fulfilled (cf. 2 Sam. 7:11–17; 4Q174 *Florilegium*). And there would be no point in introducing Joseph at the outset as being 'of the house of David' (Luke 1:27) if the fulfilment were to be by some other means, discounting entirely his relevance. Yet there remains within the range of traditions concerning Mary's motherhood the persistent whisper of a different thought, that is to say, illegitimacy.

This thought is by no means within the horizon of the term 'son of Mary'. Despite the suspicions of many a commentator, and the allegations of more than one rabbinic report about Jesus, Jewish sources dealing with persons living across a wide time span have been assembled to show that a so-called matronymic does not suggest illegitimacy. Thus, three high priests are called 'sons of Kamith' and would have been disqualified from priesthood by illegitimacy, but their mother was famously a woman of conspicuous piety and discretion (Josephus, *Antiquities* 18:34; 20:16; Ilan 1992: 30–32). However, what does not come through via Mark's 'son of Mary' language is left on the table, as it were, by pre-Matthean tradition.

A tradition-historical analysis of the story of the dream of Joseph (Matt. 1:18–25; cf. Catchpole 2000: 73–80; Soares Prabhu 1976: 243–53) is the place to start. I have argued elsewhere that later Matthean expansions of an earlier pre-Matthean version of this story can be detected in (i) the link with the earlier genealogy, 'Now the birth of Jesus the Messiah took place in this way' (Matt. 1:18a); (ii) 'from the Holy Spirit' (v. 18b), which anticipates and, in narrative terms, weakens the force of the angel's message (v. 20); (iii) 'and unwilling to expose her to public disgrace . . . quietly' (v. 19), which skews the reference to Joseph's righteousness and unrealistically forgets the fact that a divorce is a public event; and (iv) the typically Matthean extended quotation from Isaiah

7:14, with its fulfilment motif and doubling of the naming of Jesus (Matt. 1:22–3). This leaves the following underlying tradition:

> 18bWhen Mary the mother [of Jesus] was engaged to Joseph, but before they lived together, she was found to be pregnant. 19Joseph, being a righteous man, planned to divorce her. 20But when he considered this, an angel of the Lord appeared to him in a dream and said, 'Do not be afraid to take Mary as your wife, for the child conceived in her is of the Holy Spirit. 21She will bear a son, and you are to name him Jesus, for he will save his people from their sins.' 24When Joseph awoke from sleep, he did as the angel of the Lord commanded him; he took her as his wife, 25but had no marital relations with her until she bore a son; and he named him Jesus.

Joseph is the hero of this story. At the start he is 'righteous', in that he recognises that violation of the bond of engagement always requires divorce procedure (Bockmuehl 2000: 17–21), and at the end he abstains from sexual intercourse with his pregnant wife, bearing in mind that 'none who has intercourse with a woman who is with child can be considered pure' (Josephus, *Against Apion* 2:202; cf. Pseudo-Phoclides, *Sentences* 186: 'Do not lay your hand upon your wife when she is pregnant'). He intends a living together (Matt. 1:20), and is told to marry (vv. 20, 24), so is not in the business of an unconsummated relationship and perpetual virginity. He is thinking about what Jewish people would regard as a proper marriage, but that is for a later date. Meanwhile, before, during and after the encounter with the angel, he is the very model of punctilious law-keeping. In the body of the story, he only deviates from the requirement to divorce his fiancée at the behest of the angel, whose message about the Holy Spirit's involvement in the pregnancy activates for the reader the memory of a series of other pregnancies in biblical literature, pregnancies brought about by normal sexual relations between a man and a woman, where God had been providentially involved (Catchpole 2000: 76–7). That was just another way of saying that what had happened, even if it represented a problem of colossal seriousness, could be set within the ever-paradoxical, unpredictable, but providential programme of God. After all, the expected child would, according to the angel and therefore according to God, be the restorer of Israel.

As for Mary, the nature of the liaison which brought about the pregnancy is left undefined – and the distinction drawn by legal texts treating this problem between a woman's being complicit or forcibly violated (Deut. 22:23–4, 25–7; Philo, *Special Laws* 3:72–8; Josephus, *Antiquities* 4:251–2; *Against Apion* 2:201) is not picked up explicitly. If the death penalty was in place at the time for both complicit partners, the initial decision of Joseph to do no more than activate divorce proceedings would suggest that forcible violation had occurred, in which case Philo's reference to the 'mercy and understanding' which the woman deserved would come into the reckoning. If the death penalty was not in place at the time, the text of Matthew leaves the background quite unexplained. On any showing, however, the colossally serious problem was a pregnancy that proved sexual intercourse to have taken place with someone other than Joseph after engagement to Joseph had been agreed. While the angelic/dream feature brings the story into the succession of many such angelic/dream stories in biblical literature, stirring the usual doubts about historicity in consequence, the desperate and all too human problem which is thus 'solved' is most unlikely to be an unhistorical Christian creation. The main restraint on such a conclusion is the multiple attestation of Joseph's fatherhood in a series of traditions. It is therefore difficult to draw conclusions with any confidence. All one can say is that either explanation – ordinary and legitimate sonship to Mary with Joseph, or illegitimate sonship to Mary and an unidentified male, with Joseph's acting later only as legal and 'official' father – provides a more credible backdrop for the subsequently strained relationship between Jesus and his mother than the suggestion of an abnormal conception can ever do.

That severely strained relationship emerges into the daylight through Mark 3:31–5 (following on Mark 3:21) and even more through Mark 6:1–6a. Once again, as elsewhere in other dislocated stories, here in Mark 6:1–6a the gospel writer very probably recasts earlier tradition and seems to have no difficulty living with the dislocations that he himself has created. There are a number of possible ways in which tradition might be separated from editorial intervention (cf. Barton 1994: 86–9), and then interpreted. Here is one such.

> [1]*He left that place and* he came to his hometown, *and his disciples followed him.* [2a]On the sabbath he began to teach in the synagogue, [2b]*and many who heard him were astonished.*

Jesus People

²ᶜThey said, 'Where did this man get all these things? What is the wisdom that has been given to this man? ²ᵈ***What deeds of power are being done by his hands!*** ³ᵃIs not this the carpenter, the son of Mary and brother of James and Joses and Judas and Simon, and are not his sisters here with us?' ³ᵇAnd they took offence at him. ⁴ᵃThen Jesus said to them, 'A prophet is not without honour, except in his hometown ⁴ᵇ***and among his relatives and in his own home.***'

⁵***And he could do no deed of power there, except that he laid his hands on a few sick people and cured them.*** ⁶ᵃ***And he was amazed at their unbelief.***

First, there are some details in the introduction that are probably pre-Marcan, notably the setting of the scene by referring to Jesus' coming to his hometown (preparing for v. 4a) and teaching (preparing for v. 2c). But 'he left that place' (v. 1a) connects the story to the preceding story about Jairus' daughter, and would not have figured in an independent story, and the disciples' following is a favourite Marcan theme. It serves his purpose to have them as witnesses, but they play no part at all in this specific incident (Barton 1994: 87).

Second, the direct speech of the residents of Nazareth (vv. 2c–3a) is said to express both astonishment (*exeplēssonto*, v. 2b) and scandal (*eskandalizonto*, v. 3b). But the two are not identical: for Mark astonishment is appreciative, especially when miracle is being highlighted (cf. 1:22; 7:37), whereas scandal is unequivocally negative (cf. 4:17; 14:27, 29). Jesus' comment (v. 4a), which is a *sine qua non* for a properly completed story (Marcus 2000: 376), presumes the negative, so even though the negative uses the 'scandal' terminology which Mark favours (Barton 1994: 89), it is the positive (v. 2b) which is probably Marcan redaction.

Third, the association of wisdom with Jesus is unparalleled in Mark, and therefore unlikely to be a Marcan creation. The term 'these things' carries no necessary implication of acts of power, though that is doubtless what it does on the Marcan level by harking back to the public miracles in Mark 5:21–43. In isolation from that Marcan context it can, in the light of Luke/Q 10:21, '. . . you have hidden *these things* from the wise and the intelligent', relate to the communication of divine wisdom through Jesus. This suggests that the double question, 'Where did this man get all these things? What is the wisdom that has been given to this man?' forms a neat synonymous parallelism, and that the reference to miracle, 'What deeds of power are being done by his hands!' is redactional. It is highly expressive of Marcan interest (cf. 1:21–2, 27–8), especially given that this whole unit of tradition brings to a climax a major section of Mark's gospel dominated by miracle (as widely agreed, cf. Marcus 2000: 62–4). In verse 2d it is, moreover, loosely and awkwardly attached, and at the same time in some tension with the final reference to limited performance of miracle (v. 5), so Marcan redaction seems likely. The same is probably true of the conclusion describing the limitation of Jesus' power (v. 5) and the confrontation with unbelief (v. 6a), two ideas which in combination serve to anticipate the similar limitation of the disciples' power in the story of the epileptic (9:14–29).

Fourth, the negativity in the Nazareth synagogue now begins to emerge as unrelated to the performance of miracle but rather a product of the presumed incompatibility of two profiles – the woodworking artisan on the one hand and the wisdom-endowed teacher on the other. The residents of Nazareth share the opinion of Jesus ben Sirach (38:24—39:5) that the two are opposed:

> [24]The wisdom of the scribe depends on the opportunity of leisure; only the one who has little business can become wise. [25]How can one become wise who handles the plough . . . [26]He sets his heart on plough-ing furrows . . . [27]So it is with every artisan . . . [28]the smith . . . [29]the potter . . . [31]All these rely on their hands, and are skilful in their own work. [32]Without them no city can be inhabited . . . [34]They maintain the fabric of the world, and their concern is for the exercise of their trade. How different the one who devotes himself to the study of the law of the Most High! [1]He seeks out the wisdom of all the ancients, and is concerned with prophecies; [2]he preserves the sayings of the famous and penetrates the subtleties of parables; [3]he seeks out the hidden meanings of proverbs and is at home with the obscurities of parables.

The prevailing view in Nazareth is clearly similar: someone who is wholly given over to woodworking is not in a position to explore tradition and communicate wisdom. Consequently, Jesus' teaching (v. 2ac), and therefore Jesus himself, must be judged inauthentic and lacking divine authorisation.

Fifth, given that there may be more than one carpenter linked to the

Nazareth community, the function of the family reference in verse 3 is to provide precise identification. It is not in any way polemical (*contra* Marcus 2000: 375). Had the phrase 'son of Mary' contained any kind of depreciation, a distancing between family and local community would result. But this is not the case. Factual identification: no more, no less. This enables us to hear the text without distraction. And the text says that, faced with the necessity of choosing between two profiles, the Nazareth people use their knowledge of and association with the family to choose the artisan profile to the exclusion of the wisdom teacher. In effect, they are saying, the family belongs to us (cf. 'with us', v. 3a), and this artisan Jesus belongs to the family, so we know what to think about him (Barton 1994: 94–5). What we, the readers, do not know from verses 2c, 3a is where the family members themselves stand on the Jesus question. In a sense, we do not need to know in order to make basic sense of the story. But we can still ask: Do they, on the Jesus issue, identify with him or with their community? Jesus provides a very clear answer. In a reference which is indeed 'especially rhetorical and emphatic' (Barton 1994: 90), he bluntly includes his family within the scandalised community. For the story to be coherent and complete, he did not need to do so. The fact that he does probably points to Marcan redaction in verse 4b: 'and among his relatives and in his own home'.

At the pre-Marcan stage of this tradition Jesus is defined by others as a woodworking artisan, and therefore not a studying and teaching scribe. Jesus is defined by himself as neither artisan nor as scribe but as prophet: 'A prophet is not without honour, except in his own hometown.' That is the essence of his vocational self-understanding. He grounds his teaching and authorisation not in persistent and settled patterns of scribal study but in a prophetic calling.

But at the Marcan stage of the tradition, while the superimposing of miracle conveys in part the interest of the evangelist, for our present purpose very much more interest attaches to the editorial adjustment in the addition of 'and among his relatives, and in his own home'. The evangelist is quite clear about alienation in the relationship between Jesus and his family. The residents of Nazareth think he belongs with his mother, his brothers and his sisters. Mark is blunt: he does not. In painting such a picture, he is following up what was said by means of the 'sandwich structure' he created in 3:21, 22–30, 31–5. Indeed he is bringing the story of Jesus' relationship to his family to a conclusion, for with 6:6a the relatives disappear from the story, never to return: 'under the cloud of unbelief (*apistia*), Jesus' family pass entirely from Mark's narrative' (Barton 1994: 91).

The earlier tradition that had opened up the question of the family's relationship to Jesus (Mark 3:21, 31–5) runs as follows:

> [21]His family . . . went out to restrain him, for people were saying, 'He has gone out of his mind' . . . [31]Then his mother and his brothers came; and standing outside, they sent to him and called him. [32]A crowd was sitting around him; and they said to him, 'Your mother and your brothers are outside, asking for you.' [33]And he replied, 'Who are my mother and my brothers?' [34]And looking at those who sat around him, he said, 'Here are my mother and my brothers! [35]Whoever does the will of God is my brother and sister and mother.'

There was a strong tendency in early Christianity to honour Jesus' family. One thinks of the historically well-grounded position of James, and the historically problematic traditions in Luke 1. So it is most unlikely that Mark would have presented such a situation of alienation, had it not been historical. For him, the position of Jesus' mother is especially problematic: the repetitious kinship references all follow the order 'mother . . . brothers . . . (sisters)', as indeed was the case in Mark 6:3, but in the concluding declaration the order is reversed, 'brother . . . sister . . . mother' (3:35). The mother is placed in the position of highest significance – for better or worse. For Mark also, the family's position, calling for Jesus from 'outside' (3:31) after having previously dismissed him as 'out of his mind' (3:21), is deeply symbolic of those 'outside' who stand over against the circle of those who truly hear, see, and receive the mystery of the kingdom (4:10–12).

For Luke (see 8:19–21), coming along later and feeling the need to reduce the negativity, and therefore confirming for our purpose that this tradition satisfies the criterion of embarrassment, tell-tale editorial changes needed to be, and were, introduced. In his recast version (i) the dismissal of Jesus as 'out of his mind' is dropped. (ii) The family do not call for Jesus from outside but rather try to reach him, only to be held back by the crowd. (iii) Jesus simply does not ask the critical question which undermines the position of the birth family, 'Who are my mother and my brothers?' (iv) The circle of those who are sitting around Jesus, exemplifying the new family, does not appear in the text. And therefore the affirmation that 'my mother and my brothers are those who hear and practise the word of God' by no means excludes the birth family. As historians, we should be more impressed by the heavy hints dropped by Mark than by the laboured rebranding of the image of Mary and Jesus' siblings by Luke.

The family rupture doubtless conditioned Jesus' attitude to his family, not excepting his mother. Further confirmation – that is, double attestation – of this conclusion is provided by the tradition in which one woman's instinctive sympathy with another *as a woman and a mother* is rather sternly corrected. For Jesus it was a matter of principled opposition to 'religious claims made on grounds of motherhood but not on grounds of discipleship' (Schüssler-Fiorenza 1995: 146). Rather, a woman, any woman, stands with a man, any man, in qualifying on a quite different basis for the beatitude at the heart of the mission of Jesus. Thus, Luke 11:27–8:

> 27A woman in the crowd raised her voice and said to him, 'Blessed is the womb that bore you and the breasts that nursed you!' 28But he said, 'Blessed rather are those who hear the word of God and do it.'

The traditional notion of a distinguished son's conduct bringing honour to his mother (cf. 1 Sam. 20:30), or the invocation of blessing on parents as a variation on the theme of calling down blessing on the son (Tobit 11:17; Sir. 3:10–11) – both are here undercut. Instead, the only honour worth counting accrues to the person who attends to the prophetic word of Jesus – and even Mary, it seems, has to learn the hard way to respect that rule. On the other hand, we know from other evidence that we have begun to assemble that there were plenty of women who did qualify, that is to say, plenty who had committed themselves to the cause of the coming kingdom, who had experienced already its healing power, and who were willing to place their resources at the disposal of Jesus and his mission (cf. the lists of named women in Mark 16:1; Luke 8:2–3). So discipleship is determinative, and the assumption of any privileged position for the birth family in general and the mother in particular firmly and critically resisted.

Jesus' own family was not the only one made dysfunctional by the call to follow, a call issued (so it seems) to men and women, husbands and wives alike. Luke/Q 12:51–3 makes the point very strongly. What it says could not be more at odds with the blueprint of family reconciliation which, we saw, defined the work of Elijah and thus of John the Baptist (Mal. 3:24/4:6; Mark 9:12a). For Jesus, Micah 7:6, a text which the great R. Eliezer ben Hyrcanus would a few years later associate with 'the footprints of the Messiah' (m. Sotah 9:15), provides the raw material but is not adopted without change. By comparison with the oracle of Micah, (i) Jesus does not pick up the warning to a man not to speak trustingly to his wife; (ii) he does not see the family tension as a matter of the younger generation's contempt for the older generation, but instead paints a picture of symmetry between the two; and (iii) he does not express disapproval, for what happens stems inexorably from his mission. Doubtless it is a matter of outcome rather than intention.

This saying belongs with a family of similarly influenced Jewish sayings about the 'young versus old' antagonisms which will bring damage to family life during the time of suffering before the new age dawns (Allison 1999: 289–94). The significantly varying versions of Matthew (10:34–6) and Luke can be explained in terms of energetic editorial alteration of an earlier Q saying, which ran:

> [51]Do you think that I came to project peace on/in the earth/land? I tell you, not peace but rather a sword. [52]For there are (will be) five people in one house, three against two and two against three. [53]For I came to divide father against son, and son against father; mother against daughter, and daughter against mother; mother in law against daughter in law, and daughter in law against mother in law.

This token household consists of two persons of the older generation (a father and his wife) and three of the younger generation (a son, his wife = his mother's daughter in law, and his sister). The disrupted relationships are those based naturally and instinctively on shared gender, and female relationships are specially emphasised. That fact itself is worth pondering. What is also worth pondering is the presence of the daughter in law. Had the intention been simply to treat inter-generational tensions, that would have been achieved very satisfactorily by a two-versus-two scheme, but this one is three-versus-two and vice versa. The presence of the daughter in law suggests that a younger married couple stands over against the son's parents, whose religious position does not (as might have been expected) determine that of the son and his wife. Instead the younger couple stands together on the basis of their united commitment to Jesus. Their marriage is compatible with their commitment. And that commitment pitches them into the tensions and antagonisms which are a feature of the final phase before the new age, the experience reflected in the surprising presence of 'persecutions' in the promise of the 'new family' (Mark 10:29).

In this light it can be appreciated how, for both Jesus and his associates, severance from the 'old' family is carefully balanced by attachment to a 'new' one. Two further traditions come into play now, the first of which is Mark 10:28–30:

> [28]Peter began to say to him, 'Lord, we have left everything and followed you.' [29]Jesus said, 'Truly I tell you, there is no one who has left house or brothers or sisters or mother or father or children or fields . . . [30]who will not receive a hundredfold now in this age – houses, brothers and sisters, mothers and children, and fields, with persecutions – and in the age to come eternal life.'

The break with family and work (again farming) is asserted once more – interestingly, without any necessary implication of leaving spouses. The gospel, we observe again, is not seen as the cause of marriage splits, and the implication must be (i) that those who followed Jesus included at least some married couples, and (ii) that even in the context of discipleship the commitment to marriage was seen as primary.

The addressees, whose gender is unspecified and therefore unrestricted, are clearly the itinerant followers of Jesus. These are the persons who, if male, are invited to consider the ravens, or who, if female, are invited to consider the lilies. For such persons, both male and female, there are provided substitute families, that is, those who in their own settled and non-itinerant setting ('houses . . . fields') offer hospitality and an experience of 're-socialisation'. Again, the setting in life is evidently that indicated in the mission charge (Mark 6:6b–13; Luke/Q 10:3–11). Those who are on the move are drawn into the family life and structures of those who remain settled, and the network of all such families is the 'new family'. Only one role within the welcoming family is not drawn into the definition of the new family experience, that is, the role of father. Fathers are left behind by those who follow Jesus, but in the new experience of community life there are no comparable 'father figures'. 'New mothers', yes, but no 'new fathers'!

The absence of 'new fathers' explains why there was clearly no place for Jesus' birth father or any 'new family'-type father in Mark 3:31–5. And that absence is reinforced by another tradition, preserved this time only in Matthew (23:8–10):

> [8]You are not to be called rabbi,
> for [only] one person is your teacher, and you are all brothers.
> [9]Do not call anyone on the earth father,
> for one is your father, the heavenly one.
> [10]Nor are you to be called instructor,
> for you have [only] one instructor, the Messiah.

In this tripartite saying, the third member overlaps with the first ('teacher' matches 'instructor'), and with its messianic allusion it sounds rather Christian. These considerations suggest that the first and the second members, which carry no Christian overtones, are probably basically pre-Matthean. However, the term 'brothers' in the first saying, which may certainly be an anticipation of the fatherhood reference in the second, is less appropriate when the teacher/learner relationship is in view, and 'brother' is also a favourite Matthean way of describing a member of the Christian community. Consequently the earlier form of the saying, at that stage containing only two members, may well have run:

> [8]You are not to be called rabbi,
> for [only] one person is your teacher, and you are all disciples.
> [9]Do not call anyone on the earth father,
> for [only] one is your father, the heavenly one.

Such a saying has a very good, though admittedly not irresistible, claim to go back to Jesus: it presupposes a situation prior to the development of Christian authoritative leadership and teaching structures; it is not likely to reflect Matthew's polemic against emergent rabbinic Judaism, given its pre-Matthean origin, but it contains an implicit criticism of well-known Pharisaic relationships of the pre-70 CE period; and its Christology is notably low and undeveloped. It suggests a 'community of equals' assembled round the one prophetic teacher, Jesus himself, and relating to God (and God alone) as their father figure.

Equality at risk: the riddle of Simon Peter

Just as it was important to clear the ground for an appreciation of the true family of Jesus by subjecting the relationship between Jesus and his mother to searching appraisal, so too for an appreciation of the defining features of the 'community of equals' it is important to subject to critical scrutiny the position of the one person who might be thought to be, as it were, more equal than the others. No gospel invests as much in the authority and function and theological conservatism of Simon Peter as the gospel of Matthew, to whom (ironically) we owe the previously quoted principle that 'one person is your teacher, and you are all disciples'. Evidently the struggle for control of the Christian community in Antioch was thought to be best served by energetic assertion of the alleged uniqueness of Simon Peter. But, we cannot forbear to ask, was what Matthew alleged the same as what the historical Jesus authorised?

We shall shortly examine the tradition of 'Jesus and the sons of Zebedee' (Mark 10:35–45), and accept one of the main arguments in favour of its historicity. On the basis of the criteria of embarrassment and plausible historical continuity, so runs that argument, the tradition is historical. (i) James and John are shown in such a bad light that the early Christian spin machine is certainly not in operation here; and (ii) within the earliest Christian community the pre-eminence of Peter was so quickly established that no one would ever in such circumstances have created a tradition in which the positions of supreme honour are sought by James and John (Sanders 1985: 147). The corollary of that argument is, of course, that the pre-eminence of Peter is not a factor in the pre-resurrection setting within which the conversation should be set. Therefore the attempt to place Peter on a religious pedestal, as it were, on the grounds of a pre-Easter confession (Mark 8:27–9) has to be questioned, and the historicity of 'You are Peter . . .' (Matt. 16:17–19) as a pre-Easter commission doubted. This last point needs to be developed by means of an assessment of those two crucially important traditions. The first will turn out to be arguably a Marcan construction. The second will turn out to be, also arguably, a Matthean expansion for his own purposes of a tradition derived from the early community in Jerusalem. Neither of them has a good claim to go back to the historical Jesus. Neither of them, therefore, introduces a personalised inequality into the life of the inner circle of the 'community of equals' assembled by Jesus.

The confession of Peter at Caesarea Philippi runs, according to Mark 8:27–33, as follows:

> [27]Jesus went on with his disciples to the villages of Caesarea Philippi; and on the way he asked his disciples, 'Who do people say that I am?' [28]And they answered him, 'John the Baptist; and others, Elijah; and still others, one of the prophets.' [29]He asked them, 'But who do you say that I am?' Peter answered him, 'You are the Messiah.' [30]And he sternly charged them not to tell anyone about him. [31]Then he began to teach them that the Son of Man must undergo great suffering, and be rejected by the elders, the chief priests and the scribes, and be killed, and after three days rise again. [32a]He said all this quite openly. [32b]And Peter took him aside and began to rebuke him. [33]But turning and looking at his disciples, he rebuked Peter and said, 'Get behind me, Satan! For you are setting your mind not on divine things but on human things.'

A strong case can be made in favour of this tradition's being the creation of Mark the evangelist, and insofar as it has an historical base, locating that base in Peter's status as the first to see the resurrected Jesus.

First, the very precise agreement between the saying about the suffering of the Son of Man in verse 31 and the course of events as told in Mark's passion narrative casts doubt on the former. Moreover, the 'Son of Man' usage here does not conform to the *modus operandi* of *bar (e)nash(a)* speech: this is no generalising statement of principle with wide applicability without any necessary involvement of the speaker (see above, p. 62). The speaker is uniquely in mind, and all other persons excluded. We note that Peter's rebuking of Jesus in verse 32b meshes with the prediction of suffering, and cannot be extricated from it.

Second, the fluctuation between secrecy and openness in verses 30, 32a reflects the characteristically Marcan secrecy scheme, the historicity of which it has proved somewhat adventurous to defend.

Third, the removal, as it were, of verses 30–32 causes the devastating rebuke of Peter in verse 33 to be juxtaposed with verses 27–9. Could it be that here we are left with an historical relic, according to which Jesus dismisses the messianic confession as a satanic temptation, and thus protects his mission from unwanted and unwarranted socio-political inferences? This is exceedingly unlikely: first, we can hardly suppose that the earliest Christian community would have preserved and transmitted a unit of tradition which undermined their central and definitive belief about Jesus (cf. 1 Cor. 15:3b); second, the balance of the tradition would require that in verse 29 a *correct* and not an incorrect view should be set over against the inadequate or incorrect views listed in verse 28; third, the notion of Peter as a mouthpiece of satanic opposition to Jesus fits easily with Mark's repeatedly negative portrayal of disciples, as well as with his portrayal of the mission of Jesus as one long confrontation with Satan.

Fourth, the list of inadequate evaluations of Jesus is artificial. Had the three options been formulated as 'in the succession of John the Baptist', 'in the succession of Elijah', and 'in the succession of the prophets', it would have been possible to find a basis for such views in authentically historical Jesus data, but the initial question and the related answer do not work that way. Moreover, the question which starts the whole conversation off presupposes that the person of Jesus is enveloped in mystery – which is a definitively Marcan but hardly historical idea. Definitively Marcan – yes indeed, for the synagogue assemblies in Capernaum (Mark 1:27) and Nazareth (6:2), and most crucially the disciples on the lake (4:41), ask questions and receive no answers.

Fifth, Mark is fond of using single-sentence affirmations about the person of Jesus, whether voiced by demons (3:11), by God (1:11; 9:7), by the centurion (15:39), or by Jesus himself (14:61–2; 15:2), so Peter's 'You are the Messiah' conforms neatly to Mark's mode.

Sixth, for Mark, the appearance of the risen one to 'the disciples and Peter', according to 16:7, hooks up very deliberately with the previous failure of them all, that is to say, the total failure of the disciples in general and Peter in particular, according to 14:27, 28, 29–31. Any specialness assigned to Peter within the continuity of the passion narrative would on that score have to be grounded in the spectacularly serious apostasy of which he had been guilty, according to 14:66–72. But if the narrative were extended to take in the gospel as a whole, it would almost certainly be relevant that Peter had been given the chief and primary position in the trio of witnesses who saw Jesus not only achieving a resurrection but also and above all appearing in anticipated resurrection mode himself: see 5:35–43; 9:2–8.

So Mark 8:27–33 preserves a reminiscence, not of the historical Jesus but of the risen Jesus; not of the pre-Easter Peter but of how Easter marked the beginning of a new chapter in his life story.

The other tradition which, according to widespread Christian supposition, though probably widespread Christian misinterpretation, attributes a special status to the pre-Easter Peter, is the sayings complex in Matthew 16:17–19:

> [17]And Jesus answered him, **'Blessed are you, Simon son of Jonah! For flesh and blood has not revealed this to you, but my Father in heaven.** [18]And I tell you, you are Peter, and on this rock I will build my church, and the gates of Hades will not prevail against it. [19a]**I will give you the keys of the kingdom of Heaven, and** [19b]whatever you bind on earth will be bound in heaven, [19c]and whatever you loose on earth will be loosed in heaven.'

Very few New Testament specialists hear in this saying addressed to Peter any echo of the voice of the historical Jesus. It is, however, important to assess the material afresh, and this can best be done by taking a number of steps:

First, this complex, made up of sayings which are neither consistent in their imagery nor mutually dependent in their content, is quite separate from the traditions which fed into the gospel of Mark. Given that evangelist's interest in Peter as the leading witness to the pre-Easter Jesus (cf. Mark 1:16; 3:16; 5:37; 9:2; and above all, 8:29!), Mark would not have excluded it, had he received it from pre-Marcan tradition. Matthew for his part shows no sign of owing to anyone other than Mark his version of the preceding conversation and confession, so there is no evidence supporting any hypothesis of an original pre-Matthean sequence involving a confession and a 'You are Peter . . .' sequel.

Second, the 'Blessed are you, Simon . . .' saying (Matt. 16:17) is very likely to be Matthew's own work (cf. Luz 2001: 356). It is tightly bound to Matthew's edited version of the confession, to which he attached the extra title 'the Son of the living God'. It is also linked to other traditions on which Matthew sets great store. The idea of 'flesh and blood', that is to say, humanity as such, being unable to discern divine truth is already present in Mark 8:33, but here in Matthew 16:17 it is part of a combination of the ideas of inaccessibility to human beings, divine revelation, the divine Sonship of Jesus, and God as his heavenly Father. This, as has rightly been pointed out (Luz 2001: 355), makes Matthew 16:16–17 an outstanding exemplar of the principles set out in Luke/Q 10:21–2:

> [21]I thank you, Father, Lord of heaven and earth, because you have hidden these things from the wise and intelligent and have revealed them to infants; yes, Father, for such was your gracious will. [22]All things have been handed over to me by my Father; and no one knows the Son except the Father, and no one knows the Father except the Son and anyone to whom the Son chooses to reveal him.

Significantly for our enquiry, Luke/Q 10:22, which is later than Luke/Q 10:21, is almost beyond doubt a reflection of post-Easter convictions about Jesus, as expressed in Matthew's version of the group appearance of the risen Jesus:

> [18]All authority in heaven and on earth has been given to me. [19]Go therefore and make disciples of all nations, baptizing them in the name of the Father and of the Son and of the Holy Spirit. (Matt. 28:18–19)

In similar vein, it may be that we should take seriously the agreement between Matthew and Paul in combining the idea of the divine revelation of the risen Son of God in a setting independent of 'flesh and blood' (see Gal. 1:15–17). That agreement may mean that when creating Matthew 16:17 the evangelist is not so much engaged in a *creatio ex nihilo* as informed by a tradition of how the earliest Christians understood appearances of the risen Jesus (Brown 1973: 88–9; Meier 2001: 235). Given his strong theological preference for the Petrine over against the Pauline, fuelled by the likelihood that his life setting was the Christian community in Antioch, where the Petrine position had triumphed over and displaced the Pauline position (Gal. 2:11–14), it may well be that the sub-text of Matthew 16:17 is a forceful reassertion of the non-Pauline theology which legitimated itself with reference to Peter.

Third, the saying in Matthew 16:19a, 'I will give you the keys of the kingdom of heaven', is also likely to be Matthew's own creation (Luz 2001: 356–7). The attached saying in 16:19bc about binding and loosing has probably been adjusted to a singular form (contrast 18:18) in order to fit a personal address to Peter. But there remains the mixing of metaphors – from opening/shutting to binding/loosing – and the awkward fact that binding/loosing has nothing to do with entry to the kingdom. While the image of opening the kingdom of God is unknown in contemporary Judaism, and the notion of the keys extremely rare, both occur in a highly polemical anti-Pharisaic Q passage in Matthew 23:13/Luke 11:52:

> Woe to you, scribes and Pharisees, hypocrites! For you lock people out of the kingdom of heaven. For you do not go in yourselves, and when others are going in, you stop them.

So it is probable that Matthew has created 16:19a in order to establish Petrine teaching authority, analogous but antithetical to Pharisaic teaching authority, and therefore set in polemical confrontation with that of the rabbinic authorities in the synagogue in Antioch, who had excluded the Christian Jews from that synagogue and who were the spiritual heirs of the Pharisees. No gospel is tougher on Pharisees than his, in itself a pointer to the religious tensions which dominate his world. Custody of the keys to the kingdom, which is ceded to the Pharisees in Matthew 23:13, is now emphatically removed from them, for they have resisted the kingdom-centred mission of Jesus and his community (Kloppenborg 1987: 142–3). But this means that for pre-Matthean material defining the status and function of Peter, we are now left with 16:18 alone:

> I tell you, you are Peter, and on this rock I will build my church, and the gates of Hades will not prevail against it.

A cluster of difficulties comes into view. In Matthew, the correspondence between 'You are the Messiah . . .' and 'You are Peter . . .', together with the need for some specific content for the word 'this' in the phrase 'on *this* rock', suggests that the rock stands for the confession of Messiahship which Peter has voiced as a representative of the disciple group (cf. 'Who do you [emphatic] say that I am?'). The reality represented by 'this rock' is related to, but not identified with, Peter personally. As far as Peter personally is concerned, there is no question of his here being renamed. The renaming of Abram as Abraham (Gen. 17:5), or of Sarai as Sarah (17:15), or of Jacob as Israel (32:28; 35:10), is not analogous, for Matthew 16:18 has no equivalent to the 'You shall not be called X, but you shall be called

Y' formulation in those cases. Matthew, while reminding his readers that Simon is the primary name – thus, 'Simon, who is called Peter' (Matt. 4:18; 10:2) – omits the Marcan detail that Jesus attached the name Peter at the time of the appointment of the twelve, and does not hesitate to use that name Peter on several occasions in advance of Matthew 16:18 (thus, 8:14; 14:28, 29; 15:15). While the name Simon appears only once (17:25) after the 'You are Peter' incident, and the name Peter becomes the norm, Matthew gives us no clue as to when the name was applied to Simon, or what it originally meant. He only exploits the potential for punning represented by the name Peter (*petros*) and the noun rock (*petra*).

In Mark, the position is a little different. Jesus personally attaches three new names at the time of appointing the twelve: in the leading trio Simon is named Peter, and James and John are named Boanerges (Mark 3:16–17). The person previously known only as Simon (1:16, 29, 30, 36) almost entirely ceases to be other than Peter ('Simon, are you asleep?' [14:37] is the one exception), and we have the impression that the new name is intended to represent Peter's new, formal, and leadership role in the group of twelve. There remains the suspicion that Mark is taking liberties in setting up such a scheme, for it does not cope well with the comparable attachment of the name Boanerges (helpfully translated as 'sons of thunder') to James and John. For them as for Simon there are, according to Mark, overtones of formal or functional specialness, for they are placed next to Simon in the list, thus separating Andrew from his brother, and together with Peter they do of course appear subsequently as privileged witnesses (Mark 5:37; 9:2; 14:33; with Andrew, 13:3). But what has the name Boanerges, and by extension the name Peter, to do with this? The suggestion has certainly been made that Boanerges expresses their 'prophetic, apocalyptic proclamation' (Balz 1994: 222–3), but the proclamation entrusted to them by Jesus was entrusted equally to all, so why should they be singled out? It seems more likely therefore that a personality trait is in mind, so that theirs is a nickname (in the same way as the five sons of Mattathias have nicknames, whose deriva-tion and meaning now defy definition, 1 Macc. 2:2–5) rather than an expression of formal status or function – whether 'thunderbolts' or 'sons of unrest, agitation' or 'persons of courageous wrath' or 'sons of restless noise', to mention a few of the suggestions that have been mooted. And, by extension, one has to ask whether the same may be true of the name Peter, given that the normal everyday sense of the underlying word *kepha* would be 'a round stone (stone, gem, hailstone, nugget)', or at most 'free-standing, round rock'. This, as has been observed, is not suitable terminology for the foundation of a building (Luz 2001: 358–9)!

It seems, then, that there is reason to be suspicious about Mark's formalising tendency and his upgrading of nicknames. What remains to be done is to exercise informed imagination in order to find a context in which an experience of Peter might be regarded as foundational ('this rock') and precisely because it happened to Peter might give rise to the pun on his name ('You are Peter'), and in consequence cause him to stand out in some special way though without in any way equating him with the rock in question. For 'this rock' stands for something to which Peter is referred, as distinct from something which refers to Peter. Just as 'I thank you . . . that you have revealed *these things* to infants' (Luke/Q 10:21) requires us to supply our own best guess as to the meaning of 'these things', so here we have to hazard a guess as to the identity of '*this* rock', this something that happened to Peter. Very little imagination is needed to equate 'this rock' with the first appearance of the risen Jesus, on which basis the earliest, Cephas-led, Christian community in Jerusalem grounded its Easter-defined life. A convergence of several factors serves to stiffen this possibility into a probability.

First, the distinct identity implied by the term 'church', the assembly of those who are gathered together as part of a self-conscious and continuing movement, is in place here (Meier 2001: 232–3). And from Paul's testimony in Galatians 1:13 we have it confirmed that the term 'church (of God)', encompassing the 'churches' (1 Thess. 2:14), was current in Jerusalem as a term for the assembled and ultimate people of God (Roloff 1994: 411–12).

Second, the combination of distinct identity and definitive christological confession implied in '*my* church' is in place here, given the previous occurrence of resurrection. That would have been seriously exaggerated in the pre-Easter phase of the Jesus movement. It was the post-Easter community whose convictions were formalised in 'Messiah died . . . and was raised . . . and appeared to Cephas . . .'

Third, it was here that the notion of the community as a building gained acceptance (cf. the 'pillars' of Gal. 2:9), as well as provoking a sharp riposte from one who was clear-headed enough to see the inherent risk that the use of foundational language for a leader's experience might slide over into the use of such language for the leader himself, thus substituting the human leader for the heavenly Christ (cf. 1 Cor. 3:10–17, 21–3).

Fourth, whatever may be the usage of the name Cephas/Kepha prior to Easter, it is striking that in its Aramaic form the name occurs only in post-Easter references. As a surname, perhaps surprisingly, it is not projected back into stories set within the pre-Easter sequence (cf. 1 Cor. 1:12; 3:22; 9:5; 15:5; Gal. 1:18; 2:9, 11, 14). Each and every one of those instances of 'Cephas' is set either in tradition emanating from the Jerusalem community or in documents recognising Peter's leading role in that community. 'Cephas' seems now to stand for the person who has seen the risen one and epitomises the earliest community. And according to Paul he is in that respect defined above all by 'gospel [and] apostolate of the circumcision' (*to euaggelion . . . apostolē tēs peritomēs*).

The outcome of our extended investigation of Matthew 16:17–19 is therefore that it contains both pre-Matthean tradition and Matthean redaction, but even the pre-Matthean tradition cannot transport us into the context of Jesus' mission. The Jerusalem community, yes: Jesus, no.

Jesus' inner circle: roles and relationships

For many of those who responded to Jesus' message of the kingdom by repenting and renewing their commitment to the fundamental principles of Israel's existence, life went on as before. They continued in their own home situations as a support network of 'peace people' (cf. Luke/Q 10:5–7), but heard no call to follow. So the 'followers' were a special sub-group, close companions of Jesus, learners drawing upon him as teacher and prophet, actively committed to mission. But then there was an even smaller sub-group, the twelve, an inner circle whose role calls for special study.

The 'twelve' are mentioned in the list of those who 'saw' the risen Jesus (1 Cor. 15:5), and some have suspected that this specific group is a post-Easter development, a reflection of the earliest Christian community's missionary commitment to the twelve tribes of Israel. This is unlikely, for several reasons:

(i) There is the fluctuation in the listing – Mark has Thaddaeus, while Luke has Jude the son of James (Mark 3:16–19/Luke 6:14–16/Acts 1:13) – which suggests that the tradition is early, certainly pre-Marcan, and that the fact of twelve was more firmly embedded than the precise recollection of the identity of all those who belonged (Sanders 1985: 101). It is worth noting that some of the persons concerned never appear in any gospel stories: they will have been known in Christian circles but not as persons who stood out in their own right.

(ii) The presence of Judas Iscariot is firmly part of the list as well as being firmly part of the story of Jesus (cf. 'one of the twelve', Mark 14:43), and it is most unlikely that his presence would be a Christian creation.

What is the significance of the twelve in the setting of the pre-Easter mission of the historical Jesus, that is to say, in the setting of an expectation of the kingdom of God which has not yet come? The answer: 'Except as a visible sign of exclusive preoccupation with Israel, none at all!' One might see them as individual representatives of, and concerned with, *present* mission to, the tribes of Israel. But those who are sent out on mission are a wider group than the twelve, and there is no reason to attach a unique missionary connotation to that inner group. The meaning is rather to be located in the *future* role that is marked out for them, against the background of Jesus' expectation and proclamation that God would rescue and restore the whole of Israel. 'There is no complete kingdom of God without a complete Israel' (Meier 2001: 153). The prospect of rule over Israel in the new age following the resurrection of the dead is documented in Jewish texts – thus:

> After this Abraham, Isaac, and Jacob will be resurrected to life and I [Judah] and my brothers will be chiefs (wielding) our sceptre in Israel: Levi, the first; I, second; Joseph, third, Benjamin, fourth; Simeon, fifth; Issachar, sixth; and all the rest in their order. (*Testament of Judah* 25:1)

It is this prospect that Jesus invokes by choosing an inner circle of twelve, and with breathtaking radicalism substituting his followers for the patriarchs. But does he envisage any order of precedence? *Testament of Judah* 25:1, instead of following the birth sequence from one to twelve, chooses the order three, four, eleven, twelve, two, nine and then the rest. A consciousness of being one of Jesus' chosen twelve might well allow space for thoughts of precedence and a 'some are more equal than others' ranking.

In the gospels there is multiple attestation for an expectation among the disciples, and affirmed by Jesus (Matt. 19:28/Luke 22:30), that in the age to come they would exercise royal authority over Israel. Moreover, in line with Jewish expectation, there is indeed interest in precedence and rank within the new royal situation (Mark 10:35–7, 40). Perhaps surprisingly, Jesus does not criticise the idea of ranking in the future kingdom; he simply prohibits it as a factor affecting relationships in the present age.

An analysis of the tradition of 'Jesus and the sons of Zebedee' clarifies this future bearing of discipleship. The historicity of the tradition has, as already mentioned, been convincingly defended. If that conclusion is correct, what may the record of the conversation between Jesus and the two brothers, the so-called 'sons of thunder', disclose as to the meaning of present life and future prospects in Jesus' inner circle?

> [35]James and John, the sons of Zebedee, came forward to him and said to him, 'Teacher, we want you to do for us whatever we ask of you.' [36]And he said to them, 'What is it you want me to do for you?' [37]And they said to him, 'Grant us to sit, one at your right hand and one at your left, in your glory.' [38]But Jesus said to them, 'You do not know what you are asking. *Are you able to drink the cup that I drink, or be baptized with the baptism that I am baptized with?'* [39]*They replied, 'We are able.' Then Jesus said to them, 'The cup that I drink you will drink; and with the baptism with which I am baptized, you will be baptized. But* [40]to sit at my right hand or at my left is not mine to grant, but it is for those for whom it has been prepared.'
>
> [41]When the ten heard this, they began to be angry with James and John. [42]So Jesus called them and said to them, 'You know that among the Gentiles those whom they regard as their rulers lord it (*katakurieu-ousin*) over them, and their great ones exercise authority (*katexousia-zousin*) over them. [43]But it is not so among you; but whoever wishes to become great among you must be your servant, [44]and whoever wishes to be first among you must be slave of all.' [45]*For the Son of Man came not to be served but to serve, and to give his life a ransom for many.*

In analysing this tradition and reconstructing its history we can take an ordered sequence of steps:

First, Mark 10:41–5 is clearly separable from 10:35–40: Jesus talks to all the disciples and not just two. It also has a parallel in Luke 22:24–7, which is meaningful in its own right and has nothing like Mark 10:35–40 preceding it.

^{24}A dispute also arose among them as to which one of them was to be regarded as the greatest. ^{25}But he said to them, 'The kings of the Gentiles lord it over them; and those in authority over them are called benefactors. ^{26}But not so among you: let the greatest among you become like the youngest, and the one who leads like the one who serves.' ^{27}*For who is greater, the one who reclines [for a meal] or the one who serves? Is it not the one who reclines? But I am among you like the one who serves.*

Moreover, we have in Mark 9:33–5 another parallel tradition in which the issue of future greatness is tackled.

> ^{33}Then they came to Capernaum; and when he was in the house he asked them, 'What were you arguing about on the way?' ^{34}But they were silent, for on the way they had argued with one another about who [should be] greatest. ^{35}He sat down, called the twelve, and said to them, 'Whoever wants to be first must be last of all and servant of all.'

The two traditions in Mark 9:33–5 and 10:41–5 match and complement each other, and confirm on the basis of double attestation that the disciples did think in these terms, and also that they received just such a servant-focused answer from Jesus.

Second, Mark 9:33–5 presently has attached to it 9:36–7, the addendum in which Jesus uses the small child as a model:

> ^{36}Then he took a little child and set it among them; and taking it in his arms, he said to them, ^{37}'Whoever receives one such child in my name, receives me, and whoever receives me receives not me but the one who sent me.'

In the final saying in verse 37 we have a variant of the mission saying using the 'sending' principle (see above on Luke/Q 10:16). That the first person in the chain of reception is typified by the child is a powerful critique of all status-driven instincts: the child has no inherent place up the pecking order of human esteem, and therefore the model of mission-centred discipleship in the here and now is to be free of all such concerns. The child will in Mark's sequence shortly be presented as the model of Christian life in general (double attestation in Mark 10:13–15,

16): now Jesus insists that those with apostolic roles are governed by, and by no means exempt from, the same status considerations. They have not as the twelve outgrown the childhood model.

Third, Mark 10:41–5 presents the critique by different means – partly by an appraisal of how authority works among the nations at large, and partly by extending the reflection on the theme of service. The formulations used in Jesus' sayings are heavily loaded. The parallelism between the two halves of verse 42b sets up an equivalence between the two verbs used: 'they exercise lordship (*katakurieuousin*) . . . they exercise authority (*katexousiazousin*)'. Both convey a strong impression of a sharp dichotomy between those who rule and those who are ruled, and both manifestly imply a 'from the top downwards' relationship. One has only to recall from other instances of the verb 'to exercise lordship' the nuances of political subjugation (Ps. 72:8) or fear-generating authority, as in the relationship of humankind to the creation (Sir. 17:4), or of demon-assisted overpowering of seven persons by another (Acts 19:16), or a leadership style of dominating others (1 Pet. 5:3). But within the parallelism between the two halves of verse 42b there is a small but significant discrepancy. Whereas 'those who rule' would have functioned in an entirely suitable way as a parallel for 'their great ones', in fact the saying refers to 'those *whom they regard as* their rulers (*hoi dokountes archein*)'. Now the verb 'to regard' does not in and of itself denote an opinion that is wrong – earlier usage is neutral and may sometimes go one way (favourably: knowledge is *regarded* as pleasant to the soul, Prov. 2:10), even if it more often goes the other (unfavourably: Lot who was *regarded* by his sons in law as joking, Gen. 19:14; a certain way may be *regarded* as right, but the outcome may be disaster, Prov. 14:12; Jesus' captors might wrongly *suppose* that he could not call for supernatural assistance, Matt. 26:53). So the verb 'to regard' does not in and of itself imply a contrast between what is perceived to be reality and what is genuinely so, that is to say, between 'apparent' rulers and the only 'true' ruler, God. The sense is rather a combination of how things are and how they are recognised as being: persons in authority *are* in that position and *are recognised as being there* by those who are below them.

Three examples make this clear: (i) When during the reign of Herod Agrippa, some young men in the city of Dora in Phoenicia caused consternation and outrage by bringing an image of Caesar into the Jewish synagogue, an angry rebuke was sent by Petronius, the Roman governor of Syria, who in the course of his letter referred to how 'even those who are regarded as eminent (*hoi dokountes autōn*) among the transgressors' made certain defensive claims. Thus, Josephus, in *Antiquities* 19:307, clearly has in mind persons who not only were leaders but also were recognised and esteemed as such.

(ii) While not having a personal reference, the phrase 'those parts of the body that *we regard as* weaker (*ta dokounta melē*)' stands in parallel with the following phrase 'those members of the body that we think (*ha dokoumen*) less honourable', thus demonstrating that the accent is placed on how things are evaluated and esteemed (1 Cor. 12:22–3).

(iii) When describing with some bitterness the Christian leaders in Jerusalem, Paul refers to them in Galatians 2:9 as 'those who were acknowledged pillars (*hoi dokountes stuloi einai*)', and in doing so makes clear a certain animus on his part towards them, and even scepticism about the way their authority is established (2:6). But the phrase he uses reflects not his opinion – which is not quite the same! – but that of the other members of the community in which they are set. They have position, a position of special and superior authority, and they have the recognition of others that goes with it.

So we begin to understand the fine-tuning of Mark 10:42b: Jesus is commenting on a pattern of authority which involves top-down lordship over others and the recognition by others which goes with it. And the sharp critique of that pattern could scarcely be more uncompromising or astringent. Deliberately using the present tense, not the future, he declares, 'It is not so among you.' By this means, attention is drawn to what is

> not a prediction but a present reality demanding responsible behaviour . . . a new form of community where the rules about power and service are different . . . a community of discipleship that stands as an alternative to the structures of power of their world . . . a subversive community that proves possible ways of exercising authority other than dominion by the strongest. (Kaminouchi 2003: 129, 139, 155)

In other words, whatever the future prospects may be, and whatever the grisly and ambition-tinged present reality may be, the definition of the community of Jesus people involves no promotion of one over another, no subjugation of one to another, no investment in hierarchy and the status that goes with it, no 'asking for positions of privilege in a hierarchy of power' (Kaminouchi 2003: 102). Here is another acutely counter-instinctive ideal, stated indicatively as a fact in order that it may act as a non-negotiable imperative.

Fourth, we have so far referred to Mark 10:41–5, but was this correct? Should we not refer to Mark 10:41–4, and see 10:45 as a later attachment? The answer is probably yes. In three respects that saying cannot but refer to Jesus, and to Jesus alone, and therefore be of limited relevance to the discussion of authentic discipleship:

(i) The language of 'having come' is the language of a messenger (cf. Job 1:14–19; Dan. 9:23; 10:14; Josephus, *Jewish War* 3:399–402: texts cited by Theissen/Merz 1998: 525), and the definitive messenger can only be Jesus.

(ii) While the language of 'ransom' can be used to interpret the demise of one human group for the benefit of another (cf. Isa. 43:1–3), it is most unlikely that the intention of the calling of those who share Jesus' prophetic mission could be their deaths for the benefit of 'the many'. To understand discipleship in terms of the total abandonment of oneself and one's earthly prospects is multiply attested – see the 'taking up the cross and denying oneself' sayings in Mark 8:34–5; Luke/Q 14:27; 17:33 – but that falls very considerably short of the idea of a transformative death. Mark's version of the eucharistic words, on the other hand, shows he is at home with the idea that Jesus' own death might have such an intention.

(iii) If the 'Son of Man' saying fits neatly into the Marcan presentation of the meaning and destiny of Jesus – and it does – it also fails to conform to the *modus operandi* of *bar (e)nash(a)* sayings. This is not a generalisation whose scope is indicated by the context, a saying that the speaker *may* apply to himself but does not have to do so. On the contrary, Mark 10:45 is a saying which *must* refer to Jesus and is most unlikely to apply to anyone else.

Once we have become alert to the likelihood that Mark 10:45 is a later attachment to 10:41–4, we are ready for the similar conclusion that Luke 22:27 is a later attachment to 22:24–6. Jesus again insists on the servant model (v. 26). The following saying (v. 27) imposes unnecessarily a very specific area of service on the tradition by recalling different roles at a meal. This suggests a tactic of illustrating the sayings about greatness by adapting them to the very particular setting of Jesus' final meal, a tactic which doubtless stirred the author of the fourth gospel to paint the moving and memorable picture of Jesus as the servant at the meal in John 13. But Luke 22:24–7 is given its present location by Luke. So, to sum up, the basic traditions on which to make a judgement about Jesus' treatment of greatness in the disciple group are Mark 10:41–4 and Luke 22:24–6.

Fifth, the discipleship model of the child, to which the tradition in Mark 9:36–7 pointed us, is another multiply attested idea, and one that has a range of implications. Two reinforcing traditions call for consideration: the famous 'suffer the little children' story (Mark 10:13–16), and the prayer that underlies the so-called Johannine thunderbolt (Luke/Q 10:21–2).

> 13People were bringing little children to him in order that he might touch them; and the disciples spoke sternly to them. 14But when Jesus saw this, he was indignant and said to them, 'Let the little children come to me; do not stop them; for it is to such as these that the kingdom of God belongs. 15*Truly, I tell you, whoever does not receive the kingdom of God as a little child will never enter it.'* 16And he took them in his arms, laid his hands on them, and blessed them.

This story originally consisted of verses 13–14, 16: in its Marcan form it has two punchlines (vv. 15, 16), a fact which is demonstrated by Matthew's later use of it. He removes verse 15, transplanting it into his teaching about humility (Matt. 18:3), and leaving behind in Matthew 19:13–14, 15 a story which makes perfect sense without Mark 10:15. But that means that originally there was a story and a separate saying about children and the kingdom of God. Multiple attestation – two sayings here, to which a third, Mark 9:36–7, can be added – strengthens our impression that we are reaching down to the bedrock of the authentic teaching of Jesus. The child for him is the model for *entry to* the kingdom, *life in* the kingdom, and also *mission for the sake of* the kingdom. Those who have the privilege of presenting the kingdom have not 'outgrown' the basic principle of entry, and they are – whether they realise it or not – committed to an outlook which simply does not buy into the conventions of honour and shame, of ambition or status.

The thanksgiving of Jesus to the Father (Luke/Q 10:21), as it is called, is assuredly a genuine saying of Jesus, but it has attracted to itself as a sort of commentary (Wanke 1980: 218) a proclamation saying (v. 22) which is more likely to belong to the post-resurrection era than to Jesus himself.

> [21]At that time Jesus said, 'I thank you, Father, Lord of heaven and earth, because you have hidden these things from the wise and intelligent and have revealed them to infants; yes, Father, for such was your gracious will.' [22]*All things have been delivered to me by my Father, and no one knows the Son except the Father, and no one knows the Father except the Son and anyone to whom the Son is willing to reveal him.*

Certain ideas are present in verse 21, which are then developed in verse 22: (i) the sense of God's fatherhood, with which the speaker's sense of sonship interlocks; (ii) the sense of an exclusive religious insight, enjoyed by some and withheld from others; (iii) the key position and role of Jesus as revealer; and (iv) an overarching sense of the mysterious and providential will of God. But those ideas are picked up and given a much heavier theological bearing in verse 22 than they ever had in verse 21. So while the 'commentary saying' has a base in the prayer, it is highly developed by comparison with the prayer. In trying to reach back to Jesus, we therefore need to assign verse 22 to the post-Easter situation and concentrate on verse 21 alone.

The prayer is one of the very few traditions in which Jesus provides a panoramic survey of his mission as a whole, and of the principles which sustain it. The 'gracious will' of the Father turns out to work completely differently from all expectation. Normally the route to wisdom is . . . wisdom! 'To the one that has, more will be given.' If you are wise, you will become wiser. If you have heroes in the tradition of wisdom, Daniel will surely figure among them, and it was Daniel who set out the principle (Dan. 2:21–3), which as a matter of fact is clean contrary to what Jesus says in his prayer:

> [21]He changes times and seasons, deposes kings and sets up kings; he gives wisdom to the wise, and knowledge to those who have understanding. [22]He reveals deep and hidden things; he knows what is in the darkness, and light dwells with him. [23]To you, O God of my ancestors, I give thanks and praise, for you have given me wisdom and power, and have now revealed to me what we asked of you . . .

The fact that Luke/Q 10:21 so consciously echoes Daniel 2:21–3 makes the divergence of the one from the other all the more arresting. Those who respond to Jesus are not the heirs to an established tradition of wisdom but the recipients of a new one. They are like children in the sense that they are models of openness to instruction, instruction that has to do with God's mysterious plan for the world, concentrated in the future, which is the future when God as king will come. They are not part of any wisdom-dominated establishment. They are given the divine wisdom, not because they already have it to some extent, but because they do not have it and are open to receive it from their sole and supreme teacher. The truth about them is that the truth is given to them – they are, above all, learners, pupils, disciples.

Discipleship in resurrection perspective

It must be evident that much of the 'following Jesus' scheme simply cannot be transplanted into any world other than his, or dictate the shape of Christian commitment in any era later than his. As has been urged wholly convincingly in connection with Jesus' sayings about discipleship and following: 'Their ethical radicalism makes Jesus' sayings absolutely impracticable as a regulative for everyday behaviour' (Theissen 1993: 36).

This impracticable radicalism should be honoured and respected. So, contrary to the assumption of some sectarian groups, the call to follow in all its rugged realism cannot sound out beyond the range of the first hearers: none but they are called to leave home and family, to be prepared to leave dead parents to be buried by others, to abandon kinship obligations, to live on the assumption that the kingdom of God is going to come soon. Jesus – and, for that matter, his followers – must be allowed to belong to their own world and time, which is far away from ours and must necessarily be so. So the problem we encounter when working with the discipleship sayings is not *how* to apply them in the post-resurrection era, but *whether* to apply them at all.

In similar vein, the position of the twelve is unrepeatable, for none but they can sit on thrones judging Israel. Their uniqueness is indicated by the care with which for obvious reasons a replacement is found for Judas Iscariot (Acts 1:15–26), but no move whatever is made to replace the martyred James (12:2). The twelve form an Israel-oriented 'college', whose function follows on from the general resurrection of the dead: James does not lose his place by dying! If then there is, for the *bene esse* of the Christian community, such a thing as apostolic succession, it takes its bearing not from the twelve but from the wider community of 'followers' and 'sent ones', among whom incidentally both men and women are represented. Consequently, in anticipation of later studies, it is worth noting that for the Christian community to defend gender discrimination in the name of the gospel, and by appeal to the maleness of the twelve, is at odds with historical Jesus evidence as well as with the radical and counter-cultural inclusiveness of the post-resurrection Christ (thus, Gal. 3:27–8).

Nevertheless, there are some principles that may truly claim to be timeless, and two may perhaps be singled out for special mention. The first concerns the thread that has achieved special prominence in the tapestry we have been considering in this chapter, namely the family. Maximum weight must be given to Jesus' endorsement of the fifth commandment. It comes at the climax of the list of demands placed before the rich ruler (Mark 10:19), and piety that places religious obligation above obedience to the fifth commandment is not piety at all (7:9–13). This has the very important corollary that the call to separate from parents and families is not a law like the fifth commandment: it is a prophetic demand, and it is vital for the understanding of the relationship between the historical Jesus and the post-Easter community that the distinction between law and demand be strictly maintained. The tendency of religious communities and leaders to erect structures of law, on the supposition that by such means they are showing due regard to the lordship of Jesus, has often proved misguided and misleading.

In this connection a very particular issue arises under the heading of Jesus and the family, namely, Jesus and *his* family. Indeed, one could go further and single out under the heading of Jesus and his family the case of Jesus and his mother. We saw how Mark goes out of his way to present the family of Jesus as dysfunctional and disunited in the face of the prophetic mission of Jesus himself. He could hardly have ventured to do so if the historical family in general and the historical Mary in particular had been sympathetic to Jesus and supportive of his mission. We may take the absence of sympathy and the lack of support as historically assured. We also saw that the historical Jesus reacted sternly and critically to a rather naïve suggestion that adulation of his mother was concomitant with recognising him (Luke 11:27–8) – historical because of appeal to the criteria of multiple attestation and embarrassment. In the face of such evidence it emerged as well-nigh incredible that the attitude of Mary – the historical Mary! – could have included an awareness of a supernatural and fatherless conception. The aggregated evidence therefore suggested that as an adherent of Jesus the historical Mary came 'on screen', as it were, in an exclusively post-resurrection setting – then and only then because that was when and only when she satisfied the principle (attested multiply in Mark 3:34, 35; Luke 11:28) that entry to the Jesus people is conditional on commitment to the word of Jesus. All of this has at least two significant corollaries.

First, the contemporary Christian tendency to bypass tradition-historical testing of the gospel material covering the Jesus/Mary relationship urgently needs attention. The need could scarcely be more cruelly exposed than by the 2005 Agreed Statement of the Anglican–Roman Catholic International Commission, which handles the text of the New Testament, and notably the traditions towards which its members are specially attracted, with conspicuous disregard for historical-critical methods. What is called 'an ecclesial and ecumenical reading' (ARCIC 2005: 8–9) works uncritically with the text as it stands. Professing to integrate what is valuable in different ways of reading and interpreting a text – historical-critical, typological, narrative, rhetorical and sociological – it dismisses critical methods as 'overly reductionist' and proceeds to ignore them. It defends its position by quoting passages indiscriminately in the interests of one version of Christian tradition. It even invests in the angel Gabriel's command of Greek perfect participles (Luke 1:28; ARCIC 2005: 17, cf. 35, 51, 52, 57)!

It may be doubted whether such an approach serves the interests of the Christian faith in a critical age. Those interests require the most careful and rigorous testing of traditions – and such testing is not appropriate only to gospel traditions other than Luke 1, the main resource of Mary-focused piety! In fairness, although it does not improve the situation, the need was already evident well before the ARCIC Report was a gleam in anyone's eye. It can be illustrated by checking the development of feasts and festivals focused on Mary from *The Book of Common Prayer (1662)*, through to the *Alternative Service Book (1980)*, and then on to *Common Worship (2000)*. It is important to remember that critical work on the gospel traditions began to flourish after *BCP* and before *ASB*, and was therefore well known to each of the commissions producing *ASB* and *CW*, not to mention the members of the ARCIC.

While there are detectable traces of engagement with critical thinking by the commission that produced the *ASB*, the tendency of the *CW* commission seems to have been in the reverse direction of more sympathetic and less critical acceptance of tradition, some of it biblical and some of it rather less so.

Thus, lines of continuity connecting all three books can be seen in 'The Purification of the Blessed Virgin Mary', renamed 'The Presentation of Christ in the Temple' (2 February), 'The Annunciation to the Blessed Virgin Mary' (25 March), 'The Visit of the Blessed Virgin Mary to Elizabeth' (31 May or 2 July), and 'St Anne, Mother of/to the Blessed Virgin Mary' (26 July). The *ASB* removed 'The Nativity/Birth of the Blessed Virgin Mary' (8 September) and 'The Conception of the Blessed Virgin Mary' (nine months earlier, 8 December), replacing them with a single so-called holy day dedicated to 'The Blessed Virgin Mary' (8 September), and thus discouraging any explicit preoccupation with the beginning of her life. It also gave a new day to 'St Joseph of Nazareth, Husband of the Blessed Virgin Mary' (19 March). With *CW*, however, a theologically significant shift is observable. First, there is the *prima facie* modest addition of Mary's supposed father Joachim to share the day dedicated to Anne. Second, rather less modest is the *reinstatement* of both 'The Conception of the Blessed Virgin Mary' (8 December) and 'The Birth of the Blessed Virgin Mary' (8 September), plus the *retention* of 'The Blessed Virgin Mary' which had replaced them (15 August) – from two such festivals (*BCP*) to one (*ASB*) to three (*CW*)!

It surely does not need saying that concerning Anne we know absolutely nothing, and concerning Joachim we also know absolutely nothing. Lurking below the surface of this move is dependence on the second-century apocryphal gospel of James – not in any way, shape or form a credible historical witness. More seriously, the singling out of Mary's own *conception* represents an overture to a tradition of thought which, it should be clear in the days of *CW* even if it was not in the time of *BCP*, substitutes piety for sustained critical analysis. What we know about the historical Mary, and why she might merit contemporary Christian reflection, suggests that a resurrection-conditioned theology might do wonders in restraining the tendency of religious people to indulge in unrestrained credulity. But when regularly repeated liturgical rites reinforce that indulgence, it takes a very great deal of stopping. And when widespread liturgical usage is seen as somehow legitimising positions which lack critical defensibility (ARCIC 2005: 46–7), things are even worse.

Second, Mary takes her place, not among the Jesus people but among the resurrection people, as someone who can genuinely serve as a pointer to a robust and realistic understanding of the Christian gospel. The dark cloud of negativity which hovers over the pre-Easter chapters of her life story is given a striking silver lining by her post-Easter commitment to the cause of her son. She came into the community of resurrection people as one whose life may well have been scarred by perhaps the most damaging and devastating experience that can overtake any woman, and she also came in as one who had kept her distance from that son who, in her ears, did not as a prophet ring true. In both respects her Christian presence is a shaft of light. For any woman, all women, who have suffered abuse of any sort, personal disrespect and devaluation, physical and/or emotional violence, or unbearable anguish, her life story may well be a witness to the compassionate healing and restorative inclusiveness of God and his community. And also for any person, man or woman, who has been unconvinced by and resistant to what turned out to be the providence of God and the central significance of Jesus, she confirms that change is possible.

That complex of family-oriented issues represented the first thread in the tapestry of 'following Jesus' which the resurrection required to be reconsidered. The second thread is the matter of hierarchical or non-hierarchical relationships within the community of Jesus people. 'It is not so among you', said the historical Jesus, at the same time as he spelt out the implications of the models personified in the child and the servant.

Perhaps the principle which is the hardest to implement of all those we have uncovered is the counter-cultural critique of the conventions of honour and shame, of status and ambition. This critique will not give the time of day to the urge to absorb into the life of faith-commitment the human tendencies to seek advantage over others, to bear down on others, to exert pressure on others, in short, to opt (consciously or unconsciously) for power. It is manifestly harder for the religious community to subject such tendencies within itself to exposure, critique and correction than it is for that community to do the same when such tendencies are detected outside its own life. Yet that is precisely what the historical Jesus did, and there is no reason to suppose that what he did was to be viewed as of temporary relevance and applicability. Robert

Runcie once said, 'Everyone nowadays wants to be known as a servant.' Doubtless he was right, but wanting to *be known as* a servant of others is not the same as wanting to *be* a servant of others. From time to time each and every one of us post-resurrection and pre-final-resurrection Christians has to undertake a health check in this respect. Some of the original disciples made the mistake of investing for status and personal gain in the commitment they had made to Jesus. From Jesus they received a brisk and bruising retort.

Institutions tend, almost by a law of nature and sociological momentum, to become pyramids, and over time the Christian Church has been markedly more thorough in its development of pyramids than in its gospel-based critique of them. Perhaps an episcopal church is especially vulnerable to the charge of having done so, but this problem is not confined to such a church, nor does it only happen when people relate subserviently to their bishops, and bishops become unduly convinced of their specialness. The same applies in non-episcopal churches *vis-à-vis* bishop-equivalents.

At the present time we can detect a growing attempt to exhibit the model of humility and servanthood by means of episcopal ritual reproduction of the foot-washing behaviour of the Johannine Jesus on Maundy Thursday. Leave aside the detectable reticence of Christian women and men to have their feet washed by bishops! More seriously, one is bound to ask whether this washing ritual is appropriate. The tradition in John 13 combines the two patterns of imitation and participation. Those present *share* in Jesus (v. 8) and they are required to *imitate* Jesus (v. 14). Insofar as the thought of a ritual enactment is present, it relates to the sharing element and concerns baptism as the formal religious rite of inclusion, washing and participation – baptism, and baptism alone. Insofar as the thought of exemplary self-humiliation is present, it concerns an action which can be robbed of its potency by being ritualised. Indeed, the act of ritualising it can hardly do other than diminish and defuse it. Within the culture of the time, which is where it belongs, the action of the Johannine Jesus is located somewhere on the spectrum between the inappropriate and the intolerable – which is why it is questioned. Within the culture of our time, which is where it must belong if it is to be acted out at all, such an action needs to be set in 'the outside world', a world in which some gesture, which takes its meaning from *contemporary* culture and is not without cost to prestige and status, may be meaningful in *contemporary* terms. That is a world in which each or every Christian leader might show authentic willingness to take a lower status in relation to other members of the community of faith.

In relation to the way authority, control, hierarchy and status work out in the community of post-Easter people, the patterns of servanthood and childhood are variations on a single theme. If we turn from the one variation to the other there is one and only one thing that can be said: What the resurrection did *not* do was to undermine in any way at all the principle that getting into the kingdom and being in the kingdom should correspond to and be modelled on the role and status of children, 'for it is to such as these that the kingdom of God belongs'. When Mark has the disciples getting very angry and indignant about the children, we can be sure that something is happening that is acutely counter-cultural and disturbingly counter-instinctive — but at the same time absolutely fundamental to the ongoing meaning of Jesus of Nazareth.

CHAPTER 3

'Waiting for' and 'waiting on': learning to pray the Jesus way

Introduction

The setting is a tiny country church nestling in the foothills of rural Wales. It's a mid-1960s summer Sunday morning, and the service is about to begin. Outside the church, on this peaceful morning all is still; the bright sunlight touches the fields and the hills, and to many it would seem so right to move from the creation to belief in a God of truth, goodness and beauty. Inside the church, the sun invades the building, warming the ancient grey stones which have seen generation after generation come to feed their sense of God, even though they have often seemed to the priest more at ease singing hymns than saying prayers. Today he is about to celebrate the Holy Communion, but he has not yet said a word. Silently he prays. Soon he will be expected to preach. But just now, all is still. He wishes it could stay that way. For words are a problem to him: How can any language be devised that can do justice to God? How can neat formulae learnt in theological college relate to what is 'revealed' – is that the right word? – in creation and country life? How can the hidden God be mediated to a world in which human beings regularly suffer and often find God-talk simply incomprehensible?

On 25 September 2000 the vicar will die in ripe old age, but although dead he will continue to speak through the succeeding years with a poem entitled 'Kneeling':

> Moments of great calm,
> Kneeling before an altar
> Of wood in a stone church

In summer: waiting for the God
To speak; the air a staircase
For silence; the sun's light
Ringing me, as though I acted
A great role. And the audiences
Still; all that close throng
Of spirits waiting, as I,
For the message.
    Prompt me, God;
But not yet. When I speak,
Though it be you who speak
Through me, something is lost.
The meaning is in the waiting.

That poem, one of R. S. Thomas's best (I believe), conveys a sense of how that most Christian of activities, worshipping in general and praying in particular, thrives on quietness, on freedom from the compulsive urge to turn everything into words. A ministry which apparently lacked the confident certainties of the typical prophet, and whose defining features were more often inner struggle and a sense that others may have regarded him as a 'crippled soul . . . limping through life on his prayers', is here epitomised in a moment of prayer. As has rightly been observed (Phillips 1986: 68), if waiting on God is the paradigm of faith, waiting for God is the aspect of that faith which emerges in this poem. And how-ever perpetually hidden and persistently silent God may be, prayer presupposes, for all its paradoxes, *a sense of God* and *a sense of being related to God*.

We might usefully look to see whether any of this shows when Jesus opens up the principles and the practice of prayer. Maybe . . . maybe not. But one thing is clear: before we even open the pages of the gospels there are good reasons to expect prayer to figure prominently in the mis-sion of Jesus. If our earlier studies were correct, the mission of Jesus was a prophetic one, spearheaded by him but enlisting his disciples. It follows that the prominence of prayer in the life and work of the typical prophet must be relevant. If a prophet is someone who 'enjoys' an intimate rela-tionship with God, someone who is sustained by a sense of God and a sense of being related to God, and who performs a mediatorial function, then the communicative process within that relationship must not be thought of as a one-way street – from God to the prophet, yes, but also from the prophet to God.

Of course, others beside prophets can and do engage in prayer (Witherington 1999: 10), so this is not something distinctive and *exclusively* prophetic, but there are quite enough examples to justify the conclusion that prayer is characteristic. 'I will look to the Lord,' said Micah (7:7), 'my God will hear me.' In that same vein, Samuel had been specially requested to intervene by prayer to ease the plight of a disobedient people, and had responded, '. . . far be it from me that I should sin against the Lord by ceasing to pray for you' (1 Sam. 12:23; cf. also 1 Kings 13:6). In retrospect he came to be regarded, with Moses, as one of the two most notable prophetic intercessors (Jer. 15:1). Similarly, the prophet Jeremiah was pressed into prayer by a combination of king and priest, indeed by the whole community: 'Please pray for us to the Lord our God' (Jer. 37:3). Likewise, 'Be good enough to listen to our plea and pray to the Lord your [*sic*] God for us', to which Jeremiah responds, 'Very well: I am going to pray to the Lord your God as you request . . .' (42:1–4). When a prophet, who feels intercession to be central to his vocation – 'Remember how I stood before you to speak good for them, to turn away your wrath from them' (18:20) – is even forbidden to pray because the alienation of the people of God has become too chronic (cf. 7:16; 11:14; 14:11), the situation is dire indeed. But the presupposition that prayer is normally at the heart of the prophet–God relationship remains in place.

Prophetic oracles are themselves sometimes presented as divine answers to prophetic initiatives in the form of prayers. So what the public sees and hears is but the projection of something intensely private, that is to say, an inter-personal encounter located on the frontier between the divine and the human. And within that encounter the traffic is, as already suggested, moving in both directions. The representative role of the prophet is a dual one: s/he represents God to the people, yes, but also the people to God. Proclamation without prayer would be a contradiction in terms, a single-sided coin. So, even after due allowance has been made for the complexity of the history of the material in the prophetic books, we cannot but take seriously the fact that those same books in all their variety point to a well-established religious tradition. They converge on the conclusion that prayer and proclamation, not proclamation alone, are complementary components of a prophetic vocation. As was rightly observed some decades ago (Lindblom 1963: 206):

> The prophets were specialists in prayer in the same measure as they were specialists in the delivering of divine oracles and the proclaiming of divine revelations. A balanced view of the prophetic commission must take both functions into account.

One further point needs to be made. The place of prayer in the frequently agonised ministry of Jeremiah in particular becomes especially relevant to our studies, given the evidence elsewhere of the influence of Jeremiah upon the historical Jesus. Who more than Jeremiah hands on to posterity the frank revelations of his own tortured prayers, which are at the heart of the intimate relationship with God out of which he speaks (e.g. Jer. 15:15–18; 16:19–20; 18:19–23)? The book which bears his name intends 'to articulate the person of Jeremiah as a model or paradigm of what a prophet is . . .', that is to say, a person 'utterly claimed by [the Lord] . . . subject to no other authority' (Brueggemann 1987: 115–16). The practice of prayer, in which he feels compelled to engage, relates directly to the vexing fact that his God is not invariably a sympathetic figure but rather at times tough, ruthless, relentless and unaccommodating in his sovereignty. Equally, the God of the historical Jesus has at times, we sometimes sense, a darker side.

So when we turn to the gospel tradition we expect to meet a prophetically defined community of disciples which is a community of prayer, preoccupied with God and centred on someone whose very existence and mission is prayer-conditioned. Some of the prayer complexes in the gospels may, just like the prophetic books in the Hebrew Bible, be the product of creative reflection by later writers, but we may be sure that their reflections are rooted in the reality of the historical Jesus. This was a major part of the impression that he made. In support of this inference, four converging pieces of evidence can be assembled.

First, if the roots of the mission of Jesus are sunk deep in the mission of John the Baptist, and they are, then the inseparability of repentance and prayer would be taken for granted within that mission. Those who look for a major intervention of God, and who prepare themselves for it, turn to prayer as a means of expressing their genuine movement back to God in repentance. See, for example, Daniel 9:3:

I turned to the Lord God to seek an answer by prayer and supplication with fasting and sackcloth and ashes. I prayed to the Lord my God and made confession . . .

Against that background we may be sure that Luke in his editorial work reflects a true perception when (i) in Luke 5:33 diff Mark 2:18 he reports that 'John's disciples, like the disciples of the Pharisees, frequently fast and pray, but your disciples eat and drink'; and (ii) in Luke 11:1 he has Jesus' disciples asking, 'Lord, teach us to pray, as John taught his disciples.'

Second, the inaugural experience of ecstatic vision immediately after Jesus' baptism, his prophetic call experience, was one that we were able to classify alongside the ecstatic vision of Peter in the course of the Cornelius narrative in Acts 10—11. We could have gone further and noted that in detailing the vision, Luke/Peter several times refers to its happening while he was praying: 'Peter went up on the roof *to pray*' . . . 'I was in the city of Joppa *praying*, and in a trance I saw a vision' (Acts 10:9; 11:5). Likewise, when the Paul of Acts receives a call to embark on gentile mission, it comes during a ecstatic trance while praying (22:17). Hardly surprisingly, Luke edits the story of what happened after Jesus was baptized: 'When all the people had been baptized, and when Jesus had been baptized *and was praying* . . .' (Luke 3:21 diff Mark 1:10).

Third, that Jesus was a miracle worker is a conclusion that has withstood the most corrosive scepticism. The evidence is overwhelming and all the stronger for being by no means restricted to the testimony of those who identified with him: it is 'common to friend and foe' (Sanders/Davies 1989: 330–31). Josephus in *Antiquities* 18:63 describes him as 'someone who performed amazing deeds' (*paradoxōn ergōn poiētēs*). But the work of healing occasionally met obstacles, as is clear from a Marcan narrative (Mark 9:14–27, 28–9) which comes to a climax with a statement of principle enunciated by Jesus, 'This kind can come out only through prayer' (9:29). This narrative is plainly intended on the level of Marcan redaction to recall the editorially amplified story of Jesus' visit to his hometown (6:1–6a), which we have already examined. According to Mark, Jesus himself was inhibited by unbelief (6:5–6a), and now it is the turn of the disciples. How can this be?

We begin by noting the carefully constructed connections between the two stories. First, the disciples, who have previously healed successfully

(Mark 6:13), now find themselves frustrated and impotent (9:18), just as Jesus, the uniquely successful healer, had been (6:5). Second, Jesus is critical of the wider clientele, pinpointing 'faithlessness' (9:19), an attitude which the epileptic's father eventually acknowledges (9:24). Until he cries out, 'I believe; help my unbelief!' he is representative of a generation which looks for a sign (8:12) but will not receive one. He is also at one with the people of Nazareth (6:6). Third, scepticism in relation to Jesus is registered by the father, with his somewhat distant words, 'If you are able . . .', just as Mark had caused the people of Nazareth to comment in distinctly reserved terms on Jesus' miracle-working achievements (6:2d). The father's scepticism is rebutted by the call for faith, 'If you are able! – everything is possible for the one who has faith' (9:23). And when the whole tone and tenor of the request for help is changed – and shown to be changed by the agonised cry, 'I believe; help my unbelief!' – then and only then does the healing take place.

That is the end of the story, except that Mark attaches an appendix, the conversation between Jesus and the disciples 'in the house' – a typical Marcan device (cf. 7:17; 10:10). Typical of Mark though it is, it nevertheless provides an interpretation of the preceding incident that is highly likely to be true to the position of Jesus. That is to say, the miracle worker is hindered from carrying out a work of healing by the absence of genuine prayer on the part of the petitioner – and true prayer, agonised prayer, helpless prayer, prayer without scepticism, totally dependent prayer, is the supreme expression of faith. When Jesus 'was not able' (6:5), and when the disciples 'were not able' (9:18, 28), he and they were held back by the lack of faith (apistia) and by the registering of a request which was not a prayer. It was testing (cf. 8:11): it was not trust.

So from these stories, interpreted on the level of the Marcan narrative, we can uncover a principle which sets prayer at the heart of the mission of Jesus, dedicated as it was to human healing and wholeness. The principle is that prayer directed to God, who is currently available in such a way that the prayer can legitimately be addressed to Jesus, is the *sine qua non* of every transforming intervention by him in human life. And this intervention, intended surely to be a typical intervention exhibiting a far-reaching principle, shows itself to be (and needing to be read as), in a true sense, a resurrection: '. . . the boy was like a corpse, so that most of them said, "He is dead", but Jesus took him by the hand and *raised him up*, and he was able to stand' (Mark 9:26–7).

Fourth, when Jesus is integrated – as he must be integrated – into the religious experience of Judaism, his life and outlook have to be related to the two great foci of that faith, Mosaic law and Jerusalem Temple. Now the positive purpose which the Temple was designed to serve shines through even when he is acting in critical prophetic mode: 'Is it not written that "my house shall be called *a house of prayer* for all the nations"?' (Mark 11:17). Some suppose this to be an early Christian commentary on the action Jesus had taken (11:15–16, cf. Sanders 1985: 66; Fredriksen 2000: 209), but without a commentary from Jesus himself the action would be quite opaque: we must suppose that Jesus himself conveyed his reasons for acting so drastically. And if so, the Temple is shown to be for him what it is for God: the place where all of humankind is intended ultimately to converge for the practice of prayer. When God's providential purposes for the world are achieved, humankind will be found united in that practice of prayer. Such is what we may call the core of the spirituality of Jesus.

Prayer, healing and wholeness

The demands voiced by Jesus sometimes seem frankly impossible! They make no concessions to circumstances or (so it often seems) human frailty. This is in part because Jesus sometimes adopts the style of the teacher of wisdom. Now wisdom teachers not only used rational argument and assumed in their hearers an openness to persuasion. They not only encapsulated the accumulated insights of human experience (and therefore often sounded, or indeed were, elderly). They also went in for unqualified demands. The demands seemed like ideals, but they were actually 'ideals with teeth', for they were meant to be observed. One such demand on Jesus' part concerns love of enemies (Luke/Q 6:27–8, 35):

> [27]Love your enemies, do good to those who hate you, [28]bless those who curse you, pray for those who abuse you . . . [35]so that you may be sons of your Father; for he makes his sun rise on the evil and the good, and sends rain on the righteous and the unrighteous.

This reconstruction of what lay beneath the surface of Matthew 5:43–7 and Luke 6:27–8, 32–5 is based on a number of necessarily tentative mini-decisions:

First, Matthew has only two demands – 'love . . . pray . . .' – whereas

Luke has four – 'love . . . do good . . . bless . . . pray'. It would be unusual for Luke to have expanded, whereas a reduction by Matthew would be understandable and would fit the fact that there are just two supporting arguments in what follows (Luke/Q 6:32–3).

Second, the tradition of Jewish thought, itself always intensely practical, makes the parallelism of 'love . . .' and 'do good . . .' natural and convincing. By contrast, the second of Matthew's supporting examples is much less powerful when it refers, not to good things done or not done but to greetings offered or withheld: a serious pointer to alienation and disrespect – Josephus uses the terms 'insolence' and 'audacity' to characterise the person who omits to greet him (*Life* 220–22) – but scarcely in the same league as the fierce enmity expressed in 'hatred' and its parallels.

Third, both the evangelists use the word 'hate', albeit in different sentences, so its original presence here is guaranteed.

Fourth, the persons whose example should not be followed are almost certainly – here there is a wide consensus among specialists – Matthew's 'tax-collectors . . . gentiles' rather than Luke's characteristic 'sinners'. But the appeal for a better standard of behaviour than that of gentiles, and therefore of the tax-collectors with whom they are paralleled, is almost certainly a later editorial addition. This is partly because we have already seen that the comparable saying in Luke/Q 12:30a is an editorial addition, and partly because the saying about loving enemies, when relieved of this material, is rounded, coherent and complete. The corollary of this conclusion is that there are strata within the tradition, and therefore that the 'love your enemies' saying is even earlier than the Q-editorial material in the source where we find it.

Fifth, Matthew's reference to God's provision of sunshine and rain is more vivid and imaginative than Luke's bland and colourless allusion to his being 'kind' (*chrēstos*). It is likely to be more original.

Finally, Luke focuses on bad persons alone – 'the ungrateful and the wicked' – whereas Matthew alludes to both good and bad – 'the evil and the good . . . the righteous and the unrighteous'. Luke's version would be ill at ease with the reference to the creation, shared by all, and may represent a shortening in order to concentrate exclusively on how to treat persecutors.

The practice and response of prayer emerges on any showing as central to Jesus' demand. It is one of the two verbal responses – 'bless . . .

pray . . .' – to human antagonism, whatever form that antagonism may take: action, attitude or speech. That it should be singled out as an expression of love in action serves to set it at the heart of Jesus' mission. Use of the criterion of multiple attestation suggests that the love principle stands uniquely just there.

David Jenkins, in his stirring account of his decade as Bishop of Durham, reports a meeting between the then Prime Minister and a group of Anglican bishops. Insisting that the bishops appeared not to recognise the Christian roots of her motivation, Margaret Thatcher reportedly declared that both Christianity and liberal market democracy 'were about freedom'. 'Oh no, Prime Minister', said the Bishop of Chester, 'Christianity is not about freedom, it is about love.' David Jenkins goes on to refer to 'the insight of faith that the love of God so informs and directs the service of God and our neighbours that it ultimately promises perfect freedom' (2002: 133). Such an insight is surely woven into the fabric of the authentic saying of Jesus about the almost impossible exercise of love, in a tradition that is on several counts remarkable:

First, the original love commandment (Lev. 19:18) had made 'the neighbour' the object of love, and had primarily in mind a fellow-Israelite (v. 17: 'any one of your kin . . . any of your people') while at the same time extending the same principle to include the resident alien (v. 34: 'you shall love the alien as yourself'). The health and wholeness of the people of God was therefore the central even if not the sole issue. But members of the people of God – then and since! – have made a habit of falling out with one another. Jesus is therefore insisting that love must take precedence over all other attitudes and actions which might be provoked by hostile actions, however outrageous, by fellow Israelites.

In view of the plural formulations which are used here, the likelihood is that opponents of Jesus' prophetic mission and of the community of his prophetic companions are in mind. At the Q stage of the use of these sayings, what is implied is not so much physical violence as ostracism, personal animosity, verbal abuse, and perhaps jeering and insulting gestures (Tuckett 1996: 304–6). The likelihood is that the same is true for the pre-Q and the Jesus stage of their development. Remarkably, those responsible for this opposition are not, however, to be treated with sectarian enmity or verbal aggression, however unfair or confrontational their conduct may be. The old biblically encouraged instinct to regard your enemies as God's enemies, and therefore piously to cultivate hate and retaliation towards them (Ps. 139:21–2), is here outlawed. This point deserves to be paused over, in order that the full implications may be realised.

Biblical and other literature is littered with material in which Jewish groups with an intense sense of being authentic interpreters of the tradition and authoritative teachers of the plan and purpose of God for his people speak vituperatively about their opponents. Their sense of being 'in' is complemented by an equally strong sense that those with whom they disagree are 'out'. Under the surface – and sometimes all too clearly on the surface! – stands the conviction that 'we identify with God, and God identifies with us, and therefore our hostility is matched by, and can even be an expression of, the hostility of God himself.' It must be admitted that a corporate consciousness formed by the experience of divinely effected liberation (from others, of course) encourages that sense of polarity. A sense of dependence on creation, by sharp contrast, concentrates on what is common and what is shared, and simply does not deal in polarities. That is one way in which Jesus' allusion to the created order is so profoundly meaningful. To this we shall shortly return.

Second, the saying underlines with striking firmness the expression of love in the form of prayer for the opponent or enemy. This is not alien to the spirit of Judaism (Luz 1989: 344), but is rather rarely attested and is quite understandably absent in the most desperate situations. The speeches of the dying martyrs during the Maccabean trauma are full of prayerful confidence in God but empty of prayerful concern for the persecutors. The latter will ultimately see their folly or succumb to judgement but will certainly not see the fulfilment of any prayer for blessing offered by their victims (Sanders/Davies 1989: 321). This supports the conclusion that, even though there are later Christian parallels (cf. Acts 7:60; Rom. 12:14; 1 Cor. 4:12: 'when reviled we bless; when persecuted, we endure'), and Jewish precedents do exist, this is authentically the demand of Jesus.

Third, the example of God might seem more than a little surprising. Examples abound in the Hebrew Bible of a judging God's withholding rain from those who resist his purpose or fall short in obedience (e.g. 1 Kings 17:1; Isa. 5:6; Amos 4:7–8; Hag. 1:10–11). And the deep instinct to resist the idea of God's treating the righteous and the unrighteous without discrimination is articulated by Josephus in his plea to the Jewish forces in Jerusalem to surrender to the Romans:

> It is surely madness to expect God to show the same treatment to the righteous as to the unrighteous. (*Jewish War* 5:407)

But instead a benevolent, non-discriminatory and non-judging God comes into view as the God of Jesus. His primary resource is not biblical history. Instead it is the creation, where God's undiscriminating provision is a matter of daily experience. It may well be that enjoyment of the fertility of the region of Galilee encouraged this emphasis on the generosity of the creator God and Father (Freyne 2004: 37–48). What is clear is that Jesus' spirituality is, for whatever reason, formed by a sense of the creator God who is as such the Father. He, like other teachers in the wisdom tradition to which he belongs (cf. Mark 6:2), appeals to what is normal in a world created and sustained by that God, rather than what is abnormal in a world marred by human sinfulness.

Fourth, the affirmation that restrained and generous conduct means that 'you will be sons of your Father' again opens up the theme of 'being what you are': all humankind is *already* by virtue of creation in such a relationship with God, and all Israelites are *already* children of God. Now they have to *be* such and to *be seen to be* such. The mission of Jesus is evidently by intention about integrity and *wholeness*.

Fifth, Jesus' demand seems all the more 'impossible' when the situation it tackles has become personal. Take the related saying about insult (Luke/Q 6:29): 'If anyone strikes you on the right cheek, offer the other also; and from anyone who grabs your coat do not withhold even your shirt.' Here again the reconstruction takes account of Matthew/Luke agreements and disagreements, and works above all from the requirement that a single theme should be exemplified in the two actions involving a person's face and dress. On this basis it turns out that neither Matthew's nor Luke's version did justice to the fine tuning of the saying, but that by making a series of choices between their divergent readings we are able to reach back to an earlier version that did.

There is a context in which a blow on the right cheek, administered with the back of the hand (in a society where it is, incorrectly of course, assumed that all properly functioning human beings are right-handed), and the violent grabbing of someone's clothing, correspond. They are two items on the Jewish list of the most serious human insults, carrying the heaviest fines.

> If a man cuffed his fellow he must pay him a *sela*. Rabbi Judah says in the name of Rabbi Jose the Galilean: 100 *zuz*. If he slapped him he must pay 200 *zuz*. If he *struck him with the back of the hand* he must pay him 400 *zuz*. If he tore his ear, plucked out his hair, spat and his spittle touched him, or *pulled his cloak off him*, or loosed a woman's hair in the street, he must pay 400 *zuz*. This is the general rule: all in accordance with a person's honour. (*m. Baba Kamma* 8:6)

Jesus asks for the principle of love, which gives rise to prayer, to set aside even the most unbearable of affronts to human dignity and honour. People who manage to respond in this way are impressively secure in their sense of the reality of God and of their acceptance by him. People like this are in the mainstream of the prophetic tradition recorded in Isaiah 50:5–8:

> [5]The Lord God has opened my ear, and I was not rebellious, I did not turn backwards. [6]I gave my back to those who struck me, and my cheeks to those who pulled off the beard; I did not hide my face from insult and spitting. [7]The Lord God helps me; therefore I have not been disgraced; therefore I have set my face like a flint, and I know that I shall not be put to shame; [8]he who vindicates me is near.

The model prayer
The New Testament gives us two versions of the prayer taught by Jesus, or so we might suppose, to his followers (Matt. 6:9–13/Luke 11:2–4). A third version, very closely related to, and almost certainly dependent on, Matthew 6:9–13, appears in Didache 8:2. Since, as we shall see, every discrepancy between Matthew's and Luke's versions is naturally and convincingly explained by the evangelists' redaction, there is no need of the hypothesis (Crossan 1991: 293) that Luke preserves the Q version while Matthew preserves the version current within his own Christian community.

How strong is the supposition that this prayer stemmed from Jesus himself? The contrary view has recently been proposed on the following grounds: (i) If it had come from Jesus we would expect wider attestation and more uniform versions of its contents. (ii) It presupposes religious separation from Judaism. To quote the objection *verbatim*:

> the establishment of such a prayer seems to represent the point where a group starts to distinguish and even separate itself from the wider religious community, and I do not believe that point was ever reached during the life of Jesus. (Crossan 1991: 294)

Against that conclusion, objection (i) is a variation on the theme that multiple attestation is a *sine qua non* for authenticity, a requirement that has rightly been severely criticised. Objection (ii) is more interesting. One must distinguish between separation from and distinct identity within the wider religious community. The prayer shows no sign of the former, and it is worth noting that there is absolutely nothing definitively Christian within it. We would expect a prayer that acted as an expression of necessarily post-Easter separate identity to contain some unmistakably Christian reference. The parallels between the prayer and the *kaddish* prayer of the synagogue worshippers suggests not separateness but identification and intensification of that longing which is turned into worship and prayer by all Jews. Just as Pharisaism represented identification and intensification *within* the community of Israel, so too does the movement within which the Lord's Prayer is generated. Separation is just not on the agenda. But what emerges on the rebound from objection (ii) is the thought that the original version of the Lord's Prayer in all likelihood not only stems from Jesus but also expresses the community sense of the 'Jesus people'. It is *a community prayer*, and as such expresses *community* longings in respect of God's rule. It also offers petitions relating to *community* poverty, *community* forgiveness for attacks upon itself (of the sort implied by the 'loving your enemies' complexes in Luke/Q 6:27–8, 35), and *community* frailty and vulnerability in the face of the testing of its loyalty to its own defining principles.

Before we anticipate too much of the tradition-historical investigation, however, we need to start at the beginning and address fundamental questions. What was in the original prayer, what does the prayer tell us about Jesus' outlook, and what did he intend to be the priorities in the minds of his closest associates?

We must begin by recognising that each of the evangelists has a particular focus of interest within the prayer. For *Luke*, who probably preserves the order of the Q source, it is the prayer for bread, as is shown by the sequence from the prayer to the following parable of the friend at midnight (Luke 11:5–8) and the 'wisdom' teaching about fatherly provision of food for children (11:9–13). For *Matthew*, moving the teaching about fatherly provision (Matt. 7:7–11), and transposing the teaching about forgiveness (Matt. 6:14–15/Mark 11:25–6) so that it follows the prayer, the primary interest is in the prayer for forgiveness. This is of a piece with his heightening of the need for such forgiving attitudes within the Christian community (Matt. 18:15–35). But we need to turn a blind eye to unoriginal contexts provided by Luke and Matthew and concentrate instead on original content.

In respect of the content of the prayer, each of the two versions has been adjusted by the gospel writer, whether Matthew or Luke. It is necessary to take account of their special interests, and also the greater likelihood that petitions would be added in Christian usage than that someone should dare to subtract any. Specifically, it is well nigh inconceivable that Luke should take a positive decision to excise two petitions with which he is in total agreement: 'May your will be done on earth, as it is in heaven . . . rescue us from the evil [one].' It is entirely conceivable, on the other hand, that an ongoing situation of need should move him to substitute 'each day' for 'this day' (cf. Luke 9:23 diff Mark 8:34 on the long-term commitment of discipleship rather than the initial shouldering of the cross). It is also entirely conceivable that he should clarify the meaning of 'debts' by introducing as a parallel 'sins', notwithstanding the cost of damaging the parallelism of the version in the source.

Before that original version of the prayer is set out, there is just one detail that needs comment. The words 'may your name be hallowed' could be a petition running in parallel with 'may your kingdom come', in which case the coming of the kingdom is the means whereby the name of God comes to be recognised and reverenced by humankind. Alternatively, they could be seen as an attachment to the address to God as Father, that is (to use a felicitous phrase), a 'doxological honorific qualifier'. Following so rapidly after the invocation of God as Father, the second of these alternatives has some attraction. It would also mean that the same instinct is at work as when elsewhere the mention of God's name immediately provokes a reaction of praise: Paul mentions the Creator and immediately adds '. . . who is blessed for ever. Amen' (Rom. 1:25). Countless Jewish speakers mention the Holy One, and immediately add 'May he be blessed for ever!' And with rather more liturgical flamboyance, the synagogue prayer (see below, p. 138), before it reaches the petition for the establishing of God's kingdom, prefaces that petition with 'Exalted and hallowed be his great name in the world which he created according to his will.' Consequently, there is a good case (Metzler 1999: 193–8) for linking very directly the name 'Father' with the honorific reference to that name – which in turn has the effect of isolating 'May your kingdom come' as the one major petition in the prayer.

So when we reverse the later Matthew/Luke developments and add together all the evidence on this issue, we are left with the following likely reconstruction of what Jesus himself actually said (using Lucan verse numbers):

> [2]Father – may your name be hallowed! –
> May your kingdom come.
> [3]Give us this day our daily bread.
> [4]And forgive us our debts,
> as we also have forgiven our debtors.
> And do not bring us to the time of trial.

The structure of the prayer is clear: (i) an address to God, placing exclusive and unelaborated emphasis on his fatherhood, and showing special recognition of and respect for his name and status as Father; then (ii) a central and controlling request for the coming of his (future) kingdom; and finally (iii) three petitions in the first person, an 'agenda for prayer' dealing with problems which the petitioners are facing in the present pre-kingdom era.

The Lord's Prayer: on divine parenthood

The address to God as 'Father' is remarkably simple and unadorned. This one aspect of God's person and relatedness to other persons is given very particular emphasis. Recognition of, and respect for, God's fatherhood is the starting place of prayer.

At first sight, the exclusive choice of God's fatherhood as the focus of prayer seems strikingly plain, even bald, by comparison with the piling up of the descriptions of God which gives the prayer of Judith such agonised intensity and so strong a feeling of bringing pressure to bear on God:

Please, please, God of my father, God of the heritage of Israel, Lord of heaven and earth, Creator of the waters, King of all your creation, hear my prayer! (Judith 9:12)

Yet the double description 'God of my father [Simeon: 9:2], God of the heritage of Israel' articulates a consciousness of the God of Israel, which underlies Jesus' address to God as 'Father'. And the triple description 'Lord of heaven and earth, Creator of the waters, King of all your creation' is matched by the way Jesus addresses God in the prayer we have already examined (Luke/Q 10:21):

> [21]At that time Jesus said, 'I thank you, Father, Lord of heaven and earth, because you have hidden these things from the wise and intelligent and have revealed them to infants; yes, Father, for such was your gracious will.'

Talk of God's fatherhood and his lordship of heaven and earth points unmistakably to his role as creator (cf. Gen. 1:1; 2:1). Jesus' formulating for his followers an unembroidered address to God as 'Father' should certainly be heard as an implicit invocation of the Jewish experience and consciousness of God. But it also brings to expression a human instinct, a sense of all life's dependence on the sustaining providence of the creator God, an outlook we have already noticed in the reference to sun and rain in the tradition about prayerful love of enemies (Luke/Q 6:35: see above, p. 130–31). As Father of Israel, God had rescued, liberated and sustained the people (cf. Ps. 103). Even more fundamentally, as creator he had set humankind within an ordered and good universe, designed to make generous provision for human wellbeing. Doubtless the mode of praying recommended by Jesus brings all that to life. As an explicit address to God it is impressively minimal by comparison with the prayer of Judith, but in respect of content it sets Jesus and his disciples at the heart of the Jewish understanding and practice of prayer.

Reference to Jewish practice makes it important to note that Jewish parallels for Jesus' address to God as '(my) Father' demonstrate that this was definitely not (as used to be claimed, rather riskily, cf. Jeremias 1967: 27–9, and indeed continues to be claimed, mistakenly) a unique way of praying in a Jewish context. Rather, it identifies with a long tradition of trustful praying to God. The two echoes of Jesus' way of praying '*Abba,*

Father' in Pauline letters (Rom. 8:15; Gal. 4:6) certainly belong in a context of community definition, but would be better described as characteristic rather than as distinctive. In what other way could the conviction that 'he is our Lord and he is our God; he is our Father and he is our God for ever' (Tobit 13:4) be turned into prayer? Moreover, two recently published Qumran texts (Martínez/Tigchelaar 1998: 737, 937–8) provide the necessary corrective:

> [14]And while all this happened, Joseph [was delivered] [15]into the hands of foreigners who consumed his strength and broke all his bones until the time of his end . . . And he became weary [16]and he summoned the powerful God to save him from their hands. And he said, 'My father and my God, do not abandon me in the hands of the gentiles [. . .] [17]do me justice, so that the poor and the afflicted do not perish.' (4Q372.14–17: *Apocryphon of Joseph*)

> [1][. . .] you, and before you I am in dread, for like the dread of God they plan evil [2][. . .] for confusion in Israel, and for something horrible in Ephraim. [3][. . . from the l]and of guilty deeds to the height of the Most High, for from generation [4][to generation . . . f]or you have not forsaken your servant [5][. . .] my Father and my Lord. (4Q460.1–5: *Narrative Work and Prayer*)

Jesus' own corresponding practice of prayer can be seen in several gospel traditions, most notably his anguished prayer in Gethsemane (Mark 14:36):

> Abba, Father, for you all things are possible; remove this cup from me; yet, not what I want, but what you want.

Of course, no one was within earshot of the Gethsemane prayer, so at best this report conveys Jesus' *ipsissima vox* rather than his *ipsissima verba*. But it harmonises easily with the evidence we have been assembling.

Let us not forget, however, that the Lord's Prayer is a *community* prayer. That is the life setting for the address to God as Father. Just as the two Qumran parallels for the addressing of God as personal Father are set in circumstances of threat and suffering, so too the connection can be noted between this prayerful address to God as Father and the sayings about corporate love of communal enemies. There it was love, expressed not only in good deeds but also in prayer, that expressed the sons' relationship with and imitation of their creator Father.

The model prayer: on hoping for a new world

The prayer for the coming of the kingdom brings the very Jewish-pattern prayer of Jesus alongside the synagogue prayer, which fact gives a firm direction to the process of interpretation:

> Magnified and sanctified be his great name in the world that he has created according to his will. May he establish his kingdom in your lifetime and in your days and in the lifetime of all the house of Israel ever speedily and at a near time.

Any discussion of Jesus' treatment of the theme of the kingdom of God has to live with the very considerable variety of nuance that his sayings convey (Sanders 1993: 169–78). Recent discussion suggests, however, that three clear 'markers' should be put in place: (i) We should not try to pour all the kingdom sayings into a single mould: there had been plenty of variety in Jewish usage, and Jesus 'plugs into' that variety. (ii) An unmistakable part of what Jesus envisaged was an intervention in the history of the Jewish people that would come *soon*. (iii) That intervention presupposes the resurrection of the dead, and inaugurates a new era, but it does not mean the end of the world, 'the space-time universe' (Wright 1992: 280–89).

The Lord's Prayer, especially in the light of the parallel in the synagogue liturgy, clearly picks up (ii). As has been accurately summed up:

> God's kingdom, to the Jew-in-the-village in the first half of the first century, meant the coming vindication of Israel, victory over the pagans, the eventual gift of peace, justice and prosperity. (Wright 1996: 204)

Jesus thus turns into prayer the central theme of his prophetic proclamation. And we can draw on three specific kingdom-traditions to provide vital clarification of that central theme. In the first, the parable of the mustard seed (Mark 4:30–32; Luke/Q 13:18–19), it is evident that Jesus' outlook is through and through traditional and signs up to the expectation that God's kingship represents the dominance of the Jewish people over all other peoples. In the second, the parable of the unjust judge (Luke 18:2–8a), Jesus' thinking is again in no way innovative. And we can see clearly the assumption that the disciples are actively praying for the effective realisation of the traditional hope of Israel. They identify with the people whose swift 'vindication' is confirmed, and also with the widow who represents such people. Her prayer is implicitly their prayer. In the third tradition, the saying about inclusion in and exclusion from the kingdom (Luke/Q 13:28–9), the outlook of Jesus becomes more prophetic and considerably less palatable. This time, traditional thinking about the kingdom clearly has to be qualified by severe and dire warning, for some of the Jewish people are in desperate danger. These are the thoughts that attach themselves to the central and controlling petition of the Lord's Prayer: 'May your kingdom come.'

First then, the positive affirmation of Israel's destiny, as seen in the original version of the parable of the mustard seed (Luke/Q 13:18–19 diff Mark 4:30–32):

> [18]What is the kingdom of God like, and to what should I compare it? [19]It is like a mustard seed, which a man took and sowed in his garden; it grew and became a tree, and the birds of the heaven came and made nests in its branches.

Some parables are *similitudes*, that is to say, they argue from how things always are in human experience. That is the way in which the logic of Mark's version of this parable works. But other parables argue from a one-off deviation from how things are in human experience, and therefore take the form of an anecdote. That is how the logic of the Q version of this parable works. It uses verbs in the past tense, not the present, and it is a story about a quite extraordinary occurrence. The extraordinariness is the linkage between the proverbially tiny mustard seed and a *tree*, a tree in whose branches birds make nests. Normally, if you plant mustard seed you won't get a tree, and if you want a tree you don't plant mustard seed. And this tree is very special. A tree with nesting birds is the biblical symbol of one nation's sovereignty over all others, whether of Israel over all the non-Israelites, or Assyria over the non-Assyrians, or Babylon over the non-Babylonians (cf. Ezek. 17:22–4; 31:5–7; Dan. 4:10–12). Jesus argues from that remarkable occurrence and declares that the fulfilment of the hope of the Jewish people is the means whereby God's rule touches the world. This is the standard pattern of Jewish thinking, very robust thinking indeed, about the future. It is imaginatively presented, but breaks no new ground.

Second, the famous parable of the unjust judge (Luke 18:1–8) is notably revealing but requires first a more extensive process of recovery and interpretation. The parable has been subjected to editorial interference by Luke, and the effect has been a change of perspective.

> [1] *Then Jesus told them a parable about their need to pray always and not to lose heart*. [2] *He said,* 'In a certain city there was a judge, who neither feared God nor had a respect for people. [3] In that city there was a widow, who kept coming to him and saying, "Grant me justice against my opponent." [4] For a while he refused; but later he said to himself, "Though I have no fear of God and no respect for anyone, [5] yet because this widow keeps bothering me, I will grant her justice, so that she may not wear me out by continual coming."' [6] And the Lord said, 'Listen to what the unjust judge says. [7] And will not God grant justice to his chosen ones who cry to him day and night, as he shows forbearance over them? [8a] I tell you, he will grant justice to them quickly. [8b] *Yet when the Son of Man comes, will he in consequence find faith on the earth?*'

The first significant consideration is Luke's attachment of a new introduction in verse 1 (something he often goes in for) and an expanded conclusion in verse 8b. These quite clearly give a new twist to the meaning of the parable. We note (i) that the need for persevering *Christian* prayer is injected elsewhere (see Luke 11:8). (ii) The parable ought to come to a climax and finale with the 'I tell you . . .' statement in verse 8a. The impact of that climax is reduced by verse 8b, which introduces ideas drawn from Luke/Q 17:20–37 (the coming of the Son of Man) and Luke/Q 12:42–6 (the coming one's finding faithfulness in his servants). (iii) Most importantly, the introduction and the ending turn the spotlight on to the widow as a model of persistent praying. Her praying becomes something that she *ought* to do, rather than something that she does though she would wish it otherwise. This is a shift from the concentration of the original parable (vv. 2–8a) on the unrighteous judge, and on the sharp contrast between him and the righteous God.

Widows in real life would vary greatly in wealth and power. But because a society with patriarchal instincts saw them primarily as women without men, they (together with orphans) often appear as stereotypical figures representing the poor, lacking necessary food and clothing, vulnerable, lonely and sorrowful, victims of injustice. In their distress they cannot do other than cry to God. Correspondingly, treatment of widows, together with orphans or aliens, is a key 'performance indicator', indeed a priority, in the practice of righteousness in society. Countless texts, some issuing dire warnings against human indifference, others affirming divine care, punctuate the biblical record to make this clear:

> Thus says the Lord: Act with justice and righteousness . . . and do no wrong or violence to the alien, the orphan and the widow . . . (Jer. 22:3)

> The Lord executes justice for the orphan and widow, and loves the strangers, providing them with food and clothing. (Deut. 10:18)

Being a stereotypical figure, the widow in Jesus' parable can also assume a representative role. She has a legal opponent, which does not necessarily mean that she is in the wrong, nor indeed that she is right and the opponent has no case. The likelihood is that as a representative of the poor, she may well offer assurance that she will liquidate her debts, but the implementation of that assurance cannot be guaranteed. This is where principles of justice may override the practice of law. Righteousness on the part of a judge would ideally take the form of the true wisdom, which is 'fear of God . . . respect for people' (vv. 2, 4). She is a test case of the practice of justice in that sense. Her release from her predicament would be a true act of righteousness and, given the recurring nuances of judgement on oppressors which is inherent in the term *ekdikēsis*, an act of judgement on an opponent.

Those whom this widow is said to represent are the 'chosen ones' (*hoi eklektoi*). On the level of Lucan reinterpretation these cannot but be Christians who are called to faithfulness and persistent prayer. But on the pre-Lucan level, and most certainly the Jesus level, the term 'chosen ones' must be expected to carry its normal sense, that is to say, members of the covenant people of Israel: 'the offspring of his servant Abraham, children of Jacob, his chosen ones' (Ps. 105:6; cf. 1 Chr. 16:13), about whom it was said much later that

> God's grace and mercy are with his chosen ones, and he watches over his holy ones. (Wisd. 4:15)

For a widow to represent Israel and to 'cry out' in agonised prayer for justice (*ekdikēsis*) in the sense of liberation from oppression is to follow the famous precedent of Judith (cf. Judith 8:35; 9:1–2; 10:1). Her story is an integral part of the story of Israel.

The immediate response of God in the situation of distress is assured. His implementation of rescuing and judging righteousness will be neither reluctant nor delayed. It will be immediate, precisely because of the already existing special relationship signalled by the phrase 'his chosen ones'.

There is, however, a certain sting in the tail as a result of the amplifying comment that 'he shows forbearance over them' (*kai makrothumei ep' autois*). The term 'forbearance' belongs unmistakably to a context in which the terms of the covenant relationship are spelt out. Indeed, more than that, it is easy to see that 'forbearance' passages use a scheme involving the following common elements: (i) a special relationship between God and certain persons, explicitly stated or implicitly presupposed; (ii) the sinful failure of God's people; (iii) the experience of suffering, imposed either directly or through a third party, and interpreted as judgement; (iv) the achieving of repentance, the re-establishment of the relationship of the people to God; (v) a prayerful appeal to God by the sufferer(s); (vi) a time note setting a limit to the period before God intervenes; and (vii) the intervention itself, depicted as mercy or righteousness in one of its verbal forms and also as judgement on the third party.

The key 'forbearance' passages depend in one way or another on Exodus 34:6–7:

> [6]The Lord, the Lord, a God merciful and gracious, *forbearing*, and abounding in mercy and faithfulness, [7]maintaining righteousness and mercy to the thousandth generation, forgiving iniquity and transgression and sin, yet by no means clearing the guilty . . .

The sevenfold scheme set out above can be seen documented in that passage and in Numbers 14:18; Psalm 86:15; 103:8; Joel 2:13; Nahum 1:3

and Wisdom 15:1. In these texts there is no retreat from the insistent theme of God's judgement of his people if they renege on their covenant commitment, but it is important to note that attention is deliberately drawn to two alternative ways in which the judgement of God may be implemented. It may be *either* final, unrestrained and overwhelming, and allowing no hope of release, *or* real but restricted in intensity. The first is retributive; the second is remedial and rehabilitative, designed to produce repentance and thus relief. In the first case, there is no forbearance; in the second, there is.

The upshot is that the original parable in Luke 18:2–8a speaks about the nation of Israel, and the 'you' to whom the application is directed in verse 8a must be persons who need the reassurance that God will do such and such for his people. Like the widow, they are praying – praying for 'justice' (*ekdikēsis*) – praying for divine intervention in favour of the nation. For all that the people of God will (according to the parable) assuredly receive justice, that message of comfort and assurance is tinged. by a disturbing and none too subtle warning. The nation is faced once again, as so many times previously, with the prospect of restrained judgement. Israel is in all seriousness offered within the terms of the covenant the opportunity to rely on God's forbearance and to repent in order to receive freedom and righteousness. In short, it is offered a restored relationship with the covenant God. Jesus speaks, not as a teacher of the Christian community but as *a prophet for the Jewish nation*: his warning is of judgement on its spiritual alienation, his call is for repentance, and his expectation is that the condition allowing immediate restoration and renewal will be met. But suppose it is not. What happens then? According to the scheme, Israel will be judged, and in those circumstances the 'chosen ones' alone become the repentant remnant – those who *are representatively Israel*, for all that they are numerically *part of Israel*.

The first example, the parable of the mustard seed, was from a Jewish point of view, traditional and triumphalist. The second example, the parable of the unjust judge, was reassuring but hinted at judgement. A third example, which does more than hint and is in fact intensely worrying, is the saying about inclusion and exclusion in relation to God's kingdom (Luke/Q 13:28–9).

[29]Many shall come from east and west (and from north and south) and sit at table with Abraham, Isaac and Jacob in the kingdom of God.

²⁸But the sons of the kingdom will be cast into outer darkness: there will be weeping and gnashing of teeth.

This drastic judgement saying (see Reiser 1997: 230–41), preserved more faithfully by Matthew and edited more thoroughly by Luke, undoubtedly permits us to listen to the voice of Jesus. He picks up a series of standard Jewish ideas. The first is the convergence of gentiles, and inseparably together with them Diaspora Jews, on Mount Zion as part of the final assembling of the peoples by God (Isa. 2:2–4; 49:22–3; 60; 66:18–23; Jer. 3:17; Zech. 8:20–23; Tobit 13:1–17). It is theoretically possible, incidentally, that those who come from east and west are not gentiles but Diaspora Jews (cf. Tobit 13:5: 'He will gather you from all the nations, among whom you have been scattered': thus, Allison 1998: 143–4). On such a basis Diaspora Jews would, according to this saying, displace Palestinian Jews. But then it would be odd that the term 'sons of the kingdom' should be applied exclusively to Jews living in Palestine, and we might ask on what basis the one set of Jews should be substituted for the other, so the traditional interpretation in terms of a straight Jew/gentile polarity remains preferable. The second standard Jewish idea is the celebratory banquet at the climax of God's programme (Isa. 25:6–10), though gentile participation in that banquet was a new thought. The third is the 'weeping and gnashing of teeth', which ultimately draws on the thought of the valley of Hinnom close by Jerusalem, the place of judgement and death (Isa. 66:24; Judith 16:17). The fourth is the presupposition of the resurrection of the dead, bringing the patriarchs to the centre of the celebration. But the essential thrust of the saying, which makes it more a threat than a promise, is contained in its conclusion: 'the sons of the kingdom will be cast into outer darkness'.

Who, we have to ask, are 'the sons of the kingdom'? The key would seem to be in the Zion-centredness of the pattern of thought upon which the saying depends. It is addressed to Jerusalem, a city which elsewhere receives a searing rebuke for its rejection of Jesus (Luke/Q 13:34–35a). The residents of Jerusalem are treated in the round in the same way as the residents of Chorazin, Bethsaida and Capernaum (Luke/Q 10:13–15) by means of a saying that attempts to shame them by advantaging gentiles (cf. Luke/Q 11:31–32). The message is the same as that of the Jerusalem-and-Temple-centred saying, 'My house shall be called a house of prayer for all the nations, but you have made it a den of robbers' (Mark 11:17). In short, God's promises will ultimately be fulfilled, but participation in that fulfilment is not unconditional, and therefore not to be taken for granted. This is at odds with the standard and almost unconditional Jewish conviction that 'all Israelites have a share in the age to come' (*m. Sanhedrin* 10:1). The Jewish people must become the Jesus people, for those who suppose they have a special relationship to the kingdom are at risk if they do not see that kingdom as the future rule of the designated messiah, Jesus, and his associates (cf. Luke/Q 22:30).

In the Lord's Prayer, especially when locked into the parable of the unjust judge, we see the interpenetration of prayer and proclamation in Jesus' prophetic mission. The phrase 'strive for his kingdom' (Luke/Q 12:31) certainly includes sharing in the prophetic task of public proclamation. But there is more to it than that. There is private prayer, at least the private prayer of the community gathered around Jesus. There is one and only one dominant concern in that prayer to which the followers of Jesus are bidden to commit themselves: everything else is more restricted than, and subordinate to, the plea: 'May your kingdom come.' For this the disciples pray with their eyes wide open to the implications – some welcome, some worrying.

The model prayer: on coping with hunger

The prayer for the provision of necessary food 'today' is almost certainly not a prayer for the arrival of the final banquet, even though this is often in mind both in biblical texts and in sayings of Jesus (Isa. 25:6–10; Luke/Q 13:28–9). A duplication of the same petition in respect of kingdom and bread would be unlikely in so terse and economical a prayer. Nor is it a prayer for so-called spiritual food. Nor is it a prayer that has any sacramental bearing: Jesus was not into anachronism. More likely, it is a prayer of dependence on God for the ordinary food which will sustain the life of the poor (followers of Jesus) in the here and now. This conclusion is reinforced and encouraged by three traditions, each of which has God's provision of ordinary food in mind – the parable of the friend at midnight (Luke/Q 11:5–8, 9–10), the teaching on fatherly provision (11:11–13), and encouragement in the face of anxiety (12:22–31).

First, the parable of the friend at midnight (Luke/Q 11:5–8, 9–10):

⁵Which of you will have a friend, and he goes to him at midnight, and says to him, 'Friend, lend me three loaves of bread, ⁶for a friend of mine has arrived and I do not have anything to set before him' – ⁷and will that person say in response, 'Do not bother me; the door has already been locked, and my children are with me in bed; I cannot get up and give you anything'? ⁸I tell you, ***even though he will not get up and give him anything because he is his friend, at least because of his persistence,*** he will get up and give him whatever he needs.

⁹So I say to you, Ask, and it will be given you; search, and you will find; knock, and the door will be opened to you. ¹⁰For everyone who asks receives, and everyone who searches finds, and for everyone who knocks, the door will be opened.

Jesus' 'Which of you . . .?' introductions are appeals to human instinct and experience (cf. Luke 14:5; 15:4). The person addressed is being asked to place him/herself in the position of someone in the story that is about to unfold. That means in turn that the conduct of the leading person in the story must follow a normal, predictable and agreed line. In other words, this is how the person in the story reacted to the situation facing him: this is how the persons addressed by the parable would react if they were in that situation. Now according to the present *Lucan* version of the parable, help in time of need is forthcoming not because of friendship but because of persistence, but there is a problem about this: the friend who calls does not in fact engage in persistent verbal pressure. He simply describes the situation and the embarrassing problem that he faces by being unable to observe the standard oriental convention of providing hospitality.

The problem is solved, however, by the inference that Luke has acted as editor here in the same way as he did in Luke 18:1. He has probably added the bold italicised section – 'even though he will not get up and give him anything because he is his friend, at least because of his persistence' – as part of his concern to encourage Christian people to be persistent in prayer. This enables us to see that in the original parable the person in the house *most certainly would* get up and provide food, and thus extricate his friend from a most embarrassing dilemma. And, says the parable, that's what God is like! He can be counted on to provide food for the needy. The existence of need is a quite sufficient reason for him to act. The application in verses 9–10 then makes explicit what has hith-erto remained implicit. It sets out generalising principles that are *not* in fact true in everyday experience, and therefore belong exclusively to a very specific sphere where God is at work.

Second, the teaching on fatherly provision (Luke/Q 11:11–13):

> [11]Which of you, being a father, if his son should ask for bread, would give him a stone; [12]or if he asked for fish would give him a snake? [13]If therefore you, even though you are evil, know how to give good gifts to your children, how much more will the heavenly Father give good things to those who ask him?

The nature of the gift of the heavenly Father varies between the two versions: 'good things' (Matthew), which fits the content and concern of the saying, and 'the Holy Spirit' (Luke), which does not match either content or concern, and reflects a favourite Lucan interest. Luke proba-bly allowed his eye to move down the page, as it were, to the saying which set the Holy Spirit at the heart and centre of the mission of Jesus: 'If I by the *Spirit* of God cast out demons, then has the kingdom of God come upon you' (Matt. 12:28/Luke 11:20). This is one of countless 'reminiscences' in the gospel tradition (Schürmann 1968: 111–25). So 'good things', a phrase which in any case often stands for food for the hungry (cf. Ps. 107:9; Isa. 55:2; Luke 1:53), should be preferred. So also should Matthew's description of the food itself, since bread and fish together form the basic Palestinian diet (cf. Mark 6:38).

Third, the ravens and lilies tradition (Luke/Q 12:22–31), which we have already examined in another connection and which, when shorn of extra elements added at a later stage, ran as follows:

> [22]Do not be anxious about your life, what you will eat, or about your body, what you will wear. [24]Consider the ravens: they neither sow nor reap nor gather into barns, and yet God feeds them. Of how much more value are you than the birds! [27]Consider the lilies, how they grow: they neither toil nor spin; yet I tell you, even Solomon in all his glory was not clothed like one of these. [28]But if God so clothes the grass of the field, which is alive today and tomorrow is thrown into the oven, how much more will he clothe you – you of little faith! [29]Therefore do not be anxious, saying, 'What shall we eat? Or what

shall we drink? Or how shall we be clothed?' [30b]Your Father knows you have need of these things. [31]Instead, strive for his kingdom, and these things will be given to you as well.

When the Lord's Prayer is correlated with the tradition about anxiety (Luke/Q 12:22–31), and when this is in turn linked to the situation of the itinerant missionaries, it emerges that prayer is answered, not by spectacular divine intervention but by human generosity and hospitality. Human beings are not only prayerful but, as the agents of God, they are the means whereby prayers are answered.

The Lord's Prayer: on forgiving and being forgiven

The prayer for forgiveness takes any Jewish person into very familiar territory:

> [2]'Forgive your neighbour the wrong he has done,' said Jesus ben Sirach, 'and then your sins will be pardoned when you pray. [3]Does anyone harbour anger gainst another, and expect healing from the Lord? [4]If one has no mercy toward another like himself, can he then seek pardon for his own sins?' (Sir. 28:2–4)

If those who pray as Jesus instructs are being asked as individuals to make Sirach's principle their own, that is eminently understandable. But in the preceding prayer for bread there was a sense of community need, and perhaps the same is true here. In the light of Luke/Q 6:27–8, 35, Jesus may be talking less to individuals and more to a community of such persons, all committed to the cause of the kingdom, all open to hostile opposition from 'those who are indebted to us', and all taking seriously in community terms what it means to relate to God as Father.

Just as the prayer for the coming of the kingdom is implicitly understood *as Jesus interprets it*, and just as the prayer for bread arises in the experience of those engaged in a mission *inaugurated by Jesus*, so this petition indicates a two-fold concern for healing and restoration as it arises in the mission, at one and the same time penitential and controversial, *of Jesus*. Those who respond to him are joining a penitential movement; those who respond to him form a community which stands for the healing of inter-personal relationships – a community of followers – 'Jesus people' both forgiven and forgiving. And the notion of a forgiving community engages directly with the presupposition of a community with opponents.

A pair of traditions serves to give a rich resonance to the theme of forgiveness, namely the story of the healing of the paralytic (Mark 2:1–5, 11–12) and the parable of the Pharisee and the tax-collector (Luke 18:10–14a). The healing of the paralytic isolates the forgiveness of sins as the most important issue in respect of human health and wellbeing. In its Marcan form (2:1-12) it is a story which has been expanded:

> [1]When he returned to Capernaum after some days, it was reported that he was at home. [2]So many gathered around that there was no longer room for them, not even in front of the door; and he was speaking the word to them. [3]Then some people came, bringing to him a paralysed man, carried by four of them. [4]And when they could not bring him to Jesus because of the crowd, they removed the roof above him; and after having dug through it, they let down the mat on which the paralytic lay. [5]When Jesus saw their faith, he said to the paralytic, 'Son, your sins are forgiven.' [6]*Now some of the scribes were sitting there, questioning in their hearts,* [7]*'Why does this fellow speak in this way? It is blasphemy! Who can forgive sins but God alone?'* [8]*At once Jesus perceived in his spirit that they were discussing these questions within themselves; and he said to them, 'Why do you raise such questions in your hearts?* [9]*Which is easier, to say to the paralytic, "Your sins are forgiven," or to say, "Stand up and take your mat and walk"?* [10]*But so that you may know that the Son of Man has authority on earth to forgive sins' –* he *said to the paralytic –* [11]'I say to you, stand up, take your mat and go to your home.' [12]And he stood up, and immediately took the mat and went out before all of them; so that they were all amazed and glorified God, saying, 'We have never seen anything like this!'

Several familiar and very well canvassed considerations suggest that verses 6–10 have been intruded into a basic miracle story. As a result the miracle story has become a controversy story. (i) From the unanimous chorus of acclamation in verse 12, no one would ever dream that severely critical opponents were present in the way that verses 6–10 suggest. (ii) The presence of the opponents is suspiciously artificial and a touch improbable in the setting of a private home. (iii) The alleged critique mounted by the opponents – note that according to no fewer than three statements (verses 6, 8ab) they say absolutely nothing (Sanders 1990: 61), and we have only Mark's word and his report of Jesus' *intuitive* sense of what they were thinking to go by – is misconceived. Since Jesus uses a passive form, 'Your sins are forgiven', in order to invoke God, he gives no genuine ground for offence. There is no question of trespassing into the exclusive territory of God, nor for that matter any thought of 'offering this final and eschatological blessing outside the official structures, to all the wrong people, and on his own authority', that is to say, conveying through the offer of forgiveness the intention to replace adherence or allegiance to Temple and Torah with personal allegiance to Jesus (Wright 1996: 272, 274). When Jesus is brought into proper focus as a prophet, and due recognition given to the massive improbability of any scheme whereby nothing could be done about forgiveness of sins committed by those who lived miles away from Temple and priesthood (cf. Sanders 1990: 62: 'Jews believed not only in sacrifice, confession and forgiveness, but also in simple repentance and forgiveness', citing many passages in the Psalms; Taylor 1997: 109–11, also citing Psalms of Solomon 3:8; 9:6; Crossley 2004: 93, also citing Jer. 3:11–25; Sir. 3:30, *et al.*), then the notion that 'Jesus was claiming to offer something he had no right to offer, on conditions he had no right to set, to people who had no right to receive it' (Wright 1996: 436) is very probably mistaken. As a corrective to all such over-interpretation we can appeal to some important precedents.

The first is the request that Moses should forgive the sin of Pharaoh. It is explicitly as intercessor, and therefore as someone intimate with God, that Moses is addressed:

> [16]I have sinned against the Lord your God, and against you. [17]Do forgive my sin just this once, and pray to the Lord your God that at the least he remove this deadly thing from me. (Exod. 10:16–17)

In similar vein, Saul addresses Samuel, already recognised as the notable intercessor (1 Sam. 12:23), and pleads in great distress:

> [24]I have sinned; for I have transgressed the commandment of the Lord and your words . . . [25]Now therefore, I pray, pardon my sin, and return with me, so that I may worship the Lord. (1 Sam. 15:24–5)

In both these cases, the person who is expected to bestow forgiveness is not acting independently of God, but is rather requested to be an inter-cessor. That is to say, in the way of prophets, each is close to God and therefore can speak on God's behalf (Kselman 1992: 832).

The third precedent is provided by the Qumran text *Prayer of Nabonidus* (4Q242.1–5), where a miracle worker says exactly the same as Jesus says, and makes as clear as may be a concern to revere and glorify God:

> [1]Words of the pr[ay]er which Nabonidus, king of [the] la[nd of Baby]lon, the [great] king, prayed [when he was afflicted] [2]by a malig-nant inflammation, by decree of the G[od Most Hi]gh, in Teiman. [I, Nabonidus,] was afflicted [by a malignant inflammation] [3]for seven years, and was banished far [from men, until I prayed to the God Most High] [4]and an exorcist forgave my sin. He was a J[ew] fr[om the exiles, who said to me:] [5]'Make a proclamation in writing, so that glory, exal[tation and hono]ur be given to the name of [the] G[od Most High].' (Martínez/Tigchelaar 1997: 487)

So the original story inherited by Mark probably consisted, give or take a few Marcan adjustments, of verses 1–5, 11–12. In it Jesus points to the part played by divine forgiveness in the achievement of human health and wholeness. This is not to say that sickness is *always* caused by sin, but rather to acknowledge the genuine and serious possibility that it *may* be a *contributory* cause. And therefore healing and wholeness for damaged and alienated human beings extends beyond the curing of physical dis-tress. All of this is complementary to the declaration by Jesus that his incorporation of physically fit outsiders as religious insiders is analogous to a healing:

> Those who are well have no need of a doctor, but those who are sick; I have come to call not the righteous but sinners. (Mark 2:17)

A striking example of a prayer for forgiveness, which opens up Jesus' vision of things, is the parable of the Pharisee and the tax-collector (Luke 18:10–14a):

> [9]*He also told this parable to some who trusted in themselves that they were righteous and regarded others with contempt.* [10]'Two men went up

to the temple to pray, one a Pharisee and the other a tax-collector. [11]The Pharisee, standing by himself, was praying thus, "God, I thank you that I am not like other people: thieves, unrighteous people, rogues, adulterers, or even like this tax-collector. [12]I fast twice a week; I give a tenth of all my income." [13]But the tax-collector, standing far off, would not even look up to heaven, but was beating his breast and saying, "God, be propitiated to me, a sinner!" [14a]I tell you, this man went down to his home "righteoused" rather than the other. [14b]*For all who exalt themselves will be humbled, but all who humble themselves will be exalted.'*

Once the introduction (v. 9) and the attached final, and elsewhere float-ing, saying (v. 14b = Matt. 18:4; 23:12; Luke 14:11) are detached, we are able to liberate the story from the later interpretative framework imposed on it by Luke. Freed of the secondary beginning and ending, the story may well no longer require us to view the Pharisee so critically and unsympathetically as talk of despising others and exalting oneself obliges us to do. Perhaps the Pharisee is, at the pre-Lucan stage, not so bad after all! Perhaps he is not less righteous than those whose standing Jesus did not dispute even when he set his priority on the 'sinners' (Mark 2:17), and perhaps he is no less righteous than the elder son whose integrity is tacitly accepted at the same time as a welcome home is given to the prodigal (Luke 15:25–32). We shall see.

First, the theme throughout is 'righteousness': the only issue in the climactic ending (Luke 18:14a) is who has been 'righteoused', given that the Pharisee had previously dismissed the tax-collector as one of the 'unrighteous' (v. 11). In this respect the ending of this parable matches the ending of the other parable of the unjust judge (v. 8a): the righteousness of the tax-collector is part of the same package, as it were, as the vindication/'righteousing' (to adopt an apt, even if ugly, word) of the elect people. Put another way, one could see the parable as Jesus' answer to the question: 'Which is the way to the renewal of the people of God – is it the way of holiness as laid down by Pharisaism, or the way of repentance as promoted by you and John the Baptist?'

Second, the two men attend the Temple in order to pray, which prob-ably means that the time is the hour of prayer, the hour of corporate worship when the morning or evening sacrifice was offered (Luke 1:10; Acts 3:1; cf. Bailey 1980: 144–6). This is not absolutely certain

(Friedrichsen 2005: 105–6), but the use of the standard terminology of sacrifice in the tax-collector's prayer is a strong hint: 'God, *be propiti-ated* . . .' (cf. Lev. 25:9; Num. 5:8; 2 Macc. 3:33). According to the narra-tive in the book of Judith, it was 'at the very time when the evening incense was being offered in the house of God in Jerusalem [that] Judith cried out to the Lord God with a loud voice' (Judith 9:1). Prayer and sacrifice went together, and it was not necessary to be present in order to identify with both. It was not even necessary to be Jewish to do so. After all, Luke's god-fearing gentile centurion based in Caesarea experi-enced an angelic vision while praying at three o'clock in the afternoon (Acts 10:3, 30). But all the available evidence suggests that observance of the hour of prayer and sacrifice expressed each individual's identification with a community, that is to say, an awareness of the presence and acces-sibility of the one true God among the Jewish people. This sense of com-munity was also presupposed by the sacrifice itself – a community rather than an individual burnt offering (Sanders 1992: 104–5), a gesture of thanksgiving, a gift in honour of God and an acted out plea for God to be well disposed:

> At these sacrifices prayers for the welfare of the community must take precedence of those for ourselves; for we are born for fellowship, and he who sets its claims above his private interests is specially acceptable to God. (Josephus, *Against Apion* 2:196)

Given this communal dimension, it is no coincidence that when the evening sacrifice was being offered far away in Jerusalem, Judith should reinforce her appearance as a mourner, and in her prayer concentrate on the paramount need of divine intervention to rescue her people (9:1; 10:3). This same strong community awareness is the implicit setting of the very contrasting prayers to God offered by the tax-collector and the Pharisee. The one exists on the edge of the community, the other at its very heart – and in so thinking they are not wrong.

Third, the sacrifice offered at the time was a lamb, whose complete burning on the altar doubtless suggested that the smoke would be inhaled pleasurably in heaven, but there was also a sense of attracting God to the place of sacrifice or celebrating the fact that he was already, and indeed always would be, there with his people (Anderson 1992: 877–8). The renewal of God's goodwill was being sought, but without any sense of achieving atonement (Sanders 1992: 105). Some defining texts suggest so (Lev. 1:4; Job 1:5), but these are quite exceptional. The Pharisee expresses thanks for God's benevolence, which he takes as read, and in so doing conforms quite naturally to the ethos of the daily burnt offering. The tax-collector, on the other hand, feels the need to pray for God's goodwill, indeed to plead for a change from judgement to renewed mercy and graciousness. In so doing he uses very loaded language: not straightforwardly 'God, be merciful to me, a sinner' but, strictly translated, 'God, be propitiated towards me, the sinner' (cf. Num. 5:8; 2 Macc. 3:33). Such language recognises the principle voiced, for example, when Solomon dedicates the Temple, reflects on the combined activity of prayer and sacrifice, and addresses God:

> [111]We cannot but praise your greatness and give thanks for your kindnesses to our house and the Hebrew people, [112]for with what other thing is it more fitting for us to appease you when wrathful (*hilasasthai mēnionta*), and, when ill disposed, to make you gracious than with our voice . . .? (Josephus, *Antiquities* 8:111–12)

While this prayer expresses the crying need of an individual, it can also fit neatly into a setting where the communal aspect is never far away in thought. The conduct of the tax-collector, even though he remains part of the people of God, has fallen short of the norms of the community, and indeed damaged the health and wellbeing of that community. If in his prayer we pick up echoes of the prayer of Daniel, a prayer of repentance on behalf of Israel, that is probably because we are intended to do so:

> [18]We do not present our supplication before you on the ground of our own righteousness, but on the ground of your great mercies. [19]O Lord, hear; O Lord, forgive . . . (Dan. 9:18–19)

Fourth, in spite of the corporate nature of the occasion, the Pharisee (by definition a 'separated' one) sets himself apart spatially. The tax-collector does the same, and indeed may even be so far apart as to position himself in the outer court (Friedrichsen 2005: 112). But the two men's reasons for separateness are a world apart. The tax-collector, it will turn out, separates himself because he believes himself to be religiously inferior to the other worshippers, which means that he accepts other people's evaluation of him. He recognises the weakness of his participation in the people of God. The Pharisee for his part separates himself because he believes himself to have been made by God ('God, I thank you . . .', Luke 18:11) to be in the mainstream of the nation's 'covenantal nomism', and he does not wish to be associated with the other worshippers. He registers with God his own self-assessment and at the same time acknowledges his debt to God. His separateness may be the sort of thing which Hillel, one of the great heroes of Pharisaism, had in mind in his celebrated warning:

> Do not keep aloof from the congregation and do not trust in yourself until the day of your death [i.e. never!], and do not judge your fellow human being until you have stood in his place. (*m. Aboth* 2:5, quoted Bailey 1980: 149)

But it is not thereby a matter of his downfall. It is altogether too much to suggest that he is 'tearing up the fabric of his own spirituality' (Bailey 1980: 150), whatever Luke may have inferred. Any tendency to depreciate him and his piety needs to take very seriously the remarkable similarity between his prayer and that laid down in later times for the rabbi on leaving the place of study, a prayer which is not for one moment regarded as open to criticism (Scott 1989: 95; Friedrichsen 2005: 94):

> I give thanks to you, O Lord my God, that you have set my portion with those who sit in the house of study and you have not set my portion with those who sit in [street] corners, for I rise early and they rise early, but I rise early for words of Torah and they rise early for frivolous talk; I labour and they labour, but I labour and receive a reward and they labour and do not receive a reward; I run and they run, but I run to the life of the future world and they run to the pit of destruction. (*b. Berakoth* 28b)

In that same vein, the Pharisee's prayer is also a self-portrait: his attention to fasts and tithing is apt, his dismissal of all other Israelites an assumption of the stereotypical worst about the tax-collector, but perhaps not necessarily an unreasonable assumption, given that from the tax-collector's own mouth comes a very negative self-assessment: 'the sinner'.

In the Pharisee's view the latter is indistinguishable from the thieving, the rapacious and the adulterous – all typical sticks with which the religious belabour their opponents, as is confirmed by (for example) the Psalms of Solomon. He is *assumed* to be like that, just as the rest of the non-Pharisaic world is *assumed* to be like that. Tax-collectors are routinely described as sinners, and this one acknowledges it with a gesture of extreme sorrow, even grief. Just as the grief-stricken David 'bewailed his son, *beating his breast*, tearing his hair and doing himself every kind of injury' (Josephus, *Antiquities* 7:252), and just as the mourners for Jesus went home 'beating their breasts' (Luke 23:48), so too does the tax-collector. In his final word, 'God, be propitiated towards me, the sinner', he accepts his generic stereotyping. But in his case, this truth turns out to be the premise of his salvation.

Fifth, the conclusion that the renewal of the tax-collector's relationship with God, which as a matter of fact confirms his true membership of the people of God, is the outcome means that from this moment onward he need no longer accept his dismissal as a separated one. Religiously, there is no need for him to stand by himself. But what about the Pharisee – does the phrase 'rather than the other' (Luke 18:14a) indicate that being 'righteoused' is what happens to the tax-collector *and not what happens to the Pharisee*? Probably not, for the point of the contrast is not the exclusion of the one but the inclusion of the other. Within the parameters of covenantal nomism the Pharisee was indeed righteous. What distinguished the two men was that one *was* righteous and therefore nothing changed, whereas the other was in response to his prayer of repentance *made* righteous, and in his life there was a massive and overwhelming change.

This parable throws a flood of light on Jesus' basic outlook. The person on the boundary of the people of God is regarded as included, and most emphatically not to be excluded. In the Temple the tax-collector availed himself of the system of worship and sacrifice and repented, renewing the 'direction of his heart'. By contrast, the Pharisee, the essentials of whose position are accurately sketched, serves to typify an alternative pattern of religion. Jesus' mission emerges once again as orientated to 'righteousness', the relationship defined by the covenant. Its objective is that the people of God should 'be what they were designed to be'. But the way to righteousness is not in Jesus' view the separatist way of Pharisaism, for all that he does not devalue it. The prayer for forgiveness is where to start; the gift of restoration and 'righteousness' is where it continues.

The model prayer: on facing the ultimate test

The final petition, again couched in plural terms, is unfortunately the least clear of all: 'Do not bring us to the time of trial.' What is meant by the term translated trial/temptation (*peirasmos*)? There are in principle three possibilities, which however turn out to merge into one another. The first envisages any testing of faithfulness that may prove too strong. This interpretation can appeal to the very close parallel in a Jewish prayer:

> Blessed is He who causes the bands of sleep to fall upon my eyes, and slumber upon my eyelids . . . May it be your will, O Lord my God, to make me lie down in peace, and set my portion in your law, and accustom me to the performance of religious duties; but do not accustom me to transgression, and do not bring me into sin, or into iniquity, *or into temptation*, or into contempt. (*b. Berakoth* 60b)

The second could be read as a religious intensification of the first, that is to say, a testing of basic religious loyalty and commitment. We might compare God's testing of Abraham (Gen. 22:1), which became a paradigm for the possible testing of Israel during a period of intense suffering (see Judith 8:26; 1 Macc. 2:52), or how he tested Hezekiah, so that the trial 'might show all that was in his heart' (2 Chr. 32:31). Such a testing by God had the purpose of checking and confirming basic religious loyalty to him, and him alone (cf. Deut. 4:34; 8:2; 13:3).

In the light of the very concentrated attention given in the Lord's Prayer to the coming of the kingdom, these two interpretations should probably take their place within a third one. That is to say, they should be subsumed under the conviction that a traumatic time of suffering may have to be passed through before God's kingdom actually arrives, 'the great time of testing and tribulation which would precede the great deliverance' (Wright 1996: 337) – the labour pains prior to the moment when God's great design is brought to birth. This would make sense of, and provide a context for, the widely distributed sayings of Jesus which take seriously the violent opposition which has already made itself felt – thus, the experience of John the Baptist, and those who come after him, including Jesus (Luke/Q 16:16) – and prepare the followers of Jesus for the trials which are to come, their handling of which will determine their status in the presence of God:

> [8]I tell you, everyone who acknowledges me before others, the Son of man will also acknowledge before the angels of God; [9]but everyone who denies me before others will be denied before the angels of God. (Luke/Q 12:8–9)

Praying in the afterglow of resurrection

Set the Lord's Prayer firmly in the mission of the historical Jesus, and it might seem to be slipping away from us in our own later setting. If Easter was a transition point, a moment for continuity *and discontinuity* with the historical Jesus, a moment when the concerns of the Jesus people were in part transcended and replaced by something new, what are we going to do and think when we find ourselves using the prayer that Jesus taught his Jewish followers to use? Plainly some of the original concerns have to be re-thought in the new post-resurrection era within which our own story of faith is told.

We can go on talking to God as Father, *but with a subtle difference* – a difference which is, or should be, meat and drink to those whose experience of human fatherhood makes the use of such terminology for God at best uneasy and at worst repugnant. Talk of God as Father inevitably sits comfortably within a world of patriarchy, which is in turn a world defined by the possession and use of power. It is talk that does little for the many thousands of children, and adults for that matter, who have experienced fatherly power as abusive exploitation and gender-driven manipulation. But the resurrection is the bringing to new life of someone who plumbed the depths of human weakness and dishonour, not to mention abuse (if the devastating connotations of crucifixion are taken into account). Not for nothing is the *Abba* prayer the Gethsemane prayer (Mark 14:36). Nothing could be further from that scene than any tendency to invoke a gender-defined God. And that is good news in the post-resurrection era when all tendencies to gender-definition in the sphere of faith are put under a severely critical microscope. That which makes mothers very special people, people who at their best can be to children what fathers even at their very best can never be – that which mothers at their best and fathers at their best can together be for those who depend upon them, the post-resurrection God of Jesus' prayer is to the members of his community. That God has to be more than each of father and mother can be; that God can certainly not be less.

We can also go on talking to God as Father because nothing has changed in our perception of him as the creator, to whom we owe everything and upon whom we unreservedly depend. If the creation speaks eloquently of an undivided humankind, the resurrection speaks persuasively of the overcoming of artificial divisions and the making real of that undivided wholeness. Every trend towards divisive religious (and other) sectarianism is a casualty of the resurrection-inspired insight into the order of creation which is given 'body' by the vindicated and risen Christ.

We can go on talking about the kingdom of God – *but with subtle and significant modifications.* At least two adjustments have to be made. First, we cannot identify with the expectation that the coming of the kingdom will take place soon, for short-term expectations evaporated many moons ago, and well-nigh 2000 years have sounded the death-knell to such convictions. Second, we cannot identify with the traditional expectation that the coming of the kingdom amounted to a new and transformed era in the history of the Jewish people. That, incidentally, means that the use of many of the psalms in Christian worship becomes extremely problematic, and the echoing of their frequent mood of paranoid nationalism extremely inappropriate, a fact that seems to have escaped the attention of most of the great multitude of liturgical revisers whose work has so dominated the agenda of Christian communities in recent decades. The fact of the matter is that the resurrection inaugurated a new era in the experience of the Jesus people, but in the event it did not turn out to be the sort of new and transformed era for which they and their contemporaries longed. What can we do, what can we think, about this?

First, the Jesus people had been encouraged by Jesus to pick up the traditional Jewish scheme, according to which God's kingship might be exercised through a surrogate human king. That means, in the hallowed language of Jewish hope, the 'Messiah', and that is the context in which we must set the convincing evidence that when Jesus looked forward to God's kingship he looked forward to his own kingly rule and that of the followers, who would sit on thrones in his glory (see Mark 10:35-7, 40;

Luke/Q 22:30). Messiahship was not an idea which the resurrection planted, its roots were already deeply sunk in the soil of Jesus' mission, and the outcome can be seen in the unfolding of a story of crucifixion. And yet, with remarkable rapidity and intellectual agility, the former Jesus people who became the resurrection people reinterpreted the hope Jesus had encouraged in them: his kingship was inaugurated by resurrection, even though they did not abandon the Jewish this-worldly and political prospect of how that messianic kingship might ultimately be effected. On that they were doubtless wrong again, but for the resurrection people – that is, the Easter people, to whom we belong! – the key reality must be that talk about God's kingship is now talk about the universal reign of the risen Jesus. Paul got that one right! Prayer for the coming kingdom, seen through the Easter lens, must therefore be a prayer for the fullest possible, indeed universal, experience of what it means to acknowledge the lordship and authority of that risen Jesus. Well might the Easter people pray:

> Heavenly Father,
> who brought new life to the world
> in the resurrection of Christ our Lord:
> grant our days to be filled with his life
> and our world to be changed for ever.

Second, let us not, however, suppose that politics can be jettisoned with a quiescent sigh of relief. For the thread of newness and discontinuity which Easter represents is inextricably intertwined with a thread of continuity. That thread has many strands. One of them has to do with *values*. If Jesus can be heard signalling that entry to and existence within God's kingdom is according to the model of childlike-ness (cf. Mark 10:14–15), that future prospect cannot but invade the world in which we currently live. The values of God, if we may speak thus, are not to be admired now and activated then: rather they are to be activated then and both admired and activated now! That means, if we press the evidence of the sayings of Jesus, that the usual co-ordinates of honour and shame have to be shifted – not something which the Christian church with its partially inevitable and partially not inevitable attachment to hierarchy will ever find easy to do – and the true index of greatness as service has, as we noted in an earlier study, to be recovered. A second strand of the thread has to do with *social awareness*. If Jesus is to be heard many times dwelling on the predicament of the poor, the hungry and the sorrowful – and he is – and if he is heard promising that such suffering will be put right – and he is – then poverty, hunger and sorrow are not good conditions to be valued but bad conditions to be rectified. The Christian community, if inspired by the historical Jesus who became the risen Christ – the Christian community, if it is being itself as a community of resurrection-galvanised hope – cannot be patient and it cannot wait and it cannot rest, and in the face of the anguish of our times it cannot pass by on the other side.

Jürgen Moltmann wrote in his book about hope, published 39 years ago and still as relevant all these years later, that

> From first to last and not merely in the epilogue, Christianity is . . . hope, forward looking and forward moving, and therefore also revolutionising and transforming the present. (1967: 16)

Quoting another distinguished theologian, the great Dane, Søren Kierkegaard, who described hope as 'a passion for what is possible', he added,

> Those who hope in Christ can no longer put up with reality as it is, but begin to suffer under it, to contradict it. Peace with God means conflict with the world, for the goad of the promised future stabs inexorably into the flesh of every unfulfilled present. If we had before our eyes only what we see, then we should cheerfully or reluctantly reconcile ourselves with things as they happen to be. That we do not reconcile ourselves, that there is no pleasant harmony between us and reality, is due to our unquenchable hope. (1967: 21–2)

Returning to the Lord's Prayer, we can go on talking about the provision of necessary bread, *but again with some care*. For one thing, those who were taught the prayer by the Lord were a select group, and they were not the people at large who had heard the message of the gospel of the kingdom. At this point, the prayer becomes in the strictest and tightest sense the exclusive prayer of the very small group, the inner circle of the Jesus people. They had left their homes – as not all followers of Jesus were, or are, asked to do. They had left their trades – as not all followers of Jesus were, or are, asked to do. They had made themselves poor, homeless, dependent, vulnerable. Like the poor they had only God to ask for support, and in the Lord's Prayer that is just what they do. Does that take the Lord's Prayer away from us? Yes and no. And the 'no' element can perhaps best be defined by the thought that the answer to the prayers of the Jesus people was to be found in the generosity of the Jesus people themselves. Within the web of community commitment to Jesus, one group could function on God's behalf as the answer to the prayers of the other group – hence, the hospitality offered by the sons of peace to those who preached and exhibited the gospel of peace.

We can go on talking about the need for forgiveness, but this time surely *with no essential change whatsoever*, for this petition touches on an overwhelming human need which is unaffected by time or space, a need felt keenly by individual human beings and a need perhaps not so easily recognised by communities. Again we touch the thread of emphatic continuity between the Jesus people and the post-resurrection community: those who gathered round the historical Jesus were responding to a mission definitively conditioned by the words of Isaiah 61:1, '. . . liberty to the captives, and release to the prisoners . . .', and their experience of the risen Jesus was designed, if all four gospels preserve an accurate recollection, to spell restoration, renewal, and release. Release means forgiveness. In this vein two features of the petition for forgiveness give cause for pause: first, the understanding of the committing of offences between human beings as the incurring of debts to both God and others, and second the fact that the same word *aphesis* does duty for both forgiveness and liberation.

The relationship between forgiving and being forgiven is a subtle one. The Lord's Prayer makes the former the precondition of, though not the reason for, the latter. In Elizabeth Gaskell's sad and tragic novel *Sylvia's Lovers* (1863) the core of the tragedy that overtakes the heroine, Sylvia Robson, is to be found in her inability to forgive. 'It's not in me to forgive, – I sometimes think it's not in me to forget,' she says. When asked to visit and comfort a dying man, against whom she bore a grudge, and when reminded, 'It's said in t'Bible, Sylvia, that we're to forgive,' she replies, 'Ay, there's some things as I know I niver forgive; and others as I can't and I won't, either.' Need anything be said?

Paul Tournier, a notable Christian psychiatrist in the Jungian tradition, who practised for many years in Geneva, set the need for forgiveness in a much wider context, speaking about two kinds of human beings, the strong and the weak:

> The truth is that human beings are much more alike than they think. What is different is the external mask, sparkling or disagreeable, their outward reaction, strong or weak. These appearances hide an identical inner personality. The external mask, the outward reaction, deceive everybody, the strong as well as the weak. All men, in fact, are weak. All are weak because all are afraid. They are all afraid of being trampled underfoot. They are all afraid of their inner weakness being discovered. They all have secret faults; they all have a bad conscience on account of certain acts which they would like to keep covered up. They are all afraid of other men and of God, of themselves, of life and of death. (1963: 20–21)

There can be no doubt that fear has a very proper place in human life – it reinforces the instinct for self-preservation, and in religion it relates to what Rudolf Otto, in his still seminal work *The Idea of the Holy* called the *mysterium tremendum et fascinans*. Very appropriately the collect for Trinity 2 encourages the Christian community to aspire to 'a perpetual fear and love of your holy name'. That sense of awe in the face of what is simultaneously fearful and attractive, is widely registered in biblical narratives, very notably in resurrection narratives, of encounters of human and divine beings. But at the same time, the gospel of the resurrection encourages us to pray the Lord's Prayer in hope that we may be liberated from that fear which is fed by a bad conscience. Resurrection people, the continuation of the Jesus people, are encouraged to worship with fear and to pray with feeling the collect for Trinity 12: '. . . pour down upon us the abundance of your mercy, forgiving us those things of which our conscience is afraid . . .' In similar vein, the collect for Trinity 21: '. . . that your faithful people may be cleansed from all their sins, and serve you *with a quiet mind.*'

All of that relates very directly to the predicament of individual persons. But what about group relationships, for we have picked up not a few hints that the petition in the Lord's Prayer envisages relationships between groups or communities in the setting of the mission of the historical Jesus? As far as we can tell, we are taken thereby into the situation of conflict between Jesus and his followers on the one hand, and Pharisees on the other. What was involved in the conflict we shall explore in the next chapter, but in advance of this, and with the theme of forgiveness in mind just now, we might usefully reflect on how an awareness of such a conflict is to be incorporated into post-Easter communal thinking.

The conflict between the Jesus movement and Pharisees revolved, as we have already begun to see, around some serious issues, most notably the question of how a holiness- and righteousness-defined strategy should be worked out for the people of God. That said, it was a disagreement *within* the community of the Jewish people. That is not, sadly, how subsequent Christian comment on Pharisaism has seen it. One recollects here how a religious group often reinforces its own sense of identity by polarising itself over against 'the other', and in the process risks distorting the reality as far as 'the other' is concerned. That recollection is very much *ad rem* in respect of how Pharisees in particular and even the Jewish people in general – the absent 'other' – are sometimes portrayed in the hymns that Christians sing, apparently without batting an eyelid. One of the most famous, doubtless owing its popularity in part to a catchy tune, runs as follows:

> I danced for the scribe and the Pharisee,
> But they would not dance and they wouldn't follow me.
> I danced for the fishermen, for James and John;
> They came with me and the Dance went on.
>
> I danced on the Sabbath and I cured the lame;
> The holy people said it was a shame.
> They whipped and they stripped and they hung me on high,
> And they left me there on a cross to die.

The obituary in *The Times* of Sydney Carter, the author of this hymn who died on 13 March 2004, declared it the best known of the three of his songs most often sung in school assemblies – 'something between a hymn and a joyful, popular outburst' which 'seems on its way to becoming an anthem for all occasions'. Sydney Carter himself was quoted as describing 'Lord of the Dance' as 'a dancing kind of song, the life of which is in the dance as much as in the verbal statement'. But it is precisely the verbal statement which is so serious a problem that one has to wonder whether, in view of the grave risk that quite indefensible attitudes to the Jewish people are here encouraged, the song should be sung at all. It is simply and emphatically not the case that 'the holy people ... whipped and they stripped and they hung [Jesus] on high, and they left [him] there on a cross to die'. Scrupulously careful historical research has established beyond all doubt that the crucifixion of Jesus, not to mention the preliminary torture (if it happened), was carried out exclusively by Roman personnel. If the involvement of leaders of the Jewish community in preliminary proceedings against Jesus is invoked, and if they alone are envisaged by the term 'holy people', then there is an historical case to be made, and indeed it can be made (cf. Josephus, *Antiquities* 18:63–4). But those leaders and/or the people they led were not the agents of crucifixion. Such a charge echoes the propaganda of an earlier age about how 'the Jews crucified Jesus', and such a charge should be given no space in Christian thinking, Christian singing, or Christian worship. Christian people often seem to be at their most unguarded when bursting into song, and they are not immune from the tendency to be polemical about others who, conveniently, happen to be absent when unguarded things are said or sung about them. It is one thing to sing in a wholly appropriate post-Easter spirit:

> I am the life that'll never, never die;
> I'll live in you if you'll live in me ...

But by then the song is arguably past redemption. Its previous content falls dangerously short of the spirit of wholeness and healing, of peace and reconciliation, which the Lord's Prayer arguably intends to put into words.

Finally, in respect of that prayer, we can go on talking about an escape from temptation, but it is as well to do so with reticence. The time-bound expectation of a time of suffering before the ultimate intervention of God as king is not one which sits naturally in the context of ongoing Christian faith and faithfulness. But set now in a new context of the resurrection of Jesus, an awareness of how human frailty always threatens to derail Christian faithfulness makes this petition timelessly relevant. As it always has been, it is a matter of praying simply for the courage to be true to our confession of the lordship of the risen Jesus, of calling upon divine firmness to reinforce human frailty, of recalling that the *peirasmos* of Jesus, in which we share through baptism and which we may share in suffering, was succeeded by the resurrection of Jesus, in which also we share.

Epilogue

We began our study with the thought that there is more to praying than asking. I suggested that that most Christian of activities, worshipping in general and praying in particular, thrives on quietness, on freedom from the compulsive urge to turn everything into words, and that it is sustained by, indeed the very breath of its life is, *a sense of God and a sense of being related to God.* The prayer traditions upon which we have concentrated have, on the other hand, been dominated by words and by requests, though a certain terseness and economy of expression has often been apparent. Perhaps it is time to develop this tendency still further.

We have more than once paused over the thanksgiving of Jesus to the Father (Luke/Q 10:21). It is assuredly a genuine saying of Jesus, but the suggestion is that it has attracted to it as a sort of commentary a proclamation saying which is more likely to belong to the post-resurrection era than to Jesus himself (Matt. 11:27/Luke 10:22):

> [21]At that time Jesus said, 'I thank you, Father, Lord of heaven and earth, because you have hidden these things from the wise and intelligent and have revealed them to infants; yes, Father, for such was your gracious will. [22]*All things have been delivered to me by my Father, and no one knows the Son except the Father, and no one knows the Father except the Son and anyone to whom the Son is willing to reveal him.'*

The thanksgiving, with its highly charged contrast between the infants and the wise, is a deeply meaningful saying. It takes us to the core and centre of what Jesus was about. But for the present the commentary saying is our concern. For all that the commentary saying is highly developed by comparison with the prayer, it certainly has a secure base in the thought of that prayer.

Its closest parallel in the gospel tradition is the self-disclosure of the risen Jesus in the gospel of Matthew:

^{18}All authority in heaven and on earth has been given to me. ^{19}Go therefore and make disciples of all nations, baptizing them in the name of the Father and the Son and the Holy Spirit . . . (Matt. 28:18–9)

The proclamation in Luke/Q 10:22 was added at the pre-Matthean and Q-editorial stage, and therefore antedates Matthew's formulation of the saying of the risen Jesus. Nevertheless, the conclusion is almost inescapable that Luke/Q 10:22 also presupposes the resurrection. Moreover, it makes a claim to exclusive possession of the knowledge of God that comes easily from the lips of the members of a minority religious group, conscious of its alienation from a mainstream community, but convinced that it stands centrally within the providence of God.

The members of this resurrection-inspired Christian community find in the prayer of Jesus the natural base for a statement about Jesus. It is also a statement about themselves. He is the unique revealer. They are drawn not simply into a special understanding but also a special knowledge – knowledge in the sense of a relationship between the Father and the Son, which through him becomes their knowledge too.

We come back by this route to another piece of R. S. Thomas's work, a poem published in 1975 in a collection entitled *Laboratories of the Spirit*. It is entitled 'Emerging', and set at a time just before his undergoing surgery, and I believe it goes to the heart of the matter of prayer:

> Not as in the old days I pray,
> God. My life is not what it was.
> Yours, too, accepts the presence of
> the machine? Once I would have asked
> healing. I go now to be doctored,
> to drink sinlessly of the blood
> of my brother, to lend my flesh
> as manuscript of the great poem
> of the scalpel. I would have knelt
> long, wrestling with you, wearing
> you down. Hear my prayer, Lord, hear
> my prayer. As though you were deaf, myriads
> of mortals have kept up their shrill
> cry, explaining your silence by
> their unfitness.

It begins to appear
this is not what prayer is about.
It is the annihilation of difference,
the consciousness of myself in you,
of you in me . . .

CHAPTER 4

Polarities confirmed or confronted: the search for wholeness

Introduction

In a wonderfully eloquent passage in his magisterial study of the Victorian Church, Owen Chadwick describes the final slow decline in the health of Archbishop William Howley. A calm and gentle soul, he was Archbishop of Canterbury during twenty years which were anything but calm, years which saw the birth of the Oxford Movement and all the attendant controversy. No man of conflict himself, Howley breathed his last on 11 February 1848:

> Amid the splendours of Lambeth palace, last of the prince-archbishops with gilt-edged paper and solemn torchlight processions and banquets in the great hall, yet bearing on his person no whiff of grandeur, as one walking through the fire unscathed, the gentlest and wisest archbishop of the century died as he had lived, fading peaceably and unobtrusively to his grave. (Chadwick 1987: 247)

How different from the tortured end of another truly great, even if flawed, Archbishop of Canterbury whose achievement was to live in even more tumultuous times and to die amid the flames for the sake of the Reformation – that reform of which many of the protagonists in conflict during Archbishop Howley's period in office so heartily disapproved. Calm for the dying Thomas Cranmer, and peace at the last, came at a higher price than it had for William Howley. His biographer records that 20 March 1556, the day before his death, was 'oddly tranquil', and even more so, the final moments on the following day.

Fire was put to the wood. In the flames, Cranmer achieved a final serenity, and he fulfilled the promise that he had made in the last shouts in the [University] church, 'forasmuch as my hand offended, writing contrary to my heart, my hand shall first be punished there-for'. (MacCulloch 1996: 599, 603)

Two archbishops, exhibiting or achieving serenity in diametrically opposed circumstances. Behind them, two movements – each, as it happens, with indissoluble links to the University Church of St Mary the Virgin in Oxford – and each fighting for its understanding of the identity of the community it cherished. Two periods of conflict, discrepant in fundamental ways but dominated by and dedicated to the task of interpreting faithfully a defining tradition.

The task of defining a community, leading it in such a way as to enable it to be true to itself, and interpreting and transmitting the tradition which enables it to be what it is – all of these concerns have a healthy and health-giving aspect. Sadly, they often have a darker and less healthy side. Internal conflict is almost always a given. Demarcating the boundaries of community life almost always gives rise to a human polarisation between those who are 'inside' and those who are 'outside'. Naturally, those who are 'inside' tend to view themselves one way, normally benignly and confidently; those implicitly designated 'outsiders' see the situation differently, often less patiently and more critically alert to the presence of both light and shade. The health of the spirit of any community is therefore best served by occasional self-examination of itself and its traditions, the face it presents to the outside world and how the outside world sees that face.

This fourth study takes us into that sort of territory. We will work on the question of where Jesus and his associates stood in relation to those outside or on the edges of the Jewish people, and how he related to issues customarily defining what it meant to be inside. In his situation, as in other comparable situations, where community identity is the cause of a great deal of trouble, it matters a lot how that community identity is understood in principle; how measures are taken to respect and preserve it in practice; how the problem of 'flaky people' on the edges is handled; and who is in power and therefore able to enforce whatever norms are laid down.

For the Jewish people, the key identity concept was 'holiness', defined in biblical texts whose authority no one disputed:

> [44]I am the Lord your God; sanctify yourselves therefore, and be holy, for I am holy . . . [45]For I am the Lord who brought you up from the Land of Egypt, to be your God; you shall be holy, for I am holy. (Lev. 11:44–5)

Significantly, this principle was framed by a statement of the distinction between the clean and the unclean in matters of food. In similar vein, the requirement to maintain the holiness of the sabbath day was conditioned by the holiness of God and of the people, and strengthened by the force of exodus experience and theology:

> [2]You shall be holy, for I the Lord your God am holy. [3]You shall each revere your mother and father, and you shall keep my sabbaths: I am the Lord your God. (Lev. 19:2–3)

> Remember that you were a slave in the land of Egypt, and the Lord your God brought you out from there . . . therefore the Lord your God commanded you to keep the sabbath day. (Deut. 5:15)

Thus the existence of Israel is defined in terms of the exodus experience and certain 'boundary markers' or 'badges of identity' – belief in one and only one God, the distinction between clean and unclean foods, the separateness of the sabbath day from all other days and, of course, the practice of male circumcision. Within precisely this scenario the Jesus of the gospels appears as a figure of conflict and division – which emphasises again the importance of the question of how the historical Jesus treated issues relating to identity. When it is seriously claimed that 'Jesus had no interest in making ritual purity a test case of covenant loyalty' (Dunn 2002: 464), or that he wanted 'to relativize these god-given markers of Israel's distinctiveness' as part of a strategy of redefining or reconstituting Israel (Wright 1996: 389, 398, 473), it is clear that the stakes are very high indeed.

Jesus the Jew and the gentiles

The twentieth century saw the flowing and then the final ebbing of a tide of assessment of the historical Jesus as a person in fundamental

---

tension with the religious principles of his people. The number of those who would nowadays seriously promote the theory that Jesus' authority threatened that of Moses has steadily shrunk. So in that sense at least, it is realised that he belonged to Judaism.

A Jesus who belonged to Judaism would be – and assuredly was – deeply conscious of the sharp dichotomy between Israel and the gentiles, the polarity that was built into the ongoing self-consciousness of his people. A Jesus who belonged to Judaism with 'evident religious intensity' (Fredriksen 2000: 239) would be – and was – a celebrant of the pilgrimage festivals that, each in their own way, recalled a divine act of liberation from gentile domination. A Jesus who belonged to Judaism would be a celebrant of the annual festival of Hanukkah (the festival of lights), commemorating the dedication of the Temple after a near-fatal gentile attack on the holy place and the holy people. Such celebration could not but reinforce a sense of Jewish separateness, for it recalled the perilous days when the Temple was desecrated, circumcision prohibited, 'the unclean and the profane' in matters of food made obligatory, sabbaths and festivals defiled. Perhaps especially hard to take would be the preserved memory of how in such a time of peril some of the nation proposed a ghastly compromise: 'Let us go and make a covenant with the gentiles around us, for since we separated from them many disasters have come upon us' (1 Macc. 1:11–15, 41–64). A Jesus who belonged to Judaism would celebrate the Passover in particular in the holy city, to which the prefect would come from his normal base in Caesarea with a reinforced military detachment, specifically to prevent the tinderbox of nationalistic sentiment from catching alight. While the liturgy of festival celebration caused the families of Israel to speak about one gentile nation, Egypt, what they could not but see watching them suspiciously at this season above all others was another gentile power, Rome. As far as foreign control was concerned, however unobtrusive and restrained that control might normally be, and however far short it fell of being an occupying power (Sanders 2002: 9–13), it must have seemed at Passover time a case of *plus ça change* . . .

What did Jesus do about this Jew/gentile polarity which was, one might say, engraved on the heart of the nation? Did he identify with the self-consciousness of the nation, or did he promote a wider and more universal vision? We can divide the question into two halves: first, how did he himself treat non-Jews, a category which may or may not include Samaritans, and second, how did he handle those legal 'badges of Israelite identity' or 'boundary markers of the Jewish people' such as circumcision, the food laws, and the sabbath?

There are a number of sayings in which gentile personnel figure, sayings that appear to be prophetic demands addressed to a Jewish audience. The affirmation of a better fate for Sodom in the final judgement than for towns rejecting the disciples' mission (Luke/Q 10:12) seems at first to involve a radically creative use of Scripture, reversing the standard Jewish view of Sodom's dire prospects and crying out to be a word of the prophetic Jesus. But perhaps we should hesitate: the point is to underline the extreme seriousness of the fate of the rejecting towns, not to promote Sodom above them. What then of the related sayings about the queen of the south and the residents of Nineveh (Luke/Q 11:31, 32)? They will act as prosecution witnesses against Jesus' contemporaries in the final judgement – but they are different from Sodom, for in their own way they took seriously the word of prophecy and wisdom. Here is a very positive appraisal by Jesus, and one that belongs firmly within a (failing) mission to Israel, but it falls short of any active attempt to draw gentiles into an experience of the kingdom-inaugurating mission of the person who presently provides wisdom and prophecy. The concern and purpose of the saying is to stir and denounce the immediate audience in Israel. Perhaps the stories of direct encounter between him and individual gentiles will take us further.

The most famous cases of contact between Jesus and gentiles are probably the healings of the centurion's servant/child (Luke/Q 7:1–10) and the Syrophoenician woman's daughter (Mark 7:24–30). Once again, caution is needed. There is some doubt about whether the centurion is in fact a gentile (Catchpole 1993: 280–308), though this is widely assumed, and there are certainly important parallels between the two stories – the illness of a child, the gesture of humility by the suppliant, pressurising argumentation addressed by the suppliant to Jesus, the dismissal of the petitioner, and the healing carried out from a distance. A further parallel between the story of the centurion's servant/child and a story about the healing of Gamaliel's son by the Galilean holy man, Hanina ben Dosa, is also striking:

> Our Rabbis taught: Once the son of R. Gamaliel fell ill. He sent two scholars to R. Hanina b. Dosa to ask him to pray for him. When he saw

them he went up to an upper chamber and prayed for him. When he came down he said to them: Go, the fever has left him. They said to him: Are you a prophet? He replied: I am neither a prophet nor the son of a prophet, but I learnt this from experience. If my prayer is fluent in my mouth, I know that he [the penitent] is accepted: but if not, I know that he is rejected. They sat down and made a note of the exact moment. When they came to R. Gamaliel, he said to them: By the temple service! You have not been a moment too soon or too late, but so it happened: at that very moment the fever left him and he asked for water to drink. (*b. Berakoth* 34b)

The parallel is so striking that both stories are said to illustrate 'a recognized charismatic pattern' (Vermes 1973: 75). But in fact that parallelism casts doubt on, rather than supporting, the historicity of both. It appears that a stylised scheme is present in both. If the historicity of the one story turns out to be suspect, we are left to work with the other, the story of the daughter of the Syrophoenician woman:

> [24]From there he set out and went away to the region of Tyre. *He entered a house and did not want anyone to know he was there. Yet he could not escape notice,* [25]but a woman whose little daughter had an unclean spirit immediately heard about him, and she came and bowed down at his feet. [26]Now the woman was a gentile, of Syrophoenician origin. She begged him to cast the demon out of her daughter. [27]He said to her, **'Let the children be fed first, for** it is not good to take the children's food and throw it to the dogs.' [28]But she answered him, 'Sir, even the dogs under the table eat the children's crumbs.' [29]Then he said to her, 'For saying that, you may go – the demon has left your daughter.' [30]So she went home, found the child lying on the bed, and the demon gone. (Mark 7:24–30)

At the beginning of this story there is evidence of Marcan intervention: the house as the place of secrecy, and the (unrealistic) preference for hiddenness (v. 24bc). Similarly, there is tension within the discouraging response of Jesus. 'Let the children be fed *first*' (v. 27a) implies order – one group *before* the other – whereas 'It is not good to take the children's food and throw it to the dogs' (v. 27b) implies exclusivity – one group *rather than* the other. It is easier to see verse 27a as a later softening of verse 27b, a softening grounded in the 'to the Jew first, and also to the Greek' missionary scheme – Pauline, yes, but congenial to Mark – rather than seeing verse 27b as a later hardening of verse 27a. Moreover, the woman's nimble repartee (v. 28) is a response to exclusivity rather than to sequence. So we conclude that the original version of the story reported Jesus' reply as simply 'It is not good to take the children's food and throw it to the dogs'. This reply can be viewed on more than one level.

First, as a statement of general principle it can be assigned to the stock of wisdom sayings, and as such it does not even need to originate with Jesus. In speaking so negatively about dogs, it picks up the dominant and widely attested tendency to view dogs as animals commanding no respect or affection, creatures that roam in cities and prey on unburied corpses (see 1 Kings 14:11; 22:38; 2 Kings 9:10; Ps. 68:23), animals which because they call forth distaste and disapproval can be made to represent evildoers (Ps. 22:16) and agents of death (Ps. 22:20). Just occasionally there are hints of a more appreciative human attitude to dogs – the protector of the flock (Josephus, *Antiquities* 4:206), the guardian of the household (Isa. 56:10; *m. Baba Kamma* 5:3), or the travelling companion (Tobit 6:2; 11:4), an animal for whom food is deliberately provided (*m. Bekhoroth* 4:4) or who is sufficiently part of the household to steal bread while it is being baked (*m. Baba Kamma* 2:3). In short, the dog as domestic pet can be distinguished from the roaming dogs outside. Thus, when Joseph's Egyptian bride Aseneth abandons her native faith and converts to Judaism, she throws away her sacrificial meal to the strange dogs with the words:

> By no means must *my dogs* eat from my dinner and from the sacrifice of the idols, but let *the strange dogs* eat those. (*Joseph and Aseneth* 10:14; cf. 13:8)

Nothing in the Mark 7:27b saying conveys any such hint – not even the diminutive form 'little dogs' (*kunaria*), which some writers have unguardedly taken to suggest appreciation rather than antagonism – while the verb 'to throw' (*ballein*) conveys a sense of distance (cf. Matt. 7:6, 'Do not *give* what is holy to dogs; and do not *throw* your pearls before swine').

Second, as a saying of Jesus in a very specific context, nothing should refine or reduce the negativity of his response: it *is* a refusal, yes, and it *is* insulting to use the image of the dog for a human being, irrespective of race. To be pro-Jewish does not require discourtesy to a non-Jew, and the temptation to defend the indefensible (e.g. by appeal to 'the sinlessness of Jesus') should be resisted. Not for nothing has Jesus' reply been described as 'morally offensive . . . insultingly cynical', posing an unanswerable question:

> How can we avoid being caught in the contradiction that children are given a higher value within the image presented, but in reality a suffering child is being denied help? (Theissen 1992: 61, 65)

It is entirely understandable that some Jewish scholars, to whose assessment we should in fairness attend, react with negativity to the saying:

> His answer was so brusque and chauvinistic that if any other Jewish teacher of the time had said such a thing Christians would never have forgiven Judaism for it . . . such harsh words that the ears of the most chauvinistic Jew must burn at them. (Klausner 1929: 294, 364; cf. Marcus 1999: 468)

> It may have been Galilean chauvinism that was responsible for Jesus' apparent antipathy towards Gentiles. For not only did he feel himself sent to the Jews alone; he qualified non-Jews, though no doubt with oratorical exaggeration, as 'dogs' and 'swine'. (Vermes 1973: 49)

Third, important light has been thrown on the saying in the human context of relations between Jews and gentiles in the rural border areas where Tyre and Galilee adjoined one another. In those areas Jews lived and worked, and doubtless it was to them that Jesus went (Theissen 1992: 66–8). But the person he met was probably a city-resident, a privileged member of the upper class, someone at home in Greek culture but also bilingual and therefore able to communicate with Jesus (Theissen 1992: 68–72). As a resident of Tyre this woman belonged to a population dependent on the surrounding area for agricultural goods (cf. Acts 12:20). For that very reason she embodied a problem for the Jewish population of the rural area of Tyre/Galilee: food was liable to be passed to the rich urban area and away from the poorer Jewish areas where it was produced. The reply she received from Jesus would almost certainly evoke a painfully accurate awareness of the economic and political situation of the area (Theissen 1992: 72–7). Moreover, the bitterness of the response matches the comment of Josephus that 'the Egyptians, the whole race without exception, and among the Phoenicians the Tyrians, are notoriously our bitterest enemies' (*Against Apion* 1:70, cited by Theissen 1992: 77). Religious sanction for such attitudes was provided by extravagant prophetic denunciations of Tyre (cf. Isa. 23; Jer. 47:4; Ezek. 27; Amos 1:9–10; Zech. 9:3–4), which liturgical texts kept ever fresh and alive (cf. Ps. 83:7). So the saying of Jesus to the woman from Tyre is heavy with Galilean prejudice, fuelled by ingrained social, political, historical, economic and religious experiences and attitudes.

This brings us to the woman's retort to Jesus' hard saying. 'Sir,' she argues, 'even the dogs under the table eat the children's crumbs.' In so speaking she, like Jesus, goes into wisdom mode with a saying which is a statement of fact grounded in observation. Like Aseneth, she presses the distinction between the dog that belongs 'out there' and is viewed with distaste, and the dog who belongs within the home. She accepts for the sake of argument that gentiles are going to be described as 'dogs', but she counters that it should be as dogs who belong to the second scenario rather than the first. Thus she changes the scene to one in which dogs are fed, not because someone throws food to them but because the food is what happens, even if unintentionally, to reach them as the children are eating. By this means she achieves her central objective, not by contesting but rather by conceding the special and primary position of the Jewish people – 'Yes, indeed, but . . .' (Mark 7:28a) – and then daring to redefine the relationship between the Jews and gentiles. It is as if she says, 'We belong inside the house [i.e. God's world], not outside.'

When Jesus does what the woman wants he acts neither because of any heartfelt compassion on his part, nor because of intellectual adroitness on her part, but rather because of her concession – 'Yes, indeed . . .' – and even more because of her irresistibly true observation – 'because of this saying . . .' This negativity of approach on Jesus' part encourages a positive assessment of the historicity of the story. It is 'against the grain' of most versions of early Christianity, committed as they were to gentile mission. But if that is right, we are left with a picture of the historical Jesus as imbued with a powerful conviction of the specialness of Israel, and of gentile contact with his Israel-defined programme being a matter of incidental secondariness rather than deliberate design. Only to a very limited extent is this story, revolving as it does around a statement of 'extreme Jewish ethnocentrism', a story about 'the transcendence of Jewish particularism' (Marcus 1999: 466, 468). Rather, any benefits accruing to gentiles are, by implication, haphazard and marginal to the main Israel-conditioned strategy. The best we can say is that Jesus listens and shows himself open to persuasion from an unlikely quarter, a Syrophoenician woman. On this basis he performs a cure of the same sort as he has repeatedly achieved for Jewish persons.

Jesus the Jew and the Samaritans

We might usefully begin with one of Jesus' alleged sayings suggesting an equally particularistic attitude to Samaritans. This most stringent saying is set by Matthew at the beginning of the mission charge to the disciples (Matt. 10:5b–6) and partially reused in the later story of the Syrophoenician woman (15:24):

> Go nowhere among the gentiles, and enter no town of the Samaritans, but go rather to the lost sheep of the house of Israel.

What are we to make of this? If the number of gentiles resident in Palestine was indeed small (Sanders 2002), they would be easily avoided, and the clear demarcation of Samaritan and Jewish spheres would make it easy to respect this prohibition. What lurks within the prohibition with its initial parallelism is the classic Jewish presupposition about, indeed prejudice towards, Samaritans as no better than gentiles.

Ethnic ambiguity was the root of the problem. Were the Samaritans, as they claimed, descendants of those members of the tribes of Ephraim and Manasseh who survived the destruction of the northern kingdom by the Assyrians in 722 BCE? Or were they, as their opponents claimed, descendants of the colonists transplanted into Samaria at that time by the Assyrians (Anderson 1992: 941)? This latter claim led to their being routinely and dismissively described as 'Cutheans', and only called Samaritans because of their tendency to assume the name of the area in which they had settled (2 Kings 17:24–41; cf. Josephus, *Antiquities* 10:184). This persistent ambiguity, which meant that the Samaritans were 'neither fully Jewish nor fully gentile' (Meier 2001: 533), made possible some aggravating manifestations of what Jewish writers regarded as moral slipperiness. The Samaritans, so the Jews claimed, were inclined to acknowledge a connection with the Jewish people when they were faring well, and to disavow all links in times of Jewish misfortune – thus, in toadying mode to Antiochus Epiphanes, 'we are distinct from them both in race and in customs', a stated preference for a connection with the Sidonians, and a proposal to dedicate the Gerizim temple to Zeus Hellenios (Josephus, *Antiquities* 12:261). Josephus put the matter bluntly and bitterly:

> The nature of the Samaritans [is that] when the Jews are in difficulties, they deny that they have any kinship with them, *thereby indeed admitting the truth*, but whenever they see some splendid bit of good fortune come to them, saying that they are related to them and tracing their line back to Ephraim and Manasseh, the descendants of Joseph. (*Antiquities* 9:291; 11:340)

The roots of such antagonism were sunk deeply into the Jewish psyche: 'Two nations my soul detests,' declared Jesus ben Sirach (50:2–6) many years earlier, 'and the third is not even a people: those who live in Seir [Edomites], and the Philistines, and the foolish people that live in Shechem [Samaritans].' Given the phenomenon of ethnic ambiguity represented by the Samaritans, it is of some interest to check how they were measured up against the 'badges of Jewish identity', namely, monotheism and the circumcision, sabbath and food laws.

On *monotheism*, the defining narrative in 2 Kings 17 speaks of these people as having been instructed in 'the law of the god of the land' and 'how they should worship the Lord', which they observed *in combination with* their earlier religious loyalties. Josephus in his retelling of the tale is more circumspect and doubtless thereby reflects the perceptions of his own time. In his account, the immigrants suffered pestilence, rather than a threat from lions (v. 25), and the pestilence was removed after they took an initiative in response to an oracle, rather than following a move by the king of Assyria (v. 27). So it came about that 'they, being instructed in the ordinances and religion of [the Most High] God, worshipped him with great zeal', that is to say, exclusively. Josephus says nothing about continuing, simultaneous worship of a range of gods (*Antiquities* 9:288–90). He has to concede that 'these same rites have continued in use even to this day among the Cutheans'. So, although he says so (as it were) through gritted teeth, he has to admit that these 'gentiles' are Moses-respecting

---

monotheists. When later the Samaritans made a somewhat disingenuous offer to help with the construction of the second Temple in Jerusalem, an offer that was brushed aside with predictable acerbity and a loaded suggestion that they might, like everyone else (i.e. gentiles), come and worship there when the building had been completed, there was some justice in their claim that 'we worship God no less than they, and pray fervently to him and have been zealous in his service . . .' (*Antiquities* 11:85).

Where do these Moses-respecting Samaritan monotheists stand on the issue of *circumcision*? The Jewish texts provide evidence of unease, even embarrassment. Anti-Samaritan polemic fastened on the (unfortunate) fact that Shechem, the city situated centrally within Samaria, was also the name of the rapist who violated Dinah, the daughter of Jacob and Leah (Gen. 34). The original narrative highlighted the willingness of the Hivites in general and the miscreant Shechem in particular to be circumcised as part of a deal to achieve marriage with Dinah and an alliance with the family of Jacob with territorial implications. Circumcised they were indeed, though it did them no good when Simeon and Levi descended upon them to wreak vengeance for what their sister had suffered.

The retelling of the story by later writers is a matter of imaginative recasting with a view to playing down the circumcision. Thus (i) *Jubilees* 30 (probably mid-first century BCE) passes over the circumcision part of the story, making the story an object lesson concerning divine judgement on anyone who defiled an Israelite virgin, and then even more emphatically an object lesson in righteousness when 'the sons of Jacob spoke, saying, "We will not give our daughter to a man who is uncircumcised because that is a reproach to us"' (30:12). One would never dream when reading *Jubilees* 30 that the Shechemites had been circumcised.

(ii) Josephus in turn (*Antiquities* 1:337–40) passes over it in total silence, pausing only to remark on Jacob's view that 'it was unlawful to marry his daughter to a foreigner'. The implication is that Shechemites (for whom read 'Samaritans') are gentiles.

(iii) *Testament of Levi* presents the avenging of Dinah as Levi's most outstanding feat (2:2). That act of vengeance was a response to a command of the intercessory angel (5:3), which naturally puts him in the right. This time, however, there is a complication: the circumcision of the Shechemites is an acknowledged fact (6:2), and the anger and sorrow of Jacob at the killing of circumcised persons admitted (6:6), but the offence is mitigated by the double argument that Levi had advised against it, and the Shechemites had wanted to rape Sarah and Rebecca as well but had been prevented from doing so by the Lord (6:8). A clear case of creative accounting in a literary sense!

What about *sabbath* and *food laws*? Here a linkage of the Samaritans with those Jews who infringed the laws of sabbath and unclean food is promoted in a very odd passage in Josephus:

> [346]When Alexander died, his empire was partitioned among his successors (the Diadochi); as for the temple on Mount Gerizim, it remained. And whenever anyone was accused by the people of Jerusalem of eating unclean food or violating the sabbath or committing any other such sin, he would flee to the Shechemites, [347]saying that he had been unjustly charged. (*Antiquities* 11:346–7)

The content of this passage borders on the absurd, but its tendency is transparently clear. Jewish persons (i.e. circumcised persons) who choose to infringe the boundary markers of the Jewish people, have a natural home with the Samaritans. The unconvincing implication is that the Samaritans, who are (unfortunately) circumcised, do infringe the other boundary markers. Whether or not this is likely in a Moses-respecting community, the message Josephus conveys is that Samaritans are a distinct people. They are and must be recognised as gentiles, while Jewish people who consort with them are and must be recognised as 'sinners'.

Instinctive antipathy and repugnance towards all things Samaritan was therefore a fact of life, and the mere mention of their name would call to mind a long historical sequence of provocative incidents involving the Temple, its primacy, its construction, its holiness and its worship. That worship had, for example, been notoriously defiled by Samaritan intruders scattering the bones of the dead one Passover time (Josephus, *Antiquities* 18:30). Not that the traffic of this sort had been all in one direction – thus, the attack on Samaria in 128 BCE by John Hyrcanus (Josephus, *Antiquities* 12:275). Such attitudes, widely held in Jewish circles and fuelled repeatedly over centuries, regularly raising bitter resentment to new levels of detestation and contempt, were evidently cordially reciprocated. It was a classic case of those who are nearest at hand in every way provoking the most corrosive animosity.

This is the backdrop for the saying attributed to Jesus in Matthew 10:5b–6. But does this prohibition of contact with gentiles in general and Samaritans in particular, and instruction only to reach out to 'the lost sheep of the house of Israel', indeed stem from Jesus? Probably not. The concern with the lost sheep of the house of Israel (v. 6) is derived by Matthew from a Marcan narrative comment that Jesus 'saw a great crowd, and had compassion for them, because they were like sheep without a shepherd' (Mark 6:34; cf. 1 Kings 22:17; Judith 11:19). This comment Matthew reformulates in direct speech in the repeated saying in Matthew 10:6; 15:24. This leaves only that part of the saying that deals with the avoidance of gentile and Samaritan space (10:5b). This saying probably not only stems from Q but is also an editorial addition: (i) The Matthew/Luke agreement in references to Samaritans next door to the mission charge (cf. Luke 9:51–6; 10:25–37) suggests that Q also referred to them here. (ii) The saying expresses the same particularistic attitude as the editorial additions in Luke/Q 6:33; 12:30a. It probably does not stem from Jesus.

A tradition which, on the other hand, almost certainly does stem from Jesus is the famous and notably subtle parable of the good Samaritan (Luke 10:30–37). It has rightly been described as 'one of the most brilliant miniature stories ever composed' (Wright 1996: 306).

Two recent studies of this famous parable have urged that its central concern is the debate about which of two laws takes precedence over the other when they come into conflict (Bauckham 1998; Bryan 2002: 177–85). Such a debate is a familiar concern when the law is being strictly interpreted. So the dilemma of the priest and the levite is said to be the conflict of two obligations. The first is the avoidance of contact impurity with a corpse – for the victim of violence might be already dead and not just at risk of dying. The second is the showing of compassion towards a fellow human being in deep trouble. The obligation to avoid corpse impurity (cf. Lev. 21:1–3; 22:3–7) was a stringent one; the obligation to respond to human need with neighbourly love (Lev. 19:18) was also imperative. How should the two religious professionals decide? Was the decision they made in favour of the corpse impurity commandment the right one? That is what the audience is asked to decide, according to these two studies.

A third study has injected a little critical restraint into this tendency in the interpretation of the parable, by pointing out that the victim of violence, the priest, the levite and the Samaritan were all travelling *from*, not *to*, Jerusalem (Luke 10:30–31). Therefore, for the priest and the levite, there was no question of protecting their purity with a view to exercising their functions in the Temple. They had already done that. Instead, according to this study, 'Jesus was attacking an emphasis on maintaining purity when outside the Temple', for 'the priest would not in fact be punished for contracting impurity and certain authorities would not have a problem with him contracting corpse impurity in the case of an abandoned corpse' (Crossley 2004: 117–20).

Just as this contribution to the discussion injected a little realism by noting the direction of the journeys, perhaps even more realism may result from noting that the victim of violence was visibly not at all dead! He was *half* dead (Luke 10:30: *ēmithanē*). If the Samaritan could see clearly that he remained half alive, why within the terms of the story should that not be equally clear to the priest and the levite? If all could see that this was no corpse by the side of the road, all talk of corpse impurity turns out to be over-subtle – a dangerous thing to say, admittedly, since one risks being regarded as not subtle enough! But from that it would follow that the proposal that the parable is about a clash between two legal principles (compassion and purity) may be mistaken. If so, is there an alternative way of reading the parable?

Attentive members of Jesus' audience would recognise the use of the 'law of three' when first the priest and then the levite had come, looked at, and done nothing for, the naked and half-dead victim of grievous bodily harm. A third person was bound to come down the road! Members of the audience would also be aware of the tendency in rulings concerned with the interpretation of Torah to deal consecutively with three typical figures – the priest, the levite and the Israelite layman. To take just one of many illustrations, this time about *peah* legislation: 'This measure is prescribed for priests, for levites, and for Israelites alike' (*m. Peah* 8:6). The audience would therefore have raced ahead in thought to the supremely predictable third person in the sequence, that is to say, the Israelite lay person . . . who duly failed to appear! Instead, there appeared a representative of the hated rival community in Samaria, a person identified with another temple. And that is surely the point. The obvious inference from the priest's and the levite's journeying *from* Jerusalem to Jericho is that their homes are not in the capital city and that they have been performing their necessary functions in the Temple.

Had the third traveller been an Israelite layman, he too could have been a Temple worshipper, and there would then be no contrast between him and the two others. But the third person was not an Israelite layman: he was, as a Samaritan, someone *who did not worship in the Jerusalem Temple*. It is important to remember the polarisation between two communities identifying with two temples. It could scarcely be clearer than in the evidence of Jewish destruction of the Samaritan temple, and Samaritan defilement of the Jewish Temple, that is to say, the polarisation so deftly formulated by the Samaritan woman in the gospel of John: 'Our ancestors worshipped on this mountain, but you say that the place where people must worship is in Jerusalem' (John 4:20). What Jesus is using that polarisation to convey is surely this, another polarisation: the quintessential Temple worshippers who do not go on to show compassion to the needy *versus* the non-Temple worshipper who does show 'mercy' (Luke 10:37).

Could greater violence be done to the feelings of Torah-respecting and Temple-loving hearers than by the introduction of such a person, this Samaritan? That must have been the reaction. But the very violence that Jesus does to the feelings of his audience is surely just another way of conveying in narrative form the prophetic principle that 'I desire mercy and not sacrifice, the knowledge of God rather than burnt offerings' (Hos. 6:6; cf. Bailey 1980: 50). The net effect is that Jesus' parable, designed to stimulate thought about love in action, turns out to convey an identical message to that which Mark's scribe formulated: love of God and especially neighbour 'is much more important than all whole burnt-offerings and sacrifices' (Mark 12:33). There is absolutely no whisper of an attack on the Temple as such, absolutely no whiff of criticism of the cult which the priest and the levite serve. To transform the essential thrust of the parable so that it 'dramatically redefines the covenant boundary of Israel, of the Torah itself, and by strong implication of the Temple cult' (Wright 1996: 307) is, if I may say so with respect, to read out of the text that which first has been read into it. The conduct of the priest and the levite may have been mistaken from Jesus' point of view, but it was scarcely so damaging that 'the whole system of Temple and sacrifice would itself be called into question'. On the contrary, their error was not their service in the Temple, it was their misjudgement of the priorities, their neglect of the *sine qua non* of authentic worship. Jesus is simply mounting a barbed and blistering critique of any worship, even worship in that most holy place in Jerusalem, which does not lead directly into loving care for those whose plight is desperate.

The shock tactics employed by Jesus in asking a Jewish audience to view a Samaritan as a moral example not only presumed the age-old Jew/Samaritan prejudice but also by implication subjected it boldly to criticism. As noted above, here and there in the gospel tradition editorial statements demand conduct *better than* that of the group of 'outsiders'. This parable does precisely the opposite: it asks for conduct to be *raised to* the level of the representative 'outsider'.

But, we may go on to ask, is the intention simply to stir a Jewish audience by an appreciative reference to a Samaritan without any matching concern to follow up in a mission in Samaria that freshness and that positivity? Stirring a Jewish audience is one thing, even the primary thing, but is it possible that something more inclusive in respect of Jesus and the Samaritan community itself might emerge? The evidence is admittedly not strong, but the unsuccessful visit to Samaria (9:51–6), included by Luke at the start of his travel narrative (9:51—18:14), at least gives cause for pause.

The story looks as if it combines pre-Lucan tradition and Lucan redaction, as indicated below, and the case for such a separation can be mounted in the following way:

> 51 *When the days drew near for him to be taken up, he set his face to go to Jerusalem.* 52a*And he sent messengers ahead of him (apesteilen aggelous pro prosōpou autou). On their way* 52bthey entered a village of the Samaritans *to make ready for him (hōs hetoimasai autōi);* 53but they did not receive him, *because his face was set on going to Jerusalem.* 54When his disciples James and John saw it, they said, 'Lord do you want us to command fire to come down from heaven and consume them?' 55But he *turned and* rebuked them. 56*Then they went on to another village.*

First, this story contains repeated reminders of the journey which is now beginning: 'he set his face to go to Jerusalem . . . his face was set on going to Jerusalem . . . they went on to another village' (vv. 51, 53b, 56). So it fits, or has been made to fit, rather firmly into Luke's overall scheme.

Second, it also has the tightest of linkages with the mission of the 70 (or 72) that follows (Luke 10:1–16), for in both there is a 'sending . . .

ahead of him/before his face' (9:52; 10:1). Those sent by Jesus are – this must be the implication – clearly separate from Jesus himself.

Third, the pattern of '[sending] messengers before [your] face who shall prepare . . .' is an unmistakable echo of what was said about John the Baptist in relation to Jesus in a Q-editorial statement (Luke/Q 7:27). Since Luke normally preserves the order of his sources, this is significant. For within the Lucan Q sequence 7:18–35 was the last block of Q material which Luke used before moving into an extended non-Q sequence involving L (Luke 7:36—8:3) and Marcan (Luke 8:4—9:50) material, and now our story (Luke 9:51–6). That proximity strongly suggests that in 9:51–6 there is a reminiscence of the earlier statement about John/Jesus.

Fourth, the suitability of that reminiscence emerges clearly when we observe that it is precisely as the preparatory Elijah-type figure (Mal. 3:1, 23/4:5) that John's position is defined in Luke/Q 7:27, and it is the Elijah-type action in Samaria of calling down fire from heaven (2 Kings 1:9–12) which the disciples suggest to Jesus. This, they apparently believe, is a fitting response to rejection, and by implication a confirmation of the special status of the person who is being rejected. For us it is significant that there is a direct line of thinking between Luke/Q 7:27 and Luke 9:54, a reminiscence of the one within the other.

Fifth, there is internal tension within the narrative. Sometimes, especially when the language comes closest to Luke/Q 7:27 or to the mission charge which follows in Luke/Q 10:1–16, we have the impression that the disciples are on their own and separate from Jesus – 'he sent messengers ahead of him' (Luke 9:52a). At other times he seems to be present – 'they did not receive *him* because his face was set on going to Jerusalem' (Luke 9:53). How are we to explain this aporia, this dislocation? Surely by suspecting the existence of an underlying tradition of a visit by Jesus, as well as disciples, to a Samaritan village. And although nothing is made of it in Luke's remodelling of that tradition, everything that is said suggests that it was a visit for the purpose of mission. That is the assumption behind 'they did not receive him' (cf. Luke/Q 10:8, 10).

So Luke is actively interventionist in the telling of this story, recollecting what had been said in recently used source material, and fashioning the story to suit his Jerusalem-aligned travel scheme. But did he create the story *ex nihilo*? That is surely rather unlikely.

Luke is himself very favourably disposed towards a mission to the

Samaritans (see Acts 1:8; 8:4–25): it would have served his purpose well to have Jesus preaching the kingdom effectively in Samaria, just as success attends the subsequent mission of the disciples (Luke/Q 10:1–20), and just as effective contact between Jesus and the centurion (Luke/Q 7:1–10) had been made to anticipate the story of the advance to the gentiles in Acts 10:1—11:18. But Luke 9:51–6 records unqualified failure. In no way does it function as an archetype for the Samaritan mission in Acts.

The important thing is that 'the Samaritans did not receive him'. One could say simply that they behaved as Samaritans did *vis-à-vis* Galilean pilgrims heading for Jerusalem some 20 years later than Jesus, according to Josephus (*Jewish War* 2:232; *Antiquities* 20:118). In this case, however, rather more seems to be involved. Having been approached (so we infer) with the message of the kingdom, they showed their rejection of it by a Sodom-like refusal of hospitality (cf. Gen. 19). Here was an imitation of the behaviour of the inhospitable (as well as morally permissive) Sodom upon which 'the Lord rained sulphur and fire out of heaven' (Gen. 19:24). And such behaviour, so the biblically aware James and John not unreasonably supposed, merits immediate divine intervention in judgement. Biblically aware they may be, but in line with the outlook of Jesus they most certainly are not. In the mission charge, Jesus took the present rejection problem seriously if due weight be given to Luke/Q 10:12: 'I tell you, on that day it will be more tolerable for Sodom than for that town', but of that there is no hint in the conversation with James and John. Nor is there any sign of sympathy with the ghastly story of Elijah's calling down fire from heaven on the soldiers of the king of Samaria (2 Kings 1:9–12). Instead, as has been brilliantly and convincingly demonstrated (Allison 2002), Jesus' response corresponds to a well-attested Jewish tradition critical of what happened in the unpleasant stories of Moses and the punishment of Korah, Dathan and Abiram (Num. 16), Elijah and the companies of soldiers (2 Kings 1:9–12), and Elisha and the mauling of the disrespectful small boys by bears (2 Kings 2:23–5). Moreover, if the Jewish tradition of unease and discomfort with these stories is, as is clearly the case, grounded in a sense of the universal compassion of the creator (cf. typically, Wisdom 11:22—12:2: Allison 2002: 470–72), and his preference for allowing time for repentance, then it matches and is matched by the historically firm evidence of Jesus' own perspective. His God is the creator, the God of universal compassion, the one who expects human reactions to the sinfulness of others to be formed by the evidence of his own indiscriminate compassion (Matt. 5:45), the one who allows a time of restraint as an opportunity for repentance (Luke 18:7b). If Jesus allowed no judgemental preoccupation with the righteous over against the unrighteous, he also disallows the same preoccupation with Samaritans, even when they reject him and his prophetic gospel.

So, once we have taken account of internal dislocations and the evidence of Lucan editorial change we are in a position to isolate pre-Lucan tradition. That tradition drops a substantial hint that Jesus' mission was not just to unambiguous Israel but also to the ambiguous community of the Samaritans. Should we be surprised by the thought of a mission to Samaria? Hardly! First, the prospect of a rule over the twelve tribes (Luke/Q 22:30), by means of which God's own kingship would be effected, would potentially draw in those who themselves, whatever doubts might be expressed by Jews, traced their ancestry to Ephraim and Manasseh and thus to Joseph, that is the Samaritans. So their forming part of Jesus' mission strategy would be consistent. Second, the introduction of the liberating rule of God would necessarily bring in its wake the liberation of Samaria, for the writ of the Roman prefect, following the post-Herodian allocation to Archelaus (Josephus, *Antiquities* 17:319), extended to Samaria as well as to Idumea and Judah.

If these inferences are correct, the polarities of Israel's situation were indeed being confronted by Jesus. The position which emerges this time is somewhat nuanced. Whereas the Jew/gentile polarity was accepted and endorsed, the Jew/Samaritan polarity was viewed more critically and constructively. In the latter context, in the response to the message of the kingdom there could be achieved the endorsement of the inclusive view of Samaritan history over against the conventional exclusive view, the overcoming of racial and religious prejudice, and the relegation to the past of a centuries-old history of hostility and provocation.

Jesus and the community of holiness

Any true Jew would see the holiness principle, which characterised and indeed distinguished the nation, as wholly non-negotiable. And the inseparability of the law from the process of giving effect to that holiness principle cannot be overestimated. Speaking of reverence for the Scriptures, Josephus declared:

For although such long ages have now passed, no one has ventured either to add, or to remove, or to alter a syllable; and it is an instinct with every Jew, from the day of his birth, to regard them as the decrees of God, to abide by them, and, if need be, cheerfully to die for them. (*Against Apion* 1:42; cf. Luke/Q 16:17)

That said, however, the holiness principle and the law that enshrined it would in practical terms need to be interpreted and applied. Here there would be room for disagreement and dispute.

As a Galilean prophet, Jesus would ordinarily have come into contact most frequently with one of the three current movements which, in their different ways, set out to implement the holiness principle and correspondingly to guide the life of the nation, that is to say, the Pharisees. They are repeatedly present in the gospel tradition as (usually, though not invariably) critical witnesses and controversial opponents of Jesus. But they constitute a perplexing problem for students of the historical Jesus. This problem essentially concerns use of the sources available to us: (i) Josephus, who had first-hand experience of membership of the Pharisaic movement during the years 56–7 CE (*Life* 12); (ii) the rabbinic material, which is heavily influenced by post-70 CE developments, with the dating of the different pieces of evidence preserved in that material being often uncertain or controversial; and (iii) the gospels, which often though not invariably adopt a very polemical attitude to the Pharisees, and sometimes level accusations which bear little resemblance to reality – for example, the two versions of an anti-Pharisaic allegation of corporate responsibility for the deaths of prophets (Matt. 23:29–31/Luke 11:47–8). They may therefore sometimes mirror later Christian–Jewish relations rather more than those between Jesus and his own contemporaries.

We therefore have a problem in interpreting and assessing the historical value of gospel traditions in which Pharisees figure. Some writers have even gone so far as to claim that those gospel traditions which are historical give no support to the idea of any cleavage at all between Jesus and the Pharisees! Whether or not that is a defensible position, it makes it all the more essential that we should do three things: first, establish what it was that gave the Pharisees their identity; second, examine with particular care and self-critical openness the history of all relevant

Christian traditions; and, third, account for the very widespread, indeed multiply attested, tradition of conflicts between Jesus and Pharisees.

In a thumbnail sketch of the essential features of Pharisaism, assembled by critical scrutiny of the three complexes of evidence, the following features emerge. First, they were 'the most accurate interpreters of the law (Josephus, *Jewish War* 2:162). That is, they set out to achieve precision in interpretation and application, and thereby inevitably developed a tradition – indeed more than one tradition – of interpretation. The authority of tradition was expressed in claims of an unbroken succession of guardians of the law from Moses to Joshua, the elders, the prophets . . . on through Judah ben Tabbai and Simeon ben Shetah . . . on to Hillel and Shammai (who flourished as BCE was replaced by CE) . . . and on to those who in later times became the heroes in the Pharisaic hall of fame (*m. Aboth* 1:1–18; Mark 7:5; Matt. 23:2: 'they sit on the seat of Moses'). Each of those great guardians of the law was remembered for a key principle that had guided their work of interpretation. Sometimes those principles were admirable and unexceptionable:

> Be the disciples of Aaron, loving peace and pursuing peace, loving mankind and bringing them near to the law. (Hillel, *m. Aboth* 1:12)

Sometimes they were less appealing:

> Let your house be opened wide and let the needy be members of your household; and do not talk much with womankind. (Jose ben Johanan of Jerusalem, *m. Aboth* 1:5)

Second, as their name probably implies (*parush* = separated one), they characteristically adhered to the principle of separation and therefore of 'purity'/'holiness'. This characteristic of the whole people was developed by them in especially thoroughgoing ways, for example, in exclusive fellowship meals where the assembled company held a common view of purity, and in washings before meals (cf. Mark 2:15; 7:3). A certain 'democratisation' of the principle of holiness led them to extend to lay people the purity rules normally incumbent on the priesthood alone, without however relaxing the inherent specialness of the priesthood itself. Thus the whole people could become 'a priestly kingdom and a holy nation' (Exod. 19:6).

Third, in addition to hand-washing and general extremely careful attention to cleanness/uncleanness, the Pharisees set great store on the law of tithing. This also has a bearing on eating practices. To practise tithing oneself was an act of conformity to law (cf. Lev. 27:30–33; Num. 18:20–32). But if the principle is right, why not bring everything within its scope (cf. Luke/Q 11:42)? And suppose that food one bought in the marketplace had, as a result of laxity on the part of the seller, not been tithed! That would be a cause of inadvertent deviation from the principle of holiness. The only safe policy then would be, as one conscientious Pharisee put it, 'I give tithes of all that I acquire' (Luke 18:12).

Fourth, according to one strand of Jewish thinking, the final coming of God would depend upon, or be hastened by, the repentance of Israel. One of the signs of repentance, reinforced by a desperate sense of longing for divine rescue, was fasting: the pattern can be seen clearly in the Israelite reaction to the threat posed by Nebuchadnezzar in the book of Judith: fasting, combined with self-humbling, heartfelt prayer and expressions of mourning (4:8–15). While some fasts were obligatory, it was always possible as a gesture of religious seriousness and penitential preparation for the age to come to embark on an even more rigorous practice of fasting. To quote again the same conscientious Pharisee, 'I fast twice a week' (Luke 18:12).

Fifth, wholly unsurprising is the concern of a holiness movement like Pharisaism with one of the key expressions of holiness, namely sabbath observance. The principle of precisely accurate interpretation of the holiness of the sabbath was always likely to be central to Pharisaic practice (cf. Mark 2:24; 3:2; Luke 13:14; 14:1).

While this is a major concern of the Pharisaic movement, it is important to recall that it would be quite incomprehensible for any Jewish person with a proper understanding of Jewishness to be less than deeply respectful of the sabbath. It was a true instinct, though a particularly nasty action, on the part of the Jewish apostate Antiochus in Antioch, during the dark days of the war with Rome, to put pressure on the Jewish community there to jeopardise their own identity in two ways – first, by offering sacrifices to gods 'in the manner of the Greeks', and so compromise monotheism, and second, to abandon sabbath observance, and so compromise their identity as the people of God (Josephus, *Jewish War* 7:50–53). It was a true instinct that also guided the writer of the first edition of the fourth gospel to rewrite synoptic tradition in his two definitive narratives of Jerusalem miracles (John 5:1–18/Mark 2:1–12, 23–8; John 9:1–34), and in doing so to expose the dilemma of the scrutinising synagogue authorities: *either* Jesus is a prophet because of his performing an amazing miracle, *or* he is a sinner, notwithstanding the miracle, because he broke the sabbath – and the outcome? Expulsion from the worshipping community of the synagogue.

The relationship between the people at large and the Pharisees is important for us. The gospels indicate three things – first, that Pharisees were in constant contact with Jesus; second, that Jesus was not himself a Pharisee; third, that the Pharisees expected Jesus to conform to their principles. How may this be understood?

Josephus claims that the Pharisees exerted wide influence over the people at large (*Antiquities* 13:298, 401), which suggests that they were not just talking to themselves about how the will of God should be defined. Rather, they had a programme for the nation. That programme they set about communicating. It seems that many Jews, while not joining Pharisaic fellowships, nevertheless respected Pharisaic rulings. Pharisaic strategy was apparently to cultivate good relationships, not only within their fellowships but also with the wider population, thereby making themselves 'extremely influential' (*Antiquities* 18:14). In the same vein, 'The Pharisees are affectionate to one another [*philallēloi*] and cultivate harmonious relations with the community' (*Jewish War* 2:166). The triple conundrum posed above can probably be resolved by bringing together several observations. (i) Pharisaic influence upon the population makes it natural that they should exert pressure on a popular movement that took a different view on key issues. (ii) The process of careful interpretation of Scripture makes it natural for the exponents to expect their view to prevail. (iii) In the main setting of Jesus' activity there was probably no other strongly influential group, so the two were almost inevitably going to prove competitors. (iv) The closeness of Jesus to the Pharisees, which we shall soon discover, makes relevant the sociological principle that the nearer two groups are to one another, the fiercer the conflict between them.

We are now able to look at some representative traditions dealing with Jesus and the Pharisees in order to check historicity and uncover the underlying causes of conflict. The key indicators of his position are his treatment of the sabbath, the cleanness/uncleanness distinction, and the practice of tithing. The main synoptic tradition about sabbath observance is Mark 2:23–8:

> [23]One sabbath he was going through the cornfields; and as they made their way his disciples began to pluck heads of grain. [24]The Pharisees said to him, 'Look, why are they doing what is not lawful on the sabbath?' [25]And he said to them, 'Have you never read what David did when he and his companions were hungry and in need of food? [26]He entered the house of God, when Abiathar was high priest, and ate the bread of the presence, which it is not lawful for any but the priests to eat, and he gave some to his companions.' [27]Then he said to them, 'The sabbath was made for humankind, and not humankind for the sabbath; [28]so the Son of Man is lord even of the sabbath.'

Suspicion concerning the historicity of this tradition has often been registered, sometimes with a hint of humour: 'What were [the Pharisees] doing in the midst of a grain field on the sabbath? Waiting on the off-chance that someone might pick grain?' (Sanders 1993: 214). Objecting to the conduct of the disciples rather than that of Jesus *might* reflect a later community consciousness, and the sudden appearance of the Pharisees in the cornfields *might* seem a little contrived. On the other hand, the criticism may be overblown. The argumentation of Jesus pre-supposes a Pharisaic partner in debate, and the identification of Jesus and his disciples, whose conduct is necessarily more obvious than that of an individual, makes the direction of the question unsurprising. Perhaps we should allow the story to represent what was remembered as *typical* of Jesus. The key elements in the story (cf. Casey 1988: 1–23) are as follows:

First, the disciples are probably walking along the edges of the cornfields and taking advantage of the *peah* provision, that is to say, the leaving of grain at the edges of the fields for the poor to 'glean' (cf. Lev. 19:9–10; 23:22; Deut. 23:25; 24:19–21; Ruth 2:1–7). The disciples of Jesus doubtless qualified to take advantage of this generous social provision, for they had become poor by following Jesus.

Second, such activity is not the same as harvesting, nor is it work which breaks the sabbath (Crossley 2004: 160–62). Even the 39 examples of sabbath-breaking work listed in *m. Shabbath* 7:2 do not include pluck-ing: 'sowing, ploughing, reaping, binding sheaves, threshing, winnow-ing . . .' but not plucking ears of corn. The critics of Jesus' disciples cannot therefore take their stand on any biblical law, but doubtless represent the stricter parties to a contemporary debate about sabbath observance. Their attitude corresponds to assertions about the eating of previously prepared food only, assertions documented in Qumran (CD 10:22–3) or Qumran-related (*Jubilees* 2:29–30; 50:9) texts as well as Philo (*Life of Moses* 2:22), but evidence of an agreed and established position at the time is lacking. It is therefore entirely right to observe (Crossley 2004: 161) that anyone who was not in sympathy with the tendency to expand biblical law would not have given the time of day to the suggestion that the disciples were doing 'what is not lawful on the sabbath'. Nevertheless, if the matter was being debated in some Pharisaic circles, the criticism had to be met with argument.

Third, Jesus' initial counter-argument appeals to the precedent of David's action in asking for, and receiving from the priest Ahimelech (not Abiathar), the shewbread (1 Sam. 21:1–6). While the timing of the two incidents matches, for the shewbread was freshly baked every sabbath eve and replaced every sabbath, there is a slight mismatch between situation and argument: in David's case it is holy or restricted food that is involved and given to an inappropriate person (Lev. 24:5–9), whereas in Jesus' case it is allegedly inappropriate activity which makes ordinary food available. Nevertheless the point is more or less clear: human need justifies a breach of the norm as currently laid down. In David's case, of course, the breach was indeed a breach of biblical law, so Jesus' retort is somewhat *ad hominem*: 'If you are against all breaches of law, what are you going to do about this one which is regarded by the biblical narrative as justified?' As an *ad hominem* argument, however, it could not bear the full weight of a compelling and convincing response.

Fourth, Jesus' next counter-argument complements the first by appealing to a principle: 'The sabbath was made for humankind, and not humankind for the sabbath' (Mark 2:27). That this is where the real weight of argument is located is indicated by the fresh introduction, 'Then he said to them . . .' What follows is a piece of very subtle argumentation, designed to establish that within the divine order the primary entity is humankind and not the sabbath: therefore the shape of sabbath observance is to be determined by the needs of human beings. This emerges from the fact that the structure of the saying – 'not A for B, but B for A' – brings it alongside other similarly formed sayings, all of which have to do with primacy within the divine order.

It is worth pausing over these sayings in order to gain a sense of how Mark 2:27 is intended to work. Thus, (i) 2 Baruch 14:18 declares that 'man was not made on account of the world, but the world on account of man,' and the context deals with the paradox of humankind's temporariness over against the world's permanence. In spite of that, humanity has been divinely appointed as administrator and so placed in a position of authority and responsibility (cf. Gen. 1:26–8; Ps. 8:6–9). That is to say, the primary entity is the one (humankind) and not the other (the world).

(ii) 2 Maccabees 5:19 affirms that 'the Lord did not choose the nation for the sake of the sanctuary, but the sanctuary for the sake of the nation.' The meaning this time is that the Temple is not immune from, but rather dependent on, what happens to the people, and it suffered during the time of Antiochus Epiphanes because of what the people did. That is to say, the primary entity is the one (the people) and not the other (the Temple).

(iii) As part of a highly controversial and somewhat convoluted argument, Paul calls Genesis 2:18–25 in aid by declaring, 'man was not made because of woman, but woman because of man' (1 Cor. 11:9). What he has in mind is more than mere priority of existence, but rather authority and lordship. In these terms, the primary entity is the one (man) and not the other (woman).

(iv) To these sayings may be added the famous statement, 'The sabbath is handed over to you, not you to it' (*Mekhilta* on Exod. 31:14; see Marcus 1999: 245). Since 'you' in this saying represents Israel, the common conviction that the sabbath is a badge of Israel's identity is in the speaker's mind, as the context of Exodus 31:14 makes abundantly clear:

> [12]The Lord said to Moses: 'You yourself are to speak *to the Israelites*: "You shall keep my sabbaths . . . [14]You shall keep the sabbath, because it is holy for you . . . [16]Therefore *the Israelites* shall keep the sabbath, observing the sabbath throughout their generations, as a perpetual covenant. [17]It is a sign for ever between me and *the people of Israel*."'

Fifth, the arguments from biblical precedent and principle come together in the conclusion: 'So the Son of Man is lord even (*kai*) of the sabbath' (Mark 2:28). If we go back to the Aramaic-speaking Jesus, then the saying can be set alongside the *bar (e)nash(a)* sayings, in which the speaker enunciates a general principle without in any way necessarily bringing himself within the range of those covered by that principle. The conduct of the disciples of Jesus is defended in terms of their qualifying as members of humankind, and not because of their link with him. The appeal is to the divine order of creation – just the sort of thing that comes to the surface in Jesus' appeal to the creator's provision of rain and sunshine for the benefit of wicked people in support of the demand to 'love your enemies' (Matt. 5:45/Luke 6:35) – just the sort of thing that comes to the surface in Jesus' appeal to Genesis 1:27; 2:24 in support of the demand to preserve a marriage (Mark 10:2–9).

From the sabbath we turn to a second issue, again an epitome of Jewish commitment to the law and another 'boundary marker', the food laws. The background situation could hardly be clearer than when the loyalists during the Maccabean period 'chose rather to die than to be defiled by food or to profane the holy covenant' (1 Macc. 1:62–3), or when Daniel, Tobit and Judith avoid defilement by not eating gentile food (Dan. 1:8–16; Tobit 1:10–11; Judith 10:5; 12:2, 19), or when twelve allegedly fine priests of Josephus' acquaintance, having been sent to Rome to give an account of themselves to Nero, 'had not forgotten the pious practices of religion, and supported themselves on figs and nuts' (*Life* 13).

According to Mark 7:19, Jesus *prima facie* abolished the very distinction upon which those food laws rested: 'thus he spoke, making all foods clean'. And under the influence of Mark 7:19, and with a resounding echo of the proposal that inaugurated the so-called, but (cf. Allison 2005: 1–9) quite inappropriately labelled, new/second quest of the historical Jesus (Käsemann 1964: 39), it has been claimed that Jesus was 'cryptically subverting the Jewish food laws' (Wright 1996: 284). He was, so it is said, showing scepticism about the distinction between clean and unclean things which formed the very religious bedrock upon which Judaism was grounded (Theissen/Merz 1998: 571).

The polar opposite interpretation of Mark 7:19 is that within the flow of the argument the foods mentioned there are not all foods in general but only those foods which, inherently clean in themselves, have been rendered unclean by being touched by unwashed hands (Crossley 2004: 191–3). By invoking consistency between two of Mark's editorial insertions in 7:3–4, 19, it is suggested that there is no clash at all between Mark's Jesus and the food laws.

Perhaps in this case neither view is entirely satisfactory. Against the first view, when Jesus is said repeatedly to specialise in the cryptic and to persist with the subversive, and therefore to be behaving characteristically in Mark 7, one cannot suppress a suspicion that invoking the cryptic is only necessary because the proposed interpretation of Jesus' sayings and conduct is simply not clear at all. Against the second view, the form of words chosen by Mark – 'making all foods clean' – is very firm and unqualified. Matthew seems to have regarded the whole comment as better omitted. As for the argument from continuity, it seems a little fragile. After all, there is a sharp break in that continuity when the *Marcan* Jesus leaves the public arena to concentrate 'in the house' on the disciples alone (Mark 7:17), just as there was when the *Marcan* Jesus did the same thing in the presentation and explanation of the typical parable (4:10–12) and in the middle of the discussion of divorce (10:10). In both cases the private instruction went beyond the public declaration. So also in 7:19, where we do well to take our bearings from Mark's very clear interest in promoting a gentile mission (note the closeness of 7:19 to the incident involving the gentile woman, 7:24–30) in which the gospel might effect unrestricted table fellowship. This might well encourage the thought that this cause would be greatly helped by having *his* Jesus pronounce all food clean. That said, and having been careful not to assume that the *Marcan* Jesus is the same as the *historical* Jesus, we need to turn to the history of the tradition in the unusually long debate in Mark 7:1–23.

First, if our initial move is to extract Mark 7:15 as it stands from its present context, then it is extremely unlikely to preserve an authentic saying (cf. Räisänen 1992: 127–49). An abolition by Jesus of the clean/unclean distinction in dietary matters, if that is what is implied, would leave the subsequent course of events and debates in the early years of the Christian movement incomprehensible. How could the early Church have come so close to tearing itself apart over such an issue if Jesus had staked out so distinctive and radical a position? It hardly makes sense, as has often been observed. But perhaps we should work on, rather than set aside, the context in which Mark 7:15 is presently set.

Second, the *cause célèbre* at the heart of the debate is not the eating of one sort of food rather than another but the 'failure' to wash hands before a meal. This may well be an infringement of the practice of the Pharisees, and not just in respect of meals taking place on special days like a festival or a sabbath (thus, Sanders 1990: 228–32). It may well flout the opinion, based on an extension of biblical law, that food touched by unwashed hands becomes unclean (Crossley 2004: 184). It does not involve the practice of 'all the Jews' (Mark 7:3) – Mark is a specialist in exaggeration! – but it may well reflect how some Jews of a strict inclination ordered their practice. As a divergence from Pharisaic norms from the time of the great founders of the different schools of interpretation, Hillel and Shammai, it quite appropriately provokes the question, 'Why do your disciples not behave in line with the tradition of the elders, but eat food with unwashed hands?' (Mark 7:5).

Third, in what follows, Jesus first picks up the reference to 'the tradition of the elders'. He mounts a counter-attack (Mark 7:6–8) which contrasts the human tradition with the divine commandment, whereas the Pharisees regarded the two as in direct continuity and harmony with one another. His tactic involves setting up a virtual *reductio ad absurdum* in a devastating critique of the sort of morally offensive situation which this human tradition has generated, the so-called *korban* (Mark 7:9–13). The debate about the *korban* may well be a unit of tradition that could exist separately and quite possibly go back to Jesus. Its presence in Mark 7 is, however, dependent on the preceding 7:6–8, which in turn depends on the LXX rendering of Isaiah 29:13 at a point where it deviates from the Hebrew text. So the earliest version of the tradition did not include Mark 7:6–13, and the Pharisees' critical question may or may not have included the words 'not behave in line with the tradition of the elders, but . . .'

Fourth, various Marcan interventions are visible in the calling of the crowd and the secret instruction of the disciples (Mark 7:14, 17–18a and therefore vv. 18b–23). Of the former the observation was made many years ago (Quesnell 1969: 94) that 'the crowd is called in v. 14 to hear and understand a statement (v. 15) which is to settle a dispute at which they were seemingly not present . . . and the explanation of which they do not hear (v. 17)'. Quite! With regard to the secret instruction of the disciples, which has the effect of severing everything after verse 15 from what precedes, we have already noted a typical Marcan tendency (cf. Mark 4:10; 10:10). A further Marcan intervention can be seen in the parenthesis explaining for the benefit of a gentile audience what is obviously a strange and unknown practice (7:3–4).

Finally, Mark has been thought by many (myself included) to be responsible for the phrase 'going into him' (*eisporeuomenon eis auton*, Mark 7:15), which is typical of his style. It is, however, symmetrical with 'coming out' (*ek . . . ekporeuomena*) and not alien to the discussion of the suggested effect on the eater of eating food which has *become* unclean. Probably we should retain it, but whether we do or don't probably does not make a great deal of difference.

We can now recover the approximate content of the original tradition:

> [2]Some of [Jesus'] disciples were eating with defiled hands, that is, without washing them. [5]So the Pharisees [and the scribes] asked him, 'Why do your disciples (not behave in line with the tradition of the elders but) eat with unwashed hands?' [15]He said to them, 'There is nothing outside a person that (by going in) can defile, but the things which come out are what defile.'

For the interpretation of Jesus' defining saying (Mark 7:15) it is important to engage with a recent scholarly proposal (Theissen/Merz 1998: 365–7, 394–5). The argument runs as follows:

First, the contrast set out in Mark 7:15 is not an intensification, asserting that defilement takes place *not only* by external things but *very much more* by what is within. Instead the text challenges quite fundamentally the view that external things are unclean: 'There is nothing . . . that *can* make unclean.' So it is a matter of principle, and the exclusive formulation does not allow any external uncleanness (pp. 365–6).

Second, a situation can readily be imagined in which this principle would be laid down – the context of radical discipleship, like that in which 'Leave the dead to bury their dead' operates. In this limited context 'on their travels the disciples may accept any food that is offered to them – regardless of whether it is clean or unclean, tithed or not tithed' (p. 366).

Third, the saying does not lay down a rigid behavioural norm, and someone who believes that external things do not cause uncleanness could still observe the purity laws 'out of respect for a tradition or in order to avoid scandal' (p. 366). In the light of this pragmatic strategy, the disputes after Easter remain comprehensible. The upshot of this argument is as follows:

> The commandment to love God and neighbour was the most important to [Jesus]. The unimportant commandments included those relating to cleanness; here he did not even share the underlying

'maxim' that there was external uncleanness which brought ritual separation from God. Here he abrogates a maxim of the Torah by an even more important (implicit) axiom, which has the relationship to God governed by the will of God and human beings and not by reified qualities. But here too he does not draw any conclusions about an abolition of the concrete norms of purity. They are unimportant but valid; however, they can be broken in particular instances.

To this highly nuanced and heavily qualified proposal some counter-arguments may be offered.

First, the question of inherently clean and unclean *foods* does not arise in the original version of the tradition reconstructed above. That tradition dealt not with *what* was eaten but *how* whatever was eaten was eaten. The behaviour of the travelling charismatics was indeed intended to conform to the mission charge in the tradition underlying Luke/Q 10:2–16, but it remains highly doubtful whether that Q mission charge contained the injunction to 'eat what is set before you' (Luke 10:8b). Rather, the influence of the gentile mission on Luke (Acts 10:15; 11:9; cf. 1 Cor. 10:25–7) seems to be on display.

Second, the word 'can' in the saying, 'There is nothing outside a person which *can* defile . . .' should not be over-pressed. Usage elsewhere in Mark suggests this. Jesus' wisdom-informed response to the question about non-fasting runs, 'The wedding guests *cannot* fast while the bridegroom is with them, can they?' (Mark 2:19a), but the sense is 'The wedding guests *do not* fast while the bridegroom is with them, do they?' Similarly, Jesus' comment on the non-following exorcist, 'No one who does a deed of power in my name will *be able* soon afterwards to speak evil of me' (Mark 9:39), but the sense is 'No one who does a deed of power in my name *will* soon afterwards speak evil of me.' Again, when the disciples in their perplexity respond to Jesus' saying about the difficulty of entry to the kingdom by asking, 'Who then *is able to* be saved?' (Mark 10:26), the sense is, 'Who then *will* be saved?'

So it becomes possible to return to the antithesis in Mark 7:15, to interpret it as a statement of relative importance rather than of exclusivity, and to stress the second half rather than the first. Jesus is by no means steering close to the wind of rejecting a key principle of the Torah. He may well be opposing a tendency to expand and extend biblical law (Crossley 2004: 200–204). Without disputing the notion of defilement as such he is saying that infinitely more important, and much more definitive of a person's condition, is the uncleanness that comes from inside – and here is the rub: his critics are failing to remember this truth. The position he adopts is antithetical to a current Pharisaic preoccupation, and instead it is with the prophetic succession that he appears to be aligning himself. If precedent be needed, here it is.

The famous attacks on the practice of sacrifice by Isaiah, Hosea and Amos in practice take the sacrificial system for granted at the same time as they appear to mount a root-and-branch critique of it.

In Isaiah's case, the divine repugnance for sacrifice – the sacrifices of Judah and Jerusalem, likened to Sodom and Gomorrah – provokes the call for a fundamental washing and cleansing. That cleansing is then defined:

> [16]Cease to do evil, [17]learn to do good; seek justice, rescue the oppressed, defend the orphan, plead for the widow. (Isa.1:16–17)

In Hosea's case, it is:

> I desire steadfast love and not sacrifice, the knowledge of God rather than burnt offerings. (Hos. 6:6)

In the case of Amos:

> [21]I hate, I despise your festivals, and I take no delight in your solemn assemblies. [22]Even though you offer me your burnt offerings and grain-offerings, I will not accept them . . . [24]Let justice roll down like waters, and righteousness like an everflowing stream. (Amos 5:21–4)

From Isaiah, Hosea and Amos to the historical Jesus is a very short step indeed. For all four, the problem is not the worship system but the worshippers. For the Jesus of Mark 7:15 as for the others, it is the condition of the critics which is itself subjected to such coruscating criticism and correction.

Further support for this interpretation of Mark 7:15 can be found in Matthew 23:25–6/Luke 11:39–41, the underlying Q version of which probably ran:

Woe to you, Pharisees, for you purify the outside of the cup and dish, but inside they are full of plunder and self-indulgence. Purify the inside of the cup . . . so that . . . clean.

To expend a lot of effort on interpreting the saying against the background of Pharisaic practice *vis-à-vis* the outside and inside of vessels is to some extent to miss the point. The charge that the cup and dish are full of plunder and self-indulgence is sufficient to show that a metaphorical portrayal of human beings and their preoccupation with their external washings is involved. While the wording of the final demand is difficult to recover from the varying Matthew/Luke wording, the point is clear: the cleanness of the person depends on doing something about any falling short of moral purity. When this saying is added to Mark 7:15, recourse to the criteria of multiple attestation and conformity to a prophetic profile suggests authenticity.

This brings us to the third issue, the matter of tithes. Not for nothing does a Pharisee, offering private prayer in the course of public worship, articulate his distinctive position thus: 'I fast twice a week; I give a tenth of all my income' (Luke 18:12). The first tithe, of agricultural produce (grain, wine and oil) and of flocks, was allotted to the levites (Num. 18:21–4), who in turn gave a second tithe of what they gained to the priests (Num. 18:25–32). Such tithed produce thus attained the status of 'holiness to the Lord' (Lev. 27:30–33; Judith 11:13); the 'second tithe' was set aside for the provision of celebratory meals in Jerusalem (Deut. 14:22–7). In another of the woes, further definition of Jesus' position comes to light (Matt. 23:23/Luke 11:42):

> [42a]Woe to you Pharisees, for you tithe mint, dill, and cummin, [42b]and have neglected the weightier matters of the law: justice and mercy and faithfulness. [42c]It is these you ought to have practised without neglecting the others.

We have explicit corroboration of the dill and cummin, though not the mint, in the rabbinic sources, but the three clearly serve to exemplify a tendency to extend, and explain in more and more detail, the range of the tithed produce. The essential thrust of Luke/Q 11:42ab is very much in line with the thrust of the other sayings we have assembled – acceptance of Pharisaic concerns, provided they did not substitute for the primary moral commitments of Israel. There can hardly be any commitment more central to the covenant-grounded holiness of Israel than 'justice, mercy and faithfulness'. In the view of some Q specialists Luke/Q 11:42c is a later addition, out of kilter with the surrounding traditions, and akin to the hard-line affirmation of the eternal validity of every requirement of the Torah, however small (Luke/Q 16:17, cf. Kloppenborg Verbin 2000: 152–3). This is arguably to invest in a distinction without a difference: there is nothing amiss in the careful tithing envisaged in Luke 11:42ac, the only thing wrong is the neglect of central ethical commitments in Luke 11:42bc.

In our study so far, much space has been given to the sayings of Jesus. But what about the actions of Jesus? There are several stories which suggest that the principles set out in the sayings caused serious conflict when translated into practice. One is the case of the woman with permanent vaginal bleeding (Mark 5:24–34), to which we shall turn later in another connection. Two other cases involve a leper and a man with a withered hand.

The story of the healing of a leper (Mark 1:40–45) has been significantly expanded by Mark. First, the perplexing statement that Jesus 'after sternly warning him threw him out' (1:43) assimilates the healing to an exorcism, a tendency that we see in Mark's way of telling stories elsewhere (cf. 'he rebuked the wind', 4:39). Second, the command to secrecy (1:44a) is part of Mark's whole secrecy complex. Third, the implicitly christological phrase 'as a testimony to them' is characteristically Marcan (cf. 6:11; 13:9). Fourth, the conclusion (1:45) is so typical of Mark in wording and scheme, that there must be doubt as to whether it existed before the story reached the evangelist. This enables us to distinguish the original story within the expanded version:

> [40]A leper came to [Jesus] begging him, and kneeling he said to him, 'If you choose, you can make me clean.' [41]Moved with anger, Jesus stretched out his hand and touched him, and said to him, 'I do choose. Be made clean!' [42]Immediately the leprosy left him, and he was made clean. [43]*After sternly warning him he sent him away at once,* [44a]*saying to him, 'See that you say nothing to anyone, but . . .'* [44b][He said to him], 'Go, show yourself to the priest, and offer for your cleansing what Moses commanded, *as a testimony to them.*' [45]*But he went out, and began to proclaim it freely, and to spread the*

word, so that Jesus could no longer go into a town openly, but stayed out in the country.

What is particularly interesting is not Jesus' rather surprising anger, perhaps (though we can hardly be sure) provoked more by indignation at human suffering than by anything the leper had said. It is the juxtaposition of (i) his respect for Moses, and the conformity to the letter of the requirement of the law of Leviticus 13—14, which would not only confirm the cure but re-admit the previously sick person to society, and (ii) his willingness to touch the sick person. Leprosy in the strict sense, being incurable, is probably not the problem, but rather some curable but defilement-causing kind of skin disease. On the other hand, leprosy proper, a condition which reduced such persons to living in isolation as 'solitary vagrants, with their clothes rent', was presumed at the time to be curable. After 'certain rites of purification', the cutting off of hair, and 'the offering of a numerous variety of sacrifices before entering the holy city', a return to normality was envisaged (Josephus, *Against Apion* 1:281–2). Whatever may have been the strict definition of the problem of the sufferer met by Jesus in Mark 1:40, waving the healer's hand over the spot, as Naaman had expected (2 Kings 5:11), might have sufficed. Jesus, however, actually touches him. Technically he incurs defilement. Some have suggested that by means of what he does and says to the leper Jesus gives effect to the idea of 'an offensive purity, [meaning that] purity, not impurity, was infectious' (cf. Theissen/Merz 1998: 229–30; similarly, Dunn 2002: 461: 'Jesus countered the contagion of impurity with the contagion of purity'). It is hard to be sure that the text does actually convey this idea, and it may therefore be safer to stay with the more straightforward inference that Jesus does indeed incur defilement. If so, he indicates that, when loving action is called for, a preoccupation with purity in the traditional sense does not loom large in his mission.

The healing of the man with a withered hand (Mark 3:1–5) is controversially timed. As a result an atmosphere of criticism is generated, to which a riposte is directed by Jesus: 'Is it lawful on the sabbath day to do good or to do harm, to save life or to kill?' The issue of bearing arms or responding to aggression even on the sabbath is obviously not the concern, though there may be an *ad hominem* hint of the decision that had had to be made in Maccabean times in Jesus' reference to saving life or killing (cf. 1 Macc. 2:29–41). What then follows is a skilful assimilation of 'to do good or to do harm' to the concession that the critics' own tradition had allowed: 'to save life or to kill'. And the antithesis is the key to the saying: the message is that failing to do good is in fact to do harm. According to more than one tradition (Matt. 25:41–5; Luke 10:31–2), that failure comes under judgement. In other words, divine care for human beings in need (cf. Mark 2:25–7) emerges all the more clearly because of the timing on a day when the defenders of a particular interpretation of sabbath observance would rule it out.

Jesus, the prosperous and the poor

Thus far, we have seen Jesus working within the parameters of Israel's distinctiveness and holiness – hence the instinctive negativity towards gentiles like the Syrophoenician woman. The only sign of a greater inclusiveness emerged in the traditions dealing with Samaritans – thus a willingness to draw the boundaries of the holy people as widely as possible, and certainly more widely than was customary. In respect of those laws which functioned as boundary markers or 'badges of identity', Jesus took a conservative stance and in no way undercut them, but he did formulate interpretative guidelines which gave primacy to compassion and inner purity. So those who heard and responded to his message *for Israel* were constituted by that response as *true, faithful and righteous Israel*. But, we may ask, what of those distinctions within the life of the community which were liable to effect marginalisation or relegation to second class citizenship? How did he engage with socio-economic and gender-driven distinctions?

At times Jesus sounds very much like a typical Jewish teacher of wisdom when commenting on issues of prosperity and poverty, though he avoids the typical wisdom teacher's tacit assumption of a 'from the top downwards' view of human society. The possibility of material preoccupations becoming an alternative to the service of God is memorably recalled in a reminder that 'there is more to life than food and clothing' (Luke/Q 12:23), and in the God versus mammon saying (Luke/Q 16:13). The necessity of investing, not simply and exclusively in the good things of life but rather with due recognition that God will at some stage call time, and death will place everything in perspective, is put across clearly in the parable of the rich fool (Luke 12:16–21) – itself a resounding echo of the wisdom tradition in Sirach 11:18–19:

18One becomes rich through diligence and self-denial, and the reward allotted to him is this: 19when he says, 'I have found rest, and now I will feast on my goods!' he does not know how long it will be until he leaves them to others and dies.

Sometimes a very sharp edge is given to this teaching, as when the parable of the rich man and Lazarus works with a stereotypical presentation of a self-sufficient and uncaring rich person, whose lavish lifestyle in respect of food and clothing sums up the man, and who, precisely because he is rich, comes under judgement (Luke 16:19–31).

Not that judgement is inevitable, as the story of the meeting with the rich ruler (Mark 10:17–22) confirms. As it stands at the head of an extended block of originally discrete sayings, this tradition is the introduction to bifocal coverage of riches/renunciation and following Jesus. Mark causes the thread of renunciation that runs through the fabric of 'following Jesus' traditions to become visible once more, and explicitly so. It must be admitted, however, that the words 'then come, follow me' (10:21) might be MarkR: they are very typical of Mark's presentation of discipleship (cf. 1:17–18), and the response of Jesus would end very suitably with '. . . and you will have treasure in heaven' (Barton 1994: 97).

17As he was setting out on a journey, a man ran up and knelt before him, and asked him, 'Good Teacher, what must I do to inherit eternal life?' 18Jesus said to him, 'Why do you call me good? No one is good but God alone. 19You know the commandments: "You shall not murder; You shall not commit adultery; You shall not steal; You shall not bear false witness; You shall not defraud; Honour your father and mother."' 20He said to him, 'Teacher, I have kept all these since my youth.' 21Jesus, looking at him, loved him and said, 'You lack one thing; go, sell what you own, and give the money to the poor, and you will have treasure in heaven; *then come, follow me.*' 22When he heard this, he was shocked and went away grieving, for he had many possessions.

This story raises a question in respect of historicity: the questioner asks about inheriting eternal life, which is odd in view of the common conviction that, apart from some notorious exceptions, 'all Israelites have a share in the world to come' (*m. Sanhedrin* 10:1). On the other hand, (i) Jesus' unnecessary detour querying the assumption of his own goodness is unlikely to be an early Christian creation; (ii) the notion of alms-giving bringing heavenly treasure for the giver is well established in Judaism, for which point of view Tobit may act as a mouthpiece: 'If you have many possessions, make your gift from them in proportion . . . so you will be laying up a good treasure for yourself against the day of necessity' (Tobit 4:8–9); (iii) the affirmation of the Decalogue is, as we have seen, in harmony with Jesus' attitude to the Mosaic law; and (iv) the pattern of voluntary poverty not only fits Jesus' attitude in principle to both poor and rich (cf. Mark 10:23, 25; Luke 12:15–21; 16:19–31) but also corresponds with the actual position of his disciples (cf. their resort to 'gleaning', Mark 2:23–8). Application of the criteria of embarrassment and coherence supports historicity.

Not surprisingly, the danger of general preoccupation with the ordinary affairs of life is especially highlighted with reference to the prospect of God's kingly rule. Thus, it is almost impossibly hard for a rich person to experience the kingdom of God (Mark 10:23, 25). And, in another arresting complex of sayings, the innocent preoccupations of the contemporaries of Jesus are fused with recollections of what happened to some anything but innocent sinners, the generations of Noah and Lot. All this is part of an insistence on the need for genuine openness to the intervention of God, which will otherwise spell disaster (Luke/Q 17:26–30):

> [26]As it was in the days of Noah, so will it be in the days of the Son of Man: [27]they ate, drank, married, were given in marriage, until the day when Noah went into the ark, and the flood came and caused them all to perish. [28]Similarly, as it was in the days of Lot: they ate, they drank, they bought, they sold, they planted, they built, [29]but on the day when Lot went out from Sodom, it rained fire and sulphur from heaven, and caused them all to perish. [30]It will be exactly like that on the day when the Son of Man is revealed.

This tradition may well have been edited in order to centre the future expectation on the Son of Man – understood, of course, to be Jesus – rather than, in line with Jesus' own norm, the 'kingdom of God'. The term 'Son of Man' here stands for one person alone rather than a group, and is out of line with normal Aramaic usage (Casey 1987: 36). So if 'Son of Man' belongs to the earliest stage of the material's history, that material is likely to be unhistorical. But if at the earliest stage the 'kingdom of God' were the term used, the matter can remain open. Then the sayings can be recognised as unusually striking, especially when set alongside, compared and contrasted with, a small collection of texts in Jewish literature where the examples of Noah and Lot are cited (cf. Catchpole 1993: 247–52). Wisdom 10:3–4, 6–8 sets Noah and Lot in a sequence of notable persons who were rescued by wisdom. According to Sirach 16:7–8 the flood generation and the Sodomites head the list of those whose misdeeds brought upon them the fiery judgement of God. In 3 Maccabees 2:4–5 the flood and the destruction of Sodom exemplify the dire prospects awaiting the exponents of injustice, vice and pride:

> [4]You destroyed those who in the past committed injustice, among whom were even giants who trusted in their strength and boldness, whom you destroyed by bringing on them a boundless flood. [5]You consumed with fire and sulphur the people of Sodom who acted arrogantly, who were notorious for their vices; and you made them an example to those who should come afterwards.

Into the mouth of Abraham, the author of *Jubilees*, probably writing in the mid-second century BCE, places dire warnings against apostasy and fornication:

> [5]And he told them the judgement of the giants and the judgements of the Sodomites just as they had been judged on account of their evil. And on account of their fornication and impurity and the corruption among themselves with fornication they died. [6]'And you guard yourself from all fornication and impurity, and from all corruption of sin, so that you might not make our name a curse . . . And you will be cursed like Sodom, and all your remnant like the sons of Gomorrah.' (20:5–6)

No less trenchant is the *Testament of Naphtali* 3:4–5:

> [4]In the firmament, in the earth, and in the sea, in all the products of his workmanship, discern the Lord who made all things, so that you do not become like Sodom, which departed from the order of nature. [5]Likewise the Watchers departed from the order of nature; the Lord

pronounced a curse on them at the Flood. On their account he
ordered that the earth be without dweller or produce.

Interestingly, Josephus seems to be aware of such a classic combination of
judgement precedents. Commenting on the sacrilege perpetrated by
John of Gischala and his associates, he wrote:

> Nor can I here refrain from uttering what my emotion bids me say. I
> believe that, had the Romans delayed to punish these reprobates, either
> the earth would have opened and swallowed up the city, or it would
> have been swept away by a flood, or have tasted anew the thunderbolts
> of the land of Sodom. For it produced a generation far more godless
> than the victims of these visitations, seeing that these men's frenzy
> involved the whole people in their ruin. (*Jewish War* 5:566)

The first example, drawing on Numbers 16:32, is out of biblical order,
thus leaving the other two from Genesis 7 and 19 as a consecutive
pairing of classic examples of divine judgement.

The exercise of comparison and contrast between these texts, bringing
to light an established tradition of interpretation, and Luke/Q 17:26–30
is revealing. All of them are, fairly obviously, judgement texts. Moreover,
the reasons for divine judgement are normally set out explicitly and
baldly. But here we run up against an oddity in the Jesus tradition. What
is wrong with 'eating, drinking, marrying and being given in marriage',
as in the setting of Noah? Answer: Absolutely nothing. Or again, what is
open to criticism in 'eating and drinking, buying and selling, planting and
building' in the context of Lot? Answer again: Absolutely nothing. In
support we may cite the instructions to the exiles via Jeremiah:

> [4]Thus says the Lord of hosts, the God of Israel, to all the exiles whom
> I have sent into exile from Jerusalem to Babylon: [5]Build houses and
> live in them; plant gardens and eat what they produce. [6]Take wives and
> have sons and daughters; take wives for your sons, and give your
> daughters in marriage, that they may bear sons and daughters; multiply
> there, and do not decrease. (Jer. 29:4–6)

All those activities are represented here and repeatedly elsewhere in the
literature as wholly innocent and unexceptional; none of them are

grounds for judgement – yet the contemporaries of Noah and Lot were commonly characterised by deviant and notoriously non-innocent activities, and so they went down in history as classic recipients of judgement! The explanation for the so-called oddity would seem to be somewhat as follows.

First, an exceptionally daring and creative handling of the Old Testament texts is taking place, which in turn means an original mind is at work. Second, before the warning based on the contemporaries of Noah/Lot can be conveyed to the speaker's audience, observable facets of the speaker's audience are being superimposed on the Noah/Lot contemporaries. The innocent contemporaries of the speaker are in consequence not faced with judgement for infamous amoral behaviour or religious apostasy: in spite of their pursuit of entirely honourable activities they face judgement. And the only explanation that in any way coheres with echoes of Jesus' prophetic preaching elsewhere is that openness to the coming judge, that is to say, God, is not forthcoming from those who are wholly taken up with the concerns of present social, economic and domestic life. In other words, the call of the prophetic gospel of Jesus is a call for detachment from those concerns which, encouraged by the wisdom tradition, constitute the standard formulae of wellbeing and prosperity.

That being so, the critique of the norms that most would take for granted almost inevitably encourages the inference that it will be the theme of poverty that points up Jesus' priorities with special clarity.

Q set the beatitudes, the first of which says something about poverty, at the start of Jesus' teaching (Matt. 5:3–12/Luke 6:20b–23). Luke not only moved Jesus' visit to Nazareth and made it inaugurate Jesus' public ministry (Luke 4:16–30/Mark 6:1–6) but also put into Jesus' mouth on that occasion a claim to be the Spirit-anointed preacher of the gospel for the poor. Both Q and Luke assuredly made a correct judgement as to the centre of gravity of Jesus' prophetic message (cf. Catchpole 1993: 81–6). So a rapid process of reconstruction of the original tradition, so that we may hear the more clearly the voice of Jesus himself, is apropos.

First, of the eight short beatitudes in Matthew, three have parallels in Luke, four articulate favourite Matthean themes, and one acts as a bridge-type transition to the long beatitude for the persecuted followers of Jesus. All but the three Matthew/Luke sayings are best attributed to Matthean editorial work.

Second, the sayings Matthew has created are all about praiseworthy human qualities. And the same is true of Matthew's version of the three that are shared with Luke. But in Luke all three short beatitudes are about human problems, from which release is needed. This suggests that Matthew has assimilated and edited these three sayings to bring them into line with his overall concern in this block of material. This means that the original versions of the sayings dealt with 'the poor . . . the hungry . . . those who [weep]'.

Third, Matthew preserved the original wording of the saying about those who weep. There are two reasons for saying this. (i) The terms 'mourn . . . comfort' appear in the adjacent Lucan woes (Luke 6:24, 25b), as well as in Matthew 5:4. Therefore they were probably present here in Q. (ii) Luke's version, by using the language of laughter, taps into a strong biblical tradition of laughter as a sign, not of innocent humour or joy but of triumph over opponents (cf. Job 22:19; Ps. 2:4; Jer. 20:7). That is doubtless why Luke places this beatitude third in the sequence. He wants to achieve a smooth transition into the long beatitude about the persecuted followers of Jesus.

Fourth, Matthew's third-person form is probably original over against Luke's second-person form, since it makes for a less smooth transition from the short sayings to the long one.

Fifth, the final long beatitude is probably a later addition at the editorial stage in Q, for three reasons: (i) it follows the rough transition; (ii) it is much longer; and (iii) it is explicitly Christian, whereas the three short sayings are not explicitly Christian at all.

Sixth, since the poor are often marked out in biblical tradition as grief-stricken (Sir. 4:1–2; 7:32–4; 38:19) and hungry (Prov. 22:9; Sir. 4:1; 34:25), the three short sayings emerge as three variations on a single theme. This fact in turn helps to explain two other features. (i) There appears to be a discrepancy between the verb in the present tense in the first saying, and the verbs in the future tense in the other two. But the use of present tenses to convey future meaning in Semitic languages suggests that the first saying should come alongside the other two by being interpreted as '. . . theirs *will be* the kingdom of God'. (ii) The first saying refers to God explicitly, whereas the others do not. But by using 'divine passives', they do so implicitly. God's action is involved throughout. The original pre-Q tradition now comes to light:

20bBlessed are the poor, for theirs is [i.e. will be] the kingdom of God.

21aBlessed are the mourners, for they will be comforted [i.e. by God].

21bBlessed are the hungry, for they will be filled [i.e. by God].

There can be little doubt that, as in the reply of Jesus to John that 'the poor have good news brought to them' (Luke/Q 7:22), this summary is intended as an activation of Isaiah 61:1–3:

> 1The Spirit of the Lord God is upon me, because the Lord has anointed me; he has sent me to bring good news to the poor, to bind up the broken-hearted, to proclaim liberty to the captives, and release to the prisoner; 2to proclaim the year of the Lord's favour, and the day of vengeance of our God; to comfort all who mourn; 3to provide for those who mourn in Zion . . .

It is important to remember that the essence of 'poverty' is not *primarily* humility or poverty of spirit. That would enable the economically prosperous to lodge a paradoxical claim to poverty, and in terms of the rich/poor stereotypes that is just not possible. The poor may *secondarily* be humble and poor in spirit, because in their distress and dependence they have no one to turn to other than God. But that is, as it were, an extension of meaning. The essence of poverty is rather powerlessness, vulnerability, deprivation, liability to exploitation and injustice, as part of which material poverty may figure. It is a social, political and economic condition, which *may* and *should* give rise to spiritual dependence.

As far as poverty and the Jewish nation are concerned, there are two key perspectives that now need to be borne in mind. (i) The poor as a group *within* Israel are just as liable as the poor in any other nation to be despised, marginalised and treated as if they do not really belong. They have no power. In no sense do they make the running in society. The announcement of a gospel for the poor will therefore envisage their rescue from powerlessness and injustice. For the first time they will count. That effectively confirms that they are just as much at the heart of, and essential to, the nation as any other group. A gospel for the poor is a gospel about the wholeness of the nation. (ii) The poor may, since the essence of poverty is powerlessness, come *to stand for* Israel, especially when she is suffering at the hands of other nations. A gospel for the poor is in these circumstances a gospel about the freedom of the nation to be itself, the people of God living in freedom and justice under God.

The position is well illustrated by the concept of the poor in the (probably Pharisaic, Jerusalem-based, first-century BCE) Psalms of Solomon, to which we turned when exploring the standard resonance of the term 'sinners'.

In the 5th psalm the psalmist acknowledges God as 'the shelter of the poor' (v. 2), and the psalmist cries out in prayer as a representative of that group looking for restoration. Although a part of Israel, the psalmist clearly regards himself as representative of the whole of Israel, suffering under the alien yoke of Pompey, and painting a self-descriptive picture of himself as poor, hungry, needy and humble:

> [8]If I am hungry, I will cry out to you, O God, and you will give me [something]. [9]You feed the birds and the fish, as you send rain to the wilderness that the grass may sprout [10]to provide pasture in the wilderness for every living thing, and if they are hungry, they will lift up their face to you. [11]You feed kings and rulers and peoples, O God, and who is the hope of the poor and needy, if not you, Lord? [12]And you will listen. For who is good and kind but you, making the humble person happy by opening your hand in mercy? . . . [18]Those who fear the Lord are happy with good things. In your kingdom, your goodness [is] upon Israel. [19]May the glory of the Lord be praised, for he is our king.

In similar vein, in the 10th psalm God is confidently expected to be 'merciful to the poor to the joy of Israel' (v. 6). The 18th psalm affirms that 'your ears listen to the hopeful prayer of the poor' (v. 3), equates the poor with Israel, and defines their future hope thus: 'a cleansing of Israel for the day of mercy in blessing, for the appointed day when his Messiah will reign' (v. 5).

This use of the idea of poverty to characterise a whole people, and in particular the circle of those represented by the psalmist(s), is on a direct trajectory from Isaiah 61:1–3 itself. There the concerns are manifestly 'the concrete issues of a community in trouble' and 'Yahweh's deeply transformative response work in the community of his people'. This involves 'powerful ministries to the weak, the powerless and the marginalized to restore them to full function in a community of well-being and joy'. This 'rehabilitation of life out of impoverishment, powerlessness and despair' has two aspects: first, 'the restoration of land, security, stability and well-being to *the community as a whole* of Jews too long in jeopardy, that is, community-wide restoration' and, second, 'the reordering of the internal economics of the community, an adjudication of the social relationships between the haves and the have-nots' (Brueggemann 1998: 212–14).

Jesus' deliberate echoing of Isaiah 61:1–3 sets his mission in the mainstream of this Zion-centred hope of Israel. Each of the two levels of meaning is vital. There is a concern for Israel in its wholeness – a wholeness of powerlessness and vulnerability – which cannot but involve political transformation. There is also the necessary corollary of concern for that part of Israel that is specially powerless and vulnerable, that is to say, the socio-economically disadvantaged. For today the poor remain poor, but (as has been said) they are promised a better tomorrow, and such a promise is 'gospel/good news'. For today the key person is the messenger of good news, the Spirit-anointed prophet; for tomorrow the key person will be the royal appointee, the messianic king who will rule in Zion over a people assembled from the farthest corners of the globe.

It is hard to resist the inference that when Jesus and his followers set out for Jerusalem, and when a formal procession of entry was arranged as he approached the city, the thought in both his mind and theirs was that the era of messianic rule and restoration for the whole people, the era of release and restoration for the marginalised and powerless among the people, was about to begin.

Jesus the man and the women

If poverty is about powerlessness and vulnerability, dependence and subordination, then that topic leads naturally into a consideration of the position and status of women, both in the immediate setting of the Jesus people and in the future setting of God's kingly rule. According to one writer:

> The Palestinian culture was one of the most patriarchal in the Mediterranean crescent. The home and family were basically the only spheres where women could play significant roles in early Judaism. (Witherington 1992: 957)

And as has truly been said, patriarchal structures and poverty are two sides of the same coin, and 'in antiquity widows and orphans were the prime paradigms of the poor and exploited' (Schüssler-Fiorenza 1999: 140–41). So, given that in Jesus traditions women, notably widows, often serve as the embodiment of poverty (cf. Mark 12:41–4; Luke 18:2–8a), it would not be surprising if the outcomes of such consideration were, first, that the status of women in contemporary society remained unchanged by Jesus' mission, in just the same way as the poor remained poor; second, that women were given a foretaste of the healing power of God's kingship; third, that the prospect for women in the new era, once it had arrived, was for a position wholly the reverse of the present, in short their being promised a better tomorrow as well. That would, however, fall some way short of saying that 'Jesus was a reformer of a patriarchal society' (Witherington 1992: 959).

We come back to the experience of involvement in the community of Jesus people, both female and male. For those women who became his followers, the step of commitment must have been determined by the atmosphere created by his contacts with women other than those who became followers, and also by the general tenor of sayings alluding to women.

The historical Jesus did not scruple to touch a leper, and thereby technically incur uncleanness from someone whose condition, according to some texts, made him little different from the dead (Mark 1:40–45). Equally, his treatment of the woman with permanent vaginal bleeding (5:24–34) is thought-provoking.

Mark takes pains to convey by a series of hints how totally intractable this woman's situation was – in much the same way as he took care to leave his readers in no doubt that anything that could possibly be done to 'solve' the problem of legion had indeed been done, and had spectacularly failed (Mark 5:3–5). With the total failure of the medical profession, which puts her in the same situation as the unfortunate Tobit (Tobit 2:10), only worse in view of the defilement caused by bleeding, and the exhaustion of her finances, the woman's dilemma is deep and insoluble.

In detail, her condition was one of permanent and defiling uncleanness (cf. Lev. 15:19–31). One cannot exaggerate the serious implications of this condition. 'She was not only defiled, she defiled anything and anyone she touched. Her illness left her personally, socially and spiritually cut off' (Guelich 1989: 296). Illustrating 'the economic impoverishment of the incurably ill' (Schüssler-Fiorenza 1999: 124), she invested her last despairing hope in Jesus. In doing so she worked with the ancient view that through physical contact transcendent power may be conveyed to the otherwise hopelessly weak and sick.

Her hope was not disappointed. Contact with Jesus proved truly transformative. But his contact with her would require him to wash afterwards. Doubtless we should assume that such washing did subsequently take place (Fredriksen 2000: 200), and not assume on the basis of an unsafe *argumentum e silentio* that it did not. That was, after all, what the holiness of the people of God was about (Lev. 15:31). The uncleanness question, which runs like an unspoken thread through the fabric of the story, is however simply not the main item on Jesus' agenda. Instead there is an affirmation of salvation and wholeness, prefaced by the intensely meaningful word 'Daughter' (Mark 5:34).

When, assuming the story is historical, Jesus moves on to touch and heal the daughter of the synagogue president (Mark 5:21-3, 35-43), the same subordination of concern about uncleanness (cf. Num. 19:11-13) to the priority of responding to human need is on display. These two stories, interwoven with one another in Mark 5:21-43, may owe their juxtaposition to one of Mark's favourite story-telling 'sandwich structures', but it is hard to resist the possibility of genuine reminiscence of Jesus' own strategy: after 12 years the one person resumes, and the other enters upon, the experience of whole and adult womanhood as designed by the creator.

From here we go to the multiply attested use of women as role models in sayings of Jesus. This undoubtedly puts us in touch with an authentic feature of his approach. The widow seeking vindication (Luke 18:2-8a) is a representative figure with whom Israel can identify. The home-based woman whose coin is lost models the mission strategy of Jesus just as much as the shepherd does (Luke 15:4-10). From the cooking of the home-based woman, just as much as from the gardening activity of the man planting mustard seed, something can be deduced about the universal scope of God's kingly rule (Luke/Q 13:18-21). Perhaps the most outstanding of all such man/woman pairings is Luke/Q 11:31-2:

> [31]The queen of the south will rise at the judgement with this generation and will condemn it, because she came from the ends of the earth to listen to the wisdom of Solomon, and see, something greater than

Solomon is here! [32]The people of Nineveh will rise up at the judgement with this generation and condemn it, because they repented at the proclamation of Jonah, and see, something greater than Jonah is here!

The 'something greater' is likely, in spite of the time of judgement's being still future, to be God's kingly rule. The presence of the kingdom provides an even greater reason than usual to attend to the ministry of the prophet and sage who is at work in Israel. As far as the proclamation of the contemporary prophet(s) is concerned, those who attend responsively are declared to be the 'children of Wisdom' (Luke/Q 7:35; cf. Sir. 39:13). As far as the wisdom of the contemporary sage – to be distinguished sharply from the sages to whom the present heavenly revelation is not disclosed – a comparison with earlier wisdom sayings about women reveals striking correspondences but at the same time a massively striking difference.

First, the correspondences: The parable of the widow seeking justice (Luke 18:2–8a) recalls Sirach 21:3; 35:17:

> The prayer of the poor goes from their lips to the ears of God, and his judgement comes speedily . . . God will not ignore the supplication of the orphan, or of the widow when she pours out her complaint.

The warning against adultery (Matt. 5:28) recalls Sirach 9:5, 8 (cf. also Prov. 6:25; Sir. 41:21):

> [5]Do not look intently at a virgin,
> or you may stumble and incur penalties for her . . .
> [8]Turn away your eyes from a shapely woman,
> and do not gaze at beauty belonging to another.

The demand to hold back from divorcing a wife (Mark 10:9) matches, at least to an extent, Sirach 7:26:

> Do you have a wife who pleases you? Do not divorce her.

Second, the non-correspondences: Nowhere in the sayings of Jesus – and this is no weak *argumentum e silentio* – nowhere do we find ourselves listening to wise sayings extolling a happy marriage and a steady wife

(Prov. 18:22; 31:10–31; Sir. 36:29). Nor do we hear the faintest whisper of a thought about women seductively fanning the flames of sexual desire in the hearts of men (Prov. 6:27; 7:10–23), and leading intelligent men astray (Sir. 19:2); women as the source of the evil in the world (Sir. 25:24); women as responsible for shame and disgrace (Sir. 42:13–14); women as desperate to marry and therefore willing to accept any man as a husband, by contrast with men's freedom to choose from a number of possible partners (Sir. 36:26). Nothing reminds us of the prolonged list of anxieties that a father (*sic*) has to cope with: when young a woman may not marry; when married she may be disliked; when a virgin she may be seduced and become pregnant; when married she may go astray or have no children (Sir. 42:9–10) – from this amazing catalogue of risk the message seems to be that the only safe woman is a sexually *passée* widow of sufficient maturity to have no thought of marriage!

In similar vein, the traditions dealing with divorce deviate from the common assumption that adultery is an act directed only against a husband. The earliest version of the multiply attested tradition about remarriage probably survived in Luke/Q 16:18:

> 18aAnyone who divorces his wife and marries another commits adultery, 18band whoever marries a woman divorced from her husband commits adultery.

This saying, when set alongside Mark 10:9, with which it cannot harmonise if it is taken to be a law, is not a law – not a law but a demand! It makes the conventional assumptions about the divorce process, that is, that only the husband can initiate it. But adultery turns out to be an offence defined by a different yardstick from that provided by law. It is an offence against the divorced wife and is committed by the remarrying husband (Luke/Q 16:18a). It is not just an offence against a married man. From the symmetry of the saying we can infer that as a wronged (divorced) person the former wife has exactly the same and equal status as a wronged (divorcing) husband.

What then of the debate about divorce itself, with its concluding demand not to engage in divorce? This has important implications not only for the experience and status of women but also in relation to the issue of whether Jesus stood foursquare within the sphere of Moses' authority. For some, this tradition is one of the few which document a tendency on his part to relativise the authority of the Torah. Its appeal to the principles of the creation has then been understood as an investment in the Jewish scheme which matches the final era to the first — *Endzeit* renewing *Urzeit* (Allison 2005: 185–91). Thus:

> The law, designed for the ordinary purposes of life, cannot be un-affected by the coming of God's reign, which brings the extraordinary. If the kingdom is at hand, then the renewal of the world is nigh, then paradise is about to be restored; and if paradise is about to be restored, then concessions to sin should no longer be needed. This is certainly the implicit logic of Mark 10:1–12. (Allison 2005: 186)

With that thought in mind, we turn to the tradition itself:

> [2]Some Pharisees came, and to test him they asked, 'Is it lawful for a man to divorce his wife?' [3]He answered them, 'What did Moses command you?' [4]They said, 'Moses allowed a man to write a certificate of dismissal and to divorce her.' [Deut. 24:1] [5]But Jesus said to them, 'With your hardness of heart in view he wrote this commandment for you. [6]But from the beginning of creation, "God made them male and female." [Gen. 1:27] [7]"For this reason a man shall leave his father and mother and be joined to his wife, [8]and the two shall become one flesh." [Gen. 2:24] So they are no longer two, but one flesh. [9]Therefore what God has joined together, let no one separate.' (Mark 10:2–9)

This debate must first be considered in terms of its shape/structure. In a remarkable way its form matches the typical form of a rabbinic (Pharisaic) discussion about the interpretation and application of a law: (i) The topic/question under discussion is introduced (thus v. 2). (ii) Someone introduces a biblical text which should answer the question (thus v. 4, quoting Deut. 24:1). (iii) Someone else relativises the effect of that biblical text by indicating that it belongs only in a very specific context and cannot be the basis for a general rule (thus v. 5: 'with your hardness of heart in view'). (iv) Someone introduces a different biblical text which can (arguably) be interpreted as the basis for a general rule (thus vv. 6–8a, 8b, quoting Gen. 1:27; 2:24). (v) The final ruling, based on the preceding argument, is formulated (thus v. 9).

What can we deduce from this Marcan unit, with its concluding declaration? First, as it stands, the logic of the wording of its conclusion should be carefully noted: it does not say 'what God has joined together, no one *can* separate' (i.e. indissolubility, and a clash with Moses) but 'what God has joined together, *let* no one separate' (i.e. dissolubility, and no clash with Moses).

Second, given the structural parallel with rabbinic discussions, it is additionally clear that no clash with Moses is envisaged: Deuteronomy 24:1 is relativised and set within a defined context, but it is not abrogated. The implication of non-abrogation is that Jesus would, like everyone else, need at some stage to state a view about the meaning of 'something objectionable in her' (Deut. 24:1), but in this context he is not entering into such detail. But there is one detail over which he does seem to pause. In the discussion there is a deliberate movement from what is 'allowed' (v. 4), that is to say, divorce as such (thus responding to the question asked, v. 2), to what is 'commanded', that is to say, the writing of 'a certificate of dismissal' (v. 5). That is particularly important for women: the Mosaic legislation may have been heavily conditioned by the holiness principle, but it also imposed an obligation on a husband which was also a protection for his wife. Jesus underlines that obligation.

Third, the key passage, upon which the 'new' conclusion is based, is Genesis 1:27. The other Genesis saying, 2:24, is introduced in order to say, in effect, that marriage is the means to achieving that *divinely created unity* of which Genesis 1:27 speaks. Of course, one might ask whether that is what Genesis 1:27 is saying! Is it not talking about humankind as the creator designed it and as it is experienced – that is, *gender-differentiated* humankind? One strand of ancient Jewish interpretation of Genesis 1:27, which might be invoked, is summed up as 'the image of the androgyne' (Meeks 1983: 88, 155) – that is, a two-in-one, male-cum-female being. Is that how marriage is seen as a counterpart or realisation?

What then of the suggestion (Allison 2005: 191) that the appeal to the created order draws on an *Endzeit-Urzeit* correspondence and makes a portion of the law irrelevant in practice? One has, with respect, to register hesitation and doubt. For this is only one of several occasions when Jesus appeals to the created order, and these look more like evidence of a creation-defined spirituality than of an end-time-conditioned vision – not, I hasten to add, that Jesus in general lacks such a vision. The created order enables people to observe the unchanging evidence of indiscriminate sunshine and rain (Matt. 5:45), and to remember the permanent divine provision for ravens (Luke/Q 12:24) as the psalmist had done (Ps. 147:9) and much as Rabbi Simeon ben Eleazar had, without needing any end-time concept, done (*m. Kiddushin 4:14*: see above, pp. 74–5). It alerts people to the underlying reason for the provision of the sabbath (Mark 2:27: cf. Gen. 2:1–3 after 1:26–7) and thus to the need to resist an extension of biblical law. That sabbath order, with which Jesus' disciples align themselves, is intended *for all time* since creation and not just for the special time when paradise is about to be restored. And when we return to the use of Genesis 1:27 in Mark 10:6, we recall a similar appeal to that text in the Qumran critique of polygamy, 'The builders of the wall . . . are caught twice in fornication: by taking two wives in their lives, even though the principle of creation is "male and female he created them"' (*CD* 4:19–21). There have to be special and clear reasons for giving a paradise-type connotation to an appeal to Genesis 1:27.

Fourth, historical doubts have often been raised over Mark 10:2–9 as a whole. Thus, would the Pharisees have asked Jesus for a ruling on the principle of divorce (unless they were not serious, which we must assume they were) when Moses had said it all? And the very academic exchange set out in Mark 10:2–9 is not what we are used to finding in the historical Jesus tradition. As a context in which Jesus sets out his declaration of the will of God, it is unusual. But whether or not the tradition of the debate as a whole is historical, there is no doubt that the climactic declaration in Mark 10:9 does not depend upon it. So it can be considered in its own right, and at the same time be related to the remarriage saying in Luke/Q 16:18. According to this saying, (i) marriage is a divine creation, which (ii) *should not* be dismantled. According to Luke/Q 16:18, marriage *cannot* be dissolved. Put the two sayings together, using the notion of social function, according to which the overarching purpose is what matters while the way of expressing that purpose may vary, and that overarching purpose seems to be an emphatic assertion of the dignity of the marriage relationship, and a demand – not, let it be repeated, a law – that it should be preserved. Precedent for the implied critical divine attitude to divorce can be found in, say, Malachi 2:16: '"For I hate divorce", says the Lord of hosts.' So a clash with Moses? No! A *legal* prohibition of divorce? No! A full-hearted affirmation that 'marriages are made in heaven'? Yes! A concern to protect the rights and extend the status of a woman? Yes, and yes again!

This is the point at which to notice that a specially striking expression of the inclusiveness of Jesus' mission as far as women are concerned emerges in references to prostitutes. In this he is the true successor of John the Baptist. Involvement with prostitutes is a sign of alienation, of abandonment of commitment to the holy people of God, and when the prodigal son becomes involved with them (Luke 15:13, 30) there is only one way out, that is, repentance (15:18). Ex-prostitutes, who were receptive to the message of the kingdom, were among those made welcome at Jesus' meals – with devastating consequences for his reputation. The evidence is to be found in Matthew 21:28–31, 32 and Luke 7:29–30.

> 28'What do you think? A man had two sons; he went to the first and said, "Son, go and work in the vineyard today." 29He answered, "I will not"; but later he changed his mind and went. 30The father went to the second and said the same; and he answered, "I go, sir"; but he did not go. 31Which of the two did the will of his father?' They said, 'The first.' Jesus said to them, 'Truly I tell you, the tax-collectors and the prostitutes are going into the kingdom of God ahead of you. 32*For John came to you in the way of righteousness and you did not believe him, but the tax-collectors and the prostitutes believed him; and even after you saw it, you did not change your minds and believe him . . .'*

> 29And all the people who heard this, including the tax-collectors, righteoused God, because they had been baptized with John's baptism. 30But by refusing to be baptized by him, the Pharisees and the lawyers rejected God's purpose for themselves.

The analysis of these obviously related traditions can proceed as follows:

First, Matthew's parable, which has certain similarities with Luke's parable of the prodigal son (Luke 15:11–32), clearly ends after verse 31: the punchline in that verse is complete and needs no amplification. That punchline is notable for singling out the two associated groups, widely despised as a matter of principle, and affirming that they are showing the way to others *vis-à-vis* entry to the kingdom. That way can only be the way of repentance, as exhibited in the parable itself.

Second, the parable and its punchline contain no reference to John the Baptist. But the addition of 21:32 to the parable is of a piece with Matthew's editorial plan of attaching 21:28–32 to the preceding material. That material covers the debate about the authority of Jesus, which he turns into a debate about the authority of John (Matt. 21:23–27/Mark 11:27–33). Some of the language of the debate, most notably the idea of believing in John (cf. Mark 11:31/Matt. 21:25), and some of the language of the parable, most notably the 'changing of mind' (Matt. 21:29), may well have penetrated the saying added in Matthew 21:32. But that saying still contains sufficient overlap with Luke 7:29–30 and the Q context in which it is set, to justify the conclusion that a Q tradition is the source. As well as the agreement in referring to John, the reception he was given by tax-collectors, the theme of righteousness, and the rejection he received from others, there are connections (i) between 'the way' and Q 7:27, 'my messenger . . . shall prepare your *way* before you', (ii) between how John 'came' and Luke/Q 7:33, 'John *came* . . .'; (iii) between the rare use of the verb 'to righteous' with a human subject in Luke 7:29 and Luke/Q 7:35, 'Wisdom is *righteoused* by her children'; and (iv) between the prostitutes and the group represented in Luke's mind by 'the sinful woman of the city', whose story is told immediately afterwards in Luke 7:36–50.

Third, once the decision has been made that Matthew 21:32/Luke 7:29–30 had a Q archetype, we can infer from Luke's normal practice in handling his sources that the archetype occupied the Lucan position. It is harder to decide whether it was in speech or narrative form. What we can say is that it picked up the immediately preceding strong endorsement of John by Jesus in the pre-Q stratum (Luke/Q 7:24–6, 28) before that was overlaid by a Q-editorial stratum subordinating John to Jesus (Luke/Q 7:27). It also prepared for the ironically true criticism of Jesus himself that in his fellowship meals he showed himself to be 'a friend of tax-collectors and sinners' (Luke/Q 7:34).

Fourth, in terms of the criteria of authenticity, the theme of openness to tax-collectors and prostitutes has thus been attested in both Matthew 21:28–31 and Luke/Q 7:29–30. And since prostitution, normally a female problem in biblical tradition, is a problem of poverty as well as morality, the inclusive gospel of the poor once again comes into focus. In the teeth of criticism from 'the righteous', who see Jesus' behaviour as that of the stubborn and rebellious son who mixes with distinctly doubtful company, Jesus himself will not be deterred, nor will he be restricted.

Polarities in resurrection perspective

The world of the historical Jesus, like most worlds before and since, was a world of flourishing polarities – holiness/separation versus assimilation, Jew versus alleged (Samaritan) or actual (gentile) non-Jew, the righteous versus the sinner, the rich versus the poor, men versus women. Not all polarities could possibly be abandoned, but all could, and emphatically should, be assessed. The religious mind, conditioned by resurrection, is obliged to engage, both personally and communally, in searching self-criticism in the face of such polarities. Christians cannot but belong to a culture, but no culture can expect to be unreservedly confirmed and affirmed by the post-resurrection, anti-discriminatory gospel. The people of God are now to be defined, not by differentiation and exclusivity but by inclusiveness. The worst thing that can happen is that the resurrection should somehow, by twisted logic and lack of insight into the very newness of the new post-resurrection world, be seen as endorsing the parameters of the old pre-resurrection world. Sometimes that will even involve standing over against the position of the historical Jesus.

The recurrent themes in all our present study has been the search for the wholeness of the people of God, a wholeness in which every person shares. That wholeness imparts dignity to each and every individual person, irrespective of whatever divisive influences may threaten to diminish or disadvantage them. The definition of the people of God is throughout a traditional one – the people of God as the Jewish people, the covenant people, holy people, people related to God and therefore obliged to match his defining qualities of holiness and righteousness. Occasionally there are hints of boldness in crossing the lines of conventional holiness-inspired taboos, but on the whole the Jesus who confronts the traditional norms is a conservative. On occasion, however much it goes against the grain, that conservative Jesus can even appear as a prejudiced Jesus, treating a harassed gentile woman with anything but compassion. Consequently, it is as well that the resurrection requires us to make decisions about (i) the extent of direct continuity from the historical Jesus to the Easter Jesus, (ii) which interpretation of the Easter Jesus we wish to acknowledge, and (iii) which comes to the same thing, which definition of the people of God we will adopt as the basis of our theology and ethics.

In the end, as indicated more than once previously, I believe we have no choice but to give our vote to the programme and manifesto of Paul! His was not the only interpretation of resurrection, but no interpretation other than his was responsible for bringing us to where we are as participants in a faith which is both universal and non-discriminatory. Under his influence – not that of his theologically energetic but doggedly conservative opponents – we are able to focus our understanding of the people of God not on covenant but on creation. We can work with and from the wholeness of humankind rather than the wholeness of the Jewish people over against the rest of humankind. We can work from the person of the risen Christ as the embodiment of a new and undivided humankind, and the Christian community as the effective realisation of that great hope. Insofar as the historical Jesus stayed with division, there is a discrepancy between him and the newness of resurrection life. Insofar as he began to open up tendencies toward the overcoming of division, there is a line of continuity between him and the resurrected one.

CHAPTER 5

Place and people in jeopardy: echoes of Jeremiah

Introduction

Our studies so far have kept on returning to the theme of prophecy – John and Jesus as prophets – prophets who were inspired by prophets – prophets in relation to their communities – prophets who disturbed the comfortable, and brought comfort to the disturbed. These considerations bring us, for reasons that will become clear, to the theme of Jesus and the Temple, that most holy of holy places for all members of the community of Israel. They also sharpen our awareness of how more than one of the prophets of Israel provided a model for, and exerted an influence on, the consciousness of Jesus. Second Isaiah is there, as we can infer from the mission charge. So is Third Isaiah, as we can infer from the beatitudes. But just as visible and vital is the complex and challenging figure of Jeremiah.

Jeremiah is the human thread connecting the next two chapters of this analysis of the Jesus people. Echoes of his very characteristic message can be detected not only in traditions recording Jesus' perspective on the Temple but also in that particularly intense community-defining tradition of the eucharistic words. And that brings us very naturally to the point of reflection on the notion of memory – not just the meaning of 'Do this in memory of me', which we shall discuss in the final chapter, but also the extent to which human memory may be regarded as a safeguard for the preservation and transmission of such important material as the Temple traditions in the gospels.

That very fine Chilean novelist Isabel Allende made some acute observations in her altogether absorbing semi-autobiographical memoir, entitled tantalisingly *My Invented Country*. The story of a person, told with self-deprecating wit and candour, this book is also to an extent the story of a country, a country so absorbed into her life that it travels with her, as it were, into exile and then to a new life in another far-distant country. Through a diplomatically peripatetic childhood, on through years of torment spent abroad during the Pinochet period, through a first marriage and then a divorce and then a second happy marriage, on through the tragic loss of a beloved daughter, a human journey from South America to a somewhat idiosyncratic Californian existence, Isabel Allende took Chile with her. But if her story is also at a very deep level the story of her country, which country is it? How can it be 'my *invented* country'? Could it be really 'that mythic country that from being missed so profoundly has replaced the real country'? Let Isabel Allende herself speak:

> I have constructed an idea of my country the way you fit together a jigsaw puzzle, by selecting pieces that fit my design and ignoring the others . . . I have also created a version of myself that has no nationality, or, more accurately, many nationalities . . . I can't pretend to know what part of my memory is reliable and how much I've invented, because the job of defining the line between them is beyond my ability. My granddaughter Andrea wrote a composition for school in which she said she liked her 'grandmother's imagination'. I asked her what she was referring to, and without hesitation she replied, 'You remember things that never happened.' Don't we all do that? I have read that the mental process of imagining and that of remembering are so much alike that they are nearly indistinguishable. Who can define reality? (2003: 178–80)

When eventually we reach the study of the eucharistic words these observations will help us to be realistic about the extent to which the traditions, hallowed by centuries of use in corporate worship, can be assessed as historically reliable. How far are they memories of what the historical Jesus did, said, and had in mind? Not even liturgical usage constitutes a cast-iron guarantee of historical authenticity, for those who participated in the original events and bequeathed a memory which subsequently turned itself into strikingly diverse liturgical formulae were themselves part of the same sort of process as Isabel Allende observes in her own work. Being present and being inventive are not opposites. They are complementary, especially when the subject matter of memory is central to an emotionally charged life story.

From this perspective we turn to a study of how Jesus positioned himself, theologically and religiously, in relation to the Temple, the holy place in Jerusalem. And once again there are some preliminary points to be made so that the parameters of this study may be clear.

First, it is extremely likely *a priori* that the attitude of Jesus to the Temple would match and be in harmony with his attitude to the law of Moses. The key relevant factors of the latter are his making the having-come-near-ness of God's future kingdom his overall frame of reference; his being favourable and respectful in principle, with no disposition to set the law aside; his prophetic emphasis on transformation of the human heart; and his insistence on a process of interpretation which dispensed with detail and stressed the major priorities of righteousness/justice, and active mercy/compassion in the face of human need.

The likely consistency of approach to Torah and Temple is worth viewing within a broader perspective. Some of those who pursue the current quest – misnamed the 'third' quest (cf. Allison 2005: 1–26) – of the historical Jesus are much inclined to find him somehow undermining, bypassing, or even substituting for, what the Temple represented. Some even go so far as to find in the final meal shared by Jesus and his disciples the founding of an alternative cult. This, if true, would have major community implications. Two notable representatives of this tendency may be cited.

According to the first reconstruction, Jesus represented a shift from sacred place to divine man, and so offered an alternative to the Temple: he was 'its functional opponent, alternative and substitute', as his miracles implied. The successor of the Baptist, whose baptism 'cast negative aspersions, be this explicit or implicit, on the Temple cult', he exercised a power and authority, for example in the cleansing of the leper (Mark 1:40–45), which stood 'on a par with or even above that of the Temple itself' (Crossan 1991: 235, 322, 354–5). The religion of Jesus, so we are told, was characterised by 'immediacy' and the total absence of 'brokers'. The essential role of the Temple for Jesus' contemporaries had thus allegedly become for him inessential. So we are told. And a particular reconstruction of the development of Christology starts to emerge as part of this package: it is plain that the stance adopted by this particular 'historical Jesus' requires a highly developed personal self-consciousness on his part.

According to the second reconstruction, ironically at many points intended to contradict the first reconstruction, Jesus, convinced that the new era of God's kingdom had dawned, transcended and bypassed the Temple system altogether (Wright 1996: 130, 432). By (allegedly) reconstituting Israel around himself, that is to say, by replacing adherence or allegiance to Temple and Torah with allegiance to himself (274), he set up 'a counter-Temple movement' (131, 437). Furthermore, the way of life he inaugurated 'had no further need of the Temple ... All that the Temple had stood for was now available through Jesus and his movement' (335, 436). Throughout his mission he 'had constantly been acting ... in a way which invited the conclusion that he thought he had a right to do and be what the Temple was and did, thereby implicitly making the Temple redundant' (362). Naturally, that also branded the whole sacrificial system as redundant. According to Mark 12:28–34, the exceptionally perceptive scribe discerned this. He recognised that love of God and the neighbour is 'much more important than all whole burnt offerings and sacrifices' (566). Such a replacement of the Temple with Jesus himself was, in traditional Jewish terms, blasphemous (526). While, according to this scheme, there is (as one would expect) a heavy Christology of messiahship involved, going far beyond what a prophet *qua* prophet would do, even this does not seem quite sufficient. To use the term 'blasphemous' leaves the distinct impression that something more than a messiah is here, and so does the notion that later Jewish tradition (*b. Sanhedrin* 43a) preserved an historical memory (*sic*) with its judgement that 'Jesus of Nazareth practised magic and *led Israel astray*' (Wright 1996: 439–42, 548–52). But, however that may be, there is without doubt nothing less than messiahship.

This is where we might recall with due and salutary realism that the second quest – what used (inappropriately, as it turned out) to be called the 'new' quest before its bright and shining newness grew a little tarnished, and before the fact that it was not 'new' anyway had been demonstrated with such devastating ruthlessness (Allison 2005: 1–26) – said the same sort of things about Jesus' approach to law. There too Christology was a formative concern – an *implicit* Christology, first detected and then exploited (Käsemann 1964: 43–4). But that proposal in all its varied manifestations turned out to have read far too much into the relevant traditions and (paradoxically) to have been insufficiently careful in attending to the history of those traditions. It lacked staying power. And, that being so, maximum care needs now to be exercised lest the same mistake be made again. The risk of exaggerated exegesis must haunt us all.

Second, it is logical to take as a working hypothesis the likely continuity between Jesus and the earliest Christian community in attitudes to the Temple. Now, the conduct of the earliest Christian community in Jerusalem seems in this respect to have been entirely traditional.

There were, according to Acts 6:1, two language-differentiated wings in that community – 'Hebrews' and 'Hellenists' (cf. Hengel 1983: 1–11). The Hebrews were devout Temple worshippers (see Acts 2:46; 3:1; 5:42), and the texts contain no hint of a permanently critical or fundamentally detached attitude to the sacrificial cult. They convey no hint that their loyalty to it was a matter of temporary provisionality or pragmatic compliance in order not to give offence (*contra* Hengel 1981: 56). If such an inference be drawn from their being the target of persecution by the Sadducean priestly nobility, then their leaders' being *exempted* from the persecution which followed the death of Stephen (Acts 8:1) also calls for explanation. The truth is that we have no reason to assign to tactical pragmatism rather than firm principle their continuing devotion to Temple worship.

Now, some at least of these 'Hebrews' had been among Jesus' closest colleagues. If being as close as that to Jesus meant being close to a subversive anti-Temple movement, containing within itself all that was needed, and having no need of the Temple and all it stood for, then it has to be said that these people were remarkably obtuse and uncomprehending. 'If [Jesus] actually explicitly opposed one of the main institutions of Judaism, he kept it secret from his disciples' (Sanders 1985: 67). Quite so! 'If Jesus had indeed acted and taught against the Temple service, then his immediate followers completely missed his point' (Fredriksen 2000: 209). Quite so, again!

Over against the Hebrews, however, there stand the Hellenists. They were the objects of some very considerable scepticism on the issue of devotion to the cult. They were allegedly accused of speaking against both Temple and law (Acts 6:11–14). Now Luke for his part insists with some vehemence that the charge was false. And unless one is going to downgrade Luke's report, and then opt for a combination of 'methinks he doth protest too much' and 'there's no smoke without fire', his insistence at least deserves to be taken seriously. In that case, the proposal that in this 'community within a community' there flourished an interpretation of the death of Jesus that spelt the end of the Temple and its cult would begin to look a little fragile. A question mark would have to be placed over the suggestion that the pre-Christian Paul breathed fire and slaughter against the Hellenistic Jewish Christians for 'their attempts to shake the foundations of Israel's existence, indeed the foundation of the whole creation' because of 'their certainty that the death of the crucified Messiah, who had vicariously taken upon himself the curse of the Law, had made the Temple obsolete as a place of everlasting atonement for the sins of Israel, and therefore the ritual Law had lost its significance as a necessary institution for salvation' (thus, Hengel 1981: 44). If this reconstruction seems to read rather a lot out of rather a little, then we can perhaps favour the contrary conclusion, namely that neither of the two groups, Hellenists or Hebrews, had a negative attitude to the Temple in principle, though their conduct would not be inconsistent with the view that the present Temple could be vulnerable.

Third, let us at this point recall a number of nods and winks concerning Jesus' own assumptions about the Temple and the sacrificial system, hints dropped without apparent design or ulterior motive, and all the more impressive for that.

(i) In Jesus' famous parable, the tax-collector who went home 'righteoused' was a different person from the one who went to the Temple to pray at the time of the offering of the sacrifices (Luke 18:10–14a). The system – or rather, God operating through the system – had brought blessing to him. The distinction between him and the Pharisee – one 'righteoused' and the other, by implication, already 'righteous' and not needing to be made so – is a distinction between two people who both came to participate in the Temple worship. It is not between contrasting models of non-participation and participation in the cult. The Temple is the 'given' in both their lives, and in the Temple the necessary trans-formation is effected by the God to whom in their different ways they both pray.

(ii) The former leper, instructed to 'go, show yourself to the priest, and offer for your cleansing what Moses commanded' (Mark 1:44), could be forgiven for failing to pick up any hint that the system he was required to respect was in fact doomed. On the contrary, there could scarcely be a clearer and more unambiguous demonstration of Jesus' affirmation of Temple, priesthood and purity laws (rightly, Sanders 1993: 129). Jesus mediates divine healing ('be cleansed', a divine passive) and looks to the priest to formalise the cure by receiving the appropriate sacrificial offering and then officially declaring the man cured. So respect for the laws of Leviticus 13—14 and the cult, bound up with one another, is promoted without qualification by Jesus. It may well be that Jesus in carrying out the cure became unclean himself, in which case the regular means for becoming clean again could be used to deal with a not uncommon problem, one which by no means implied the slightest disrespect for the law (Crossley 2004: 87–92). The Jesus of this story is unswervingly pro-law and pro-Temple.

(iii) There is more to the highly commended scribe of Mark 12:28–34 than meets the eye. The summing up of the paramount human obligation to love God and the neighbour unites Jesus and several Jewish writers. According to Philo, who in this respect is wholly representative, the focus of synagogue teaching on Mosaic instruction was as follows:

> Among the vast number of particular truths and principles there studied, there stand out practically high above the others two main heads: one of duty to God as shown by piety and holiness, one of duty to men as shown by humanity and justice. (*Special Laws* 2:62–3; similarly *Testament of Issachar* 5:2; *Testament of Dan* 5:3; cited by Lührmann 1987: 206–7)

No one steeped in Jewish tradition would disagree. But this very agreement also implies a consensus that everything else, *however important*, was less important. So for the scribe to clarify the implication by drawing on, say, 1 Samuel 15:22 or Hosea 6:6 is to say something neither new nor radical. Samuel's rebuke to Saul is a statement of principle, provoked by Saul's distorted conduct in wishing to offer sacrifice despite disobedience (1 Sam. 15:15, 21). Hosea's insistence on the priority of steadfast love over sacrifice asserts a hierarchy of obligation, not an antithesis designed to include one and exclude another. Both are separated by some considerable distance from any declaration of the redundancy of the sacrificial system (thus, Wright 1996: 566). In the same terms, the narrator of the book of Judith was hardly devaluing the institution of sacrifice by making the heroine declare:

For every sacrifice as a fragrant offering is a small thing, and the fat of all whole burnt offerings is a very little thing; but whoever fears the Lord is great for ever. (16:16)

If so, there is something seriously amiss, a major misapprehension, immediately afterwards:

When they arrived at Jerusalem, they worshipped God. As soon as the people were purified, they offered their burnt offerings, their freewill offerings, and their gifts. (16:18)

(iv) Finally, that same theme of acceptable worship's being dependent on acceptable worshippers comes through loudly and clearly in Matthew 5:23–4, where there is not the faintest echo of a community of disciples replacing the Temple, or of processes of worship that set aside the obligation to offer sacrifice:

23When you are offering your gift at the altar, if you remember that your brother or sister has something against you, 24leave your gift there before the altar and go; first be reconciled to your brother or sister, and then come and offer your gift.

Imagine a member of Jesus' audience in Galilee, who has made the minimally three-day-long journey to Jerusalem (Josephus, *Life* 269) in order to offer sacrifice. That person is told that achieving an interpersonal relationship of peace, following the recollection of some cause of offence, has to be given such priority over the cultic observance that a journey from Jerusalem to Galilee and back should precede the offering of the sacrifice! Imagine actually leaving the sacrifice in the Temple while reparation takes place! A typically extreme formulation on Jesus' part – what has been called 'a categorical, hyperbolically sharpened exemplary demand'! – spells out what it means in the fullest sense to be one of 'the peace people' (Luke/Q 10:6), but at the same time 'it is valid for Matthew *and for Jesus* [my italics] that the cultic law is not abrogated by the command of reconciliation' (Luz 1989: 289).

Fourth among our preliminary points, it is important to bear in mind a broad distinction between two perspectives, the *programmatic* and the *prophetic*. The *programmatic* outlook stresses God's control of history and therefore his having a plan that will definitely be implemented. Such a thought provides comfort for the people of God when battered and beleaguered (cf. Dan. 2; 7; 11). And in this setting we are in the realm of *prediction*. In this vein, if the agent of God announces that God will destroy the Temple – and, conceivably, replace it – he definitely will do it. His plan is, as it were, set in concrete, non-negotiable. Over against the programmatic, however, we have the prophetic. The *prophetic* outlook and strategy contains within itself, explicitly or implicitly, an element of conditionality. This time we are in the realm of *threat*. And in this vein, dire and devastating declarations may be voiced, but the spoken or unspoken presumption is that if human beings respond, then God may change his mind and (for instance) not impose his threatened judgement. If his agent announces that he will destroy the Temple, that does not necessarily mean that he will do it! Jeremiah (18:5–11) puts the matter beyond the range of doubt.

> ⁵Then the word of the Lord came to me: ⁶Can I not do with you, O house of Israel, just as this potter has done? says the Lord. Just like the clay in the potter's hand, so are you in my hand, O house of Israel. ⁷At one moment I may declare concerning a nation or a kingdom, that I will pluck up and break down and destroy it, ⁸but if that nation, concerning which I have spoken, turns from its evil, *I will change my mind* about the disaster that I intended to bring on it. ⁹And at another moment I may declare concerning a nation or a kingdom that I will build and plant it, ¹⁰but if it does evil in my sight, not listening to my voice, then *I will change my mind* about the good that I had intended to do to it. ¹¹Now, therefore, say to the people of Judah and the inhabitants of Jerusalem: Thus says the Lord: Look, I am a potter shaping evil and devising a plan against you. Turn now, all of you from your evil way, and amend your ways and your doings.

Fifth, the inseparability of people and Temple cannot be too heavily stressed and must be borne in mind throughout our investigation. It is not too much to say that whenever we are talking about the Temple we are talking about the community of the people of God. Two revealing texts make the point powerfully.

(i) The writer of 2 Maccabees, reflecting on the depressing tragedy of what occurred under Antiochus Epiphanes, declared in 5:15–20:

^{15}Antiochus dared to enter the most holy temple in all the world . . . ^{17}he was elated in spirit, and did not perceive that the Lord was angered for a little while because of the sins of those who lived in the city, and that was the reason he was disregarding the holy place. ^{18}But if it had not happened that they were involved in many sins, this man would have been flogged and turned back from his rash act . . . ^{19}But the Lord did not choose the nation for the sake of the holy place, but the place for the sake of the nation. ^{20}Therefore the place itself shared in the misfortunes that befell the nation and afterwards participated in its benefits; and what was forsaken in the wrath of the Almighty was restored again in all its glory when the great Lord became reconciled.

Such a text makes clear that whatever is said about the Temple is essentially a comment on the condition, standing, and prospects of the people. It also suggests that talk of positive restoration is essentially an extension of talk about retributive judgement.

(ii) The writer of the book of Tobit has some enthusiastic things to say about the Temple in two appendices to his book. In the first appendix (chapter 13), a psalm of praise, he looks forward to the liberation of the city, the return of the dispersed Jews, and the attraction of the gentiles to the bright light of the world (cf. Matt. 5:14). He exclaims:

^{9}O Jerusalem, the holy city, he scourged you for the deeds of your hands, and will again have mercy on the children of the righteous. ^{10}Acknowledge the Lord for he is good, and bless the King of the ages, so that his tent may be rebuilt in you in joy.

Then in the second appendix (chapter 14), dominated by Tobit's farewell discourse, he declares:

^{4}Everything that was spoken by the prophets of Israel, whom God sent, will occur. None of all their words will fail, but all will come true in their appointed times . . . All our kindred will be scattered . . . and the whole land of Israel will be desolate, even Samaria and Jerusalem will be desolate. And the temple of God will be burned to the ground, and it will be desolate for a while.

5But God will again have mercy on them, and God will bring them back into the land of Israel; and they will rebuild the temple of God, but not like the first one until the period when the times of fulfilment shall come. After this they all will return from their exile and will rebuild Jerusalem in splendour; and in it the temple of God will be rebuilt, just as the prophets of Israel have said concerning it. 6Then the nations in the whole world will all be converted and worship God in truth . . .

This text reads like a programme, for all that it highlights the prophets, and within that programme the revival of the fortunes, and the renewal of the integrity, of the people is matched by the glorification of the restored Solomonic Temple (Moore 1996: 290). The one is inseparable from the other. Both *together* are caught up in the fundamental pattern: God 'scourges', and then gives effect to his mercy (Nickelsburg 1981: 30–35). Tobit, previously blind but now with sight restored, understood and personally exhibited the principle: 'Though he scourged me, he has had mercy upon me' (11:15). From his own experience he went on to generalise: 'Blessed be God . . . he scourges, and he shows mercy' (13:2). Again, 'he will scourge you for your iniquities, but he will again show mercy on all of you' (13:5, 9). The scheme is clear: (i) whatever happens to the Temple is but a projection of what happens to the people, and (ii) talk of restoration is a necessary corollary of talk of judgement on the part of a God who is ultimately merciful.

Finally, a point needs to be made about method, a point stimulated by an acute awareness that the Temple sayings attributed to Jesus represent just about as difficult a problem as any encountered by the student of the historical Jesus. So at this point, a health warning – this will be the most difficult chapter in this book! There are two ways of setting about this testing task – *either* one can build up a picture from scratch by assessing each of the traditions singly, deciding what they positively demand concerning the status of the speaker, *or* one can decide in advance on an overall view about the speaker's self-awareness, and then fit the individual conclusions within that overall view. The former is normally the safe and appropriately cautious route to travel, but the latter is sometimes favoured. In the case of Jesus' Temple sayings, this might happen if we were to decide that one of them, let us say, positively demanded that the speaker presumed his messianic status. Then the other pieces of data, which by themselves might demand no more than a prophetic self-awareness on Jesus' part, would have to be fitted, unless of course that did violence in some way to their implications, into the messianic scheme.

It is therefore worth checking at this early stage whether the messianic category is in fact available as an historical reality within the mission of the historical Jesus. We might not need it, but on the other hand we might. So is it there for us to use, if we choose? The answer is yes, and not simply because of the evidence of the traditions in Mark 10:35–7, 40 and Luke/Q 22:30, which we have already studied. In those two cases, the assignment of future, subordinate, judicial roles to followers of Jesus can hardly be other than an extension of his own future kingly role and status. The implication is clear enough. But more can be added.

That the earliest post-Easter community affirmed *ab initio*, in spite of the grim and alien evidence of suffering and death, that Jesus was 'Christ' may not be doubted (cf. 1 Cor. 15:3b). That this issue was the ground of his Roman execution should almost certainly not be doubted (though it has been: Catchpole 1984: 328–9 – *mea culpa*). Admittedly the primary passion account is a stylised narrative, upon which reliance should not be placed without due caution, but the *titulus* in Mark 15:26 conforms to the convention of public exposure of the ground of execution (Dio Cassius, *Roman History* 54.3.7; Suetonius, *Gaius Caligula* 32.2; *Domitian* 10), and uses language which is unusual for the early Christians. The term 'king of the Jews' is natural when non-Jewish people are speaking (Josephus, *Jewish War* 1:282; *Antiquities* 14:36; Matt. 2:2). Moreover, Mark 15:2 (cf. 14:62, variant reading: *su legeis hoti egō eimi*), in using the formulation, 'You say so' (*su legeis*), conveys something less than a bold and uncompromising confession and opts instead for a guarded, in-explicit form. This form, if parallels are taken into account, indicates a preference for not taking responsibility for the idea, while acknowledg-ing its validity, subject to nuanced interpretation, and for avoiding the dangerous consequences of unguarded and explicit affirmation. This can be recognised in the light of the following text:

> When Rabbi (Judah) was dying in Sepphoris, the men of that place declared, 'Whoever comes and announces that Rabbi is dead will be put to death by us.' Bar Kappara went, looked through a window, and squeezed himself in, his head being wrapped and his garments torn, and exclaimed, 'My brothers, sons of Jedayah, hear me! hear me! Angels

and mortals have taken hold of the tablets of the covenant. The angels were victorious and have snatched the tablets.' They cried, 'Rabbi is dead!' He said to them, '*You have said it*; I have not said it.'

Why did he not say it? Because it is written, 'He that utters a bad report is a fool.' [Prov. 10:18] They tore their garments [so violently] that the sound of the tearing reached Gufta three miles away, and the text was applied: 'The excellency of knowledge is that wisdom preserves the life of him that has it.' [Eccles. 7:12] (*Koheleth R* 7:12)

So we have available to us both the categories of prophet and messiah as we try to determine the authenticity, meaning and strategic community bearing of each of the sayings of Jesus about the Temple.

First variation: from grandeur to rubble

Specialists in gospel study have given concentrated attention to the shocking saying with which the admiring enthusiasm of the Galilean visitors to Jerusalem and its Temple is greeted by the Jesus of Mark:

Do you see these great buildings? Not one stone will be left here upon another; all will be thrown down. (Mark 13:2)

This saying forms the preface to Jesus' farewell discourse. Just as Jacob's farewell discourse to his sons in Genesis 49:1–27, and Paul's farewell discourse to the community elders from Ephesus in Acts 20:18–35, look forward respectively to the post-Jacob and post-Pauline situation, so too does Jesus' farewell discourse in Mark 13:5–37 look forward to the post-Jesus situation. It brings him into direct contact with the later Christian situation for which Mark writes. In Jacob's case, it is a matter of 'Gather around, that I may tell you what will happen to you in days to come' (Gen. 49:1). In Paul's case, it is a matter of 'I know that after I have gone, savage wolves will come in among you, not sparing the flock' (Acts 20:29). Each departing leader dons the mantle of seer. A figure of the past is thus, as it were, made contemporary with the present audience. And so it is with the Jesus of Mark. A discourse, which mirrors the exposed and insecure situation of a later generation of Christian believers, becomes a device whereby the departing seer speaks directly to them. And the saying that provokes the discourse can therefore fairly claim to be among the most important of all the sayings of Jesus transmitted by this evangelist.

All that may be true of the Jesus of Mark in relation to the community of Mark, but did the historical Jesus say it? Might it, on the other hand, be something attributed to him but in fact presupposing the Roman destruction of Jerusalem and its Temple? Might it be the creation of Mark, simply serving Mark's own purpose?

It would be possible to mount a case in favour of Mark's being the creator of the saying. One could draw on evidence of a certain degree of negativity in his attitude to the Temple. One might cite, for example, the enclosing of the 'cleansing' of the Temple in the tradition of the cursing of the fig tree, so that, as is always the case with Marcan 'sandwich structures', the one conditions and colours the reader's understanding of the other. In this case, the (slightly unfair) charge of untimely fruitlessness evokes the curse of timeless fruitlessness (Mark 11:13–14, 20–21). Passing from tree to Temple, the message is painfully clear.

An even stronger case can, however, be mounted in favour of Mark 13:2 as a pre-Marcan saying. It starts with the recognition that this saying contrasts sharply with another close by in Mark 13:14:

> But when you see the desolating sacrilege set up where he ought not to be (let the reader understand), then those in Judea must flee to the mountains.

The contrast should not be weakened by suggesting that verse 2 refers to God acting in judgement by means of the Romans, and verse 14 to the Roman invasion as such (Wright 1996: 511). No, in verse 14 we certainly have a human, not a divine action, but it is an act of defilement, not an act of destruction; an action focused on a personal object – 'set up where *he* ought not to be' – rather than an action with no such focus; an action described in writing, not in speech; a communication veiled in coded language – 'let the reader understand' – not in clear discourse. These points of difference suggest strongly that the two sayings in verses 2 and 14 do not really belong together at all (Theissen 1992: 128–37). And while the saying in verse 2 may be important, it is the inauthentic saying in verse 14 in which Mark invests.

When the reader does, as instructed, understand the talk of 'desolating sacrilege', s/he notices that the loaded language used points to the 'desolating sacrilege erected on the altar of burnt offering' (1 Macc. 1:54), to which Daniel alluded more than once (9:27; 12:11):

^{27}He shall make a strong covenant with many for one week, and for half of the week he shall make sacrifice and offering cease; and in their place shall be a desolating sacrilege, until the decreed end is poured out upon the desolator . . . ^{11}From the time that the regular burnt-offering is taken away and the desolating sacrilege is set up, there shall be one thousand two hundred and ninety days.

With a series of other allusions to Daniel scattered through Mark 13, and particularly in parts which show not the faintest tinge of Christian colouring, the scene is set for the conclusion that under the surface of Mark 13 there lurks what we may call a Jewish memorandum (cf. Theissen 1992: 130–32). Arguably, it consisted of Mark 13:7–8, 14–20, 24–7. This memorandum has its own life setting, a setting in which events have stirred both memories and fears – memories of the religious mayhem and devastation brought about by Antiochus Epiphanes in 168–165 BCE, and fears that somehow this devastation might happen again. Actually, such memories and fears must logically be at home in more than one setting – first, the setting in which the memorandum belongs when existing by itself, and second, the setting in which that memorandum is thought by Mark to have become relevant once again. Logically, again, that must mean that the first time (memorandum time, pre-Marcan time) the threat and the fears were not in fact realised, whereas the second time (memorandum-quoting time, Marcan time) the threat is thought to be reviving and the fears coming to life once more.

What, we may ask, was the setting in life of the memorandum? Highly likely, the late 30s CE. The Roman emperor Tiberius died on 17 March of the year 37 CE, and was succeeded by Gaius Caligula. Gaius began well, according to Josephus, but:

> . . . as time went on, he ceased to think of himself as a man and, as he imagined himself a god because of the greatness of his empire, he was moved to disregard the divine power in all his official acts. (*Antiquities* 18:256)

And so it came about that in the year 38 CE the plan was devised to erect statues of Caligula, not only in Jewish synagogues, which was bad enough, but also in the Temple itself:

[203][Gaius] gave orders that . . . a colossal statue coated with gold, should be set up in the Temple of the mother city . . . [603]in the inmost part of the Temple in the special sanctuary itself, into which the High Priest enters once a year only on the Fast as it is called, to offer incense and to pray according to ancestral practice for a full supply of blessings and prosperity and peace for all mankind. (Philo, *Embassy to Gaius* 203, 306)

The Temple was to be converted into 'a temple of his own to bear the name of Gaius, the new Zeus made manifest' (*Embassy* 347). Against a background of 'rumours of war' (Josephus, *Jewish War* 2:187), the plan went ahead. Entirely predictably, opposition in the Jewish community was fierce and frenzied. The situation was only eased by the adroit manoeuvring of Petronius, the Roman legate to Syria, and (to the intense relief of all concerned) by the assassination of Gaius himself on 24 January of the year 41 CE.

What, we may go on to ask, was the setting in life of the edited quotation of the memorandum and of the gospel of Mark? As already noted, a time when the old fears have been renewed, and recourse made to the same reflections and the same reactions – a time of national unrest and cosmic disturbance, a time when the nightmare of another personalised desecration of the Temple wakens the readers in terror, a time when it is still possible to leave the holy city and make for the mountains, that is, a time when Roman armies have not yet encircled Jerusalem – very likely, a time in the late 60s CE (Hengel 1985: 14–28). And what does that do for Mark 13:2? It demonstrates that it is set in a document, the gospel of Mark, which antedates the Roman sacking of city and Temple in late August of the year 70 CE.

That earlier setting is confirmed by the discrepancy between what the saying envisages – that is, total destruction leaving 'not one stone upon another' – and what actually happened – that is, destruction by fire (Sanders 1993: 257). It is also supported by the account of the strikingly parallel threat voiced in advance by the lone Jeremiah-inspired figure, Jesus ben Ananias:

[300]Four years before the war, when the city was enjoying profound peace and prosperity, there came to the feast at which it is the custom of all Jews to erect tabernacles to God, one Jesus, son of Ananias, a rude peasant, who, [301]standing in the Temple, suddenly began to cry out, 'A

voice from the east, a voice from the west, a voice from the four winds; a voice against Jerusalem and the sanctuary, a voice against the bridegroom and the bride, a voice against all the people.' [Jer. 7:34] Day and night he went about all the alleys with this cry on his lips ...

[306]During the whole period up to the outbreak of war he neither approached nor was seen talking to any of the citizens, but daily, like a prayer that he had learnt, repeated his lament, 'Woe to Jerusalem.' ... [308]His cries were loudest at the festivals.

So for seven years and five months he continued his wail, his voice never flagging nor his strength exhausted, until in the siege, having seen his prediction verified, he found his rest. For, while going his round and shouting in piercing tones from the wall, 'Woe once more to the city and to the people and to the Temple', [309]as he added a last word, 'and woe to me also', a stone hurled from the rampart struck him and killed him on the spot. (Josephus, *Jewish War* 6:300–309)

In the declaration of Mark 13:2 against city and Temple, and doubtless by implication against the human community as well, it becomes ever more likely that we hear the voice of the historical Jesus. (i) The argument thus far has shown that the gospel of Mark, and therefore the saying, antedates the Jewish war with Rome. (ii) The dark warning of Jesus ben Ananias confirms that this sort of threat is naturally set in advance of that war. (iii) The author of destruction is not Jesus himself but God. (iv) On the basis of multiple attestation, authenticity is positively supported by the evidence elsewhere of Jeremiah-speak, as well as by the evidence elsewhere of negative announcements by Jesus concerning Temple and city. And if that be accepted, then we can indeed hear the historical Jesus announcing a future act of divine destruction – though the reason for such a disturbing message is left entirely unclear.

Second variation: from presence to absence

From the probably authentic tradition in Mark 13:2 we move to the one relevant tradition in Q which bears explicitly and directly on the Jesus/Temple question. This is the *Lament over Jerusalem* (Luke/Q 13:34–5). And as we do so, we have to be aware that an announcement of divine departure is both premise and preface of an altogether grim occurrence of destruction. God cannot be present with his people if the place of his presence is sacked or goes up in flames. If it is sacked or burnt, he is not there. And if he is not there, the implications are dire for the community whose self-understanding and covenantal election are bound up with his presence among them.

While painting a picture of the flames devouring the Temple at the climax of the war with Rome, Josephus assembled the record of so-called portents that should have been interpreted as warnings of a disaster to come. One was the opening of the gate of the Temple by other than human agents:

> The learned understood that the security of the Temple was dissolving of its own accord and that the opening of the gate meant a present to the enemy, interpreting the portent in their own minds as *indicative of coming desolation*. (*Jewish War* 6:296)

That is the interpretative context in which to set the announcement of divine withdrawal:

> [299]At the feast which is called Pentecost, the priests on entering the inner court of the temple by night, as their custom was in the discharge of their liturgical duties, reported that they were conscious, first of a commotion and a din, [300]and after that of a voice, as of a host, '*We are departing hence (metabainomen enteuthen)*.' (*Jewish War* 6:299–300)

Later in his narrative, Josephus puts into the mouth of Eleazar, the leader of the doomed Masada rebels, some observations which doubtless represent his own point of view:

> We ought to have read God's purpose and to have recognized that the Jewish race, once beloved of him, had been doomed to perdition. For had he continued to be gracious, or but lightly incensed, he would never have overlooked such wholesale destruction or *have abandoned his most holy city* to be burnt and razed to the ground by our enemies. (*Jewish War* 7:328)

This last speech of Eleazar recalls Josephus' own extended apologia as the clouds of war gathered around the Jerusalem community, city and Temple. God's presence is the only ground of security; his departure a

---

tragic development that clears the way for the defeat of a people and the destruction of a shrine:

> My belief is that *the Deity has fled from the holy places* and taken his stand on the side of those with whom you are now at war. (*Jewish War* 5:415)

That is the thought world of the *Lament*, wherever it may happen to have originated.

A detailed study of this tradition needs initially to consider the possibility of a link with other content-related traditions. The argument that follows will suggest two such links – first with the woe against those whose ancestors had made martyrs of prophets (Luke/Q 11:47–8), and second with the condemnation of 'this generation' in the light of Wisdom's plan (Luke/Q 11:49–51).

First, the final *woe*. Both Matthew and Luke, while recognisably depending on a common source, have clearly gone in for drastic revision of that source. Matthew's version (23:29–31) accuses allegedly hypocritical scribes and Pharisees of dissociating themselves from their fathers who shed the blood of prophets, whereas (so says this Jesus) an acknowledgement of a filial relationship with the murderers implies identification with and shared responsibility for what they did. In other words, the contemporary generation, which has not killed anyone, carries the same burden of responsibility as those who had. Luke's version (11:47–8) accuses unidentified hearers of approving of the murders simply by virtue of building tombs for those who had been murdered.

It has to be said that, however brilliant they may be elsewhere, neither Matthew nor Luke gain high marks for logical thinking at this point – 'somewhat defective . . . tortuous' is a dry but fair comment (Tuckett 1996: 308–9). The content of the version on which they drew is obscured by their disagreements with one another. But at least this much seems clear: the underlying tradition exploited the filial relationship with an earlier generation that had assassinated prophets, and the later generation, the audience addressed by 'Jesus', inherits their guilt even without engaging in murderous deeds of their own. Given the early Christian tendency to hold 'the Jews' responsible for the deaths of prophets *and Jesus* (Mark 12:1–9; Acts 7:52; 1 Thess. 2:15), this is more than a little interesting. It opens up the possibility of an echo of the voice of the historical Jesus.

The not unrelated questions that immediately arise are: (i) How exactly can guilt be passed on from one generation to another? (ii) What, if anything, has the contemporary generation done which falls short of murder and yet brings upon it such a burden of guilt and liability to judgement? A possible answer to question (i) might be that the sins of Israel have previously been judged in a restrained and forbearing way in order to draw a response of repentance (see above, pp. 142–3, on Luke 18:7). Now, however, the continuing rejection of God and his emissaries has brought the unrepentant to the point where the measure of sinfulness is filled to the brim and overflows. The outcome is unrestrained and immoderate, that is to say, final judgement. A possible answer to question (ii) might be that the present generation stands at the end of the process of God's dealings with his people and has indeed refused to repent in the face of the last appeal (Tuckett 1996: 310). These tentative answers turn out to be strikingly consonant with Matthew's reference to 'filling up the measure of your fathers' (23:32) and his echo of the preaching of John the Baptist (23:33). Perhaps in this respect Matthew got it right!

Second, if the Wisdom-centred *oracle* (Luke/Q 11:49–51) was preceded by this *woe*, did it in turn precede the *Lament* (Luke/Q 13:34–35)? Here a choice has to be made between the sequences of Q material in Matthew and Luke.

In Luke's sequence of Q material the *Lament* comes not long after the sayings which depict gentiles coming to the final banquet (Luke/Q 13:28–9) and then the reversal of 'first' and 'last' (Luke/Q 13:30). Having used those Q traditions, Luke struck out on his own with the non-Q narrative tradition about Jesus' departure from Galilee (Luke 13:31–3). This set the journey under the shadow of the personal threat to Jesus from Herod Antipas, and its conclusion (v. 33b) amply prepared for the *Lament*: 'It is impossible for a prophet to be killed away from Jerusalem.' After that, it was natural and understandable that Luke in editorially active mode should decide to add the *Lament*. Consequently, many Q specialists are convinced that, notwithstanding Luke's normal tendency to preserve the order of Q, he has this time changed that order while Matthew has preserved it (cf. Robinson 1998).

Matthew's Q sequence brings together two traditions (Luke/Q 11:49–51; 13:34–5) in his 23:34–6, 37–9 which are not only extremely close to one another in language and outlook but also exhibit common dependence on the story of the martyrdom of Zechariah the son of

Jehoiada in 2 Chronicles 24:19–23. This would mean that, at least in Q, the *Lament* followed immediately on the woe dealing with the killing of prophets (Luke/Q 11:47–8/Matt. 23:29–31) and also the *Oracle of Wisdom* (Luke 11:49–51/Matt. 23:34–6). Hypothetical this may be, but it is still not a bad working hypothesis. In what follows, we shall do just that and work with it.

The Wisdom oracle itself raises literary questions – first concerning wording, and second concerning strata. From due consideration of these questions the following reconstruction, distinguishing strata within the text, will be proposed:

> [49]Therefore also the Wisdom of God said, 'I will send to them prophets and emissaries, some of whom they will kill and persecute', [50a]so that this generation may be charged with the shed blood of all the prophets, [50b]*since the foundation of the world,* [51a]*from the blood of Abel to the blood of Zechariah, who perished between the altar and the sanctuary.* [51b]Yes, I tell you, it will be charged against this generation.

As to wording, Matthew has repeatedly intervened: (i) it is far easier to think of his changing from Wisdom to Jesus as the speaker, especially in view of his keenness to equate Jesus with Wisdom (11:2–19, 28–30), than it is to think of Luke's making the reverse change; (ii) those sent are likely to include apostles – in the Jewish sense of messengers (cf. 1 Kings 14:6), not the Christian sense of church leaders – rather than wise men and scribes, especially in view of Matthew's incorporation of the scribal role in his Christian perspective (13:52); (iii) Matthew's distinctive prediction of crucifixion, scourging in synagogues, and pursuit from one city to another is in line with his use of Mark 13:9–13 already in the mission charge (10:17–23).

As to strata within the tradition, there has been rather more disagreement and debate. The two decisions that have to be made concern, first, the extent of the speech of Wisdom and, second, the provenance of the 'from Abel to Zechariah' reference.

First, there are the two I-figures, Wisdom and then the speaker contemporary with 'this generation'. If Wisdom's speech were to be attributed to some lost document, as some suggest (following Bultmann 1963: 114), there would be a question as to where the quotation from that document ended. This might be somewhere within the oracle, or perhaps even somewhere within the following *Lament*. Then what the contemporary of 'this generation' says would arguably become a sort of superimposed Christian updating of the sort found in the Qumran community's self-centred interpretation of ancient texts (Robinson 1998: 245–6). But if Wisdom's speech had no earlier and separate existence, the question of when a literary quotation ends simply does not arise. Then it is just a case of the contemporary speaker's using the device of looking at the present in the light of the past, and specifically a past that is said to be under divine control by virtue of being mapped out in advance by the figure of Wisdom. As soon as we move from predictive speech to 'present' speech, we have in other words left the speech of Wisdom behind, but it was actually the contemporary speaker all the time! This would be the more attractive hypothesis of the two unless, that is, we find that in the following *Lament* things are said which positively demand a 'supra-historical entity' like Wisdom, to the exclusion of an historical entity speaking in the name of Wisdom.

Second, the Abel–Zechariah reference needs to be set in its context. The contemporary speaker makes the speech of Wisdom look *forward* to future prophetic missions: 'I will send to them prophets and emissaries', the two terms being of course synonymous. So Wisdom stands at a point in the history of Israel when prophets have not yet appeared on the scene. Furthermore, prophets as such are involved, not just rejected prophets, because Wisdom says, '. . . *some of them* they will kill and persecute.' So no prophets have yet been sent at the point in time when Wisdom speaks prospectively. When we reach the first declaration in verse 50a of the charge against this (*sic*) generation, solemnly reinforced by a second such declaration in the first person in verse 51b (just as the initial injunction to fear in Luke/Q 12:5 is followed by a solemn repetition, 'Yes, I tell you, fear him!'), none but the contemporary speaker is involved. This would suggest that the 'quotation' ends with verse 49b. Short though it is, it packs a powerful theological punch by its creative combination of two schemes in a few words (Tuckett 1996: 170). The first scheme is Wisdom's issuing of an appeal that is rejected (cf. Prov. 1:20–33). And the second scheme is the so-called deuteronomistic view of history as being shaped by recurrent rejection of prophets (cf. 1 Kings 18:4, 13; 19:10, 14; 2 Kings 17:7–20; Ezra 9:11; Neh. 9:26; Jer. 7:25–34; 25:3–14; 26:2–6; 29:17–20; 44:2–10; cf. Steck 1967).

This latter scheme consists of four basic elements: (i) The people are disobedient throughout the pre-exilic period in the promised land. (ii) In the forbearance of God they are warned by prophets. (iii) They remain obstinate, and reject the message of the prophet or the prophet himself – or even murder him. (iv) The judgement of God is imposed. When the first element has to be adapted for the post-exilic period, two more elements are attached: (v) Renewed demands for national repentance are issued, followed by (vi) the prospect of restoration for a repentant Israel and judgement on her enemies (Tuckett 1996: 168–9).

After the 'quotation' in verse 49 and the attached announcement in verse 50a there then follows the panoramic and retrospective statement in verses 50b–51a: 'since the foundation of the world, from the blood of Abel to the blood of Zechariah, who perished between the altar and the sanctuary'. Here we have a retrospective look back to creation (v. 50b), and an amplifying clarification (v. 51a). In verse 51a the person named Zechariah is almost certainly Zechariah the son of Jehoiada (2 Chr. 24:20–22) – not, incidentally, Zechariah the son of Berechiah (Zech. 1:1; Matt. 23:35). Matthew got that one wrong. With the right Zechariah, there (nearly) ends the whole story set out in the Hebrew Bible, from first book to last, from Genesis to 2 Chronicles. Now for the Chronicler, Zechariah was definitely a prophet. The text not only says in 2 Chronicles 24:20 that 'the spirit of God took possession of him' but also links him in the preceding verse 19 to the generalisation that '[the Lord] sent prophets among them to bring them back to the Lord; they testified against them, but they would not listen' (cf. also 2 Chr. 36:15–16, which epitomises the whole history as one of recurrent and, typically, rejected prophetic missions). But equally for the Chronicler, Zechariah was not the last prophet in his narrative: there were others still to come, some anonymous (2 Chr. 25:15–16), others named, like Isaiah (26:22; 32:20, 32), Oded (28:9), and Jeremiah (36:12). So Zechariah at (almost) the end of the scriptural narrative is not the last prophet. Abel at (almost) the beginning of the scriptural narrative is not a prophet at all, nor in any meaningful sense a 'sent' one. So the point about the Abel–Zechariah *inclusio* is that those two persons are martyrs. Zechariah is not the last *prophet*, but he is the last *martyr*. As such, he together with Abel makes the Bible something more than 'the law and the prophets' (Luke/Q 16:16). It is a history of martyrs.

The main point in verse 50b in the above reconstruction is therefore more martyrdom than prophecy. Some of the martyrs happened to be prophets (v. 50b), which is not quite the same as saying (v. 49) that some of the prophets were martyrs (v. 49). If, then, there are fault lines between verses 50b–51a and what precedes and follows them, we can set out the tradition in such a way as to distinguish earlier tradition from later redaction, as was indeed done above.

For the redactor, God's judgement cannot have been the abandonment of Jerusalem or its temple in 587 BCE. After all, Zechariah himself belongs to a time considerably in advance of the exile, and the biblical record framed by Genesis and Chronicles extends far beyond the exile. The precise timing and manner of the judgement is therefore left open in verses 50b–51a, but in verses 49–50a, 51b, the earlier tradition, the speaker of the oracle removes the uncertainty and applies the closure. *This* is the time: '*this* generation'. But the audience might ask, what has this generation done to deserve it? And why should it be *this* generation and not a succeeding generation? The oracle does not specify explicitly, but in that respect it matches the preceding woe on those whose fathers murdered prophets. The presumption must be a contemporary refusal to heed prophetic missions and messages. That refusal, if in the succession of the earlier rejections envisaged by Wisdom, does not have to be actual killing (cf. '*some* of them'), but rejection it is, all the same. And because this is the time of final reckoning it must be the last time, that is to say, the time immediately before the great climax of Israel's history. So Wisdom, who spoke in advance of all the prophetic missions to Israel, initiating them all from first to last, is taken to stand behind the last of them, the contemporary mission, implicitly that of the speaker who is none other than Jesus. His is the voice that declares with inspired authority, 'Yes, I tell you . . .' His is the vision which sees time about to reach its end point in judgement. The last, fatal, disastrous offence, which fills to the brim the cup of the nation's responsibility for such rejections, is . . . again he does not specify. Nevertheless, whatever it is causes dark and unrelieved pessimism to reign supreme.

This brings us to the goal of this whole study, the *Lament over Jerusalem* in Luke/Q 13:34–5. Its wording is easy to recover. Internal strata are admittedly more disputed, but the case will be made for verse 35b as a later addition to the original lament:

[34]Jerusalem, Jerusalem, the city that kills the prophets and stones those who are sent to you! How often have I desired to gather your children

together as a hen gathers her brood under her wings, and you were not willing! 35aSee, your house/sanctuary is left to you. 35b*And I tell you, you will not see me until the time comes when you say, 'Blessed is he who comes in the name of the Lord.'*

This lament certainly could be voiced by 'a supra-historical entity'. It could be, but it doesn't have to be, for the speaker could just as easily be heard as a duly authorised representative and mouthpiece of a supra-historical entity. All that the speaker has done in the past is attempt often to 'gather' (*episunagagein*) the children of Jerusalem (maybe the city and its resident population, but more likely the nation at one and the same time embodied in Jerusalem and due to be assembled in Jerusalem, cf. Tan 1997: 126). That attempt at 'gathering' must have been done on behalf of Wisdom, but not by a succession of persons like the earlier prophets and emissaries. While Jerusalem is here addressed directly, her children constitute the whole of Israel (cf. Baruch 4:5–29). These 'sons and daughters of Jerusalem' represent the widest possible community of those who regard the 'house' as *their* house, who prize the connection with *their* holy city, and whose 'being gathered to that defined place' (cf. *episunagagein*) constitutes the ultimate end-time assembly envisaged in many earlier texts (e.g. Tobit 13:9, 12–13; 14:7; 2 Macc. 1:27–8). Only one person has a mission which is dedicated to the realisation of that end-time hope. He must be the contemporary speaker. He can without strain or tension be set in the succession of the prophets and 'sent ones', and yet has a higher status than any of them by virtue of where he stands within the divine scheme. So it is that in Luke/Q 13:34–35a, that contemporary speaker draws together the past and a future so imminent that the tense of the verb (*aphietai*) is present. In Luke/Q 11:49–50a, 51b the words of Wisdom concern exclusively the long-term future, and the contemporary speaker who takes his/her cue from Wisdom addresses a future stretching no further than the present generation. In other words, Wisdom's prospective announcement in the one tradition has no match in the second. In the second, the speaker is not Wisdom herself but Wisdom's agent.

In detail, (i) there are some very substantial thematic connections between Wisdom's speech and its amplification in verses 49–50a, 51b, and what the following *Lament* in verses 34–35a says. First-person I-speech occurs in both; so do the prophets; so does divine sending; so does prophetic martyrdom. There are also (ii) substantial thematic connections between the editorial addition in verses 50b–51a and the oracle directed at Jerusalem: a specific focus on Jerusalem, death by stoning (2 Chr. 24:21), and divine abandonment (cf. 2 Chr. 24:20: 'Because you have forsaken the Lord, he has also forsaken you'). Since the debt to 2 Chronicles 24 can be seen in what is secondary in the oracle but primary in the lament (unless of course the words 'and stones those who are sent to you' are an editorial addition, which possibility can scarcely be ruled out), the likelihood is that this was what attracted the two traditions to one another, or alternatively what led the one to be edited in the light of the other. That may mean that the *literary* connection between the two on the level of Q may not go back prior to Q, whereas the *thematic* connection between the two can be taken seriously irrespective of the literary history involved.

The *Lament* reaches its climax in the statement that 'your house is left to you' (v. 35a). Up to and including that statement, the lament/oracle is complete in itself – an address, an accusation, an announcement of judgement, and the judgement itself. That judgement is couched in terms of a 'divine passive', so that 'your house is left' signals the departure neither of Wisdom nor of the speaker but of *God*. What then follows is markedly different in tone. The use of Psalm 118:26, 'Blessed is he who comes in the name of the Lord', or 'Blessed in the name of the Lord is the one who comes', belongs normally to the arrival of pilgrims in Jerusalem for the festival (cf. Mark 11:9). The mood of such a moment is joyful and celebratory. Unmistakable echoes of such a greeting and its matching mood are conveyed by Psalms of Solomon 8:15–17 (text in Charlesworth 2: 659), where the totally misguided and morally torpid leaders of the Jerusalem community fall over themselves to welcome the warmongering Pompey.

> 15God brought someone from the end of the earth, one who attacks in strength;
> > He declared war against Jerusalem and her land.
> 16The leaders of the country met him with joy. They said to him,
> > 'May your way be blessed. Come, enter in peace.'
> 17They graded the rough roads before his coming;
> > They opened the gates of Jerusalem, they crowned her city walls.

In just such a vein, verse 35b is a speech of glad welcome to someone. Is that someone God, as was the case in 'your house *is left*'?

Assuming that it is, forswearing literary criticism, relying on the Lucan order of the two quotations of Psalm 118:26 in Luke 13:35; 19:38, and then moving directly to history, the proposal that Jesus' entry to Jerusalem is 'the symbol and embodiment of YHWH's return to Zion', sees the light of day (Wright 1996: 639). Unfortunately for this proposal, those two quotations of Psalm 118:26 are in Matthew in reverse sequence. It is illegitimate to read straight from an evangelist's redaction to history; there is nothing in the primary story of Jesus' entry to Jerusalem to encourage the thought of God's return to Zion; and the 'coming one' in the Q tradition is in any case not God (cf. Luke/Q 3:16; 7:19). No, it is someone else, the Son of Man (cf. Luke/Q 12:35–8, 39–40, 42–6; 19:12–13, 15–26).

So the underlying oracle talked only about judgement and referred to God's leaving 'your house' – that is, removing his presence, which the Jewish people prized, from their (*sic*) house. An editorial layer, consisting of verse 35b, superimposed the Christian notion of Jesus the Son of Man who had been on earth, and then went up to God in heaven. His withdrawal is a sign of God's temporary judgement. And the implication is that he will finally come from heaven to earth to be welcomed by a responsive and repentant Israel. Here, for the mission of the Q Christians to the nation of Israel, personified in its capital city of Jerusalem, is the silver lining of hope within the dark cloud of judgement. Here, expressed in alternative language, is a restatement of the hope for the celebratory banquet to which 'the many' will be drawn after the exclusion of the Jerusalem-based 'sons of the kingdom' (Luke/Q 13:28–9).

If this admittedly speculative reconstruction is right – a forlorn hope, perhaps! – the underlying pre-editorial material would have taken off from a woe against those who had not themselves killed prophets but were still not being allowed to escape identification with those of their ancestors who had done so. From there it would have run as follows:

> [49]Therefore also the Wisdom of God said, 'I will send them prophets and emissaries, some of whom they will kill and persecute', [50a]so that this generation may be charged with the shed blood of all the prophets. [51b]Yes, I tell you, it will be charged against this generation.
>
> [34a]Jerusalem, Jerusalem, the city that kills the prophets and stones

those who are sent to you! [34b]How often have I desired to gather your children together as a hen gathers her brood under her wings, and you were not willing! [35a]See, your house/sanctuary is left to you.

By virtue of the movement into first-person speech in verse 51b the following first-person speaker in verse 34b must be Jesus. The distinction between the speaker and Wisdom must carry over. The relationship can certainly be – indeed is likely to be – one in which the speaker of the *Lament* understands himself as one sent by Wisdom. Indeed, he is not just any sent one but the last one. His rejection – there is no implication of his being murdered – brings about the abandonment of 'your house', that is to say, the departure of God from the place that is prized as the place of his presence. We should give maximum attention to the fact that the ultimate judgement envisaged by both traditions is an act of God: for the first time in the oracle God comes into the reckoning with 'this generation may be charged . . . it will be charged against this generation' and 'See, your house/sanctuary is left to you' brings God implicitly into the reckoning for the first time in the *Lament*.

In setting its sights on the Jerusalem community, the earliest pre-Q tradition targets the whole community of Israel, the community that identifies and is identified with the holy city and the holy place. The tradition has recourse to, indeed updates, the deuteronomistic view of rejected prophetic missions in interpreting the rejected prophetic mission of Jesus. This view, as the classic texts indicate, is especially firmly championed by Jeremiah, just as the abandonment of the house is also part of the content of the judgement he announced (cf. Jer. 12:7; 22:5). Jeremiah is the prophet in whose shoes the contemporary speaker, the Jesus of the tradition, implicitly claims to stand. Is that speaker, is that Jesus, the historical Jesus? Or do we have to fall in line with the suggestion that Luke/Q 11:49–51; 13:34–5 'cannot logically, in terms of what they say, be ascribed to Jesus . . . indeed cannot be ascribed to a human at all, but only to "a superhuman, divine authority"' (Robinson 1998: 246)?

Such a conclusion would not be the natural outcome of the argument so far. Instead, a case would be better mounted in favour of the authenticity of this tradition, using the three criteria of multiple attestation, dissimilarity and coherence:

(i) The speaker identifies with the prophets and messengers of God – which Jesus did on numerous occasions.

(ii) The speaker thinks of the present generation as the last one – which matches the urgency of Jesus' own mission, and his sense that the time immediately before the great climax has been reached. One recalls here the praise of John as 'a prophet . . . and more than a prophet' (Luke/Q 7:26), with the corollary that he stands on the brink of the kingdom's inauguration that Jesus himself begins to effect. One thinks of 'the law and the prophets until John' (Luke/Q 16:16), with John balanced precariously on the demarcation line between the era of the prophets and the new but controversial and kingdom-defined mission of Jesus.

(iii) The speaker may well review repeated visits to Jerusalem – which Jesus as an observant Jew must have made, and Jesus on a prophetic mission to all Israel needed to make. But, as we have seen, on another level Jerusalem represents Israel, and it is Israel to which Jesus' mission has been dedicated and intensively pursued.

(iv) The speaker laments the unresponsiveness of a community personified in a city – which Jesus does elsewhere, in the woes over Chorazin, Bethsaida and Capernaum (Luke/Q 10:13–15).

(v) The speaker does not accuse his contemporaries of having killed any prophet – which was frequently done in early Christian polemic. He evidently looks for a response of repentance – which Jesus did times without number.

(vi) In announcing the dreadful outcome of national obduracy, namely that 'your house is left to you', a prophetic precedent is prophetically invoked (cf. Jer. 12:7; 22:5), and therefore no recourse to the events of 70 CE is required in order to make sense of the tradition (*contra* Robinson 1998: 238).

Finally, (vii) the speaker speaks for Wisdom but is not equated with Wisdom – as happened early in Christian thought.

So a case can indeed be mounted in favour of the authenticity of this sayings material. It is not a cast-iron case, but at the same time it is not negligible. If it carries any conviction, then there is one final observation to make, and it is this. One topic lurks unmistakably in the background of these sayings of Jesus: destruction!

Third variation: from destruction to replacement

The saying about the destruction and replacement of the Temple by Jesus himself appears in two versions and in two separate but integrally related Marcan contexts. The first version, Mark 14:58, presently set within the tradition of the proceedings against him by the Jewish authorities (14:55–65), runs:

> We heard him say, 'I will destroy this temple that is made with hands, and in three days I will build another, not made with hands.'

The second version, Mark 15:29, set within the narrative of the crucifixion, runs:

> Aha! You who would destroy the temple and build it in three days . . .

Objections on procedural grounds to the historicity of the setting of the first version need not detain us. We learnt long ago that sayings move around in the gospel tradition, and even the most suspicious of settings says nothing either way about the historicity of a saying. All we need note *en passant* is that the handling of the case of Jesus could easily have followed the same lines as that of his later namesake, Jesus ben Ananias, that is to say, a handing over of the offender by the priestly authorities to the Roman prefect for his decision. Whatever the gospels may say, Josephus is clear that those Jewish authorities' objections to Jesus decisively influenced the prefect's decision:

> Pilate, upon hearing him accused by men of the highest standing among us, had condemned him to be crucified . . . (*Antiquities* 18:64)

Whether the saying about destruction and rebuilding can be interpreted satisfactorily; whether it is in whole or in part historical; whether it originally belonged in a context known to us (for example, the event of Mark 11:15–16, cf. Sanders 1985: 75–6); and whether it pinpoints the issue which was determinative in Jesus' case – all these are of some moment in our explorations.

Central to the meaning of Mark 14:58 are the phrases 'this . . . made

---

with hands ... another, not made with hands' (*touton cheiropoiēton ... allon acheiropoiēton*), and the identity of the 'I' who speaks.

First, the word '(an)other'. On every other occasion in his gospel, when Mark uses the term 'other' (*allos*) he has in mind 'another of the same sort' and not 'another of a different sort' – other seeds (4:5–8), other boats (4:36), other human beings with opinions (8:28), other messengers (12:4–5, 9), other commandments (12:31–2), and so on. This immediately undermines the hypothesis that what will be built is not a bricks-and-mortar building but a substitute Temple-like human community, 'a temple only in a metaphorical sense' (Juel 1977: 156), the sort of thing the Qumran community had in mind when using Temple imagery about itself (Donahue 1976: 69–71, 77).

Second, the contrasting terms 'made with hands ... not made with hands' (cf. Lohse 1974: 436). Much is often made of the fact that 'made with hands' can be just a synonym for 'idolatrous', and there are plenty of supporting texts from Leviticus 26:1, 30 LXX to Judith 8:18 and Wisdom 14:8, and on to Philo's imaginative report of Moses' despairing comment on the bull of Exodus 32:

> Whoever holds that none of *the works of men's hands*, nor any created things, are gods, but that there is one God only, the Ruler of the universe, let him join me. (*Life of Moses* 2:168)

But usage is not uniform, not all instances work in that way, and much depends on contexts. (i) It should be wholly inconceivable that Mark would wish to describe as idolatrous a building which was at the heart of the religion of Judaism, and which he himself had again and again referred to with respect: 'my house' (11:17) is typical. (ii) The term *cheiropoiētos* appears in Josephus, *Antiquities* 4:55 for a fire lit by human beings rather than one 'kindled at the bidding of God, brilliant and of the fiercest heat'; in Josephus, *Jewish War* 1:419–21 (cf. *Antiquities* 15:324) for a mound which is artificially constructed rather than a feature of the natural creation; in *Jewish War* 7:294 for a fortress made impregnable both by human construction and by nature (*phusei te kai cheiropoiētōs*). The term appears also in Philo, *Life of Moses* 2:88, in a highly appreciative description of the furnishing of the sanctuary, from which all negativity or thought of idolatry is a million miles away:

> It was necessary that in framing a temple of man's making (*hieron cheiropoiēton*) dedicated to the Father and Ruler of All, he should take substances like those with which that Ruler made the All.

The interpretation of Mark 14:58 would therefore be greatly assisted by a recovered awareness of the inherent neutrality of the term 'made with hands'. There is nothing inherently wrong with the first building, which every Jew knew to have been authorised and endorsed by God. The second, which replaces it, is superior simply and solely, and of course overwhelmingly, because it is the work of God.

One may note that the term 'not made with hands' drives a wedge between what Mark 14:58 envisages and what was achieved by Herod, 'the king of the Jews' (Josephus, *Antiquities* 15:380–423), that is, the pulling down of parts of the second Temple prior to an extensive and more splendid rebuilding. The qualifications conveyed by 'made with hands . . . not made with hands' fit better when God authorises both buildings (second Temple and end-time Temple) but builds the second one differently, that is, by direct action without human, though possibly with superhuman and transcendent, agency.

Third, apart from being Jesus himself, who is the 'I' who speaks – allegedly? The answer emerges when we take careful note of the contexts in which the two versions of the saying are set.

The first version, Mark 14:58, has a context shrouded in uncertainty. Did Jesus say what some say he said? Over what exactly did the witnesses disagree? Did the alleged saying in whatever form have any appreciable effect on the proceedings? If we only had Mark 14:55–65 we would be quite uncertain in the face of observations like: 'Many gave false testimony against him, and their testimony did not agree. Some stood up and gave false testimony against him, saying, "We heard him say . . ." But even on this point their testimony did not agree' (Mark 14:56–7, 58a, 59). Our uncertainty is, however, dispelled by the Marcan crucifixion narrative, within which the second version, Mark 15:29, is set.

Three schematic features of the Marcan crucifixion narrative impress the reader, most obviously. The first is an artificial division of time into three-hour periods, which has the effect of imposing what might be called 'a unity of divine control' on all that happens. The second is the creative use of four allusions to Psalm 22, ending with the anguished cry, 'My God, my God, why have you abandoned me?', which deliberately drives a wedge between Jesus and the courageous and confident martyrs of Jewish history, and prepares for the bright light of resurrection by intensifying the deep darkness of death. The third, and by far the most important for our present purpose, is the use of the scheme involving a testing to the point of death of the righteous servant of God and his claims (cf. Wisdom 2—5; Nickelsburg 1972: 58–62).

The essence of the 'narrative drama' in Wisdom 2—5 is that *what the righteous servant of God actually said* is under sceptical scrutiny. The essence of the matching Marcan narrative scheme is therefore that *what Jesus had actually said* is under sceptical scrutiny. According to the sceptics, it will only be shown to be true if the righteous man – or Jesus – does not die. But in fact both the righteous man and Jesus do die. Nevertheless, the sceptics will not have it all their own way. The truth of what they have doubted will overtake them when they have an experience of 'seeing' – in the case of the righteous man when he is seen among the angels (Wisdom 5:2), and in the case of Jesus, when and how? The amplification of the messianic claim in Mark 14:62 speaks of the opponents 'seeing' him exalted and then coming, while the very circumstances of his death not only convince a representative opponent of the truth of what had been resisted *vis-à-vis* his person (15:37, 39), but they do so in a particularly spectacular way. They provide a forward-looking sign of the destruction of the Temple (15:38), his prediction of which had provoked such intense criticism. The truth of the saying will be demonstrated, but *post mortem* and in a way that the critics do not expect.

How and when will Jesus' act of destruction and rebuilding occur? This is where the tearing of the Temple curtain comes into its own. Within the narrative in Mark 15 it seems to interrupt the smooth sequence of events, which fact serves only to highlight its great importance:

> [37]Then Jesus gave a loud cry and breathed his last. [38]**And the curtain of the temple was torn in two, from top to bottom.** [39]Now when the centurion, who stood facing him, saw that in this way he breathed his last, he said, 'Truly this man was God's Son!'

The curtain of the Temple mentioned here could be either the one which separates the holy place, the sanctuary, from the rest of the Temple site, or it could be the curtain which replaces the Temple doors when they are open during the day (Schneider 1965: 629; Juel 1977: 141). The term used for 'temple', *vaos* rather than *hieron*, cannot be pressed into service in favour of the first possibility (*contra* Juel 1977: 127), since the two words are constantly used as synonyms. The second possibility allows a remarkable correspondence between this damaging occurrence and the similar occurrences listed by Josephus as portents of the destruction of the city and the Temple (Juel 1977: 140–42). Foremost among these is the opening of the eastern gate of the Temple (*Jewish War* 6:293–6) at midnight by a supernatural agency – as strong as 20 men! – at Passover in the year 66 CE. According to a rabbinic text, this is said to have happened more than once, and to have been interpreted by Rabbi Johanan ben Zakkai as a forewarning of the Temple's destruction (*b. Yoma* 39b). In the context of Mark 15, therefore, the invasive verse 38 suggests just such an advance sign of destruction in association with the death of Jesus.

At the moment of Jesus' death, therefore, according to Mark 15:22–39, what he had indeed said would happen has still not happened, but an advance sign has been provided. The question that remains, then, is when Jesus will actually do what he has said he will do in the Temple saying. This brings us back to the related question of the identity of the 'I' who speaks.

(i) The logic of the crucifixion narrative is that the event belongs to the end-time, that is to say, when the Son of Man comes from heaven. There is no room for any other event when Jesus will carry out this act of destruction and building. If the crucifixion narrative is about the testing of what Jesus had said in the official Jewish hearing, then the one part of what he had said that remains unquoted is Mark 14:62:

> You will see the Son of Man seated at the right hand of the Power, and coming with the clouds of heaven.

What Mark 14:62 has done is to equate the Danielic Son of Man with Jesus and to superimpose, as it were, this person on 'the Messiah, the Son of the Blessed One', whose heavenly (*sic*) enthronement is conveyed by the allusion to Psalm 110:1. The explicit testing of Jesus' Messiahship in Mark 15:31–2 therefore also involves an implicit testing of Jesus' Son-of-Man-ship.

(ii) Elsewhere in the gospel of Mark we observe the same sort of thinking. Thus, in Mark 8:27–38 the Messiahship of Jesus (v. 29) has to be understood in a very particular way. Room must be found not only for death but also for the ultimate exercise of the authority of the one who comes with the angels, the one whose Father is God, the one who comes to judge, that is to say, the Son of Man – again, of course, equated with Jesus (v. 38). Similarly, in Mark 13 the pre-Marcan memorandum had spoken in Danielic terms about the concluding climax of events with the coming Son of Man. Naturally, there was no equation of this figure with Jesus in such earlier, non-Christian tradition. But Mark's editorial provision of a new context makes this Son of Man-centred climax unmistakably Jesus-centred (cf. vv. 28–37) and indeed one which is above all integrated with the destruction of the Temple (cf. vv. 2, 4). So Mark, writing before the climax of events in the year 70 CE, looks forward eagerly to the end-time demonstration of the ultimate truth of Jesus' saying about his own personal action of Temple destruction and building. But, and this is important for our enquiry into the history of the tradition, his 'I' is Jesus as Son of Man. The evangelist has done what the earliest versions of the sayings about the coming Son of Man did not do, whether in Mark 13:26 or Luke/Q 12:8–9: he has equated the coming Son of Man with Jesus.

That the coming Son of Man, now a heavenly figure, should on God's behalf destroy the 'made with hands' Temple and proceed to build a 'not made with hands' replacement is entirely logical and consistent. It taps into a pattern of Jewish thought which probably goes back to the pre-70 CE situation, and which is documented in *Sibylline Oracles* 5 and 4 Ezra 13 (cf. Bryan 2002: 193–5). In those texts the allusion to Daniel 7 is significant: the appearance of 'a blessed man [who] came from the expanses of heaven' to act on God's behalf to build a glorious temple 'in the last time of holy people when God, who thunders on high, founder of the greatest temple, accomplishes these things' (*Sib. Or.* 5:414–33). Similarly, 'something like the figure of a man [coming] up out of the heart of the sea . . . and behold, that man flew with the clouds of heaven' on his way to the implementation of a terrifying judgement. This Danielic figure turns out to be 'he whom the Most High has been keeping for many ages', and of whom it is said further that 'my son will be revealed, whom you saw as a man coming up from the sea' (4 Ezra 13:1–4, 26, 32). Within this tradition messianic traits are discernible in the profile of the heavenly person, which might be thought to bring these texts alongside the thought pattern of the Qumran text *4QFlorilegium*

(4Q174), but a normally human Messiah acting as God's agent would not qualify within the terms of the 'made with hands . . . not made with hands' antithesis.

Once the effects of the Marcan editorial superimposition of the 'Jesus = the heavenly Son of Man' equation are subtracted, we can infer with reasonable confidence that the archetype of Mark 14:58 may have been, using 'divine passives' throughout:

> This temple made with hands will be destroyed,
> and in the course of three days another not made with hands will be built.

Is this a saying of the historical Jesus? Reference is often made to the supposed embarrassment of the evangelists (cf. typically, Sanders 1985: 71–6; Allison 1998: 99–100), which is taken to strengthen the case for authenticity. This argument has probably been overstated. In the gospel of Mark, for example, the impressive confusion about the disagreement of the witnesses, and the non-viability of their testimony (Mark 14:55–6, 59) turns out not to stem from any embarrassment but from a carefully constructed scheme, belonging to the pre-70 CE situation, and reflecting Mark's very definite expectations about Jesus' future action. In investigating the authenticity of the saying we have therefore to abandon the embarrassment argument. We can, however, appeal not only to coherence but also to the very distinctiveness of what Jesus says when it is set alongside the sprinkling of Jewish texts which also, each in their own way, speak about the end-time Temple that God will provide (cf. Sanders 1985: 77–88; Allison 1998: 100–101; Fredriksen 2000: 210).

We have already noted Tobit 13—14, though the rebuilt house of God mentioned there is probably, from the point of view of someone purporting to write in the eighth century BCE, the second Temple rather than its end-time successor. The same may apply in the case of *Jubilees* 1:15–17, purporting to review for Moses' benefit the history of Israel up to the exile and the post-exilic restoration:

> [15]And afterward they will turn to me from among the nations . . . and I shall gather them from the midst of all the nations . . . When they seek me with all their heart and with all their soul, I shall reveal to them an abundance of peace in righteousness . . . [17]And I shall build my

sanctuary in their midst, and I shall dwell with them. (Text in Charlesworth II 1985: 53)

On the other hand, firmer support can be found in 1 Enoch 90:28–9; 91:12 and 11Q19 29:7–10.

[90] [28]Then I stood still, looking at that ancient house being transformed: All the pillars and all the columns were pulled out; and the ornaments of that house were packed and taken out together with them and abandoned in a certain place in the South of the land. [29]I went on seeing until the Lord of the sheep brought about a new house, greater and loftier than the first one, and set it up in the first location which had been covered up – all its pillars were new, the columns new, and the ornaments new as well as greater than those of the first, (that is) the old (house) which was gone. [91] [12]Then after that there shall occur the second eighth week – the week of righteousness . . . At its completion, they shall acquire great things through their righteousness. A house shall be built for the Great King in glory for evermore. (1 Enoch 90:28–9; 91:12; text in Charlesworth I 1983: 71, 73)

[7]They shall be for me a people and I will be for them for ever; and I shall dwell [8]with them for ever and always. I shall sanctify my [te]mple with my glory, for I shall make my glory reside [9]over it until the day of creation, when I shall create my temple, [10]establishing it for myself for all days, according to the covenant which I made with Jacob at Bethel. (11Q19 29:7–10; cf. Martínez/Tigchelaar 1998: 1251)

An important impression is conveyed when these apparent precedents are set alongside the gospel traditions of Temple sayings attributed to Jesus. They are comparable but *different*. The Jewish texts are promissory, hopeful, unthreatening, inoffensive – emphasising the building that will take place. To use an important distinction (Sanders 1985: 71), they represent prediction rather than threat. The Jesus material, on the other hand, is threatening. As was the case with Mark 13:2, in the light of the reaction by the authorities to the matching declaration by Jesus ben Ananias, so it is with Mark 14:58/15:29. Every variant of that saying provokes an adverse reaction in its own context. The emphasis is plainly perceived to be on destruction. While it would be possible to see the replacement Temple as implying the very welcome arrival of the end-time, the devastating treatment of the pre-end-time Temple is what attracts attention. Jesus, in other words, is not simply voicing an acceptable variation on a well-accepted Jewish theme. He is speaking *un*acceptably, controversially, dangerously, prophetically.

So this exercise of testing the tradition history of Mark 14:58 points towards the authenticity of its archetype and serves to reinforce the position of Mark 13:2 and Luke/Q 13:34–35a. Multiple attestation comes into its own, especially when the first half of the saying is recognised as containing the primary thrust. While the second half, dealing with replacement, is attested only once, a securer place among the authentic sayings of Jesus can be assigned to the threat of divine judgement. And if that conclusion is correct, it suggests that we should very definitely place Jesus in the succession of Jeremiah (cf. 26:1–19).

> [4]Thus says the Lord: If you will not listen to me, to walk in my law that I have set before you, [5]and to heed the words of my servants the prophets whom I sent to you urgently – though you have not heeded – [6]then I will make this house like Shiloh, and I will make this city a curse for all the nations of the earth . . . [8]Then the priests and the prophets and all the people laid hold of him, saying, 'You shall die! . . .'

That passage is itself very closely related to the oracle in Jeremiah 7:1–15, which contributes to the comment attached to the tradition of Jesus' action in the Temple, to which we now turn. Threats to the Temple, for all the diversity of their formulations, are but variations on the theme of the peril in which a community, identifying with the Temple, presently finds itself. The disturbing and thoroughly unwelcome prophetic voice is a call to realism and repentance.

Fourth variation: a shock to the system

> [15]Then they came to Jerusalem. And he entered the temple and began to drive out those who were selling and those who were buying in the temple, and he overturned the tables of the money-changers and the seats of those who sold doves; [16]and he would not allow anyone to carry a vessel through the temple. [17]He was teaching and saying, 'Is it

not written, "My house shall be called a house of prayer for all the nations"? But you have made it a den of robbers.' (Mark 11:15–17)

Virtually everyone agrees that the incident in the Temple took place. Agreement about its meaning is another matter. Failure to agree may be in part because due emphasis has not always been given to all aspects of Jesus' intervention (Bryan 2002: 208): the expulsion of buyers and sellers, the overturning of the money-changers' tables and the dove-sellers' seats, and the obstructing of the movement of vessels through the Temple. It may also have been caused by interpreters' dogged insistence on trying to make sense of the incident without recourse to the explanation provided – which they have had some difficulty in doing successfully. And finally it may also have been caused by the manifest imprecision of the text itself. What exactly was being bought and sold, apart from doves? The text does not say. And what exactly was in the vessels that would have been carried through the Temple? The text again does not say. Hence the apt comment that this is 'less an illuminating episode than an episode that needs to be illuminated' (Allison 1998: 98).

Yet its importance cannot be doubted, as the history of the discussion proves. Many have seen it as indicating why the authorities moved against Jesus, even though the scale of the event was insufficiently large to provoke an immediate response from the ever-watchful contingent of Roman soldiers, alert to every hint of trouble at festival time. Some, going rather further, have seen in it the other side of the coin represented by the Last Supper, two events which allegedly interpret one another and combine to make Jesus the inaugurator of a new cult (Theissen/Merz 1998: 431–2). So the stakes are high, but caution has never been more necessary.

At the outset the scope of the tradition needs to be clarified. Here one must recall that any later addition to a tradition must serve some Christian purpose, while if a tradition is to survive in and be transmitted by the early Christian community it must be complete and meaningful in its own right. Now it is almost impossible to imagine a Christian purpose in attaching the statement that 'he would not allow anyone to carry anything through the temple', so verse 16 must be original as a sequel to verse 15. But what about verse 17? Notwithstanding the hesitation of some, there would be too much obscurity about verses 15–16 in isolation, so the original unit should be taken as verses 15–17. This point can be reinforced.

If Jesus' action in the Temple functions as, at the very least, a public and prophetic sign in the same way as Isaiah's nakedness, or Jeremiah's smashed pot and his yoke of straps and bars, or Ezekiel's baggage (Isa. 20:1–2; Jer. 19:1–2, 10; 27:1–2; Ezek. 12:1–9: correctly, Wright 1996: 415), then we must note that in each case the observable action was followed by public explanation (Isa. 20:3–6; Jer. 19:3–9, 11–15; 27:3–15; Ezek. 12:10–16). It is surely correct that 'all these signs would be difficult to understand without verbal interpretation' (Sanders 1993: 253). In the case of Mark 11:15–16, the only proposed candidate for such verbal interpretation other than Mark 11:17 is the saying about the destruction and replacement of the Temple in Mark 14:58. The Temple event and that saying are said to form a unity and to be 'mutually supportive' (Sanders 1985: 75, 364). Now it is certainly in principle conceivable that the saying in Mark 14:58 might originally have belonged in such a setting, as in John 2:13–19, and that it later became detached (Theissen/Merz 1998: 432, 459). But John's version is neither primary nor independent. He, like Matthew and Luke, appears to have no source other than Mark. So unless we find that we cannot make sense of verse 17 as a credible clarification of verses 15–16, it is worth persevering with it. And perseverance involves weighing up what each of the two texts, Isaiah 56:7 and Jeremiah 7:11, have to say, and what might be the effect of combining the two.

As far as Isaiah 56:7 is concerned – '. . . my house shall be called a house of prayer for all peoples' – the context of that saying provides very important controls. The surrounding unit of material consists of verses 1–8, held together by two formal 'Thus says the Lord . . .' declarations (vv. 1, 8). The beatitude, 'Happy is the mortal . . .' (v. 2) is followed by a *chiasmus* dealing with two special categories: the foreigner (v. 3a), the eunuch (v. 3b), the eunuchs (vv. 4–5) and the foreigners (vv. 6–7). That beatitude, referring to 'this' and mentioning the opposite of 'right', namely 'evil', picks up the requirement to 'maintain justice, and do what is right' but also introduces the key issue of the sabbath, which then forms the connecting thread in the treatment of the two special cases (vv. 2, 4, 6). Overarching the whole scenario, introduced by verse 1, is 'the coming new age, awaiting its near fulfilment' (Childs 2001: 426), which is amplified in verse 8 by the gathering of both scattered Israelites and the 'others'. In advance of the imminent future when salvation and deliverance will arrive – and here there is an echo of Second Isaiah's own announcement (46:13) – there is thus just one stipulation for the present: 'Maintain justice and do what is right' (56:1). That is to say, 'righteousness', a synonym for God's saving intervention, is to be anticipated in 'righteousness', a synonym for the good life. Such conduct is set within a covenant framework, represented by the sabbath, and the condition, both necessary and sufficient, of participation in the new era by *any* human person is laid down.

Of the two cases of the eunuch and the foreigner, the first could himself be either Israelite or gentile (cf. Schneider 1964: 766). If Jewish, he is legally set apart from the assembly of Israel (cf. Deut. 23:1–3), but the boundary-transcending strategy of the God who is about to act overcomes that restriction. The eunuch is in any case not the major concern of the oracle, being brought within the framework of what is said about the foreigner, who is its real focus. But for the one as for the other, a note of hope and inclusiveness is struck. Neither foreigner nor eunuch need look to the future and fear separation from Israel, or the rejection of their application for membership of Judaism (Brueggemann 1998: 170). Both have genuinely been brought within the scope of the covenant, with circumcision in the case of the gentile proselyte being presumed by the reference to their joining themselves to the Lord (Isa. 56:6: Whybray 1975: 198). Both observe the sabbath and hold firmly to that covenant; both conform to 'the norms appropriate to a life lived under torah' (Childs 2001: 458). Both serve God; both please God. Both benefit from, rather than being disadvantaged by, 'a radical torah obligation to order the community of covenant so as to bind in mutuality the strong and the weak, the rich and the poor' (Brueggemann 1998: 168–9), for that is indeed how 'righteousness' and 'right' are to be understood. Both can look forward with confidence to sharing in the pilgrimage of the scattered people of God to Jerusalem and God's house of prayer there (v. 8).

The implications of 'my house shall be called a house of prayer for all peoples' are spelt out very clearly (v. 7a):

> these I will bring to my holy mountain, and make them joyful in my house of prayer; their burnt offerings and their sacrifices will be accepted on my altar.

It has been well said of Third Isaiah that 'the chapters begin and end with an open-hearted generosity towards foreigners which is unmatched by anything else in the Old Testament' (Emmerson 1992: 55). If it is true that 56:1–8 and 66:18–21 together unite and clasp the whole book together, then the generous welcome in the first passage is made even more pointed by the inclusion of foreigners in nothing less than priestly and levitical service in the second (66:21; cf. 60:7; 61:6). There is a down side, however – an implied critique of 'the apathetic, self-centred leadership' (Emmerson 1992:102) of the contemporary establishment and the fatal inattention to ethical principles which presently scars national life. The positive theme of inclusion has a negative counterpart. That said, there could scarcely be a more unqualified confirmation of the special election of Israel, or of the 'badges of identity' of which the sabbath is typical, or of the special place of the Temple, or of the sacrificial regime which is central to its existence. Specifically, the sacrifices are exemplified by the burnt offerings, that is, the daily sacrifices offered by the Jewish community in order to honour God, to show him gratitude, or to gain his favour (Sanders 1992: 105). Gentiles will come in as full participants, though actually they are gentiles who have ceased to be gentiles and instead have become Jewish proselytes. The inclusiveness which draws them in

> pertains not randomly to any foreigner but those *with deep Yahwist intention*. Yahweh is the recruiter and the welcome committee. As a consequence, the foreigners are inducted into *the full life of the worshipping community*, participating in both prayer and sacrifice. They are welcome! (Brueggemann 1998: 172; my italics)

The outcome is therefore no different an understanding of the Temple here from that which a later generation of priests invoked when faced with the threat from Nicanor: 'You chose this house to be called by your name, and to be *for your people* a house of prayer and supplication' (1 Macc. 7:37). For Isaiah likewise, 'your people', now including all the proselytes, means Israel.

What Isaiah 56:7 contributes, therefore, is a reminder of a coming new era of salvation and deliverance. It is just around the corner for Israel, and it will centre on the worship of the Temple. It has not yet come, but it soon will. In advance of its coming there is one central demand –

covenant faithfulness, 'righteousness'. Anyone, emphatically anyone and everyone, who meets the demand is 'in'. Woe betide anyone, whatever their pedigree, who falls short.

But what happens if there is indeed a falling short of this 'righteousness'? This is where Jeremiah 7:11 provides a chilling answer. The accusation '. . . but you have made it a den of robbers' is drawn from that prophet's Temple sermon (7:3–12, cf. 26:1–6, 12–15). It not only complements the preceding Isaiah 56:7 citation but also *conveys the critical thrust*.

This critical thrust is essentially that the presence of God in the Temple is wrongly being taken for granted by the nation. The threefold repetition, 'The temple of the Lord, the temple of the Lord, the temple of the Lord', is not in this case as it is on other occasions (cf. Holladay 1986: 242) a liturgical or even a magical formula. An intense and overwhelming disclosure to Isaiah of the Lord's heavenly glory was accompanied by the threefold acclamation, 'Holy, holy, holy . . .' (Isaiah 6:3); an intense and agonised plea that the nation should hear a word of doom for King Coniah was prefaced by 'O land, land, land . . .' (Jer. 22:29). Similarly here, the nation itself voices a particularly intense conviction that the Temple is the place of God's presence, and consequently the guarantee of its security. So strong is the conviction that Jeremiah feels the need to keep coming back to that idea (Jer. 7:7, 12, 14). But the conviction is wrong, and the people are mistaken. What they think is certain is in fact conditional (v. 3). Unless the conditions are met, their threefold invocation of the Temple becomes a formula of ghastly hollowness, a demonstration of self-deception, a tragic misunderstanding of the fact that the one who wants to be present is in fact absent.

> The word that Jeremiah speaks calls in question whether the congregation worshipping in the temple is any longer in the presence of Yahweh. (McKane 1986: 159)

But why should such a devastating message be conveyed to the nation? Answer: because of alleged indifference to 'righteousness' as expressed in the Ten Commandments and in the demand for compassion towards the foreigner and the poor (Jer. 7:5–6, 9). For God to return, repentance is a necessary condition: 'Amend your ways and your doings, and let me dwell with you in this place' (v. 3). Such a call for repentance is nothing new. It has been issued repeatedly, but always in vain, by a sequence of prophets, whose experience evokes the deuteronomistic pattern (v. 13). Rejection of such an intense and insistent prophetic call brings only one thing, judgement. And judgement means two equivalent and inseparable things: the destruction of the Temple (v. 14) and the abandonment of the chosen people (v. 15). The fate of the Temple is therefore in the hands of the people; the fate of the people is in their own hands, too – will they shake off the habit of covenant-breaking behaviour outside the Temple, followed by appearance at worship in the Temple? To repent or not to repent: that is the question. The problem is not the place of worship, which in spite of everything remains 'this house which is called by my name' (v. 10), nor is it the system of worship. The problem is simply and solely the worshippers.

When those worshippers are branded 'robbers', and the Temple transformed from its true purpose into 'a den', that is to say, a place of refuge where criminal covenant-breakers can seek refuge (McKane 1986: 163), the diagnosis is unambiguously moral rather than political. So if we come forward from Jeremiah to Jesus, it is more than a little unconvincing to accuse the conservative and somewhat collaborationist Temple hierarchy of turning the Temple into a headquarters of anti-Roman resistance and a 'talisman of nationalist violence', and to read such ideas into the term 'robbers' (*leistai*) (Wright 1996: 420). Caiaphas, due to become a veteran of the policy of expedient co-operation with Pilate, could doubtless be and indeed was accused of many things, but surely not that. Such an idea is a red herring. In any case, the criticism does not seem to be targeted at the hierarchy alone (Bryan 2002: 219–20). If we go back from Jesus to Jeremiah, what is clear is that *a people* guilty of recurrent *abdication of covenant responsibilities* is being indicted. It is the covenant-breaking people that is warned that what God did once in Shiloh he will do again: he will destroy the Temple, unless ... unless they repent and return to righteousness.

All of this suggests that Jesus is painting on a bigger canvas than that of members of the priestly establishment and their ethics. It would, of course, be quite feasible in principle that Jesus should criticise their conduct. Plenty of precedent exists in one era after another for prophetic attacks on priestly behaviour (Evans 2001: 167–9). Plenty of evidence points to priestly self-seeking and corruption in the era of Jesus, including the over-charging of women for the doves needing to be offered after miscarriages, or indeed of the poor in general. In principle no stretching of the imagination is involved in thinking of undue commercialisation or oppressive profiteering in collection of the Temple tax (Bauckham 1988: 79), though it is important to observe that such a criticism would fall some way short of 'a radical objection to the tax itself' (thus, Bauckham 1988: 75). But what is feasible in principle is ultimately unconvincing. Jesus' word interpreting his action is *a word for Israel about Israel*. Over against the tendency to single out the conduct of the authorities, that is, the Temple establishment, as the sole target, what begins to be apparent is that *all the people in a solidarity of identification* is the target, and the identification of the people and the Temple makes the latter the obvious place in which to make a point about the people.

This brings us naturally to some more data suggesting the same conclusion. The tradition of Jesus' action directs the spotlight at 'selling . . . buying . . . money-changers . . . those who sold doves'. All have to do with money, and the same may well be true of the ambiguous carrying of vessels, that is, either the movement of some sacrificial items like corn, wine and oil for use as a burnt offering by those who were unable to provide anything else in association with the morning and evening sacrifice, or the transporting of money to the treasury (Bryan 2002: 212–13). The changing of money can only be with a view to payment of the half-shekel Temple tax.

The payment of this tax was, or was thought to be, biblically rooted in Exodus 30:11–16 and Nehemiah 10:32–3, where the range of concerns which the tax supports is very comprehensively drawn:

> [32]the service of the house of our God: [33]the rows of bread, the regular grain-offering, the regular burnt-offering, the sabbaths, the new moons, the appointed festivals, the sacred donations, and the sin-offerings to make atonement for Israel, and all the work of the house of our God. (Neh. 10:32–3)

In similar vein, the *Letter of Aristeas* 40 refers to such support for 'the sacrifices and the other requirements', and Josephus (*Antiquities* 3:194–6) expounds the Exodus passage: 'The sum thus collected was expended on the needs of the tabernacle.' So it was evidently intended to cover the whole range of Temple commitments, including the provision of sacrifice but a good deal else besides. Virtually every Jewish male over 20 years of age, who was neither a priest nor an Essene – members of the Qumran community were a law unto themselves and paid just once in a lifetime – was intended to make annual payment at Passover time in support of all that the Temple was and did.

A key text referring to the Temple tax runs as follows:

> On the 15th [of Adar] the tables [of the money-changers] were set up in the provinces; and on the 25th [of Adar] they were set up in the Temple. After they were set up in the Temple they began to exact pledges [from such as had not paid]. From whom did they exact pledges? From Levites, Israelites, proselytes, and freed slaves, but not from women, slaves, or minors. If the father had begun to pay the Shekel on behalf of [his son that was] a minor, he may never again cease to pay it. They did not exact pledges from the priests, in the interests of peace. (*m. Shekalim* 1:3)

This text, which has been played down as idealistic, in fact shows itself to be realistic. It tacitly concedes that not everyone did pay. Some resorted to pledges, and of course pledges might or might not be fulfilled. In the case of non-fulfilment it would doubtless be necessary to emphasise the principle on which the payment rested, which may explain some of the evidence cited by those who question the estab-lished status of the tax. Second, the priests did not pay 'in the interests of peace', a phrase which is used elsewhere to indicate an intention to impose order and control on a situation of potential disorder and dispute (cf. *m. Gittin* 5:8–9; cf. 1 Cor. 14:33). Priestly payment of the tax looks as if it had been fiercely argued, doubtless because of the special relation-ship of the priesthood to the Temple, and the text records a decision which had been intended to resolve the argument.

So here was a tax, paid by Jews near and far, Palestinian and Diaspora – only Jews, never Samaritans, never gentiles (*m. Shekalim* 1:3–5) – and, according to Philo (*Special Laws* 1:76–8), accumulating *in toto* massive sums of money: 'the revenues of the temple . . . given with the utmost zeal' in hope of 'release from slavery or healing of diseases and the enjoy-ment of liberty fully secured and also complete preservation from dan-ger'. For those who paid, it evidently represented 'an expression of Jewish identity . . . a symbol of Israel's election . . . fundamentally connected with the ransom of all Israel from Egypt, the signal moment of God's election of Israel' (Bryan 2002: 215–16).

But let us return to the question: did everyone in fact pay? And was the grounding in the biblical texts regarded by everyone as convincing? In spite of the piling up of evidence in favour of that conclusion – thus, 'that it was paid is one of the things about first-century Judaism that is most certain' (Sanders 1992: 156) – a similarly strong case can be made for its being rooted in a Pharisaic interpretation of biblical texts, its introduction only in the early first century BCE, and its remaining controversial and in need of spirited defence by leading rabbis such as Johanan ben Zakkai (Horbury 1984: 277–82). Indeed, he not only mounted a defence but also attributed the disaster of the Jewish war to widespread failure to pay the tax. The balance of the evidence suggests that the *principle* of the tax had become well-established, but the *practice* may have been less firm. All this would mean that any question directed to Jesus about his payment or non-payment of the tax would, on the first premise, be a question about his attitude to the Torah, his support for the Temple, and his identification with the self-consciousness of the Jewish nation. On the second premise, it would be a question about whether he was willing to follow the dominant Pharisaic line for whatever reason, or alternatively claim the freedom not to pay which others may have claimed.

Interference by Jesus with the arrangements for the payment of the Temple tax (Mark 11:15–16) could undoubtedly be seen by some, though not certainly by all, as a critical act *vis-à-vis* the relationship between God and the chosen people, the maintenance of that relationship by means of the system of worship in general and sacrifice in particular, and the status of the Temple as the focus of piety. Would it be viewed in an even more serious light than that, namely as a gesture of very specific protest against the principle of that tax? This is of course possible and has indeed been argued, using the rather obscure tradition of Jesus' declaration about the tax in Matthew 17:24–7 as a platform. Here is the text of that tradition, with unoriginal elements indicated.

> [24]When they reached Capernaum, the collectors of the temple tax came to Peter and said, 'Does your teacher not pay the temple tax?' [25]*He said, 'Yes, he does.'* [25]*And when he came home, Jesus spoke of it first, asking,* [Jesus said,] 'What do you think, Simon? From whom do kings of the earth take toll or tribute? From their sons or from others?'

²⁶When Peter said, 'From others', Jesus said to him, 'Then the sons are free. ²⁷*However, so that we do not give offence to them, go to the lake and cast a hook; take the first fish that comes up; and when you open its mouth, you will find a coin . . .* Take [a coin] and give it to them for you and me.'

As always, we need when checking out the historicity of a tradition to consider first its history. In this case, much suspicion may attach to the frame of the story, the very possible dependence on the similar frame of the Marcan tradition of the dispute about greatness (Mark 9:33–7) which Matthew will use immediately afterwards; the unprovoked initiative taken by Jesus in raising the subject with Peter at precisely the right time (cf. Mark 9:33); the discussion in the privacy of the home (cf. 9:33); the reference to not giving offence (*hina mē skandalisōmen autous*, cf. 9:43–7); and above all the manifestly legendary and arbitrary recourse to the fish. The frame is, however, notable for its implication that while Jesus might not pay the tax, in fact he does so. But *why* does he pay it? Is it a matter of principle or alternatively of mere accommodating pragmatism? Everything hangs on the central saying, 'From whom do the kings of the earth . . .?'

The essential thrust of that saying depends on how the logic of the argument from the earthly kings to the implicit figure of God in heaven is to be understood. The two alternative options would seem to be 'as with the kings, so with God' and 'as with the kings, so *not* with God'. The first option is the one that has been taken for granted since time immemorial, which may of course mean that even to consider the second option is absurdly foolhardy. The first option normally takes the 'sons' of 'the kings of the earth' as family members, and the 'others' as people outside the family. The exemption of family members *vis-à-vis* toll and tribute stems from the ruler's fatherhood rather than his kingship. The 'others' who know him only as king have to do the paying. The implicit application would then be that sonship in the situation of Jesus carries with it exemption from payment of the Temple tax − *either* for those who as Israelites are sons of their heavenly Father (Horbury 1984: 283) *or* for Jesus and his disciples, who are supposedly sons of the heavenly Father in a way that all other Israelites are not (Sanders 1990: 50–51). Hence, the inference has been drawn that for Jesus 'theocratic taxation, levied in God's name, is inappropriate in view of God's fatherhood' (Bauckham 1988: 74). Since we do not have to hand any secure evidence that Jesus understood the sonship of his disciples as distinct or different in kind from the sonship of the rest of Israel, it is more likely on this hypothesis that Jesus affirms the freedom of Israel in the matter of the tax and, if the logic is followed through consistently, the non-freedom and the obligation of those who are not sons – that is to say, gentiles – to pay the tax. This is where the argument starts to get into difficulty, for the Temple tax cannot be a requirement laid upon those who are not members of the community of Israel. One might be able to ease the problem by suggesting that, since God is both king and father of Israel, the matter is actually left open. In other words, the tax does not *have* to be paid by any Israelite, for it would not be a function of a filial relationship. If it *is* paid, it would be a voluntary gesture of respect for kingship. The Temple tax would then be seen as neither prohibited nor mandatory, but rather a matter of free choice. But this interpretation is less than compelling.

At this point one might very hesitantly suggest that the second option, for all that it seems *prima facie* counter-intuitive, might be thought to work rather better than the first. Elsewhere, when Jesus invokes the situation of earthly rulers, the intention is to set up a contrast (cf. Luke/Q 7:25; Mark 10:41–4; Luke 22:25–6) rather than a comparison (cf. Matt. 18:23; 22:2): 'It is not so among you', and so on. In other words, 'this is how it is with earthly rulers, but in the sphere under consideration it is different.' The question asked by Jesus belongs in the tradition of wisdom – 'this is how it is, isn't it?' – and yet it doesn't quite work. The answer, namely, that tax is paid by others and not by family members, has no parallel in the regime of the Temple tax. That tax is paid by Israel or it is not paid at all. Put otherwise, Jesus is not setting up such a parallel. On the basis of the second option, therefore, Jesus is not asserting freedom to choose whether to make at most a wholly voluntary payment, that is, freedom not to pay at all. Rather, he confirms the obligation to pay the Temple tax because the sons of the heavenly Father – Jews in general, and the disciples, too, as part of their involvement in the community life of God's people – are *not* free of such an obligation in the way that family members of earthly kings are. In other words, precisely in the situation where God is known as both king and father, the tax should be paid in support of his house, the Temple.

We must not assume too readily that by 'Jesus' we can understand 'the historical Jesus'. The earliest form of the tradition must be pre-70 CE, for there is little point in arguing about the payment of the Temple tax when the Temple is no longer there. But it is not possible to prove beyond a peradventure that the tradition could not be recording an early Christian but post-Jesus clarification of a stance on this particular issue.

If, however, the tradition does go back to the historical Jesus, then his attitude to the Temple tax turns out to be affirmative, and the attractiveness of interpreting the incident in the Temple as an attack on the tax is severely reduced, indeed reduced to zero. In practical terms, an attack on the Temple tax could hardly be other than an attack on what kept the Temple going and indeed on what was paid by all and sundry for precisely that reason. It would inevitably be an attack on the Temple itself. But the whole tendency of the Temple traditions which we have been surveying is towards a quite different conclusion.

That conclusion and the point on which all such evidence converges is Jesus' prophetic announcement of the near kingdom; his insistence on the alienation of the people from 'righteousness'; his call for repentance; his communication of the peril in which the people stood if they took for granted their security and the presence of God in the Temple; and his warning that instead of performing its divinely planned purpose when the new era dawned, the Temple would be destroyed and its worship disrupted if the people did not take stock and return to covenant faithfulness. This is the Jesus whose voice we have heard in the other Temple traditions. This is Jesus acting like a prophet, speaking like a prophet, and in no way smuggling into the situation any more developed a Christology than that.

Immediately after the incident in the Temple Mark reports the question about authority (Mark 11:27–33), which itself throws light on what had happened:

> 27As he was walking in the temple, the chief priests, the scribes, and the elders came to him 28and said, 'By what authority are you doing these things?' 29Jesus said to them, 'I will ask you one question; answer me, and I will tell you by what authority I do these things. 30Did the baptism of John come from heaven, or was it of human origin? Answer me.' 31They argued with one another, 'If we say, "From heaven", he will say, "Why then did you not believe him?" 32But shall we say, "Of human origin"?' – they were afraid of the crowd, for all regarded John

as truly a prophet. [33]So they answered Jesus, 'We do not know.' And Jesus said to them, 'Neither will I tell you by what authority I am doing these things.'

Three considerations serve to tighten the connection between this story and the preceding Temple incident: (i) the term 'these things' (vv. 28, 29, 33), pointing back to some preceding occurrence; (ii) the rare appearance of the 'chief priests' on any scene of Jesus' activity (v. 27), this time understandably linked with what has just taken place on their territory (v. 18); and (iii) the difficulty of imagining verses 27–33 existing as a separate unit of tradition serving any useful Christian purpose. Once the connection, which stands at least a chance of being pre-Marcan as well as Marcan, is established, the key issue is the logic of Jesus' response to the interrogation. Why does he answer the question about his own authority by introducing the topic of John the Baptist's status?

The possibility that Jesus is implying that his own authorisation occurred within the setting of John's work appeals to some, who go on to refer to the declaration by the heavenly voice (Mark 1:11) which is then in turn interpreted in messianic terms (cf. Wright 1996: 537). But this does not really work, for the experience of the heavenly voice is private and known only to Jesus (cf. above, pp. 45–6), and is also quite distinct from the experience of baptism. Put otherwise, Jesus' authority is not a function of John's baptism. So we turn to an alternative, namely that Jesus is implying that the decision about his own validity and authorisation is the same as the decision about the validity and authorisation of John, the person with whom he had been personally associated and who was defined by his baptism. In other words, the choice about himself is, as it was about John, a matter of 'of heaven or of human origin . . . of human origin [versus] truly a prophet'. If that is so, then the inference is that Jesus' authority is, in his view, *prophetic* authority. What has happened is intrinsically prophetic, not intrinsically messianic. This inference is in harmony with the fact that if the two biblical quotations in Mark 11:17 are an intrinsic part of the pre-Marcan tradition of the Temple incident and of the historical reality it records, then it is important that Jesus is lining himself up with two members of the *prophetic* succession (Isaiah and Jeremiah) and, moreover, quoting two *prophetic* passages, neither of which has any kingly/messianic reference whatever.

Finally, the interpretation of the event by means of the combination of Isaiah 56:7 and Jeremiah 7:11 links confident short-term expectation of an intervention by God to save and liberate his people, and denunciation of certain persons. This reminds us strongly of Luke/Q 13:28–9, an indubitably authentic saying of Jesus himself, and one to which we have frequently found ourselves returning. The saying and the incident with explanation attached share (i) a focus on Jerusalem/Zion; (ii) an appreciative outlook on the traditions of Israel; (iii) an act of expulsion, that is, of judgement on Jewish persons; and (iv) a pilgrimage to Zion and the Temple by gentiles:

> 29Many shall come from east and west (and from north and south) and sit at table with Abraham, Isaac and Jacob in the kingdom of God. 28But the sons of the kingdom will be cast into outer darkness: there will be weeping and gnashing of teeth.

So Jesus' action turns out to be a deeply symbolic prophetic gesture. It is directed at the whole community (leaders and led, i.e. all those represented by sellers and buyers of the necessary wherewithal of sacrifice). It has a judgement component and also a component of appeal for a response (see Jer. 7:3–7) to the hitherto rejected announcement of the near kingdom. The judgement component picks up the standard equivalence of Temple and community, and envisages removal of the divine presence and/or the destruction of the Temple in the face of community obduracy. In this respect there is a deep underlying agreement between this tradition and the threat in Mark 13:2 and the lament over Jerusalem in Luke/Q 13:34–35a. And suppose the nation proved obdurate in the face of prophetic warning, and suppose therefore that the Temple were indeed destroyed, what would need to happen in order that the ultimate providential purpose of God be effected? Surely the provision by God of a new Temple for a new people. And in that case there is a deep underlying agreement between Jesus' interpreted action in the Temple and the earliest version of the destruction and building tradition in Mark 14:58. All in all, we seem to be in contact with the historical Jesus and his deliberate evocation of the memory of the prophet Jeremiah.

That evocation and that memory have not yet, however, been exhausted. Only with the final meal and the eucharistic words do the full implications for the people of God and the Jesus people finally emerge.

CHAPTER 6

Celebrating in the darkness: 'They shall be my people'

Introduction

Anyone who knows and appreciates the novels of Anthony Trollope will remember the Revd Francis Arabin. For Trollope he's a sort of hero, being a sworn foe of evangelicalism and a very serious and solemn representative of the Oxford Movement that Trollope much liked. We know he's a hero because in the story of *Barchester Towers* he also gets the girl in the end! That adroit political manipulator, the archdeacon, Dr Grantly, would probably have been much more fun to spend an evening with, but it was the Revd Francis Arabin, a man unworried by schism, who was the pretext for the following comments by Anthony Trollope:

> We are much too apt to look at schism in our church as an unmitigated evil. Moderate schism, if there may be such a thing, at any rate calls attention to the subject, draws in supporters who would otherwise have been inattentive to the matter, and teaches men to think upon religion. (1978: 158)

Well, thinking upon religion has to be a good thing, and there is plenty of moderate – not to mention immoderate – schism around when it comes to the interpretation of the eucharistic words, the centre of attention in this chapter. A good deal of the schism is made inevitable by the apparent reluctance of ecclesiastical interpreters to recognise that recourse to tradition history is not an optional extra but a *sine qua non*. Of course, within the parameters of concern to articulate the Christian faith in a way which reflects *our* concerns and *our* thought forms, a certain process of intellectual translation has to be undertaken. But if thereby violence is done to what we think Jesus said and meant, that is something different. And reluctance to explore and be guided by tradition history cannot be defended, still less advocated. Nor can inattention to the cardinal principle that the meaning of what may be attributed to Jesus would need to make sense to him as speaker and to his disciples as hearers. The more we read into 'his' sayings a meaning which he and they could not have comprehended, but which we claim to be essential and non-negotiable, the more we have to be willing to abandon their authenticity. But if we allow in principle the possibility that Jesus might have said something which we can recover, and might in the process have meant to convey (and indeed succeeded in conveying) some meaning which first-century CE Palestinian Jews could comprehend, then recourse to tradition history comes into its own. Not that a commitment to the 'history of tradition' enterprise does anything but send us straight into a jungle of problems that are very difficult to solve.

The route we need to take in this final part of our exploration involves reflection on how Jesus' death relates theologically to his mission in general and his attitude to the Temple in particular. This will have important implications for the community of Jesus people. But before we undertake a special study of the eucharistic words it is as well to clear the ground.

Jesus and atonement

A clear logical distinction needs to be drawn between *intention* (thus: 'Jesus came into the world in order to die') and *result* (thus: 'Jesus died, but the aim of his mission was not to die but to call Israel to prepare for the inauguration of God's kingdom').

The *intention* scheme involves attaching meaning to a death *in advance*, which makes that death *theologically necessary*. Many Christians take this position for granted, not only as their own position but also as the position that, in their view, Jesus *must* have adopted. Whether they are making a secure historian's judgement may be doubted, for an historian is bound to feel the force of two critical objections. The first is that the sayings attributed to Jesus and putting this view forward are extraordinarily easily matched with, and in principle may not only reflect but be generated by, convictions held energetically by the earliest Christians. The second is that on such a basis the eventual death would need to inform and 'indwell' those sayings of Jesus which would seem to epitomise the concerns of his mission, most notably 'kingdom of God' sayings. That is just what it does not do.

The *result* scheme, on the other hand, takes seriously a genuine sense of the tragic. It takes seriously the conflict that, with dispiriting normality, comes the way of the typical prophet, and it accepts that in one sense any such prophetic mission may end in 'failure'. But it does not see the ultimate outcome of the conflict or the 'failure' of the mission as inexorable or inevitable, and certainly not designed or desired. In the end it may attach meaning to the death, but more likely does so at the time when *either* that death has come to be regarded as inevitable *or* it is being viewed retrospectively and interpreted with the help of the well-stocked treasury of Jewish reflection on the deaths of martyrs. Thus: 'I, like my brothers, give up body and life for the law of our ancestors, appealing to God to show mercy soon to our nation . . .' (2 Macc. 7:37); 'I [Eleazar] am dying . . . for the sake of the law. Be merciful to your people, and let our punishment suffice for them. Make my blood their purification, and take my life in exchange for theirs' (4 Macc. 6:27–9); 'They [the martyrs] became . . . a ransom for the sin of our nation' (4 Macc. 17:21); and 'These gave over their bodies in suffering for the sake of religion . . . Because of them the nation gained peace' (4 Macc. 18:3–4).

Those Maccabean martyrdoms in fact serve us rather well as a possible parallel for the death of Jesus: they *came to be* understood as atoning, but at the time they were tragedies which could only be deeply regretted. Moreover, their coming to be understood as atoning was not seen as carrying any negative implications for the sacrificial system. As a matter of history, the ravaging intervention of Antiochus Epiphanes had vandalised the Temple and the sacrificial cult had been rendered non-operative at the time they died; but as a matter of theology and religion, their supposedly atoning deaths in no way jeopardised the restoration of regular sacrificial and cultic activity.

The setting of Jesus' mission is one in which the Temple and its sacrificial system are together a working reality. That working reality brings about atonement for Israel in conjunction with repentance for those who acknowledge failure. Jesus, as we have seen, shows every sign of respecting the Temple cult.

It is important theologically, as we have seen, that the closest followers of Jesus, having made the decision to move from Galilee to Jerusalem after Easter, continued to worship regularly in the Temple and remained dependent on the sacrificial system. They plainly did not see the death of Jesus as a sacrifice that set aside or rendered the sacrifices obsolete. In similar vein, it was perfectly possible to use the *imagery* of Passover to draw out the implications of Jesus' death (see the tradition in 1 Cor. 5:7), without thereby setting aside the celebration of the Jewish festival. The idea of a once-for-all sacrifice that replaces the Temple sacrifices was probably the theological achievement of the pioneers of world-wide Christian mission, operating in a context where Greeks and Romans were familiar with religious notions of dying persons acting as scape-goats, and of voluntary human deaths functioning vicariously as expia-tory sacrifices (cf. Hengel 1981: 13–31). There the linguistic and religious categories were already current among educated gentiles before the Christian missionaries came over the horizon. Only in that context does it become necessary to speak of a life that is *intended* to be laid down in death.

Two circumstantial considerations suggest that Jesus might have reck-oned with the *logical* possibility, as distinct from the *theological* necessity, of martyrdom. The first would be the fate of John the Baptist, with whom he had been so closely associated. The second would be the expe-rience of finding his preaching rejected (cf. Luke/Q 10:13–15; 13:34–35a; 16:16/Matt. 11:12–13). The multiply attested presence of the deuteronomistic scheme as a generalisation about the prophetic experi-ence of rejection (which sometimes, though not always, goes as far as assassination) would open up the theoretical possibility, though no more than that. We should again note, however, that the deaths of the prophets were in every case unfortunate tragedies, not intentional means of atonement.

This is the point at which we need to consider the few – relatively few – sayings attributed to Jesus which envisage future suffering and death. It is not always easy to be sure that they stem from Jesus himself. Whatever may be the truth about that, the small group of such sayings deserves analysis and assessment.

The dispute about fasting (Mark 2:18–20) is one such and may be discussed first. This tradition, in its final form, refers to a future time when, following the removal of the bridegroom, the practice of fasting will be renewed as a gesture of mourning. As always, the history of the tradition needs to be examined (cf. Taylor 1997: 203–11). The text runs as follows:

> [18]Now John's disciples and the Pharisees were fasting; and people came and said to him, 'Why are John's disciples and the disciples of the Pharisees fasting, but your disciples are not fasting?' [19a]Jesus said to them, 'The wedding guests cannot fast while the bridegroom is with them, can they? [19b]*As long as they have the bridegroom with them, they cannot fast.* [20]*The days will come when the bridegroom has been taken away from them, and then in that day they will fast . . .*'

First, the practice of fasting is a 'given' in the practice of Judaism (cf. Isa. 58:1–9, and Day of Atonement texts), and it is inconceivable that Jesus and his disciples should not have recognised the statutory fasts. Therefore the issue here is the practice of *additional* fast days by Pharisees (cf. Luke 18:12), which the disciples of John apparently did, and those of Jesus might be expected to, observe. The problem is apparently that John's disciples indeed did, but the disciples of Jesus had come not to do so.

Second, Jesus' defence is a wisdom-type appeal to a commonplace of everyday life, about which he therefore expects everyone to agree: 'The wedding guests cannot fast while the bridegroom is with them, can they?' The fact that the bridegroom is *any* bridegroom simply rules out the idea that he has in mind, and is applying to himself, some christological term. For that there is in any case a complete absence of evidence. So all that Jesus is doing is affirming that in the setting of his own mission there is something to celebrate – some occasion analogous to that most joyful of events, a wedding.

Third, the bold italicized material, verses 19b–20, consists of a bridge section, opening up thought about the time after the bridegroom has left the wedding party, and then a climactic statement of how fasting will break out after his departure. But here we leave the realm of everyday experience in which Jesus had been working in verse 19a, and in doing so we encounter the problem that when the bridegroom conventionally leaves and is escorted to the bedroom with his new wife (cf. Tobit 8:1), the idea of fasting never for one moment crosses the minds of the assembled company!

So the upshot is that the bold italicized section, verses 19b–20, is at odds with the underlying unit of tradition, verses 18–19a, and reflects the later assimilation of the practice of *some* Christians to Pharisaic norms – we recall the respect in which the highly conservative James, brother of Jesus, came to be held in Pharisaic circles (cf. Josephus, *Antiquities* 20:201), and the Lucan report that the company of Jerusalem believers included some hard-line Pharisees (Acts 15:5). On the other hand, verses 18–19a make no reference at all to any expectation of a period of time after the present celebratory era. And the crucial corollary is therefore that the history of the tradition in Mark 2:18–20 gives no support at all to the idea that Jesus anticipated a crisis in the form of his death. We cannot yet say that he did not. But Mark 2:18–20, suitably treated, does not encourage us to say that he did.

From the dispute about fasting we turn to the sayings about the suffering Son of Man (e.g. Mark 8:31; 9:31; 10:33–4). These sayings play a very important role in Mark's theological scheme, but do they go back before Mark? They have no precise parallel in Q. Q is not reticent about unresponsiveness and rejection (cf. Luke/Q 7:34; 9:58; 13:34), but that is not the same as undergoing death. It is hypothetically possible that under the surface of the Marcan Son of Man sayings there is a *bar (e)nash(a)* saying which read, 'A man (*bar enash*) dies, and after three days will rise again.' This would be a general statement of resurrection hope, not confined to Jesus himself, and drawing on the idiom of 'on the third day' = 'after a short time' (cf. Hos. 6:2). This would then be a confident affirmation of general resurrection, which is implicit in Luke/Q 13:28–9 and explicit in Mark 12:18–27. Again, we have no indication of anything special in connection with Jesus' death – in fact, quite the opposite!

What then of another death-focused saying, one which is known by both Q and Mark and deals with 'taking up the cross and following Jesus' (see Mark 8:34; Luke/Q 14:27)? This doubly attested saying is probably intended not so much as a call to literal martyrdom as a metaphorical call to self-denial and abandonment of the assumptions and comforts of normal existence for the sake of the kingdom. This interpretation is confirmed, partly by the preceding saying about hatred of families, (Luke/Q 14:26), and partly by the accompanying Marcan sayings (8:35–7). These pick up the wisdom-type idea that prosperity and riches do not provide the wherewithal to pay one's way out of the jaws of death (cf. Ps. 49:7–8), and ask for that idea to feed into the call to discipleship. The call to abandon human security, since death is 'the ultimate leveller of all human beings' (Anderson 1972: 376), for the sake of identification with Jesus 'merely' activates the principle which applies to everyone. Jesus' own literal death, and any religious necessity or theological meaning attached to it, is not in view.

A concluding piece of evidence is provided by Mark 10:35–45, which makes a specially important contribution to this discussion. As we saw during our study of the meaning of 'following Jesus', this looks like an amalgamation of three separate traditions: (i) the question of greatness in Jesus' future kingdom, verses 35–7, 40; (ii) sayings about suffering as represented by a future cup/baptism, verses 38–9; and (iii) the dispute about greatness, verses 41–5 (cf. Mark 9:33–7).

The sayings about the cup/baptism could well go back to Jesus, for the language is very unusual and atypical of Christian usage. Evidently they belong to a phase of his mission when the storm clouds have gathered. Jesus is gripped by the expectation of having to pass through the period of trauma that precedes the arrival of God's kingdom. But the experience he anticipates is neither unique nor atoning. As for the ransom saying (Mark 10:45b), we have already noted (p. 111) that this shows every sign of being a later attachment which does not work in the way that authentic *bar (e)nash(a)* sayings have to work. It is highly unlikely to be a saying of the historical Jesus.

In sum, therefore, the most likely conclusion from a study of Jesus' death in relation to his future expectation can be formulated in terms of the clear logical distinction with which we began. The evidence encourages no thought of *intention*. We are not pushed in the direction of the view that Jesus came into the world in order to die. Instead, we are pushed towards *result*. Put another way: Jesus died, but the aim of his mission was not to die but to call Israel to prepare for the inauguration of God's kingdom.

Meal and meaning

When we turn to the tradition of Jesus' last meal with his disciples, the historical task is complicated by the fact that we have to allow for powerful influence on the preservation and adaptation and growth of the sayings from the direction of the regular practice of the early Church. There is a further complication, indeed one which causes even more difficulty and confusion: we ourselves in the twenty-first century cannot possibly read these sayings without the conditioning brought about by many centuries of disagreement, debate, and division as to their meaning. Those disputes have been between churches and also within churches. They have sometimes rather sadly illustrated the recurrent truth that what people – Christian people included – can be least clear about they are prepared to be most aggressively assertive about.

The first thing to note is that the dating of Jesus' last meal with his disciples is very uncertain. Did it take place at the same time as the celebration of the Passover meal (thus, Jeremias 1966: 41–62), or was it timed for the preceding evening (thus, Theissen/Merz 1998: 424–7)? It is very hard to tell.

In favour of Passover are the following hints: (i) The meal was eaten in Jerusalem, (ii) not in the afternoon but at night, and (iii) by 'reclining' persons. (iv) Jesus broke bread during the course of the meal. (v) Red wine was drunk, that is, *if* he referred to 'my blood', and (vi) words of interpretation were spoken over bread and cup.

Against Passover, on the other hand, stand the following considerations: (i) In none of the traditions is any reference made to a lamb. (ii) An alternative chronology is set out by John 13:1; 18:28; 19:31 and Jewish tradition: 'On the day before Passover Jesus of Nazareth was hanged.' (iii) Possible reminiscence of earlier timing is provided by Mark 14:1–2: '. . . not on the Passover . . .' (iv) The difficulty of timing proceedings against Jesus on the night of Passover, if that is when they took place, is formidable. (v) Early Christian investment in Passover symbolism when interpreting the meaning of Jesus may have exerted an influence. Finally, (vi) Christian celebration of the Lord's Supper did not take place annually at Passover time but more regularly, probably weekly, when the community came together.

The case against a Passover timing is probably stronger than the case in favour. But in any case, what is clear is that the general context and atmosphere of the event is that of the Passover festival. This is also important in view of the fact that the actual eucharistic words themselves do not demand, dictate or depend on either of the two possible timings of the meal (Smith 1993: 107). Jesus could have modelled his words on the Passover formulae even if the meal anticipated the festival celebration itself. This point is conceded by the pre-eminent modern advocate of the Passover timing:

It should be emphasized that the Last Supper would still be surrounded by the atmosphere of the Passover even if it should have occurred on the evening before the feast. (Jeremias 1966: 88)

Such a Passover context and atmosphere is especially firmly conveyed by Luke's narrative. After the disciples – in this version, Peter and John (Luke 22:8 diff Mark 14:12, 'his disciples') – have prepared the Passover (Luke 22:7–13), the evangelist moves straight into the meal (22:14–18, 19–20). He leaves the discussion of the betrayal until afterwards so that it can initiate a post-meal farewell discourse (22:21–3, 24–38). Before we reach the actual eucharistic institution, Luke provides a distinct prelude to the meal:

> [14]When the hour came, he took his place at the table, and the apostles with him. [15]He said to them, 'I have eagerly desired (*epithumia epethumēsa*) to eat this Passover with you before I suffer; [16]for I tell you, I will not eat it until it is fulfilled in the kingdom of God.' [17]Then he took a cup, and giving thanks he said, 'Take this and divide it among yourselves; [18]for I tell you that from now on I will not drink of the fruit of the vine until the kingdom of God comes.'

There has been some speculation about whether Jesus' statement of 'eager desire' may imply a longing that was not fulfilled, and also about whether Luke has a separate non-Marcan source for this material in 22:14–18.

The first question is fairly easily answered: the longing *is* fulfilled. (i) Luke's own narrative makes clear that this was a Passover that Jesus was indeed intending to share. The instructions are for preparation 'that *we* may eat the Passover' (22:8). The message for the householder is about a place 'where *I* may eat the Passover with my disciples' (v. 12). And when Jesus says, 'I will not drink *from now on* . . .' (v. 18), the time note refers to a situation that obtains in future but not at the moment of speaking (cf. Luke 22:69 diff Mark 14:62). (ii) Although in several Lucan instances of 'to desire', the longing is not fulfilled (cf. 15:16; 16:21; 17:22), the verb 'to desire' (*epithumeō*) is generally neutral as far as fulfilment is concerned: sometimes the longing is not fulfilled (thus, many men longed to marry Judith, but to their chagrin longed in vain: Judith 16:22), but most times the longing is definitely satisfied (e.g. Num. 11:4; Deut. 12:20; 2 Sam. 23:15; Ps. 106:14–15). We are therefore dealing with 'an ardent, real, attainable wish, now being accomplished or realized' (Fitzmyer 1985: 1396).

The second question about a possible non-Marcan source for Luke is probably to be answered 'no' (*pace* Fitzmyer 1985: 1386). In Luke 22:15–18, the narrative describes a participatory Jesus, seriously intending to eat the Passover – the reference is to the whole (cf. v. 8) and not to a part of the celebration – and then drinking from the cup which is shared by the apostles. The disciples' sharing in the meal as a whole is given added intensity by the double warning, lightened by the traditional expectation of the final banquet (cf. Luke/Q 13:28–9), that this is a farewell meal and Jesus is about to die. That double warning looks like an edited version of Mark 14:25, 'Truly, I tell you, I will never again drink of the fruit of the vine until that day when I drink it new in the kingdom of God.' Mark's positioning of that saying, a warning of death rather than a commitment to fasting, leaves open the very awkward, even grotesque, possibility that Jesus himself had shared the cup, probably the third cup, the so-called 'cup of blessing', which he had interpreted with reference to himself (Mark 14:24). There was therefore every reason for Luke to move the saying to a safer position, introducing for that purpose one of the two earlier Passover cups, one shared by Jesus as well, but not interpreted with reference to himself, as well as broadening its span of reference to the whole celebration (Luke 22:16). The most likely conclusion is that Luke is creatively and reflectively at work, and that in so doing he is using Mark, and Mark alone.

So much for Luke, but what about Matthew? He also uses Mark, and his editing shows a tendency to make the tradition independent and liturgically useful – thus the identity of the persons involved is specified, the word over the cup is transformed into direct speech, and the imperatives 'eat . . . drink' are added. He also adds the interpretative phrase, 'for the forgiveness of sins' (cf. Matt. 26:28). His source, Mark 14:22–4, runs:

> [22]While they were eating, he took bread, and after blessing it he broke it, gave it to them, and said, 'Take, this is my body.' [23]Then he took a cup, and after giving thanks he gave it to them, and all of them drank from it. [24]He said to them, 'This is my blood of the covenant, which is poured out for many.'

Matthew shows no sign of having any version other than that one he received from Mark, so we can work with Mark as a basic source and, for the purpose of this present historical exploration, set Matthew on one side.

Luke's version of the eucharistic words plunges us into the text-critical maelstrom caused by an overwhelmingly large number of manuscripts which contain 22:19b–20, and a small number which end with 'he broke it and gave it to them saying, "This is my body"' (v. 19a).

> ¹⁹ᵃThen he took bread, and when he had given thanks, he broke it and gave to it to them, saying, 'This is my body, ¹⁹ᵇwhich is given for you. Do this in remembrance of me.' ²⁰And he did the same with the cup after supper, saying, 'This cup *that is poured out for you* is the new covenant in my blood.'

The shorter reading is the more difficult, and a process of abbreviation is hard to understand, so it has appealed to many writers and biblical translators (cf. Evans 1990: 786–8). On the other hand, in spite of the difficulties, the longer version remains persuasive to the majority of scholars (cf. Fitzmyer 1985: 1387–8; Theissen/Merz 1998: 417).

If we were to vote for the shorter text, there would be nothing to disconnect Luke 22:19a from Mark 14:22, and therefore nothing to encourage the conclusion that Luke knew some tradition other than Mark. If, on the other hand, we vote for the longer text, we find in Luke a slightly different version from that of Mark, even if it occasionally shows the influence of Mark. For example, the phrase 'that is poured out for you' (*to huper humōn ekchunnomenon*) is a nominative formulation, matching 'this cup' (*touto to potērion*), rather than a dative formulation, which it should be in order to match 'in my blood' (*en tōi haimati mou*) (Evans 1990: 791; Smith 1993: 76). The fact that it is a *mismatch* points to Lucan editorial activity under Marcan influence (cf. Mark 14:24: *to huper pollōn ekchunnomenon*), and the possibility of an underlying tradition in which no such phrase figured. This takes us on to notice that at several points Luke agrees with Paul (1 Cor. 11:23–5) against Mark. And Paul is quite explicit that he is depending on earlier tradition: 'I *received* from the Lord what I also *handed on* to you, that the Lord Jesus on the night when he was handed over . . .' So Luke's deviations from Mark are not all his editorial work, but rather signs of his dependence on the same source as Paul used. Paul's version presently reads:

²³For I received from the Lord what I also handed on to you, that the Lord Jesus on the night when he was handed over took bread, ²⁴and when he had given thanks, he broke it and said, 'This is my body that is for you. Do this in remembrance of me.' ²⁵In the same way, after supper, he took the cup, saying, 'This cup is the new covenant in my blood. Do this, as often as you drink it, in remembrance of me.'

As already noted, Paul's and Luke's versions are themselves not identical. (i) Paul lacks both Luke's 'given', which can easily be there because Luke wanted symmetry with 'poured out', and also Luke's 'which is poured out for you', on which we have already commented. (ii) Paul includes a second command, 'Do this in remembrance of me.' The repetition of this command serves to give symmetry to the two interpretative sayings, and symmetry in turn is beloved of those whose stock in trade is polished liturgical texts: it is more likely to have been added to the Pauline tradition than subtracted from the version preserved by Luke.

From the two accounts provided by Luke (22:19–20) and Paul we can, therefore, with due tentativeness reconstruct what was probably in the tradition they received:

> ¹⁹ᵃThen he took bread, and when he had given thanks, he broke it and gave to them, saying, 'This is my body ¹⁹ᵇwhich is for you. Do this in remembrance of me.' ²⁰And he did the same with the cup after supper, saying, 'This cup is the new covenant in my blood.'

The Luke/Paul agreements against Mark are as follows: (i) The word over the bread includes 'which is for you. Do this in remembrance of me.' (ii) There is an intervening meal: 'likewise *after supper* he took the cup . . .' (iii) The word of interpretation over the cup is asymmetrical with the preceding saying, that is, by beginning, 'This cup is . . .' rather than 'This is . . .' It also echoes Jeremiah 31:31–4 in respect of 'the *new* covenant'. This is where the process of reconstruction and choice between alternative possibilities can begin in earnest.

From what follows it will be clear that the tradition underlying Luke/Paul looks at every point but one more original than the tradition preserved by Mark.

First, the *intervening meal* is more likely to have been excluded than inserted, so it is original! Without it the two eucharistic components are held very firmly together; with it they are kept somewhat apart. The influence of liturgical worship is more likely to have brought them together than to have separated them. But that means that the two sayings over bread and cup must be independently comprehensible, which means in turn that the explanatory phrase 'which is for you' is likely to have been present. It was possible for it to be dropped when the word over the cup had been associated more immediately with the word over the bread and included a 'for . . .' element (Smith 1993: 117). Therefore the earliest tradition of *the word over the bread* consisted of: 'This is my body which is for you.'

Second, the original *word over the cup* is more likely to have been asymmetrical than symmetrical in relation to the word over the bread: again the later tendency is likely to have been towards rather than away from symmetry. Therefore the wording in the earliest tradition was probably: 'This cup is the new covenant in my blood.'

Third, the injunction, 'Do this in remembrance of me' (absent from Mark; present once in Luke; present twice in Paul) is uncertain, though it would fit into a Passover framework. Without a high degree of confidence, we might include it, but it is more likely to stem from early Christian worship, where the assembled community entered into the memory of Jesus.

If we were to assign it to the earliest tradition, and even pave the way for its possible attribution to Jesus, the question of meaning would be quite sensitive. In the mouth of Jesus, the command to the disciples, 'Do this . . .', could only refer to their eating of the bread and drinking of the cup. They do nothing else. They are in no position to do anything else. At that point in time the 'remembrance' could not be their looking back to something that happened in the past – hence the suggestion that the words mean 'that God will remember me' (thus, Lev. 24:7; Num. 10:9–10: cf. Jeremias 1966: 237–55).

This suggestion is hardly persuasive, however, especially when a Passover setting is taken into account. There the remembering is done by those who are present. It would therefore seem preferable to render the text as 'that you may remember me', encouraged by the definitive Passover text, 'This day shall be for you a memorial day' (Exod. 12:14, cf. also Josephus, *Antiquities* 17:213, describing the festival of unleavened bread as being called 'passover, being a commemoration (*hupomnēma*) of their departure from Egypt'), and other references to human remembrance such as Wisdom 16:6: 'They were troubled . . . and received a token for a deliverance to *remind* them of your law's command.' That same meaning was doubtless also involved in early Christian understanding of the Lord's Supper (1 Cor. 11:20). That is probably where it exclusively belongs, rather than with Jesus himself.

Fourth, attached to the word of interpretation over the cup there is the saying, 'Truly I say to you, I will never again drink of the fruit of the vine until that day when I drink it new in the kingdom of God' (Mark 14:25).

To summarise, then, we have tentatively recovered the earliest form of the tradition. Using the synoptic and Pauline material, we have found that it consisted of a two-part narrative describing actions of Jesus on either side of an intervening meal, and the following sayings:

> 'This is my body which is for you.'
> 'This cup is the new covenant in my blood. Truly I say to you, I will never again drink of the fruit of the vine until that day when I drink it new in the kingdom of God.'

Before addressing the question of what Jesus may have meant, we must pause just once more over the logically prior question of whether this tradition is in whole, or only in part, the words of Jesus himself.

At this point a view has to be taken, however tentatively, concerning the phrase 'in my blood'. A reference to blood fits well within the Marcan version's reworking of the Exodus 24:8 saying, 'See the blood of the covenant that the Lord has made with you . . .', but it does not fit at all well with the classic *new* covenant text of Jeremiah 31:31. That text does not envisage the offering of sacrifice as the basis for the renewed relationship between the Lord and Israel-Judah. Furthermore, as has been pointed out (Theissen/Merz 1998: 422), the idea of the new covenant is similarly espoused in the Qumran community as the self-description of itself as it sets out to be Israel, and no inauguration by sacrifice is envisaged for the sake of the fulfilment of that hope (cf. CD 6:19; 8:21). So it is entirely plausible (thus, Theissen/Merz 1998: 423) that the word over the cup consisted only of

> 'This cup is the new covenant. Truly I say to you, I will never again

drink of the fruit of the vine until that day when I drink it new in the kingdom of God.'

The absence of the phrase 'in my blood' leaves the first part of this second word of interpretation without a reference to Jesus himself, that is, anything corresponding to 'This is *my* body ...' Some may regard this as a defect. But the fact is that the first word of interpretation, by referring to Jesus' body, envisages Jesus as a whole person (see below), and conveys a complete message about him and his role in the divine plan. In conveying that message it needs no amplification, nor does it require to be seen as the first part of a two-part declaration.

We can reinforce that suggestion. The subsequent modification of the proposed original saying by the removal of 'new', the addition of 'in my blood', and eventually the substitution of 'This is ...' for 'This cup is ...', is readily understandable in terms of later developments. A post-resurrection effort to come to terms with the perplexing *brutum factum* of Jesus' death, assisted by reflection on such scriptural material as would enable the ideology of sacrifice and even atonement to be exploited, is sufficient explanation.

To move to the question of meaning might provoke a crisis of confidence for any modern interpreter: how, we might ask, can we hope to succeed when Christians have in the course of two millennia contended with one another for widely divergent understandings? Should we even try, rather than allowing each reader/hearer who re-uses these words to attach whatever meaning they will, and then invoking a reader-response-inspired suggestion that absolutely any interpretation can count as right and absolutely no interpretation can be said to be wrong? Well, that way lies an investment in theological confusion, even chaos, for the clashing interpretations of these words which Christian history brings into view cannot all be 'right', and we owe it to ourselves as responsible historians, sensitive to that same Christian history, to try and do better. That said, if we make a serious attempt at determining the essential meaning of these texts, it would seem that our best hope is to work within the framework of Judaism at the time of Jesus, and therefore to hold with total and unwavering seriousness to the principle that any viable interpretation must pass the test of being comprehensible to Jesus and his companions within that framework. This is absolutely crucial. Later Christians may impose their own interpretations, but each and all of us have to be careful lest in doing so we impose a meaning which is attractive to us, maybe even treasured by our particular Christian tradition, but alien to those who were there in the first place.

If the historical Jesus said, 'This is my body which is for you,' the following considerations should probably guide the process of interpretation:

First, as already noted, the saying has to be meaningful in its own right, at least provisionally, since the parallel saying over the cup is separated from it by a considerable interval of time. It is perfectly possible that the second saying should supplement the meaning of the first, but the first must be clear by itself.

Second, the term 'body' in Jewish thinking stands for the person rather than 'flesh and blood' reality, so the saying is symbolic and arguably gives no encouragement to the later notion of 'real presence'. The bread *represents* and *symbolises* Jesus. Eating the bread therefore effectively seals the already existing bond of commitment. That commitment is to him, that is to say, to what he and his mission have represented, and to the God whose real and royal presence in the mission of Jesus has been affirmed from start to finish.

The symbolic intention is confirmed by the parallel with the word of interpretation over the unleavened bread in the Passover meal: 'This is the bread of affliction . . .' (Deut. 16:3). Anything other than a symbolic meaning would have been quite incomprehensible within a Jewish thought world, to which emphatically both the disciples and Jesus belonged.

Third, within the general Passover context in which these words were voiced, the analogy of the word of interpretation of the unleavened bread would almost certainly come to the minds of the hearers. And if so, the interpretation set out in *m. Pesach* 10:5 would condition not only 'This is . . .' but also '. . . for you':

> In every generation a man must so regard himself as if he came forth himself out of Egypt, for it is written, 'You shall tell your child on that day, It is because of what the Lord did *for me* when I came out of Egypt.' [Exod. 13:8] Therefore we are bound to give thanks, to praise, to glorify, to honour, to exalt, to extol, and to bless him who wrought all these wonders *for our fathers and for us*. He brought us out from bondage to freedom, from sorrow to gladness, and from mourning to

a Festival-day, and from darkness to great light, and from servitude to redemption; so let us say before him the *Hallelujah* [Pss. 113–14, or more likely just Psalm 113: cf. *m. Pesach* 10:6].

Thus, it begins to emerge that the phrase 'for you' (*huper humōn*) does not take us into the thought world of sacrifice, still less of atonement, which in any case was not required to give meaning to the Passover phrases 'for me . . . for our fathers and for us'. It is important to stay with what is actually *demanded* by the saying rather than what might be imposed upon it. Even an advocate of the view that Jesus attached atoning and salvific significance to his impending death, observes that the breaking of the bread

> may adumbrate the violent death that awaits Jesus, but this may be a theological rereading of the story through later Christian interpretation and eucharistic tradition . . . The breaking of the bread probably has nothing to do with the atoning value of Jesus' sacrifice. (Evans 2001: 389–90)

There is, of course, no shortage of texts using *huper*-formulae with nuances of sacrifice. Two such are the report that 'some of the priests came out to greet [Nicanor] peaceably and to show him the burnt offering that was being offered for (*huper*) the king' (1 Macc. 7:33), or, again with reference to the burnt offering, 'Accept this sacrifice on behalf of (*huper*) all your people Israel' (2 Macc. 1:26). But in such texts while the allusion to sacrifice is present, the notion of atonement is absent. We must again recall that burnt offerings were not expiatory (Sanders 1992: 104–5) but rather a means of pleasing God and encouraging him to be well disposed to the person or persons concerned. When a burnt offering is offered in the Temple 'for' (*huper*) a foreign power, there can be no thought of atonement but only a gesture of human respect with a view to securing God's favour.

> [77][God] did not forbid the payment of homage of another sort, secondary to that paid to God, to worthy men; such honours do we confer upon the emperors and the people of Rome. For them we offer perpetual sacrifices; and not only do we perform these ceremonies daily, at the expense of the whole Jewish community, but, while we

offer no other victims in our corporate capacity, even for the [imperial] family, we jointly accord to the emperors alone this signal honour which we pay to no other individual. (Josephus, *Against Apion* 2:77; cf. Philo, *Embassy to Gaius* 156–7)

This brings us to a series of examples of *huper*-formulae carrying no sacrificial overtones. Many of them are statements of purpose or of the cause for which a person is taking a defined action. Thus, 'for you' (Judg. 9:17) means 'for your freedom'; 'for the sake of our people' (2 Sam. 10:12) means 'with a view to their freedom'; a series of texts use the preposition 'for' to define the good cause for which a person acts or even suffers, whether it be life and/or law, religion and/or national identity, family and/or people (Wisd. 16:24; 1 Macc. 2:40, 50; 9:44; 16:3; 2 Macc. 6:28; 14:38; 3 Macc. 1:23; 4 Macc. 1:8, 10; 6:22; 11:2, 15; 14:6; 15:12, 26; 16:13). Thus, in similar vein, two passages from Josephus can be drawn into the discussion (cf. Fitzmyer 1985: 1401):

(i) According to Josephus (*Antiquities* 13:5), Jonathan, brother of Judas Maccabeus, responded to the plea 'not to suffer the nation to be without a defender or be destroyed by its afflictions'. He therefore declared himself ready to die [for his countrymen] (*huper autōn*), in imitation of his brother 'who in concern for his countrymen had died on behalf of the liberty of them all (*huper tēs hapantōn eleutherias*)'. It had already been affirmed that Judas 'had had the fortitude to do and suffer all things for (*huper*) the liberty of his fellow-citizens'. In so doing, he had 'left behind him the greatest and most glorious memorial (*mnēmeion: sic*) – to have freed his nation and rescued them from slavery' (*Antiquities* 12:433–4). The language used carries no nuance of sacrifice or substitution but rather of self-giving for the sake of a cause like the liberation of the community, a cause with which the person concerned is identified.

(ii) According to Josephus (*Jewish War* 2:201), Petronius, the legate of Gaius Caligula, was reduced by the dogged intransigence of the Jewish community in the face of the threat to erect the Emperor's statue in the Temple, to saying,

It is better that I should take the risk. Either, God aiding me, I shall prevail with Caesar and have the satisfaction of saving myself as well as you, or, if his indignation is aroused, I am ready on behalf of the lives of so many (*huper tosoutōn*) to surrender my own.

The language is again the language of identification, not sacrifice in the strict sense of the word.

So, we ask, did the historical Jesus say, 'This is my body which is for you'? Three key ideas come to the fore, which sound familiar to those engaged in the quest for the historical Jesus. They therefore benefit from the use of the criteria of multiple attestation and coherence. Those ideas are, (i) the consciousness of his centrality in the kingdom-centred plan of God; (ii) the relationship of involvement and identification that binds him and his disciples; and (iii) the recognition that the cause for which he stands takes precedence over all life and even death. In those terms there is encouragement to say 'yes' to the question. If so, the death which casts a shadow over this last fellowship meal is not some kind of trans-action with God, but rather the unwelcome final experience which rounds off a whole life devoted to unswerving commitment to the wellbeing of Israel.

One further point is worth noting now. On the basis of the above reconstruction it can be seen that it is only the bread saying which has an explicit first-person reference: the cup saying does not. That fact would inevitably give the bread saying a certain pre-eminence, which in turn may explain why the term 'the breaking of bread' was used to describe the fellowship meal of the earliest Christians (cf. Acts 2:42; 20:7).

We can now move on to the word over the cup, 'This cup is the new covenant.' If the historical Jesus is the speaker, the following considerations guide the meaning:

First, neither a cup nor the contents of a cup *are* a covenant, so the meaning is again clearly symbolic: the implied 'is' means 'represents'. And again the action of drinking is vital. It implies sharing and benefiting, ratifying a commitment to be and to represent the renewed people of God. Already they are, by eating, involved with Jesus, and by drinking, committed to being what Israel is intended to be — which is what the language of 'the new covenant' is all about.

Second, the 'new covenant' is, as we have seen, that of Jeremiah 31:31–4. That passage does not include or require any reference to death. What is presumed is a moment of mutual commitment between God

Jesus People

and a people, and also an engagement with the sinfulness and alienation of that people. Their relationship with him has been strained by disobedience, but now God is being held to his undertaking to repair and renew. In activating such language to interpret an experience of the 12 – a highly symbolic number, of course – it is implied that in their receipt of forgiveness and of divine action to transform human persons at the core of their being they embody, not a new Israel, but *Israel*! The new covenant involves the 'old' law, not a new law, and a renewed people, not a new people:

> [31]The days are surely coming, says the Lord, when I will make a new covenant with the house of Israel and the house of Judah ... [33b]I will put my law within them, and I will write it on their hearts; and I will be their God, and they shall be my people ... [34b]They shall all know me, from the least of them to the greatest of them ... I will forgive their iniquity, and I will remember their sin no more.

So did the historical Jesus say, 'This cup is the new covenant'? Once again the key ideas are familiar, and therefore again they benefit from the use of the criteria of multiple attestation and coherence. The demand for a righteousness that is realised at the heart of a human person's existence, the purpose of establishing through the disciples a people whose being was truly representative of Israel, and the debt to Jeremiah, all encourage a 'yes' answer to the question.

Finally, did the historical Jesus say, 'Truly I say to you, I will never again drink of the fruit of the vine until that day when I drink it new in the kingdom of God'? Very few gospel specialists deny it. There is more division over whether the saying is an announcement that this is the last of the fellowship meals shared by Jesus and his disciples, and therefore a prediction of death, or a vow of abstinence. The former is more likely than the latter, for the following reasons.

The word of interpretation, 'This cup is the new covenant', has no personal reference to Jesus, and therefore does not prohibit the possibility of Jesus' drinking it. And the formulation, 'I will never again ... until ...' (*ouketi ou mē ... heōs*) is not intended to exclude the moment of speaking: when Luke edited Mark 14:25 in Luke 22:16, 'I will not eat it until ...', it was the eating of 'this Passover' which was envisaged, and Luke 22:8, 11 (Mark 14:12, 14) had previously indicated that the Passover

---

would be eaten by Jesus as well as by his companions. So while the notion of abstinence for the sake of the redemption of Israel (Jeremias 1966: 207–18) is not at odds with the concerns of the historical Jesus, it is probably not required by the tenor of Jesus' saying.

Taking the alternative view, we can draw the following conclusion. Jesus sees this meal as the last of the sequence in which he and his disciples have shared wine. His impending death is recognised as inevitable, but he looks forward to the ultimate meal when, restored and vindicated by resurrection, he once again drinks wine with them. That meal in God's kingdom is both the substance of the hope to which he had alluded many times (cf. Luke/Q 13:28–9) and the continuation of the inclusive fellowship meals that had been a hallmark of his controversial mission (Mark 2:16; Luke/Q 7:34). As it has been so memorably expressed (Jeremias 1966: 262):

> Table fellowship with Jesus is an anticipatory gift of his final consummation. Even now God's lost children may come home and sit down at their Father's table.

Celebrating in resurrection light

The recovery of the text and the meaning of the original eucharistic words of Jesus can facilitate a radical clearance of ideas, specifically of those ideas that arguably confuse or divert attention from the real heart of the matter. For a start, we are able to infer with confidence that Jesus died – such was the *outcome* – but Jesus did not come into the world to die – such was not the *intention*. So the centre of gravity of his mission was all that had gone before, and all that had gone before was no mere introduction to the great and overwhelming climax. To put the matter tersely, the problem of what should be the appropriate mood in which to celebrate Good Friday is also resolved: not joy because of an atoning human self-sacrifice, but solemn grief at the dark and tragic cutting short of a human life. Liberation from theories of sacrificial atonement enables us to take death not *less* seriously but *more* seriously. And that makes it possible to emerge the more joyfully into the celebration of resurrection life.

As always, every theological proposition must submit to the scrutiny of the insistent question: 'What sort of God are we presupposing in this, that, or the other proposal?' In this case, we have to refine the question and try to analyse what sort of God we have in mind if we think of the death of a human being as the *sine qua non* of the liberation of humankind from its many ills. Is God, as it were, boxed into a system of his own devising, and unable freely to forgive? Is God not mirrored in the overflowingly generous and unconditionally forgiving father, so vividly and movingly portrayed in the parable of the prodigal son? Is not this God the God of Jesus of Nazareth?

If the death of Jesus is freed of the interpretative apparatus of sacrificial atonement, we can understand a number of historically non-contentious features of early Christianity.

First, we can understand why the earliest Christians made no alteration to their habits of worship but continued to attend the Temple, something that is almost incomprehensible if an atonement achieved by Jesus had spelt the abrogation of the Jewish sacrifices. Better surely to say that they celebrated Jesus but, quite distinctly, relied on the Temple cult. In the long term, when the cult was brought to an almost unbearable end during the war with Rome, the principle to which the rabbis resorted was a principle that they (and we!) too could make foundational (Hos. 6:6):

> I desire steadfast love and not sacrifice,
> the knowledge of God rather than burnt-offerings.

Second, we can make sense of a multitude of full-blooded – by no means milk-and-water! – theological statements in the New Testament which present the unencumbered *brutum factum* of Jesus' tragic, even if obediently endured, death as the prelude to the mind-blowing reversal of resurrection. Just one example may suffice. In his letter to the Philippians (2:6–11) Paul adopts (and adapts) a piece of early Christian verse, which he probably did not write himself, but with which he unreservedly agreed. Without the faintest echo of recourse to atonement-type thinking, it declared among other things (and I try to give the sense):

> ... he humbled himself and became obedient right through life to the
> point of death. Therefore [because of his record of obedience from one
> end of life to the other] God in his grace exalted him ...

Third, Paul, the theological giant of the first century CE, occasionally – but only occasionally, and then when drawing on the thoughts of others

---

for tactical or other reasons – used the vocabulary of atonement. But, we may ask, was his heart in it? Almost certainly not! The view of the death of Jesus that controls his Christian understanding majors on participation, solidarity, involvement – participation, solidarity, involvement in death which brings in its wake the very same experience of sharing in resurrection.

So we come back to where we started. Christian people are definitively *Easter people, resurrection people*. They do not rely on an atoning death in the past, nor are they sustained by any form of renewed offering of that which cannot be renewed in the present. They are people who, when they gather in eucharistic celebration, take a stance *vis-à-vis* those elements in the mission of the historical Jesus that represent *continuity across the Easter divide*. By eating, they signal their participation in him and in it, and their joy in liberation. By drinking, they signal their experience of the new covenant and the old commitment and the new hearts effected by the God of the future. He makes, has made, and will make, all things new until his providential programme for humankind is celebrated in the sharing of 'the fruit of the vine . . . in the kingdom of God'.

CONCLUSION

Jewish people, Jesus people and Easter people

The results achieved by the six preceding studies of the mission of the historical Jesus and its community dimension converge on the following outcome. In its broadest sense, though not its only sense, the community of Jesus was the community of Israel.

The religious awareness of that community of Israel can be gauged in a number of ways. Over against all other nations, the holiness of this people was crystallised in a covenant with God, with commitments on both sides being recognised as essential to the harmony of the relationship it was designed to perpetuate. Within the whole complex of law which articulated the commitments of Israel to her God and vice versa, those laws which functioned as boundary markers or badges of identity gained special prominence in times of trauma, but their significance was no less vital in times of calm. The historical Jesus caused no disturbance whatever to that situation. If the arguments put forward in this book carry conviction, the tendency of some very distinguished and prominent writers within what is often called 'the third quest' is probably mistaken. Insofar as Jesus' position, unswerving on monotheism (on that everyone agrees), was wholly unthreatening in respect of circumcision, sabbath and food laws, he was at one with each and every other member of his people. That he attracted criticism for his position on *how* a law should be interpreted and applied, which he did, is not the same as attracting criticism for setting a law aside, which he did not.

Much the same may be said of his position *vis-à-vis* the Temple, though it is a good deal more difficult to extract from a small number of notoriously controverted traditions exactly where he stood. The proposal

---

of this book is that the Temple remained for him the extraordinarily special but essentially vulnerable 'holy place' of God's presence, the very epitome in bricks and mortar of the covenant commitment. As the place of God's presence it epitomised the people who loved it and worshipped there. As the place of God's possible absence it epitomised its dependence on the religious integrity of those who prized it. Again, the tendency of some very powerful contributors to the contemporary quest to open up space, for whatever reason, between Jesus and the Temple, and all that it represented as well as all that happened within it, is probably mistaken.

If Jesus belongs to the Jewish people, is committed to the religious parameters within which the history and religion of the Jewish people are set, and even at times exhibits the instinctive prejudices of the Jewish people *vis-à-vis* other nations, we are not surprised that his mission should be directed exclusively to the Jewish people. An instinct for inclusiveness and a capacity for courageous confrontation with prejudice certainly characterises his adoption of a broader definition of the people of God which allows the Samaritans to be inside rather than outside. But with regard to gentiles, we cannot forget the reluctant response to the Syrophoenician mother in her hour of need. Nor can we forget that even when gentiles figure appreciatively in his sayings, those sayings are directed negatively towards a Jewish audience rather than positively towards gentile hearers.

If Jesus is so traditional, why then was he a problem to any of his contemporaries? Well, why was Jeremiah? Why was Hosea? Why was Amos? Why, a little later, was Jesus ben Ananias? Those who work within Israel cannot expect to be accepted gladly and warmly if their sense of calling is prophetic. The controversies that raged in respect of the understanding of law and Temple were fuelled by Jesus' prophetic commitment to his people and his God. The kingdom of God was not just a future hope but was also beginning to invade the present. It was not just comfort and freedom, it was also threat and menace. It did not just offer heartening restoration, it also demanded already in the present an openness to God, a transformation of values, a return to basic ethical priorities, a compassionate commitment to wholeness. Those who saw the covenant as a charter of a people's rights or even an all-risks insurance policy, but not to a sufficient degree (from Jesus' point of view) a charter of responsibilities, were always going to take offence at such a prophetic message. Like John before him, Jesus was set on renewal. Like John before him

Jesus was set on 'righteousness', a reality very much at home within the covenant, a reality expressive of God's transforming intervention, a reality which needed *to be made real* in human conduct, whether in relation to God himself or to other human persons.

So the Jewish people, the whole people, were Jesus people in the fullest and richest sense. And yet an observation like that immediately requires qualification. For the Jesus people were also, like the Baptist's people, a people within a people, a people released from the prospect of judgement threatening, like fire or water, to overwhelm them. Prophetic divisiveness in the face of reserved responses, whether of indifference or overt hostility, was inevitable. In the face of receptivity, on the other hand, there came into being a people within a people who were, when theology overtook arithmetic, not *a part of Israel* but rather *Israel itself*. What one might call the realisation and enrichment of categories could be seen in the mission of the agents of Jesus, which he regarded as his own mission. These messengers, themselves voluntarily poor and designedly vulnerable, would need hospitality in an ordinary way, and would give and receive peace greetings in an ordinary way. But the mission intensified the ordinary. Peace people, 'sons of peace', were not just the all and sundry of courteous Israelites, but rather became those who actually received the message and on that basis provided hospitality to the messengers. In no formal sense did they constitute a community. But in a loose sense they did, for within the wide community they opted into a narrower community of those who took seriously the kingdom-centred message of Jesus. From his paradoxical prophetic perspective, one can say, they opted into being what they already were, the people of God. By contrast with those who did not, they were 'the Jesus people'.

There was nothing loose about the sense in which the immediate home-leaving, property-leaving, work-leaving 'followers' of Jesus set about realising the hope of Israel in the face of the coming kingdom. They experienced and exhibited – or were, despite their inadequacies, intended to exhibit – the defining principles of Jesus' mission. In their distinctiveness and in their togetherness, in their identification with Jesus and perhaps most visibly in their controversial celebrations with Jesus, they showed what the life of the 'Jesus people' was all about. Within the parameters of Israel's life, especially as treated prophetically, they with him encapsulated the life of the 'new covenant'. In one very vital sense, as Jesus' prophetic predecessor Jeremiah had made abundantly clear, the 'new covenant' was nothing other than the old covenant (if that risky term may be employed) but it was now effected between the same God and a new people – no, better than that, a renewed people. The members of that renewed people were involved in a project of realisation, that is to say, making real that knowledge of God as king and Father which had always been at the heart of Israel's experience. In the process, they reordered their priorities away from the concerns of the present age. They accepted, however reluctantly, the new non-hierarchical order of a 'community of equals'. They accepted poverty and the implications of a message centred on poverty, that is to say, God's offer of a better tomorrow for the poor of today, God's unqualified concern for the whole of his (poor and often powerless) people, God's estimation of the poor as equal members of his people along with the non-poor, and his critical and even judgemental scrutiny of those with little understanding of the life-sapping trinity in unity of poverty, grief and hunger. They had no option but to accept the freedom from gender discrimination that established women, listening to the silent message of the lilies, alongside men, attending to the message of the ravens, within the community of active and 'following' companions of Jesus, and the intense commitment to the cause of the kingdom that went with it.

Who was this Jesus who called and commissioned, who bore with and taught, these 'Jesus people'? What, if anything, was so special about him? Participants in both the, strictly speaking, misnamed second and third quests have produced schemes which tend to promote him above the level of a prophet, and thus to maximise the continuity and ease the transition from the historical Jesus to the post-Easter Messiah (cf. 1 Cor. 15:3b). This is not by any means always born of a theological concern, but it undoubtedly conditions the varied historical constructions that they build. Now, let it be said, it is wholly unsurprising that an historian who has a commitment to the community of faith, as I do, cannot be other than him/herself when going about his/her work. All that can be asked is open and critical self-awareness. Nevertheless, the conditioning does introduce the risk of making the historical Jesus more than he was. He was a prophet. He was also more than a prophet. But we might usefully pause to ask how he himself understood the notion of being 'more than a prophet'. When he described the major human influence upon him, John the Baptist, as 'a prophet, yes indeed, and more than a prophet' (Luke/Q 7:26), what seems to have been in mind was where John stood in relation to God's coming kingdom. In other words, God's great work was reaching a crescendo and coming to its climax. When he used the biblical figures of Solomon and Jonah as yardsticks of wisdom and prophecy, claiming that in connection with himself 'something greater' than both was being made available (Luke/Q 11:31–2), what seems to have been in mind was where he stood in relation to that same coming kingdom. Until it came, he by the exercise of his prophetic and Spirit-energised charismatic power was able to introduce in a partial way the freedom and wholeness that characterised the new era (Luke/Q 11:20). When it came, he would – or so he believed – enter for the first time into the exercise of royal power over Israel, and doubtless over all the other nations in line with classic Jewish expectations. The mustard seed would become a tree. As far as the historical Jesus was concerned, however, he remained the one whom his people recognised as the end-time prophet.

Recognising him as that ultimate prophet was for the 'Jesus people' not a matter of registering agreement with a proposition, or associating oneself with something that could be demonstrated, or even aligning oneself with a decision and authorisation issued by an establishment of some sort. As was always the case with communities or even individuals in relation to charismatic figures, the commitment arose simply and solely from a sense that this person rang true. When at least some of them found themselves endowed with his charisma, there was doubtless all the more reason to believe that the cause was truly God-inspired. The implication of belonging to the 'Jesus people' was therefore becoming in consequence 'Spirit people'. Thus they became the nucleus of those who, according to John the baptizer and mentor of Jesus, would be baptized in Spirit.

When this Jesus, this ultimate prophet, fell foul of the authorities his people were almost as exposed as he was. Not that the authorities did anything drastic about them – itself one of the most tantalising features of the train of events which led to what seemed like the total collapse of his cause and his claims as the fateful Passover festival unfolded in that never to be forgotten year. The apparently serene indifference of the authorities to the 'Jesus people' could not, however, mask – perhaps in a real sense it confirmed with almost unbearable firmness – the collapse and disintegration of a community. If so, the Easter happenings had not only personal but also communal implications. God, so they believed, had raised and vindicated his ultimate prophetic emissary, inaugurating in an unexpected way and with unexpected definition the royal authority which Jesus had anticipated when Israel's history entered its final phase. Comparably, the scattered 'Jesus people' were brought together on the basis of a new step of faith. No one actually *proved* that Jesus had been raised, and no one could be dismissed as necessarily perverse or obdurate if they found themselves incapable of such a step of faith. For those who found they could manage it, however, it was another case of Jesus ringing true.

That was the moment in time when the Jesus people became the Easter people. Released from an almost unbearable trauma, they now found themselves facing a virtually limitless task, that is to say, working out how far their community life was new and discontinuous with what they had known previously, and how far the continuity was so important and unimpaired that they had still to hear ringing in their ears the echo of the voice of the historical Jesus.

Publications mentioned in the text

Allende, I. (2003), *My Invented Country. A Memoir*, London: HarperCollins.

Allison, D. C. (1998), *Jesus of Nazareth: Millenarian Prophet*, Minneapolis: Augsburg Fortress.

Allison, D. C. (1999), 'Q 12:51–53 and Mark 9:11–13 and the Messianic Woes', in B. Chilton & C. A. Evans, eds, *Authenticating the Words of Jesus*, Leiden: Brill, pp. 289–310.

Allison, D. C. (2002), 'Rejecting Violent Judgment: Luke 9:52–56 and its Relatives', *Journal of Biblical Literature* 121: 459–78.

Allison, D. C. (2005), *Resurrecting Jesus*, London: T. & T. Clark.

Anderson, A. A. (1972), *Psalms I*, London: Oliphants.

Anderson, G. A. (1992), 'Sacrifice and Sacrificial Offerings', *Anchor Bible Dictionary* 5: 870–86.

Anderson, R. T. (1992), 'Samaritans', *Anchor Bible Dictionary* 5: 940–47.

Anglican–Roman Catholic International Commission (2005), *Mary: Grace and Hope in Christ*, London: Morehouse.

Bailey, K. E. (1976, repr. 1983), *Poet and Peasant*, Grand Rapids: Eerdmans.

Bailey, K. E. (1980, repr. 1983), *Through Peasant Eyes*, Grand Rapids: Eerdmans.

Balz, H. R. (1994), '*Boanērges*', in H. Balz & G. Schneider, *Exegetical Dictionary of the New Testament I*, Grand Rapids: Eerdmans, pp. 222–3.

Barton, S. C. (1994), *Discipleship and Family Ties in Mark and Matthew*, SNTSMS 80, Cambridge: CUP.

Bauckham, R. (1988), 'Jesus' Demonstration in the Temple', in B. Lindars, ed., *Law and Religion*, Cambridge: James Clarke, pp. 72–89.

Bauckham, R. (1994), 'The Brothers and Sisters of Jesus: An Epiphanian Response to John P. Meier', *Catholic Biblical Quarterly* 56: 686–700.

Bauckham, R. (1998), 'The Scrupulous Priest and the Good Samaritan: Jesus' Parabolic Interpretation of the Law of Moses', *New Testament Studies* 44: 475–89.

Bauckham, R. (2002), *Gospel Women. Studies in the Named Women in the Gospels*, Edinburgh: T. & T. Clark.

Bockmuehl, M. (2000), *Jewish Law in Gentile Churches*, Edinburgh: T. & T. Clark.

Borg, M. J. (1999), 'An Appreciative Disagreement', in C. C. Newman, ed., *Jesus and the Restoration of Israel. A Critical Assessment of N. T. Wright's 'Jesus and the Victory of God'*, Carlisle: Paternoster, pp. 227–43.

Brown, R. E., Donfried, K. P., & Reumann, J., eds (1973), *Peter in the New Testament*, London: Chapman.

Brueggemann, W. (1987), 'The Book of Jeremiah: Portrait of a Prophet', in J. L. Mays & P. Achtemeier, eds, *Interpreting the Prophets*, Philadelphia: Fortress, pp. 113–29.

Brueggemann, W. (1998), *Isaiah 40—66*, Westminster Bible Commentaries, Louisville, KY: WJK.

Bryan, S. M. (2002), *Jesus and Israel's Traditions of Judgement and Restoration*, SNTS Monographs 117, Cambridge: CUP.

Bultmann, R. (1963), *The History of the Synoptic Tradition*, Oxford: Blackwell.

Burgansky, I. (1971), 'Simeon ben Eleazar', *Encyclopaedia Judaica* 14: 1555.

Casey, M. (1985), 'The Jackals and the Son of Man (Matt. 8:20 // Luke 9:58)', *Journal for the Study of the New Testament* 23: 3–22.

Casey, M. (1987), 'General, Generic and Indefinite: The Use of the Term "Son of Man" in Aramaic Sources and in the Teaching of Jesus', *Journal for the Study of the New Testament* 29: 21–56.

Casey, M. (1988), 'Culture and Historicity: The Plucking of the Grain (Mark 2:23–28)', *New Testament Studies* 34: 1–23.

Catchpole, D. (1984), 'The "triumphal" entry', in E. Bammel & C. F. D. Moule, eds, *Jesus and the Politics of His Day*, Cambridge: CUP, pp. 319–34.

Catchpole, D. (1993), *The Quest for Q*, Edinburgh: T. & T. Clark.

Catchpole, D. (2000), *Resurrection People. Studies in the Resurrection Narratives of the Gospels*, London: Darton, Longman & Todd.

Chadwick, O. (1987), *The Victorian Church I*, London: SCM, 3rd edn.

Charlesworth, J. H. (1983/1985), *The Old Testament Pseudepigrapha I–II*, London: Darton, Longman & Todd.

Childs, B. S. (2001), *Isaiah*, Old Testament Library, Louisville, KY: WJK.

Chilton, B. D. (2002), 'John the Baptist: His Immersion and his Death', in S. E. Porter & A. R. Cross, eds, *Dimensions of Baptism: Biblical and Theological Studies*, JSNTS 234, Sheffield: Sheffield Academic Press, pp. 25–44.

Crossan, J. D. (1991), *The Historical Jesus. The Life of a Mediterranean Jewish Peasant*, Edinburgh: T. & T. Clark.

Crossley, J. G. (2004), *The Date of Mark's Gospel. Insight from the Law in Earliest Christianity*, JSNTS 266, London: T. & T. Clark.

Donahue, J. R. (1976), 'Temple, Trial, and Royal Christology (Mark 14:53–65)', in W. H. Kelber, ed., *The Passion in Mark*, Philadelphia: Fortress, pp. 61–79.

Dunn, J. D. G. (2002), 'Jesus and Purity: An Ongoing Debate', *New Testament Studies* 48: 449–67.

Emmerson, G. I. (1992), *Isaiah 56—66*, OT Guides, Sheffield: Sheffield Academic Press.

Evans, C. A. (2001), *Mark 8:27—16:20*, Word Bible Commentary 34B, Nashville: Nelson.

Evans, C. A. (2002), 'The Baptism of John in a Typological Context', in S. E. Porter & A. R. Cross, eds, *Dimensions of Baptism: Biblical and Theological Studies*, JSNTS 234, Sheffield: Sheffield Academic Press, pp. 45–71.

Evans, C. F. (1990), *Saint Luke*, London: SCM.

Fitzmyer, J. A. (1985), *The Gospel according to Luke X—XXIV*, Anchor Bible 28A, New York: Doubleday.

Fredriksen, P. (2000), *Jesus of Nazareth, King of the Jews*, London: Macmillan.

Freyne, S. (2004), *Jesus, a Jewish Galilean*, London: T. & T. Clark.

Friedrichsen, T. A. (2005), 'The Temple, a Pharisee, and the Kingdom of God: Rereading a Jesus Parable (Luke 18:10–14a)', *Journal of Biblical Literature* 124: 89–119.

Gaskell, E. (1986), *Sylvia's Lovers*, Oxford: OUP.

Guelich, R. A. (1989), *Mark 1—8:26*, Word Biblical Commentaries 34A, Dallas: Word Books.

Hardy, T. (1988), *Tess of the D'Urbervilles*, The World's Classics, Oxford: OUP.

Hengel, M. (1981), *The Atonement*, London: SCM.

Hengel, M. (1981), *The Charismatic Leader and His Followers*, Edinburgh: T. & T. Clark.

Hengel, M. (1983), *Between Jesus and Paul*, London: SCM.

Hengel, M. (1985), *Studies in the Gospel of Mark*, London: SCM.

Hill, A. E. (1998), *Malachi*, Anchor Bible 25D, New York: Doubleday.

Holladay, W. L. (1986), *Jeremiah*, Hermeneia Commentary, Vol. 1, Philadelphia: Fortress.

Horbury, W. (1984), 'The Temple tax', in E. Bammel and C. F. D. Moule, eds, *Jesus and the Politics of His Day*, Cambridge: CUP, pp. 265–86.

Ilan, T. (1992), '"Man born of woman . . ." (Job 14:1): The Phenomenon of Men bearing Metronymes at the Time of Jesus', *Novum Testamentum* 34: 23–45.

Jenkins, D. E. (2002), *The Calling of a Cuckoo*, London: Continuum.

Jeremias, J. (1966), *The Eucharistic Words of Jesus*, London: SCM.

Jeremias, J. (1967), *The Prayers of Jesus*, London: SCM.

Juel, D. (1977), *Messiah and Temple*, Missoula: Scholars Press.

Kaminouchi, A. de M. (2003), *'But It Is Not So Among You': Echoes of Power in Mark 10.32–45*, JSNTS 249, London: T. & T. Clark.

Käsemann, E. (1964), 'The problem of the historical Jesus', in *Essays on New Testament Themes*, London: SCM, pp. 15–47.

Klausner, J. (1929), *Jesus of Nazareth*, London: George Allen & Unwin.

Kloppenborg, J. (1987), *The Formation of Q*, Philadelphia: Fortress.

Kloppenborg Verbin, J. (2000), *Excavating Q*, Edinburgh: T. & T. Clark.

Kselman, J. S. (1992), 'Forgiveness', *Anchor Bible Dictionary* 2: 831–3.

Lindars, B. (1983), *Jesus Son of Man*, London: SPCK.

Lindblom, J. (1963), *Prophecy in Ancient Israel*, Oxford: Blackwell.

Lohse, E. (1973), '*Cheiropoiētos*', *TDNT* 9: 436.

Lührmann, D. (1987), *Das Markusevangelium*, Tübingen: Mohr.

Luz, U. (1989), *Matthew 1—7*, Edinburgh: T. & T. Clark.

Luz, U. (2001), *Matthew 8—20*, Minneapolis: Fortress.

MacCulloch, D. (1996), *Thomas Cranmer*, Yale: Yale University Press.

Marcus, J. (1999), *Mark 1—8*, Anchor Bible 27, New York: Doubleday.

Martínez, F. G. & Tigchelaar, E. J. C. (1997/1998), *The Dead Sea Scrolls Study Edition I–II*, Leiden/Grand Rapids: Brill/Eerdmans.

McKane, W. (1986), *A Critical and Exegetical Commentary on Jeremiah*, ICC, Vol. 1, Edinburgh: T. & T. Clark.

Meeks, W. A. (1983), *The First Urban Christians*, New Haven: Yale University Press.

Meier, J. P. (1992), 'John the Baptist in Josephus: Philology and Exegesis', *Journal of Biblical Literature* 111: 225–37.

Meier, J. P. (2001), *A Marginal Jew. Rethinking the Historical Jesus III*, New York: Doubleday.

Metzler, N. (1999), 'The Lord's Prayer: Second Thoughts on the First Petition', in B. Chilton & C. A. Evans, eds, *Authenticating the Words of Jesus*, Brill: Leiden, pp. 187–202.

Meyer, B. F. (1979), *The Aims of Jesus*, London: SCM.

Meyer, L. V. (1992), 'Remnant', *Anchor Bible Dictionary* 5: 669–71.

Moltmann, J. (1967), *A Theology of Hope*, London: SCM.

Moore, C. A. (1996), *Tobit*, Anchor Bible 40A, New York: Doubleday.

Nickelsburg, G. W. E. (1972), *Resurrection, Immortality, and Eternal Life in Intertestamental Judaism*, Cambridge, Mass.: Harvard University Press.

Nickelsburg, G. W. E. (1981), *Jewish Literature between the Bible and the Mishnah*, London: SCM.

Otto, R. (1958), *The Idea of the Holy*, repr. London: OUP.

Paul, S. M. (1991), *Amos*, Hermeneia, Minneapolis: Augsburg Fortress.

Phillips, D. Z. (1986), *R. S. Thomas: Poet of the Hidden God*, London: Macmillan.

Quesnell, Q. (1969), *The Mind of Mark*, Analecta Biblica 38, Rome: Pontifical Biblical Institute.

Räisänen, H. (1992), 'Jesus and the Food Laws: Reflections on Mark 7:15', repr. in *Jesus, Paul and Torah*, JSNTS 43, Sheffield: Sheffield Academic Press, pp. 127–49.

Reiser, M. (1997), *Jesus and Judgment*, Minneapolis: Fortress.

Robinson, J. M. (1998), 'The Sequence of Q: The Lament over Jerusalem', in R. Hoppe & U. Busse, eds, *Von Jesus zum Christus*, Festschrift P. Hoffmann, Berlin: de Gruyter, pp. 225–60.

Roloff, J. (1994), '*ekklēsia*', *EDNT* 1: 410–15.

Sanders, E. P. (1985), *Jesus and Judaism*, London: SCM.

Sanders, E. P. (1990), *Jewish Law from Jesus to the Mishnah*, London: SCM.

Sanders, E. P. (1992), *Judaism: Practice and Belief 63 BCE – 66 CE*, London: SCM.

Sanders, E. P. (1993), *The Historical Figure of Jesus*, London: Penguin.

Sanders, E. P. (2002), 'Jesus' Galilee', in I. Dunderberg, C. Tuckett & K. Syreeni, eds., *Fair Play. Diversity and Conflicts in early Christianity*, Essays in Honour of Heikki Räisänen, Leiden: Brill, pp. 3–41.

Sanders, E. P. & Davies, M. (1989), *Studying the Synoptic Gospels*, London: SCM.

Schmitt, J. J. (1992), 'Prophecy', *Anchor Bible Dictionary* 5: 477–502.

Schneider, C. (1964), '*eunouchos*', *TDNT* 2: 765–8.

Schneider, C. (1965), '*katapetasma*', *TDNT* 3: 628–30.

Schürmann, H. (1968), 'Die vorösterlichen Anfänge der Logientradition', 'Sprachliche Reminiszenzen an abgeänderte oder ausgelassene Bestandteile der Redequelle im Lukas- und Matthäusevangelium', and 'Wer daher eines dieser geringsten Gebote auflöst . . .', repr. in *Traditionsgeschichtliche Untersuchungen zu den synoptischen Evangelien*, Düsseldorf: Patmos, pp. 39–65, 111–25, 126–36.

Schüssler-Fiorenza, E. (1995), *In Memory of Her*, London: SCM, 2nd edn.

Scott, B. B. (1989), *Hear Then the Parable*, Minneapolis: Fortress.

Smith, B. D. (1993), *Jesus' Last Passover Meal*, Lampeter: Edwin Mellen.

Soares Prabhu, G. M. (1976), *The Formula Quotations in the Infancy Narrative of Matthew*, Analecta Biblica 63, Rome: Biblical Institute Press.

Steck, O. H. (1967), *Israel und das gewaltsame Geschick der Propheten*, WMANT 23, Neukirchen: Neukirchener Verlag.

Tan, K. H. (1997), *The Zion traditions and the aims of Jesus*, SNTSMS 91, Cambridge: CUP.

Taylor, J. E. (1997), *John the Baptist Within Second Temple Judaism,* London: SPCK.

Theissen, G. (1992), *The Gospels in Context. Social and Political History in the Synoptic Tradition,* Edinburgh: T. & T. Clark.

Theissen, G. (1993), *Social Reality and the Early Christians,* Edinburgh: T. & T. Clark.

Theissen, G. & Merz, A. (1998), *The Historical Jesus. A Comprehensive Guide,* London: SCM.

Thomas, R. S. (2001), *Collected Poems 1945–1990,* London: Phoenix.

Tournier, P. (1963), *The Strong and the Weak,* London: SCM.

Trollope, A. (1978), *Barchester Towers,* repr. London: Dent.

Trumbower, J. A. (1994), 'The Role of Malachi in the Career of John the Baptist', in C. A. Evans & W. R. Stegner, eds, *The Gospels and the Scriptures of Israel,* JSNTS 104, Sheffield: Sheffield Academic Press, pp. 28–41.

Tuckett, C. M. (1996), *Q and the History of Early Christianity,* Edinburgh: T. & T. Clark.

Vermes, G. (1973), *Jesus the Jew,* London: Collins.

Vielhauer, P. (1965), 'Das Benedictus des Zacharias (Lk 1:68–79)', repr. in *Aufsätze zum Neuen Testament,* München: Kaiser Verlag, pp. 28–46.

Wanke, J. (1980), 'Kommentarworte. Kommentierungen von Herrenworten', *Biblische Zeitschrift* 24: 208–33.

Webb, R. L. (1991), *John the Baptizer and Prophet. A Socio-Historical Study,* JSNTS 62, Sheffield: Sheffield Academic Press.

Weber, M. (1987), 'Prophets and the Routinisation of Charisma', in R. Gill, ed., *Theology and Sociology. A Reader,* London: Geoffrey Chapman, pp. 36–45.

Whybray, R. N. (1975), *Isaiah 40—66,* New Century Bible, London: Oliphants.

Witherington, B. (1992), 'Women (NT)', *Anchor Bible Dictionary* 6: 957–61.

Witherington, B. (1999), *Jesus the Seer,* Peabody, MS: Hendrickson.

Wrede, W. (1971), *The Messianic Secret,* Eng. trans., Cambridge: James Clarke.

Wright, N. T. (1992), *The New Testament and the People of God,* London: SPCK.

Wright, N. T. (1996), *Jesus and the Victory of God,* London: SPCK.

Wright, N. T. (1999), 'In Grateful Dialogue', in C. C. Newman, ed., *Jesus and the Restoration of Israel. A Critical Assessment of N. T. Wright's 'Jesus and the Victory of God',* Carlisle: Paternoster, pp. 244–77.

Wright, R. B. (1985), 'Psalms of Solomon', in J. H. Charlesworth, ed., *The Old Testament Pseudepigrapha II,* London: DLT, pp. 639–70.

Index of ancient texts

1. Old Testament

Index of ancient texts

6. Philo

7. Rabbinic works

Mishnah

Index of modern authors

Allende, I., 226–8
Allison, D. C., 59, 94, 144, 187, 196,
219–20, 228–9, 261, 264
Anderson, A. A., 284
Anderson, G. A., 153
Anderson, R. T., 178
Anglican–Roman Catholic International
Commission 116, 118

Bailey, K. E., 65–6, 83–4, 153, 155, 184
Balz, H. R., 103
Barton, S. C., 67, 88–9, 91
Bauckham, R., 77, 84–5, 182, 270, 274
Bockmuehl, M., 87
Borg, M. J., 55
Brown, R. E., 101
Brueggemann, W., 124, 266–7
Bryan, S. M., 23, 27–8, 31, 182, 260, 264,
269–70, 272
Bultmann, R., 246
Burgansky, I., 75

Carter, S., 164
Casey, M., 62–3, 193, 207
Catchpole, D., 19, 76, 86–7, 173, 208, 237
Chadwick, O., 169
Charlesworth, J. H., 251, 262
Childs, B. S., 265–6
Chilton, B. D., 5, 39
Crossan, J. D., 132–3, 228
Crossley, J. G., 150, 183, 193–4, 196, 198,
200, 232

Davies, M., 59, 125, 130
Donahue, J. R., 256
Donfried, K. P., 101
Dunn, J. D. G., 12, 171, 204

Emmerson, G. I., 267
Evans, C. A., 14, 36, 269, 294
Evans, C. F., 288

Fitzmyer, J. A., 287–8, 295
Fredriksen, P., 127, 172, 216, 261
Freyne, S., 75, 131
Friedrichsen, T. A., 153–5

Gaskell, E., 162
Guelich, R. A., 215

Hardy, T., 1, 3
Hengel, M., 3, 64, 230, 231, 241, 281
Hill, A. E., 21–2
Holladay, W. L., 268
Horbury, W., 272–3

Ilan, T., 85–6

Jenkins, D. E., 129
Jeremias, J., 136, 285–6, 290, 298
Juel, D., 259

Kaminouchi, A. de M., 110–11
Käsemann, E., 196, 229
Klausner, J., 176
Kloppenborg, J., 103
Kloppenborg Verbin, J., 3, 203
Kselman, J. S., 151

Lindars, B., 63–4
Lindblom, J., 124
Lohse, E., 256
Lührmann, D., 232
Luz, U., 100–1, 104, 130

MacCulloch, D., 170.,
Marcus, J., 45, 48, 89–91, 178
Martínez, F. G. 31, 137, 151, 262
McKane, W., 268–9
Meeks, W. A., 220
Meier, J P., 8, 101, 104, 106, 201
Merz, A., 11, 12, 16, 24, 78, 111, 196, 199,
204, 264–5, 285, 288, 291–2

Metzler, N., 135
Meyer, B. F., 15
Meyer, L. V., 7
Moltmann, J., 161
Moore, C. A., 236

Nickelsburg, G. W. E ., 236, 258

Otto, R., 163

Paul, S. M., 37
Phillips, D. Z., 122

Quesnell, Q., 198

Räisänen, H., 197
Reiser, M., 144
Reumann, J., 101
Robinson, J. M., 245, 247, 253
Roloff, J., 104

Sanders, E. P., 9, 59, 93, 97, 105, 125, 127,
    130, 138, 149–50, 153–4, 172, 178, 193,
    197, 230, 232, 241, 255, 261–2, 265, 267,
    272–3
Schmitt, J. J., 5
Schneider, C., 259, 266
Schürmann, H., x, 147
Schüssler-Fiorenza, E., 93, 215–16
Scott, B. B., 155

Smith, B. D., 285, 288, 290
Soares Prabhu, G. M., 86
Steck, O. H., 248

Tan, K. H., 250
Taylor, J. E., 12–14, 34, 37, 45–7, 150, 282
Theissen, G., 11, 12, 16, 24, 30, 61, 68, 76,
    78, 111, 114, 176–7, 196, 199, 204,
    239–40, 264–5, 285, 288, 291–2
Thomas, R. S., 121, 167
Throckmorton, B. H., xi
Tigchelaar, E. J. C. 31, 137, 151, 262
Tournier, P., 163
Trollope, A., 54, 278
Trumbower, J. A., 35
Tuckett, C. M., 129, 244–5, 247–8

Vermes, G., 174, 176
Vielhauer, P., 19

Wanke, J., 113
Webb, R. L., 12, 14–15, 34, 40
Weber, M., 5
Whybray, R. N., 266
Witherington, B., 123, 214–15
Wrede, W., 26
Wright, N. T., 12, 39, 55–7, 81, 138, 150,
    157, 171, 182, 184, 196, 229, 232, 239,
    252, 265, 269, 276
Wright, R. B., 79